# Inventing Tomorrow

H.G. Wells for the BBC Home Service, 1943.

# Inventing Tomorrow

H. G. Wells and the
Twentieth Century

Sarah Cole

Columbia University Press

New York

Columbia University Press
*Publishers Since 1893*
New York    Chichester, West Sussex
cup.columbia.edu

Library of Congress Cataloging-in-Publication Data
Names: Cole, Sarah, author.
Title: Inventing tomorrow : H. G. Wells and the twentieth century / Sarah Cole.
Description: New York : Columbia University Press, [2020] |
Includes bibliographical references and index.
Identifiers: LCCN 2019006298 (print) | LCCN 2019016439 (ebook) |
ISBN 9780231193122 (cloth) | ISBN 9780231193139 (pbk.) | ISBN 9780231550161 (e-book)
Subjects: LCSH: Wells, H. G. (Herbert George), 1866–1946—Criticism and
interpretation. | English fiction—20th century—History and criticism. |
Modernism (Literature)—Great Britain.
Classification: LCC PR5777 (ebook) | LCC PR5777 .C58 2020 (print) |
DDC 823/.912—dc23
LC record available at https://lccn.loc.gov/2019006298

Cover design: Julia Kushnirsky
Cover photograph: © GRANGER

*For Freddie and Anna*

# Contents

# Acknowledgments

I f there is one thing that H. G. Wells teaches, it is that we are never alone; we are connected in a thousand ways to one another and we gain our most profound significance through these attachments. Writing this book has powerfully reinforced this insight. I am incredibly fortunate to have benefited from the deep engagement and warm encouragement of many friends, fellow scholars, and research institutions. It is a great pleasure to take a moment to offer thanks to some of those who have made this book possible.

Many colleagues at Columbia University have contributed to my thinking and have acted as inspirations, mentors, readers, and allies. I have learned immensely from dear friends in the Department of English and Comparative Literature, who have helped to shape this book through many conversations over the years and through their astonishing intelligence. I wish in particular to thank Rachel Adams, Nicholas Dames, Austin Graham, Matthew Hart, Jean Howard, Marianne Hirsch, Edward Mendelson, Julie Peters, Bruce Robbins, Gauri Viswanathan and William Worthen. The Department of English and Comparative Literature has been an unstinting source of generosity and guidance, and I am immensely appreciative to have it as my academic and institutional home.

My intellectual home over the last two decades has been the modernist studies community. I wish to thank the Modernist Studies Association for many opportunities to present my work and to learn from so many wonderful scholars at the annual convention; the NYNJ Modernism Seminar for providing exceptionally stimulating and wide-ranging discussion among local modernists and distinguished visitors at our biannual meetings; the 20/21 colloquium in the Department of English and Comparative Literature, where graduate students and faculty test out new ideas; and the many departments, conferences, and colloquia that have generously invited me to present work on this project.

My colleagues in modernist studies are a source of unending creativity and spirit, and their intellectual energy has sustained my work on Wells. It would be hard to acknowledge them adequately. Several of these brilliant and gracious peers warrant my warmest thanks for their attention to this book and for their intellectual companionship: Robert Caserio, Santanu Das, Jed Esty, Doug Mao, Kate McLoughlin, John Plotz, Victoria Rosner, and Rebecca Walkowitz. Two readers in particular have helped me to conceive and shape this project at every stage, and I wish to express my deep gratitude for their friendship and wisdom. Vincent Sherry has been a reader, critic, and supporter, lending his sparkling intelligence to the project at every stage. And Paul Saint-Amour has aided in untold ways. I have learned from his luminous ideas as an astute reader and an unparalleled friend.

I am indebted to many wonderful students at Columbia who have helped this book along, including those adventurous undergraduate and graduate students who were curious enough to enroll in courses on H. G. Wells, and many others who have shared in this project as part of our modernist community. I wish particularly to thank Nolan Gear, Will Glovinsky, Shannon Jilek, Diana Rose Newby, Jonathan Reeve, Kate Trebuss, and Ameya Tripathi for their truly superb work as research assistants. I also owe a great debt to Jessica Lilien, who lent her expert help in the last stages of publication.

I am thrilled to be publishing *Inventing Tomorrow* with Columbia University Press. Philip Leventhal has been an absolutely ideal editor: wise, attentive, practical, and a great enthusiast for the project. I am enormously grateful for his time and thoughtfulness at every stage. Robert Fellman has been a superb copy editor, and I appreciate Michael Haskell for shepherding the book through production.

Special thanks go to the John Simon Guggenheim Foundation for its support in providing a fellowship. I wish also to thank the New York Public Library Berg Collection for the use of its materials, and the wonderful staff at the University of Illinois Rare Book and Manuscript Library, whose Wells collection is an extraordinary trove. The H. G. Wells Society has offered enthusiastic support, and I am indebted to its members for their work in sustaining scholarship on Wells.

Finally, I express my deepest gratitude for my closest friends and my family. It is hard for me to imagine writing a book, or doing anything else, without the friendship of Ramie Targoff, a participant and partner at every step. My sister and brother, Felicia Cole and Adam Cole, are great allies and enthusiasts. Rosalind

Vogelbaum, my mother-in-law, has been a wonderful part of my family here in New York and a tremendous help in the ongoing effort to balance work and family. I am grateful beyond words to my loving parents and step-parents, Robert Cole and Eleanor Swift, Belle Cole and the late David Wilson, for their boundless generosity and for the unconditional support they have lavished on me. And finally, it is a joy to acknowledge the three people who fill my world with love, inspiration, and humor: my husband, Martin Aaron Vogelbaum, and my children, Frederick Cole Vogelbaum and Anna Elizabeth Vogelbaum. I dedicate this book to Freddie and Anna, who have brought me more happiness, every single day, than I would have thought possible. If there is a tomorrow to invent, it will be for them.

Parts of chapter 2 have been previously published: "H. G. Wells and the Wartime Imagination," *Modernist Cultures* 12, no. 1 (2017): 16–35; and "Civilians Writing the War: Metaphor, Proximity, Action" in *The First World War: Literature, Culture, Modernity*, ed. Santanu Das and Kate McLoughlin (London: British Academy, 2018), 99–113. I thank Edinburgh University Press and the Publications of the British Academy for permission to republish.

# Inventing
# Tomorrow

# Introduction

## I. THE WELLS FACTOR

There is nothing fixed about literary history. Like all narratives, it is made, and can, therefore, be remade. It is the ambition of this book to rewrite the literary history of the twentieth century in England, to reconsider its motivations and ideals, and to suggest proliferating possibilities for how literature might interact with the world. My alternative literary history follows from a reading of a key figure in twentieth-century imaginative life who has been largely overlooked by academics and in the general public, H. G. Wells. Wells changes the narrative in a variety of ways, mostly because his goal for literature was so ambitious: nothing less than world peace and the future of humanity were at stake, and Wells believed in an engaged readership that would be as immense and heterogeneous as the population itself. Wells's soaring ideals seem extravagant today, after a century in which a small band of mostly modernist writers have shaped academic curricula and determined aesthetic valuations, but *Inventing Tomorrow*, I hope, will help us to re-view the literary culture of the first half of the twentieth century and find there a principle of writing oriented around breadth and action. Wells had the highest of expectations for literature to produce change; he wrote of and for a future that he believed his writing could usher into being.

Such ideals jar against contemporary expectations for literature, yet Wells speaks to us today with exceptional clarity and relevance. Writing for a full fifty years, from 1895 to 1946, he produced a prodigious body of work—formidable in its ambition, variety, originality, readership, and sheer drive—addressing nearly every issue from this long period that engages scholarship today.[1] Wells wrote passionately about big topics of human experience, including war, violence, class, economics, gender, sex, history, science (in all its spheres), technology, ecology, education, governance, the past, the future, and humanity, and his works on these large subjects reached millions of readers throughout the world. His writings offer great pleasures of discovery, the product of exuberant energy and inexhaustible creative innovation. Reading Wells today introduces an entirely surprising and invigorating voice from this generative period in literary history, a writer and cultural presence who endlessly addled his contemporaries and redefined his world with brio and conviction, as he took the measure of human life in space and time with a unique power of creative expression. "It is an attempt," he wrote of his historical endeavors, "to tell how our present state of affairs [in 1919], this distressed and multifarious human life about us, arose in the course of vast ages and out of the inanimate clash of matter, and to estimate the quality and amount and range of the hopes with which it now faces its destiny."[2] Wells's irrepressible mind afforded the twentieth century with some of its most resilient figures, on such subjects as the future; the place of mankind in the planet and in time; the potential to visualize the world in jarring, uncanny ways; and the ferocious, annihilating reality of our own destructive capabilities. He gave us concepts like "time machine" (his first novel, 1895), "war of the worlds" (from his 1898 novel of Martian invasion), "the war that will end war" (from a 1914 pamphlet), and "atomic bomb" (from a 1914 novel; the first time an "atomic bomb" had been envisioned), as well as setting the template for modern utopias and fictional forecast. And he was the first major writer to overlay the age and size of the universe onto all of his writing, rescaling the cosmos and humanity's place in it.

To resurrect Wells today is to rediscover the literary landscape of the first half of the twentieth century, and yet, perhaps more importantly, we find in Wells a path that literary culture chose not to take, and are invited to think anew about some of the century's ingrained assumptions about literary values and ambitions. "In diverse forms and spirits we are making over the world," Wells wrote in 1934, "so that the primary desires and emotions, the drama of the immediate individual life will be subordinate more and more, generation by generation, to beauty and truth, to universal interests and mightier aims. That is our common role."[3] Wells believed that writing could and should change the course of history, and his unabashed efforts to propel the human cause forward into a peaceful futurity offered a vista for literature that, at the time, had serious credence. As indicated neatly in a 1934 *Punch* cartoon of Wells as a seal with the globe balanced on his nose (caption: "Mr. H. G. Wells Thinks It Ought to Be Quite Easy," see figure 1) or another in which he tosses the globe like a beach ball, Wells's peers recognized that he had the boldest of agendas for his writing, scaled to the world. It was this unabashed claim for literature that Virginia Woolf,

J. L. Carstairs, "Mr. H. G. Wells Thinks It Ought to Be Quite Easy," *Punch*, December 5, 1934.

Punch Cartoon Library / TopFoto.

characteristically, attacked in Wells, counterpointing such ambitions with the work of her cohort, who, she canonically asserted, produce works of art that are complete in themselves, not hitched to grander projects. *Inventing Tomorrow* asks us to return to this exact moment in literary and cultural history, when the question of how literature would engage the public world was fundamentally up for grabs. Wells gives us one ideal; modernism, another. We can reconstruct the alternative perspective projected by Wells, discovering that he asked many essential questions about literature—about what kinds of imaginative life we might lead and to what ends. Viewed from the vantage of the twenty-first century, his projects and assertions seem so strange, as if literature had always been destined to go in the direction set for it by Wells's modernist peers, where form leads the way in experiment and where the political goal of literature can only be expressed obliquely and never directed at a mass readership. The objective of *Inventing Tomorrow* is, in the first instance, to place Wells within and among the known modernists, as one of the period's great literary innovators, and, second, to show how his writing also clashes with modernist values as they have been enshrined by literary critics over the last seventy years. In the end, this double relation to modernism is not as contradictory as it seems. Instead, reading Wells helps uncover a thriving form of literary accomplishment, germinating alongside the more familiar works from this period, and together producing, perhaps, a broader and more capacious modernism.

Two passages set the stage for this intricate web of connections and divergences. One holds a prime place in academic literary culture; the other holds none. Both come from essays on the modern novel, and both were written in England in the decade of the 1910s.

The first:

> If a writer were a free man and not a slave, if he could write what he chose, not what he must, if he could base his work upon his own feeling and not upon convention, there would be no plot, no comedy, no tragedy, no love interest or catastrophe in the accepted style, and perhaps not a single button sewn on as the Bond Street tailors would have it. Life is not a series of gig lamps symmetrically arranged; life is a luminous halo, a semi-transparent envelope surrounding us from the beginning of consciousness to the end.... We are not pleading merely for courage and sincerity; we are suggesting that the proper stuff of fiction is a little other than custom would have us believe it ... everything is the proper stuff of fiction, every feeling, every thought; every quality of brain and spirit is drawn upon; no perception comes amiss.[4]

And the second:

> You see now the scope of the claim I am making for the novel; it is to be the social mediator, the vehicle of understanding, the instrument of self-examination, the parade of morals and the exchange of manners, the factory of customs, the criticism of laws and institutions and of social dogmas and ideas.... [I]f I may presume to speak for other novelists, I would say it is not so much a demand we make as an intention we proclaim. We are going to write, subject only to our limitations, about the whole of human life.... We are going to write about it all. We are going to write about business and finance and politics and precedence and pretentiousness and decorum and indecorum, until a thousand pretences and ten thousand impostures shrivel in the cold, clean air of our elucidations.... We are going to appeal to the young and the hopeful and the curious, against the established, the dignified, and defensive. Before we have done, we will have all of life within the scope of the novel.[5]

The first passage comes from Virginia Woolf's manifesto "Modern Fiction" (1925, in earlier form, 1919), which stands today as perhaps *the* canonical statement of modernist fictional goals and methods. The second is from an essay entitled "The Contemporary Novel," delivered by Wells as an address in 1911 and published in the *Atlantic Monthly* in 1912 (in book form, 1914), one of Wells's most extensive treatments of the novel's intervention in culture. The question of why we have remembered one of this pair, Woolf's, to the point of fetishism, and forgotten the other is not difficult to answer, since it comes straight from the heart of modernist domination over subsequent literary categories and values.[6] More importantly, though, I would have us ask, what have we lost in this combination of saturation and amnesia? This is, at heart, the motivating question of this book. Its answers will unfold as we read Wells's works, reweighting the significance of his writings in conversation with those of his contemporaries. That such a realignment is vastly more accurate to the reading habits of the first half of the twentieth century, when modernist artists were read by a small cohort, mostly in their original languages, and Wells was read by millions of people across the world, often in translation, adds additional motivation to reconsider these texts and personalities.

There is, very clearly, much that is divergent and even at odds in these short works I am using as metonyms for their authors, but at their core are some deeply shared beliefs and some surprisingly continuous expressions. Both are brash, courageous statements of intent for the present and future of fiction, bespeaking a powerful will to break the shackles of the inherited novel form, dispense with the restraints of convention and decorum, and make the novel new by making it capacious, flexible, daring, and serious. The watchword for each of the essays is "free." "If the writer were a free man and not a slave," Woolf begins her wish list for literature, and Wells's demand is "for an absolutely free hand for the novelist in his choice of topic and incident, and in his method of treatment" (*ELW*, 146). Enjoining such freedom, these writers appeal to the young, who, it is implied, are ready and willing to have their perceptions and expectations upset. The call for generational torch passing stands at the basis of these and other such statements of artistic creed; it is typical of the genre of literary manifesto.[7] For both, the strong implication is that social life, with all its mores, restrictions, and possibilities—what Wells in his essay calls "conduct"—is the larger target. It is not only fiction that is being updated but, to use Woolf's key word in her essay, "life."

Fiction is enlisted as the pivotal textual space in which to enact these generational principles of upheaval. "So far as I can see," Wells reflects, "it is the only medium through which we can discuss the great majority of problems which are being raised in such bristling multitude by our contemporary social development" (*ELW*, 141). Woolf calls her cohort "moderns" (as distinct from the repudiated "materialists") and, as is well known, claims a shift in literary emphasis: from the unimportant and transitory facts of material conditions to the richness of interior life. For Wells, the list of the novel's subjects is long and conspicuously more external ("business and finance and politics and precedence and pretentiousness and decorum and indecorum"), suggesting a primary role for literature in adjudicating the individual within her social and biological cosmos. There is no setting, situation, conflict, problem, or idea that is de facto prohibited in Wells's generous expression. Woolf, by some contrast, is keen to lay down a few rules, indeed, a great variety of them, as indicated by all her "nos" and "nots" ("*no* plot, *no* comedy, *no* tragedy, *no* love interest or catastrophe in the accepted style, and perhaps *not* a single button sewn on as the Bond Street tailors would have it. Life is *not* a series of gig-lamps symmetrically arranged"). Her invitational gesture at the end of the essay thus comes with caveats—no "perception" comes amiss, but many other things do. Wells is thinking big, as is typical for him, and is ready to embrace any kind of writing. For his clarion call, the key word, next to "free," is "hopeful" ("the young and the hopeful and the curious"), as he envisions a limitless field of possibility for the novel, which he imagines reshaping sociality in a wide sense.

Much, then, unites these statements; of differences, I want to isolate just the one already indicated, since it bears strongly on the question of why and how Wells has been eclipsed in academic estimation. Woolf has a scythe in her hand as she slashes through the terrain of contemporary literature; her famous clustering and denigration of Wells, Arnold Bennett, and John Galsworthy as "materialists" whose work is, in essence, comforting, unchallenging, and overly focused on externalities brilliantly organizes the field according to her new alignments. It is a strategy of who's in and who's out, with names named. Wells, by contrast, writes in a spirit of spaciousness, comfortable with multiple approaches. The opening part of the essay (a fairly long segment) attacks critics for demanding norms and standards of the novel—of length, say, or subject matter. He battles against any idea of fiction as easy reading or as conforming to preconceived rules. Wells's largest point is that the novel cannot be hemmed in. He makes no style demands; it is not, in that sense, a typical literary manifesto. Rather, Wells's contribution is to imagine an extensive role and scope for the novel. "Today," he writes, ". . . we live . . . in a period of adventurous and insurgent thought, in an intellectual spring unprecedented in the world's history. . . . And it is inevitable that the novel . . . should reflect and co-operate in the atmosphere and uncertainties and changing variety of this seething and creative time" (*ELW,* 140–41).

Over Wells's long writing career, the novel as a specific form for his ambitions often gave way to other genres, but in "The Contemporary Novel," he is ready to imagine the novel swelling to encompass the transformational energy he brought to the full gamut of his writing. "We intend to have it all": Wells's open invitation contrasts with Woolf's club making, and it also indicates something else, which is how this kind of nondiscrimination ultimately might work against Wells, who stakes out no clearly recognizable location in the critical scheme. When he is most specialized (in the scientific fantasies, say), he can be placed and assessed; when he is most encompassing, where are the demarcation lines we need to write literary history? But the view of Wells as *inviting* is one to maintain since it enforces the idea that reading his works might help stretch the parameters of the period's literature and highlights his own endless willingness to experiment. Right up to his death a month before his eightieth birthday, Wells never stopped reinventing the forms he felt were needed to rejuvenate his society, even when that took him away from the novel form, which, in the end, was no more sacred to Wells than the buttons sewn on by Bond Street tailors were to Woolf. And so we ask, what has the loss of this alternative paradigm meant for our understanding of the period? How can Wells deliver us a different twentieth century?

In fact, many of the most pressing topics of concern to scholars today shift and change in the new prism cast by Wells's work. On the subject of war, Wells's writing pushed his contemporaries to see and understand a fact that was only just beginning to dawn on the cultures of the turn of the century: that it would be the civilian quite as much as the soldier who would become the ultimate victim of modern warfare. Throughout his life and in many different genres, Wells explored war's logic in relation to humanity's precarious condition. Beginning well before World War I, when war crashed into modernism, and tirelessly up through the 1940s, he wrote movingly and presciently about the costs and material tragedies of modern warfare, evolving an image of the civilian as casualty that remains equally urgent today. At the same time, Wells was never content simply to document (or even to predict) the effects of war on the civilian. Instead, one of his primary achievements was the construction of a form of civilian activism against war, in which his famous pamphlet "The War That Will End War" became the opening salvo in a lifelong effort. This effort also produced a major declaration of human rights, a great deal of work in and for extranational organizations like the League of Nations, and an array of other writings meant to activate readers against war.

Wells was a writer who looked at systems, and his cosmos is penetrated by the insights of biology, chemistry, and physics, and by the principles of scientific knowledge. His tales of scientific fantasy are only the beginning; he figured the experience of humanity hinging on the realities (and speculative possibilities) of the universe as studied and, from there, vividly imagined. But although Wells shares with some modernists an interest in the new physics of relativity, which posited a fundamental disorientation at the heart of perceptual experience, Wells's basis was biology, and his motivation was to understand and plumb "the science of life," as he called it. Wells's enormous body of writing constitutes a restless investigation of what it means for the human species to live in the world, conceived in biological, ecological, and evolutionary terms. Viewed as species, human beings find themselves caught in contradictory nets of aspiration and extinction, individuality and collectivity. Wells's writings place individual people in various larger streams, with startling, often jarring results; the "life" he chased throughout his writing was precarious and biological as well as bewildering and otherworldly.

Given the long timescales at which the biological and physical universe operates, it is not surprising to find Wells at the very heart of contemporary experimentations with time. Indeed, he went back to first principles with time, and as the inventor of the first literary time machine, it is not surprising that his innovations would be extensive. Above all, Wells lived in the future, and his works abound in all manner of forward temporal play. Wells believed that we have a moral responsibility to look forward with both creativity and scientific acumen. As scholars throughout literary studies turn to temporality as a primary area of interest, and as the geological scales governing the earth come into vivid focus in our era of climate peril, the return to Wells as someone who took the future as the essential temporality becomes especially pertinent. He provides a new window into the 1914 generation, a vanguard of writers that seems, in retrospect, strangely both open and closed to its own precarious position in vast systems of time and space.

In all of his radical configurations of human experience in the world, Wells's words went out to enormous numbers of readers. To reconstruct his unique voice is to recreate a major factor in the cultural life of the first half of the twentieth century. We know that modernism constructed the audience it needed and that the gulf between modernist erudition and popular culture may not have been entirely rigid. But what we have not noticed is the readership that Wells forged, such that, for instance, *The Outline of History* could sell up to two million copies in its first decade. Wells carved out a textual and, later, media space of ample dimensions and was read by people whose class, language, and education varied extensively. Part of what it means to read Wells, then, is to reenter the period's own reading habits, almost to enter its collective unconscious. Such an audience was, I want to stress, created; we can track its formation in his style and voice. Wells sustained a readership that spanned class, political, and national distinctions, but there is one boundary left to cross, still, today: that of literary history.

## II. GETTING TO KNOW WELLS

Who was Wells, and how did he factor in the life and minds of his contemporaries? His massive body of writing offers a window into the scope and generativity of his thought over five decades, and these many texts will be our guide to his thought and influence. There is an unmistakable Wellsian quality to all of his work—he has his distinctive voice—at the same time that his output was remarkable for its diversity and range. He was a genre pioneer of the first order, producing texts that cut across familiar literary categories: novels shift back and forth into essay, warmly embracing the novel of ideas; history, economics, and science are rebuilt for a newly envisioned mass audience; the manifesto stakes important ground in human rights and world community; prophecy and anticipation take unprecedented priority; and every kind of fantasy and speculation is given textual form, setting the course for science fiction as a genre. As a journalist alone, Wells was formidable, having written hundreds of newspaper articles over the decades, published in many venues in England and around the world. Nor was his reach limited to the written word, with both film and radio central to his thought and output from as early as his first novel, *The Time Machine* (1895), which has a genetic tie to early film, swelling in the 1920s and '30s when his media presence soared (including radio, a complementarity well captured by Orson Welles's famous 1938 adaptation of *The War of the Worlds*), and of course Hollywood has never forgotten him.[8]

Wells's writing acts as a guide to his culture, telling the story of its darkest fears and brightest ambitions, conjoining unbelievable optimism with the direst insight into catastrophe and failure. Such swings through the optimism-pessimism spectrum are a striking feature of Wells's writing. One of the most persistent misprisions about Wells is that his works can be read for their message, that they are univocal and polemical—yet, in fact, they almost always function dialectically, with contradictory voices, visions, perspectives, and moods in constant interplay, resolved, if at all, only through an imperfect and unreliable synthesis. His ability to catch his culture's darkest tendencies and its most soaring ambitions represents one aspect of this ubiquitous duality across his thought. Yet if Wells frames and refracts his culture's self-image, he was unlike any of his peers in his mix of attributes and accomplishments, from his background as the son of a shopkeeper and a lady's maid, whose own life's calling was supposed to be as a draper, to his scientific training on a scholarship, to his vast textual output, to his public stature, to his famous prescience. Wells was a unique figure in the society at large and he sat at the center of several overlapping literary, cultural, and scientific milieus, replete with accomplished friends. These friendships were not always stable, and Wells was apt to engage in often public, at times bitter, debates with many of his acquaintances and friends. Yet these worlds were invigorated by his presence. The writer to whom he was most often compared during his lifetime was Charles Dickens. In world letters, his closest parallel would be Rabindranath Tagore. Imagine if, today, we were just recognizing the genius and importance of Dickens or Tagore; that is where we stand with Wells.

In his own day there was no mistaking his stature. Virginia Woolf called him "the most famous of living English novelists" (1938), and George Orwell wrote that "thinking people who were born about the beginning of this century are in some sense Wells's own creation.... The minds of all of us, and therefore the physical world, would be perceptibly different if Wells had never existed."[9] In an obituary reflection in 1946, Jorge Luis Borges wrote that "like Quevedo, like Voltaire, like Goethe, like some others, Wells is less a man of letters than a literature.... I think [his scientific romances] will be incorporated ... into the general memory of the species and even transcend the fame of their creator or the extinction of the language in which they were written."[10] Wells's works were translated into multiple languages, in many cases within months of publication. He was sought by political figures around the world, invited for private meetings with both Roosevelts, Lenin, and Stalin, whom he interviewed in 1934 (published in the *New Statesman* in what became a famous and much-criticized conversation), not to mention a host of English political figures, such as Churchill, who read all his works in succession and quoted from them in his speeches ("I read everything you write").[11] As one critic notes, "When Wells dropped in on Charlie Chaplin or Stalin or Lenin or whoever happened to be the President of the United States for a well-publicised chat about the meaning of life, it seemed the most natural thing in the world."[12] *The Outline of History* (1920), his huge illustrated work of world history, from the origin of the planet up to the present (actually the future), can only be described as a phenomenon in terms of its sales, its longevity in print (in a variety of ever-changing editions), its penetration into culture (including much noisy controversy), and its influence on the marketplace of ideas. *The Outline* today remains one of the most widely read history books of all time.[13]

Wells, in other words, stood for something in his culture; he was a writer but also, almost, a living principle. To understand what that principle entailed and meant will reveal crucial aspects of Wells's time, providing new insight into the literary culture of his era. It is an idea of the writer as waging a public and unending battle against whatever is expected—against convention, the past, the stranglehold of national identity, against complacency and blindness and smug self-satisfaction, even against the present. These negative principles are, in Wells's understanding, a constant threat to liberty, expression, happiness, and peace and are always being recharged; more, they can also come from within. In engaging the world at its most dangerous and recalcitrant, Wells was also continually pressing himself to keep experimenting and innovating. Thus, part of what Wells meant for his contemporaries is that he was visibly out there, taking stock of the present, predicting the future, restless and critical but also, fundamentally, optimistic. Above all, he made it his project to construct a new future—to invent tomorrow—one that would be less violent, ugly, and unjust than his present, even as he offered up some of the era's most memorable visions of dystopia and extinction.

By about 1914, many across the culture expected this kind of large public reckoning from him, and they looked for it in print and in other media as well. One thinks of his film *The Man Who Could Work Miracles* (1936), in which an early short story is retrofitted to include, essentially, Wells in the present, spreading forth his familiar messages and having his visions tested in front of our eyes. That the original story is submerged beneath the idea of the author—not named within the film, but not needed—gives a sense of how far that author's persona had penetrated into mainstream culture. In Borges's language, Wells is set into the frame of world literature, in a span running from the Greeks to the present and as part of a canon that notably has no primary language (Spanish, Greek, English, French, and German are all referenced) and indeed is envisioned as breaking free of language. As with the others on the list, Borges sees Wells's work having the almost unparalleled quality of lifting itself out of its own particularities of time, place, and culture. He is, in that sense, a writer of and for the globe, a *world* writer, and it is significant in this respect that Wells's dominant subject aimed to be the story and fate of all human beings.

There is no precise equivalent in our current moment for the kind of public figure that Wells cut, the mixture of fiction writer, social commentator, political aggravator, all-round prognosticator, and worldwide educator whose voice sounded beyond any of these specific realms. No doubt, this is one reason we have misrecognized him. Wells seemed, in his moment, to be everywhere, a kind of fulcrum for thought and ideas. In his scholarship on time machines and modernism, Charles Tung has noted such intellectual permeation, pointing out that popular science writers of the 1920s and '30s felt no need to cite Wells, since his work was so ingrained as to be recognizable to any reader. Olaf Stapledon commented in a letter to Wells, "A man does not record his debt to the air he breathes in common with everyone else."[14] But there is more to Wells's status than familiarity or even his ability to capture something in his era; rather, he created the conditions for that exemplarity. One of Wells's least recognized accomplishments is that he was able to develop a voice to engage a huge and diverse public and to write works that were challenging in such a way that their idiosyncratic, often radical ideas seemed to belong effortlessly in the cultural conversation. He is not, that is, a "popular" writer, in the sense of being comforting, unchallenging, or derivative, attempting to give a mainstream audience what it expects to find. If each generation of critics has found its own language for contrasting elite with popular literature—or, in our current critical moment, for thinking through their mutuality and complicity—such efforts are particularly challenging when it comes to Wells. In this book, I will largely use terms such as "widely read" to indicate that the qualitative or genre distinctions signaled by "popular" often confuse more than they clarify for Wells, whose stories were often uncomfortable ones, meant to trouble and stimulate his readers, driven by the most intractable concepts and problems. Yet he wrote for and reached an immense and diverse population of readers.

One key element in all of this was science. The most formative intellectual experience in Wells's life were his three years (1884–1887) as a science student at the Normal School of Science (later Royal College of Science) in South Kensington, where he had won a scholarship, a life-changing opportunity that lifted him out of the thankless, low-level teaching career that was his immediate lot before reaching London (this too a nearly miraculous escape from his hated and destined life in the drapery trade). "The day when I walked from my lodging in Westbourne Park across Kensington Gardens to the Normal School of Science, signed on at the entrance to that burly red-brick and terra-cotta building and went up by the lift to the biological laboratory was one of the great days of my life," he recalled fifty years later (*EA*, 159). At the Normal School, a college founded with the idea of educating future science teachers, Wells had the utter good fortune to study for one year with Thomas Henry Huxley, the great biologist, evolutionist, and exponent of Darwin's work and the leading scientific educator of his day. The learning of these years colored all of Wells's thought and profoundly shaped his role as a public intellectual. Science was not only a theme in Wells's work but his orienting vision, and it forms a pivotal aspect of his public image. As Peter Kemp writes, Wells's *"persona* was, in many ways, that of science-teacher to the human race. His mission in life, he felt, was to make man aware of his place in nature. In keeping with this, he likes to regard himself as a biologically trained observer of the human species."[15] Engrossed in the spheres of biology, chemistry, and physics and governed by the principle of ecology, Wells's worldview powerfully anticipates frames of thought and reference that, much later in the century, came to orient culture. If it is a cliché that Wells was "ahead of his time," it is also one that needs to be taken seriously, reconciling his scientific proclivity with his larger literary and cultural undertakings. At the same time, Wells richly articulated many of the scientific theories animating his contemporaries as he brought late-nineteenth-century science into bracing and often unsettling literary life.

In noting Wells's scientific orientation, we might pause to register how these ideas could be perverted into ugly visions of perfecting the population or an icy rationalism about human worth that at times sounds little better, in fact, than Wells's famous Martians, "intellects vast and cool and unsympathetic." In an uncanny way, Wells seemed to write his own worst tendencies into his fictions, as in *The War of the Worlds*, where the Martians' exterminatory treatment of their human victims outstrips but shares something with Wells's own hyperrationalism about who will and will not have a place in the perfected world he often imagined. These are deeply troubling habits of mind about people and populations that characterize aspects of his thought at the broad social level. In

Wells's works, the undertow to his soaring ability to think at large scale and to employ a vibrant hybrid of scientific imagining is this willingness to let human beings occasionally seem like mere residue. As the political theorist Duncan Bell argues of Wells and race, Wells repudiated the prevailing racist theories and beliefs of his contemporaries yet also maintained "eugenic commitments [which] undercut his putative anti-racism" in a body of work that struggles profoundly over the meaning and reach of equality as a principle.[16] In a world-picture that hungered for completeness and harmony, the problem of those who cannot or will not participate invited a kind of ferocity. Strangely, Wells's contemporaries seemed generally unbothered by these visions of a future world casting off its weakest members (he was much more likely to be attacked for his stance against Christianity than for such eugenic reveries), but for us, they haunt and trouble a universe of writing that mostly pushed toward ideals of harmony, collectivity, and peace. Such is the Wellsian reality, however: part of his profound idiosyncrasy is found in his swiveling through and among contrary impulses, many of these hovering out at the end of the spectrum of what is comfortable or acceptable. Perhaps it is not surprising, then, that his first novel, *The Time Machine*, figures humanity split into two species, predator and prey, ruthless and gentle, as if Wells were looking into his own mental habits, prefiguring at the outset how his own doubled imagination would tend.

Wells was unique as a public voice, but he could occupy this dynamic, unfixed position of artist, scientific thinker, and general cultural force in part because such a role existed. One thinks of others, such as G. K. Chesterton, Rudyard Kipling, or George Bernard Shaw, who also achieved wide authority in a cultural field of indefinite borders. If one history of the early twentieth century is of specialization, familiar from sociological accounts and crystallized in modernist values, an emphasis on the disciplines can leave us ill attuned to the phenomenon of Wells and these others, insofar as the updated, modern role of "man of letters" he occupied runs squarely against modern disciplinarity. "Man of letters," however, may be misleading as a term, implying too much gentility, not the persona sought by Wells, born into the lowest rung of the middle classes (service, shopkeeping, trades) and distrusting the institutions of intellectual refinement, such as Oxford/Cambridge and the established literary societies. And the epithet obscures his distinctive orientation toward science. But the idea of a kind of *generalist* writer and thinker with a hand in many areas of thought, art, education, culture, and even politics is one to revive in our understanding of this half-century. Crucially, this role was not solely a carryover from nineteenth-century models (Matthew Arnold, John Ruskin, or Thomas Carlyle, say), since a key aspect of Wells's aptitude was his attunement to the specific technologies of modernity. His universe palpitated with the latest prospects of global interconnection, the power of media and of information as it moves with lightning speed around the world, the reality of mass warfare, the new possibilities of creating shared world knowledge. Unlike those Victorian precursors, Wells had no romance for the past; he looked with deep skepticism at all forms of conservative idealism.

It is of the utmost importance, however, that reading Wells today is not solely a way to rediscover in new terms the literary period of the first half of the twentieth century (though it is that); his works are, in themselves, engrossing, brilliant, and complex. They can be disconcerting—or downright troubling—as well as haunting, yet they are also often extremely funny, capturing the ironies of social behavior and of literary fashion. Indeed, one disorienting feature of Wells's writing is how often a given work might cross from satire, vivid and amusing, into a ferocious, dark vision of humanity (and back again). The contradictory structure of his thought has significant formal and tonal effects as his works swing and swerve to account for the alternately bleak and exuberant visions he balances. His writings are often feats of imagination, stimulations to thought, and powerful insights into our contemporary culture's propensities and crises around such issues as war and human precarity. Those still well known to readers—though rarely included in literary-critical assessments of the period—include *The Time Machine* (1895), *The Island of Doctor Moreau* (1896), *The Invisible Man* (1897), *The War of the Worlds* (1898), *The War in the Air* (1908), *Tono-Bungay* (1909), *The History of Mr. Polly* (1910), *The Outline of History* (1920), *Experiment in Autobiography* (1934), "The Door in the Wall" (1906), and "The Country of the Blind" (1904). But I believe readers today will also find his more obscure works enormously stimulating and arresting. Several examples among scores of relatively unknown texts to note up front are *Mr. Britling Sees It Through* (1916), Wells's great war novel, written in medias res and capturing the experience of civilian life in riveting terms; *The World of William Clissold* (1926), an eight-hundred-page novel-cum-rumination at large on the state of life after the war, very much in the spirit of Montaigne, which sets new standards for the novel of ideas; *Things to Come* (film, 1936), Wells's biggest movie in both budget and concept, a deeply flawed and also marvelous epic of world destruction and ambiguous rejuvenation; *The Croquet Player* (1936), a gripping little novella that harks back to some of Wells's scientific fantasies, now set firmly in the fascist moment and distilling 1930s questions of humanity and civilization in stark terms; and *The Rights of Man* (1940), Wells's declaration of human rights, simple prose that startlingly encapsulates the moral culture of the decades that followed his death. Each of these, be it noted, was written after the First

World War had begun, and they run to the end of the 1930s, hence fully postdating the time when Wells is supposed to have dried up, as the critical commonplace has uniformly proclaimed. Even those who admire and champion Wells today almost always discount his work after 1910. Wells, it is averred, was an Edwardian or a late Victorian, his great powers expressed in those early scientific romances, in short stories, and in *Tono-Bungay*, seen as a brilliant novel to round off the Edwardian moment.[17]

This is true, but he is also a modernist of the first order, and his work upsets these literary periods with the same ease that it challenges neat genre distinctions.[18] Wells's writing stuns us for its continuous adaptability to time and change (itself one of his great themes), over the full fifty years of his writing life, and his work casts productive doubt on the stranglehold of our periodizing gestures. And modernists took note: they attacked him, made him their foil, nurtured and ended deep friendships with him, and in several cases had sexual relationships with him. As Ford Madox Ford noted in 1938, casting himself as the defender of modernism, "In the kingdom of letters Mr. Wells and I have been the leaders of opposing forces for nearly the whole of this century."[19] He was under their collective skin like no other single writer of the period, and this alone might provoke us to scrutinize these rich dialectics.

## III. WELLS AND THE MODERNISTS

In his status as modernist antimodernist, Wells stands at a humming crossroads. Engaging with his work offers an opportunity to reexamine some of literary criticism's operating assumptions about modernism and modernity, in keeping with the broad reevaluation of these principles currently transforming literary scholarship. Wells constructs his own standards and writes his own worlds, and in this sense he is fully able to set the terms and reorient the period. At the same time, in the chapters that follow, modernism has a pivotal role; it is, in many cases, the ground against which I will be positioning Wells.[20] Modernism is the interlocutor here because, quite simply, it is the literary practice that has lived on from this period and because academic literary culture has been molded, in essential ways, in its image. Ever being refreshed, the idea of modernism is ready for an infusion of the new ideas that emerge, as a deluge, from Wells's works. Nevertheless, one could just as easily come to Wells from other points of view—he was a major figure in the contexts of socialism, gender politics, utopian futures, and, of course, science fiction—but the general area where he has been most thoroughly and consequentially overlooked, and where his presence would be most startling and transformative, is in literature—not specified by genre—and especially modernism. This mobile, complex interaction has several dimensions, including (a) literary history and the supremacy of a rather narrow view of modernism in establishing taste and aesthetic values; (b) the role of Wells as straw man for his modernist peers as they attempted to clear literary and cultural space for themselves; (c) the actual friendships and disagreements between Wells and some preeminent modernists; and (d) the many shared preoccupations, thematic overlaps, and even—counterintuitive as this might seem—formal congruencies of these two different forces in twentieth-century thought and writing.[21]

Given how enormous Wells's place was in the first half of the century and how drastically it has diminished, we should be clear about how that happened. In part, as I have suggested, Wells suffered from his own productivity, with the sheer volume of his output ensuring a certain fatigue as the decades passed and a suspicion that quality could never keep up with such quantity. Too, Wells's insistence that writing could and should change the world came to seem increasingly naïve as totalitarianism and World War II closed in on Europe. But the primary answer to the question of Wells's neglect is modernism itself. As many English and Anglophone modernists liked to depict it, the literary world was organized by clear antagonisms and binaries, with Wells (often bundled with others, "Wells and Shaw" or Woolf's "materialists") lined up against themselves, as that which their very modernity must challenge.[22] As such, it would be difficult to overstate their success in carving the literary field according to the logic of modernist versus all other approaches.

For the purposes of this book, "modernism" is offered in its most generalized aspect, with reference primarily (though not exclusively) to literature in the English language from the period of Wells's writing life. Most broadly, literary modernism is the attempt to create appropriate textual conditions, in significant part via formal innovation, to gain the measure of the modern world, with all of its sensory disjunctions and novelties, its technologies, and the economic and affective consequences of global capitalism in the twentieth century. In these terms, Wells exemplifies the idea. In my many citations to modernism, however, I mean to designate three overlapping quantities, all of which follow from this broad concept but have served to narrow and filter it in particular directions. First are the practitioners, literary figures from the 1890s through the 1940s who came to dominate the tastemaking, canon-building, and curricular apparatus of the period from midcentury to the present. In this sense, it is a straightforward period moniker, qualitative in nature. Second, and most central, modernism here refers to the literary values, priorities, and biases spread by those practitioners, their followers, and their institutional promoters. Specific principles that tend to attach to modernism in this range, of importance to an analysis of Wells, include the primacy of subjectivism and the interior life of the mind, indirection and elusiveness (sometimes registered as "difficulty," unreliability, illegibility, readerly disorientation), the banishment of political discussion or definitive position taking, the belief that the work of art is autonomous, and the eschewing of popular appeal. From all of these, Wells departs; they are not his creeds. In considering Wells, these and related literary values come under pressure as we wonder whether a more capacious modernism can be asserted that makes room for alternative strategies and beliefs. Finally, the third meaning I have in mind is the modernism that extends, via these precepts and the legacy of the writers who first articulated them, into the present, in the form both of modernist scholarship and the continuation of modernist practices in contemporary literature. The ongoing process in which contemporary authors reinvigorate modernism has been well articulated in an influential essay in *PMLA*, "Metamodernism," by David James and Urmila Seshagiri: "A growing number of contemporary novelists," they write, "place a conception of modernism as revolution at the heart of their fictions, styling their twenty-first century literary innovations as explicit engagements with the innovations of early-twentieth-century writing."[23] What makes metamodernism so consequential is its articulation of the way contemporary writers update and maintain modernism as a norm, as if it were the inevitable literary formation to define its era and to set the course for what has followed.

For Wells, the dominance of modernist literary values has been overwhelming. His enormous energy took directions quite his own, and these do not line up with the primary aesthetic objectives named here, as they have been interpreted and amalgamated into literary culture. He was not, for one thing, particularly moved by minute changes of the mind nor, for the most part, motivated to create characters of intricate emotional depth. He wrote of and for the species, not the individual—though in his philosophical writings, he continually insists that only the individual, never the category, can be known, in a strenuous rebuttal of Platonism or idealism. These approaches to the intricate life of people simply signify differently from the emphases among many of his peers. Or again, when it comes to how the novelist appears in his recognizable voice, Wells and modernism take rival tacks. Modernism, at least in one of its most influential iterations, sought narrative methods that would bring the sensory present into immediacy. The illusion is of unmediated contact with the world: texts are swarmed with impressions, sense perceptions, and the tide of memory, the author as if invisible. As Joyce put it simply, "I want the reader to understand always through suggestion rather than direct statement."[24] Wells, by contrast, was a master at constructing didactic spaces within his novels, blending fiction with essay and interleaving direct, often intricate analysis of matters like economics, social change, and history, articulated as such, into his literary creations. He is hyperpresent in all of his writing. These effects will be treated more fully in chapter 1, but up front, I would have us begin by asking: why do literary critics (and our students) assume that such tactics are regrettable? Why is it always preferable for a novelist to tell us subtly and obliquely what she thinks rather than simply argue it? Only when we ask these questions can we wrench the actual literary moment free of our encrusted assumptions and biases.

In this sense, we need to retrain ourselves as literary interlocutors, to pose, as if from first principles, questions like, "Why is the intricate life of the semiconscious mind the most important aspect of character?"; "What is wrong with telling, as distinct from showing?"; "Does each novel need to be entirely sui generis, standing alone, or can it be placed within an oeuvre, receiving its significance in part within that larger body of work?" In fact, Wells's works cannot best be read singly; they should be read by the numbers, as they were during his life, when work after work appeared more or less continuously in serial venues and as books. His works do not operate as perfect wholes, and his genius is rarely expressed at the level of the line or paragraph. And now the difficult part: to recognize that *this is not a failing*. It is a signature, a way of entering Wells's vast and living textual world. Wells worked at a different scale, and this scalar eccentricity invites us to retrofit our reading practice to newly enlarged dimensions.

The astonishing success of Woolf and her peers, not only as the privileged artists read today in the academy but as the originating points for latter-day modernist ideals and legacies, has, as its collateral effect, obscured other voices from the period, no matter how far-reaching these were at the time. These dynamics have been revealed and challenged in the last two decades in the robust study of popular modernism, which has gone far to confront the preponderance of modernism as a monolith with its small cadre of writers dominating cultural memory.[25] Scholars have demonstrated the deep indebtedness of modernism to popular forms; resurrected neglected writers; unearthed ties between modernists and other, often forgotten or marginalized areas of cultural activity; studied modernists' own interests in creating audiences and marketing their work; and reintegrated genre fiction into our understanding of the literary scene. All of this important work in expanding and enriching the way we read the multiplicity and heterogeneity of the period figures into an analysis of Wells. Moreover, recent decades have decentered modernism from Europe and the United States and expanded its timescale, as in the influential work of Susan Stanford Friedman, who has helped to open modernism out to robust historical and geographical spans. Even Friedman, however, retains the essential aesthetic values still associated with an earlier account of modernism; it is these that allow her to claim an extended modernism in the first place. But Wells challenges these distinctions at the root, and the discrepancy he reveals between current neglect and contemporaneous importance (and also between academic attention and influence in mainstream culture) points in especially glaring ways to the paucity of received literary inheritance.

In this book, the writer who will come back most frequently as foil and double for Wells is Woolf. They were not friends, though they met at various occasions over the years. The Woolfs attended his wife's funeral in 1928, and they published two of his pamphlets, *Democracy Under Revision* (1927) and *The Common Sense of World Peace* (1929) at the Hogarth Press.[26] Leonard Woolf and Wells knew each other from their mutual involvement in the League of Nations during and after the war and interacted again in antifascist contexts in the 1930s. At least one extended visit was planned but never realized, a weekend stay of the Woolfs with the Wellses for Easter 1922; this represents a particularly rich might-have-been, as one wonders how they would have fared together in a relaxed and prolonged social situation, these two paragons of the intelligentsia of the early twentieth century, each a great social force in her/his (overlapping) sphere.[27] In her diaries, Woolf is predictably contemptuous of Wells the person—she imagines with horror what it would be like to be married to him, and when they meet for an evening in 1937, she cannot help but think, "Had one seen him behind a counter he wd. have seemed the very type of busy little grocer." Yet she also reveals her insecurity in the face of his enormous public stature ("the warmth & clamour of Wells' fame seems to reach me, this chilly rainy evening," she writes in 1926, and ten years later, "I suppose [he has] the greatest circulation in the whole world").[28] In her published work, as we know, she attacks Wells frequently, including in a very funny and quite insightful 1918 review of his novel *Joan and Peter*.

But Woolf and Wells are, I believe, kindred spirits in ways that have never been acknowledged by critics, not to mention themselves. Their interests and convictions were often stunningly similar, from their disparagement of bastions of elitism such as Oxford and Cambridge to their lifelong pacifism and suspicion of the institutions enforcing patriarchal dominance. As a woman and a lower-middle-class man, they share a marginalization with respect to power that energized their writing and directed their political vision. Both wrote works that deeply challenge their readers, seeming to shake the very bases of human (and literary) security, unleashing a vision of the most poignant vulnerability. Yet, in other ways, their writing bounds and surges with optimism. Their very unlikeness in style and sensibility might, in fact, help us see them as two major stars in necessary gravitational relation to each other. Woolf currently stands at the very center of modernist studies. Wells stares at us from the shadows. At least for these pages, I propose that we let our imaginations rove in new directions around Bloomsbury and other intellectual cultures, to defamiliarize the literary practices that have been so thoroughly normalized in academic hierarchies. I believe Wells warrants an analysis that centers on his work, not to keep the arrangement for all time, but rather to give the period a distinctive new set of directing cues and, from there, to revive an unfamiliar host of collective undertakings.

Woolf is the foil I have chosen; in actual life, other modernists had meaningful connections with him, such as his partner of ten years, Rebecca West; another romantic partner, Dorothy Richardson; Henry James; Joseph Conrad; E. M. Forster; and D. H. Lawrence. For each of these, the critique is complicated by the fluid dynamics of intimacy, friendship, and influence. West and Wells, who had a child, naturally developed long-lasting and deep ties, with significant consequences for their work. Richardson, too, was involved with Wells at a pivotal time in her writing career, and he figures as a character in her opus *Pilgrimage*. In the case of Lawrence, we should add Wells to our list of important influences for his extensive writings on class, economics, and the condition of England (including in *Tono-Bungay*, a novel Lawrence admired) and for his overt treatment of the theme of sexual emancipation for women. More, as a prophet and preacher of sorts, Wells offered Lawrence a model he dearly sought, a large figure against and in relation to whom Lawrence could set his own writing.

Forster, too, has Wells on his mind more acutely than is generally considered. In *Aspects of the Novel* (1927), he comes back regularly to Wells, who in surprising ways penetrates to the heart of *Aspects*, with its famous demarcation between flat and round characters. As Forster writes, "all Wells' characters are as flat as a photograph." Yet he goes on to think about how, nevertheless, they live and matter: "But the photographs are agitated with such vigour that we forget their complexities lie on the surface. . . . A Wells character cannot indeed be summed up in a single phrase; he is tethered much more to observation, he does not create types. Nevertheless his people seldom pulsate by their own strength. It is the deft and powerful hands of their maker that shake them and trick the reader into a sense of depth."[29] That Wells (like Dickens, to whom Forster compares Wells several times) succeeds in the area where he should—by the general logic of *Aspects*—fail is something that makes Wells particularly interesting for Forster's manifesto. The "deft and powerful hands of their maker" is the key, and Forster recognizes the forceful presence of Wells across his works as their defining feature, for better and for worse.

Among these writers, it is Conrad who stands closest to Wells (excepting Wells's lovers), since the work of each of these two erstwhile neighbors was so clearly and openly engaged with the other's. It is an intriguing friendship that ran for about a decade before it ended. There is a gap in the record when their friendship ends, which has led to speculations—did they have a quarrel? Was it the differences in their views of art? For us, what matters most is not the break, but to notice how their writings over a decade spar, refer back and forth, and engender one another in very explicit and formative ways.[30] Conrad dedicated *The Secret Agent* to Wells in 1907:

> TO H. G. WELLS
> THE CHRONICLER OF MR. LEWISHAM'S LOVE
> THE BIOGRAPHER OF KIPPS AND
> THE HISTORIAN OF THE AGES TO COME
> THIS SIMPLE TALE OF THE XIX CENTURY
> IS AFFECTIONATELY OFFERED[31]

It is a gesture that leaps out from a different modernism from what is familiar, the phrase "the historian of the ages to come" an especially resonant depiction of Wells's play with time, the affection and sense of appreciation apparent. As Conrad wrote to Wells in a letter in which he transcribed the dedication, "in this definition I have stated what the perfect novelist should be—chronicler, Biographer and Historian."[32] It is also apt from a thematic point of view, since Wells had written the most wildly popular fiction in the period about silent terror, *The Invisible Man*, which Conrad had read and which, as his close friend Ford Madox Ford recalled, "made an extremely marked impression on [him]."[33] He also proposed having *The Invisible Man* translated into Polish. Most revealing is the interaction of *Heart of Darkness* with several of Wells's works, earlier and later. *Heart of Darkness* is notably indebted to both *The Time Machine* and *The Island of Doctor Moreau* (the former in the frame narrative and general setup, the latter in the character of Kurtz as an iteration of Moreau), and critics have also found thematic ties with *The War of the Worlds* and *The Sleeper Awakes*. As Conrad wrote in 1898, when he was writing *Heart of Darkness*, "I have lived on terms of close intimacy with you, referring to you many a page of my work, and continuing many sentences by the light of your criticism."[34] And

Wells returns the favor in his most ambitious novel, *Tono-Bungay*, which includes an elaborately Conradian episode.[35] As with Woolf, Conrad can be placed as another gravitational figure in relation to Wells, whose writing becomes unfamiliar, shot through with a whole new energy and set of perspectives, when we set it next to Wells's.

Conrad and Wells make a compelling duo in part because they confuse the map critics have constructed for where writers and intellectuals of the period belong. If we attempt to look out from the shadows cast by the famous expatriate cohort in Paris after the war or by Bloomsbury, for example, Wells can be found in his own clusters and groups. These included the Fabians, with whom he was involved from 1903 to 1908, when he left the group after a tumultuous and productive half-decade of activity. Significant names for literary history in this community include Wells's longtime friend and nemesis George Bernard Shaw, with whom he was always associated in the public mind during his life. Arnold Bennett was a friend for three decades, and his friendships with Stephen Crane and George Gissing, who asked for him at his deathbed, also form a compelling part of the literary conversation of these years. Wells had deep ties with several people in the science community, most prominently Richard Gregory, one of his lifelong friends (from the Normal School of Science) and the editor of *Nature*, along with Julian Huxley, with whom he cowrote *The Science of Life* (1929). And of course, there were his numerous love affairs. For literary purposes, the most significant was his ten-year relationship with Rebecca West.[36] The affair with Dorothy Richardson lasted for two years and ended unhappily, though in later years they remained on warm terms. There were also relationships (sometimes sexual, sometimes not) with Vernon Lee and Violet Hunt and a long-lasting connection with the American feminist and birth-control advocate Margaret Sanger. Wells's many affairs (chronicled by him in the posthumous *H. G. Wells in Love* and, more amusingly, by David Lodge in *A Man of Parts*) can be productively viewed as a form of unconventionality that struck at the root of normative culture and held implications for the period's literary output. Beyond the long list of names of his sexual partners, Wells's attitude of confrontational gender, family, and social identity is signaled by his early divorce from his cousin (1893); his unconventional marriage to his second wife, Amy Catherine Robbins (called Jane); the complex arrangements that grew up around his other partners, including his children with Rebecca West and with the young and brilliant socialist Amber Reeve; the fact that so many of his lovers were extremely impressive women; and the way he continually wrote all of these into his published work—and in many cases they wrote him into theirs.

Finally, to name just one more evocative community, in *Group Portrait*, Nicholas Delbanco resurrects an intensely productive and appealing group of five writers who lived in the same region of Kent and Sussex, south of London, in the first decade of the twentieth century, among whom he traces a delicate web of friendship, collaboration, and, in some cases, conflict: Wells, Conrad, Ford, Crane, and James. These intricate relationships and collaborations are, in Delbanco's estimation, above all about productivity and the creation of great works of literature: "Ford wrote at book-length on Conrad and James; Conrad wrote essays on Crane and James; Wells wrote about them all. Inveterate biographers and autobiographers, they have left much language behind. There were letters, volumes, and dedications exchanged, plans formed and shelved, agents shared. These men took trips together, formulated joint aesthetics, wrote books in the same room."[37] Delbanco is mostly concerned with literary output, how these friends collaborated or spurred one another on, helping engender some defining works of this period that are not often placed side by side.

From a literary-historical perspective, though, one pair dazzles for their long friendship and their ultimate severance, Wells and Henry James. I parse this friendship in some detail for two reasons: first, because it gives texture, poignancy, and explanatory power to the dialectical relation I am attempting to establish in this book between Wells and modernism and, second, because it reopens the very real, raw case, which has seemed not only closed but foreclosed, of what literature was going to do and how it was going to be canonized in the modern period. Theirs was a public and famous break, and the story of their attachment and its demise was, up until about 1975, a staple in literary criticism. Because their rupture occurred partially in published form, with James's letters released in 1920, from early on it assumed the appearance of a literary parable. A volume of their correspondence and related texts, edited by Leon Edel and Gordon N. Ray, was published in 1958, offering readers an engrossing, concentrated, ultimately saddening narrative of this strange relationship. What *Henry James and H. G. Wells: A Record of Their Friendship, Their Debate on the Art of Fiction, and Their Quarrel* dramatizes as if in real time, and what literary history used to see as a vibrant, living story about the aesthetic practices and values of the twentieth century, is an intricate interleaving of personalities with literary principles. Forster mentions the debate in *Aspects of the Novel* as a "matter of great literary importance" (interestingly, Forster confesses that "my own prejudices are with Wells").[38] The friendship and its spectacular demise show us two writers thinking together and, in a sense, through each other, about the nature and value of their medium and their métier and about whether it is possible for entirely different—even oppositional—approaches to literature to cohabitate harmoniously in a friendship. This story, in its textual manifestations, helps introduce *Inventing Tomorrow* because it shows, in stark terms, how a dynamic, beguiling interaction between two powerful intellectuals, and the writerly ideals for which they stood, became swallowed and trivialized by the monolith of academic modernism, leaving us poorer in our conception of what the creative imagination of these years in fact generated.

The communication has a distinctive flavor. In his letters of over fifteen years, James often praises Wells elaborately, responding to Wells's books as they were published and as Wells sent them to him; he seems to have read a great number of them, if not all, in this period from 1898 to 1915. He also critiques these works, which, one senses, he loves and loathes in equal measure. The loving is, in most cases, responsive to the pervasive presence of Wells's own personality coursing through all of his works (a quality of Wells's prose suggested also by Forster); the discomfort stems from several sources, most notably James's increasing sense that Wells is insensitive to actual human motive, behavior, and speech, that he can be sloppy, and, to use a word he repeats several times, that he is "cheeky" ("Indeed your Cheek is positively the very sign and stamp of your genius").[39] Equally striking in James's voice, however, are an erotic undertow and a fulsome praise of Wells as the standout of his generation. That term, "generation," returns frequently in James's letters and ultimately in his essay "The Younger Generation," which was the opening salvo in their break. "You are for me," James wrote in a letter, "the most interesting 'literary man' of your generation" (Edel and Ray, *James and Wells*, 103). If one were psychoanalyzing James, this question of his being the elder statesman and Wells representing both the promise and the threat from below would be a fruitful one to plumb. Two representative sequences:

> Reading a book of yours is a great circumstance and solemnity—a great experience—to me and surrounded with grave forms and rites. . . . I *taste* you immensely as I take you in—that is I go on tasting and tasting, and it is as if, while this lasts, I had my mouth very full. . . . You have *force* as really no one has it, and in the fashion of some irresistible chemical dissolvent, so that reading you is really being "acted upon" in a manner that is akin to conscience and anguish.
>
> (110–11)

> Take these fevered lines tonight then simply for a sign of my admiring, panting, more or less gasping impression and absorption of your book [*The Future in America*]. When I think of the brevity of the process, of the direct and immediate experience, from which it springs, the intensity and superiority of the

projection of the realization leave me, I confess, quite wonderstricken, and I ask myself if such a quantity of *important* observation—so *many* of such—have ever before sprung into life under so concentrated a squeeze.

(114)

James, we might say, is lavish in his attention to Wells the writer and, even more, to the man whose aura always seems to be invigorating the pages of his books. By contrast, the few letters we have from Wells seem relatively cold, despite several that heap praise on James and adopt a tone of self-deprecation, not surprising given their difference in age and status. In these exchanges, Wells regularly demeans his own work as mere ephemera, a rhetorical move that reaches its culmination in the final exchange of letters, constituting their break, when Wells declares, "I had rather be called a journalist than an artist, that is the essence of it" (264). As in any epistolary correspondence, the interplay of present and absent constitutes a strong current of potential meaning, and, in this case, one intuits the time spent together, talking about topics such as books and aesthetic principles and their shared acquaintances. They seem to have genuinely liked each other, and Wells also sustained a warm and mutual friendship with Henry's brother, William James. Equally visible in tone and gesture, if not fully articulated, are the stark divergences in literary values that would eventually open a chasm too wide to be bridged.

And so when two published works erupt into the private dialogue, unleashing into the public realm the refrain of criticism that had sounded on James's part intermittently throughout their correspondence and in ferocious bursts from Wells, it is as if the relationship simultaneously culminates and reveals itself as alive with emotion and consequences. The public breach began with James, whose "The Younger Generation," published in the *Times Literary Supplement* (later in *Notes on Novelists*) in 1914, treated Wells's texts as a case study, along with Bennett, Conrad, Lawrence, and others, of a kind of writing that, as he puts it, holds too closely to the project of mere "saturation." His critique is that Wells and Bennett in particular "squeeze out to the utmost the plump and more or less juicy orange of a particular acquainted state and let this affirmation of energy, however directed or undirected, constitute for them the 'treatment' of the theme" (182–83). He also produces some dubious phrases in his appraisal of Wells, such as when he compares Wells's writing to "turn[ing] out his mind and its contents upon us . . . as from a high window forever open" (190). Gone are all the statements of force, admiration, genius. The piece is characterized by familiar Jamesian restraint and obliqueness, but for Wells, there was no mistaking the

harshness. Too, the language was recycled very closely from their private correspondence, which perhaps added to Wells's sense of outrage.

No matter the trigger, Wells's response was extremely harsh. As was often the
case with Wells, he tried his friendships through a public rift, this one irreconcilable. Inserted into his novel *Boon* (1915), as part of a comic-satiric scene in
which many famous living novelists (along with some fictional ones) assemble
for a party at a friend's villa, comes an ad hominem attack on James's style and
priorities, alongside a lengthy parody of James's writing. The most notorious and
oft-cited passage in his attack is this one (in the words of the character Boon):

> "His vast paragraphs sweat and struggle; they could not sweat and elbow and
> struggle more if God Himself was the processional meaning to which they
> sought to come. And all for tales of nothingness . . . It is a leviathan retrieving
> pebbles. It is a magnificent but painful hippopotamus resolved at any cost, even
> at the cost of its dignity, upon picking up a pea which has got into a corner of its
> den. Most things, it insists, are beyond it, but it can, at any rate, modestly, and
> with an artistic singleness of mind, pick up that pea . . ."[40]

Such is the tenor of *Boon*'s blistering attack, whose fury is only multiplied by
the addition of Wells's parody (which, it must be said, is quite brilliant). It was a
scorched-earth assault whose scope and vulgarity of manners stunned and
wounded James. At the level of content, Wells's largest point about James's fiction
is that he shaves and shaves at what can be permitted into the novel and then concentrates excessively on those minute and, to Wells, trivial situations we recognize as the Jamesian scene. The attack goes on for several pages, along these lines:

> "In practice James's selection becomes just omission and nothing more. He
> omits everything that demands digressive treatment or collateral statement. . . .
> All that much of humanity he clears out before he begins his story. It's like
> cleaning rabbits for the table. . . . Then with the eviscerated people he has
> invented he begins to make up stories. What stories they are! . . . These people
> cleared for artistic treatment never make lusty love, never go to angry war, never
> shout at an election or perspire at poker . . ."
>
> (*Boon*, 98–99, ellipses added)

Significantly, the key charge here—of triviality—is precisely the same leveled at
Wells and his fellow "materialists" by Woolf in "Modern Fiction." Wells and modernism agree that literature should be hungering after what matters, should

stake its ground on the significant and the real. But they differ on what these are and on how to capture them. After a brief exchange following the publication of *Boon*, in which James comes out looking much the more attractive, the correspondence—and friendship—ends.

The crucial point to extract from the Wells-James debacle is the way it both precipitated and continues to exemplify a spirit of antagonism between Wells and modernism. As precipitation, it is clear that when Wells repudiated James, he was also solidifying a persona for himself in opposition to what he called the "Art Form" approach to the novel. In his *Experiment in Autobiography* (1934), he looks back on these events with little remorse and summarizes the differences in these terms:

> [Henry James] was a very important figure in the literary world at that time and a shrewd and penetrating critic of the technique by which he lived.... From his point of view there were not so much "novels" as The Novel, and it was a very high and important achievement. He thought of it as an Art Form and of novelists as artists of a very special and exalted type. He was concerned about their greatness and repute. He saw us all as Masters or would-be Masters ... I was by nature and education unsympathetic with this mental disposition.
>
> (*EA*, 410–11)

> All this talk I had with Conrad and Hueffer and James about the just word, the perfect expression, about this or that being "written" or not written, bothered me, set me interrogating myself, threw me into a heart-searching defensive attitude.... But in the end I revolted altogether and refused to play their game. "I am a journalist," I declared, "I refuse to play the 'artist.' If sometimes I am an artist it is a freak of the gods. I am a journalist all the time and what I write *goes now*—and will presently die."
>
> (*EA*, 531–32)

The key word, as striking here as it was in Wells's final letter to James in 1915, is "journalist." There is something brave and counterintuitive to contemporary literary-critical standards in proclaiming oneself a journalist whose work is not meant to last.[41] By "journalist" Wells means to conjure two qualities: that the work is in and of its place in time, hence ephemeral, and also that the writing is engaged with the present in an active, interventionist spirit, aiming to inject new ideas and produce change. In this sense, Wells overtly embraces a stance that faces off against modernism (here James, Conrad, and Ford), which, as he presents it, was obsessed with posterity and demanded, at least nominally, that the work of art transcend the political situation of its moment. In other words, if James defends his concept of the novel in terms that stress a purity and integrity of vision, what is less recognizable to us is the deliberate stance that the writer might be choosing—as distinct from being consigned to—a position of present-ness. To be clear, it is not my view, nor is such entailed, that Wells's work actually is merely temporal or dated but that he is staking out a different role for fiction from what literary history, deeply invested in the idea that literature must be capable of sustaining itself over time within a canon, takes as a premise. Wells's vision of life, including literary life, was fundamentally biological, and in the biological universe, nothing is forever. Each agent has a place in ensuring the longevity and well-being of the species. It is this model of fiction as entering the stream of ongoing life that drew Wells and fed his experimentation.

## IV. WELLS AND LITERARY STUDIES

The James debate is above all symptomatic: Wells was up against the literary values for which James stood, and in offering himself as something entirely other, he came, as those values were enshrined, to be drastically reduced in significance and appeal. Indeed, the academy has rather blindly followed modernism's lead in underrating Wells, dismissing him on grounds of his very success, his ardent view that literature can and should affect positive change in the world, and his willingness to experiment with forms traditionally viewed as nonserious (or nonliterary).[42] And Wells's toxic words toward his peers and on subjects such as the "unfit" have not helped him. To the extent that Wells is considered by literary scholars, it is much more likely to be in the context of Victorian studies than modernism, for reasons that, once again, are not far to seek (modernism designating a style and mode, Victorian a chronological span; plus the fact that it is his early works that are esteemed today). An easy Google Books tabulation of references in its vast archive to Wells and to Woolf illustrates the story in graphic form, pinpointing the year in which the trends reverse—when references to Woolf begin to exceed those of Wells—at 1955. This accords well with what we know of literary history, since it was at midcentury that modernism became solidified and canonized, under the influence of F. R. Leavis, the *Scrutiny* group in England, and the New Critics in the United States, all of whose judgments spread around the world in the form of curricula, criticism, and the institutionalization of a particular kind of literary discernment. General readership is equally tenuous, despite the publication of a superb though very limited series of his works by Penguin in 2005, edited by the distinguished Wells critic Patrick Parrinder, and of a smaller series from Oxford World's Classics, all science-fiction titles. The vast bulk of Wells's writing remains out of print, and the only sustained attention and appreciation continues to be in the area of science fiction.[43]

There is more to this academic neglect than nonappearance, however; the other, even more entrenched issue is the surprisingly oppositional nature of so much of the criticism that we do have. This comes in several forms and dates back over a century, to the time when Wells's presence began to be felt. His formulations about culture, war, and the future were often simplified and misconstrued, right from the moment of inception. Such is the price of fame and his extreme prolixity, as well as, in Wells's case, an entirely uncensored approach to writing and a willingness to air all of his views, however contradictory or unappetizing (witness the skewering of his friend James in print).[44] The most direct and straightforward pattern today comes from critics who simply assume that Woolf and other modernists were accurate when they attacked Wells, that, for instance, Wells's writing is similar in some way to that of Bennett and Galsworthy; or that it stands as "materialist" to Woolf's modernist; or that he represents solely a midway era, the Edwardian, a short span that had a flavor of its own and was stamped out in 1914. A second symptom of contemporary criticism, which is essentially universal, is to reiterate the commonplace about the extreme deterioration marking Wells's career, where some aspect of the early oeuvre is taken seriously (the scientific romances, the short stories, *Tono-Bungay*) while the rest is happily consigned to oblivion. In fact, I think it fair to say that there is not a single work of Wells criticism or literary biography that does not either assume or directly state where and how his work diminished in quality and interest.[45] A third symptom of contemporary critical misprision can be considered as a grouping syndrome, where Wells is figured often as "a Wells or a Shaw" or "writers like Wells," as somehow typifying a literary phenomenon—which is particularly odd given his genuine idiosyncrasy and the sui generis nature of his public persona and vast output. A fourth category is best understood in terms of what Eve Sedgwick has influentially described as "paranoid" or "symptomatic" reading, in which some of Wells's least palatable statements or views are taken to stand as the full story, the underlying explanatory reality of his enormous body of work. Scholars and critics in the academy have learned to diagnose in the ugly statement a pervading fever, but are less capable of registering a massive body of writing that carries along multiple, competing views and strands, where it becomes crucial to balance the scales and assess the meaning and impact of different articulations within the internal body of work.

Finally, and most seriously, critics simply discredit Wells, and in many cases they do so because he fails to stand in line with modernism. I offer here just one case in point, though the examples could be greatly multiplied. Debra Rae Cohen's "Getting the Frame Into the Picture: Wells, West, and the Mid-War Novel" is an excellent piece written by a thoughtful, accomplished scholar; at the same time, its adherence to modernist principles has led Cohen to read Wells in ways that diminish his work and reproduce the narrative learned from modernism itself. Wells is deftly opposed in the essay to Rebecca West, with West's slim novella *The Return of the Soldier* (1918) treated as a rich and rewarding literary account of the war then underway and as a riposte to her lover's hugely successful war novel, *Mr. Britling Sees It Through* (1916); his is read through an unbendingly modernist prism and the novel essentially repudiated. That there is a gender dimension to this hierarchical and combative set-up should go without saying: we are meant to root for West, and it would be difficult to argue against such advocacy in principle. Cohen's summary of her argument reveals these dynamics crisply:

> *The Return of the Soldier*, in fact, takes on—in the sense of combating, rather than imitating—many features of *Mr. Britling Sees It Through*: in its sparseness, its visuality, its embrace of the modernist principle of "show, don't tell," its foregrounding of the processes of representation through the flawed observations of its unreliable narrator, it implicitly counters Wells's own conviction that a "novel of ideas" must necessarily center on explicit discussion, on "magnified and crystallized conversations and meditations" ("The Novel of Ideas," 220)....
> While both novels function as home front diagnoses, *in medias res*, of the national flaws that let England into war, West's work is assertively darker, pointedly striking down the very structural consolations in which Wells's novel allows itself to indulge.[46]

Cohen's reading represents a strong embrace of modernist values, from indirection, to unreliable narration, to the emphasis on perception over description, to the focus on representation's own mechanisms, to its darkness and antireligiosity, and to its refusal of closure. These priorities are enunciated in the present but are also carried forward from the period, reproducing Woolf's dyad, with modernists making the right literary and political moves and Wells standing for something aggressive and conventional. This I fervently oppose as a way of approaching all the issues at stake: modernism's stranglehold on reading techniques; the actual quality of Wells's texts, which are almost inevitably obscured under these strictures; the way the disagreements of that moment get projected outward as if for all time (whether it is West or James or Woolf being positioned against Wells), each party standing for a principle we either embrace or deplore; and, underpinning all of these, an unwillingness to challenge our own expectations. On the other hand, insofar as Cohen is arguing that West constructs her novella in response to Wells's, she is placing Wells and modernism in a more intricate and more interesting conversation.

Scholars of modernism have largely missed or misread Wells, but several other groups do write in sustained, compelling ways about his work. These merit a word of notice up front: scholars of the nineteenth century, who see him as an interesting phenomenon at the end of their era, exposing many of its anxieties and fascinations; science-fiction critics, who take his writing as foundational; and the small cadre of Wellsians who have done heroic work to keep his books in publication and to write comprehensively about his massive career. The H. G. Wells Society is modest as an author society, located in England with a largely UK membership, but its journal, *The Wellsian*, its annual conference, and its fostering of Wells scholarship all are crucial sustaining features for the study of Wells's work and life. A number of scholars in this community have written extensively on his work—notably Patrick Parrinder, John Huntington, John Hammond, Michael Sherborne, and Simon James—on subjects ranging across the huge panorama of Wells's interests, including science, the world state, technology, war, and sex.[47] Hammond's book *H. G. Wells and the Modern Novel* represents a particularly welcome addition to Wells scholarship within the context of modernism (the debate with James is rendered thoughtfully and extensively, for instance), as Hammond argues that Wells came much closer to modernist technique than is usually averred.[48] In a more recent study, *Maps of Utopia*, Simon James approaches Wells's extensive writing career according to a trajectory of "what Wells thinks the world might be . . . what it actually is . . . what it should be . . . and finally what he fears it might become," moving nimbly across genres and considering Wells's rise in the context of late-Victorian cultural histories.[49] Any book-length study of Wells has to contend with the fact of his enormous bibliography. The majority of author-focused work on Wells carves out a limited sphere, either in thematic or generic terms, the vast preponderance of these focusing on the science fiction. Those aiming for comprehensiveness often find themselves with myriad summaries and mini-sections to account for the enormousness of the bibliography. These strategies are not universal; along with Hammond and James, I might highlight Peter Kemp's book *H. G. Wells and the Culminating Ape*, published in 1982, which brilliantly analyzes Wells's biological imagination as it characterizes his full writing career, the book's aim being to disclose what Kemp diagnoses as his obsessional personality across his texts. Though my own reading of Wells diverges starkly from Kemp's, his book represents an admirably engaged account of Wells's full body of work, organized around ideas and themes in the biological sphere.

It is only in science fiction that Wells's reputation is well established. Although Wells may not have been the first writer to stake out the terrain of science-themed writings in the mode of speculation, he was undoubtedly the most influential.[50] Here is Darko Suvin, the acknowledged founder of modern science-fiction scholarship:

> With all his strengths and weaknesses, Wells remains the central writer and nodal point in the tradition of modern science fiction. He collected, as it were, all the main influences of earlier writings . . . and transformed them in his own image, whereupon they entered the treasury of subsequent science fiction. He invented a new thing under the sun in the story of time traveling without the help of dreams. He codified, for better or worse, the notions of invasion from space and cosmic catastrophe ("The Star"), of social and biological degeneration, of the fourth dimension, of the future megalopolis. . . . [Several listed] summits of Wells's are a demonstration of what is possible in science fiction, of the cognitive shudder peculiar to it. . . . For all his vacillations, his fundamental historical lesson is that the stifling bourgeois society is but a short moment in a menacing but also open-ended human evolution under the stars.[51]

Suvin's account of Wells clarifies that it is the mix of plots/stories with his unique writerly qualities that together generate the peculiar configurations of science fiction as it has come down to us. These tropes and forms are so familiar, having penetrated pop culture to an enormous degree, that one might forget that their universalism today had its earlier inception in the particularities of Wells's culture and of his genius. Like Suvin and Bernard Bergonzi, who sees Wells's early writings as constellating fin-de-siècle culture, Roger Luckhurst attributes Wells's foundational stature to the signal ways in which his work brings together multiple strands in the late-Victorian imagination, such as mechanization, class politics, and evolution, funneled through a far-seeing, highly creative series of speculations. As Luckhurst writes, "It is from within this crucible of mixed elements [in his early works] that Wells was to forge a scientized framework for his fiction and political writings and the evolutionary paradigm that dominated English scientific romance before, and to some extent after, 1945."[52] Among the key features critics such as Suvin, Luckhurst, Bergonzi, and others have noted is that Wells implants his fantastic elements within a realist universe governed by recognizable laws and patterns, one of the staples of science fiction. The ramifications of Wells's occupying the position of "realist of the fantastic," as Conrad first called him, will emerge at different times in this book.[53] As Wells wrote, "The writer of fantastic stories . . . must help [the reader] in every possible unobtrusive way to *domesticate* the impossible hypothesis. . . . As soon as the magic trick has been done the whole business of the fantasy writer is to keep everything else human and real."[54]

Too, in an early reading, Suvin credited Wells's works with formulating the "cognitive estrangement" he sees as the elemental characteristic of science fiction. For Suvin, cognitive estrangement means that the tale is encountered as other to our recognizable universe while remaining nevertheless ultimately legible and valuable according to familiar norms and patterns. Estrangement, like the uncanny, is both known and just beyond the accessible.[55] Suvin also argues that science fiction typically depends upon what he called the "*novum*," the novelty or innovation that engenders whatever alternative world or system the text needs for its verisimilitude, another Wellsian trope.[56] Other science-fiction scholars assessing Wells's contributions stress motif—the garden, door, or other aperture into a different world; the play with scientific principles or new technologies; the emphasis on time; the juxtaposition of other worlds and states of existence. In all of these ways—thematic, formal, cognitive—Wells helped inaugurate a century (and counting) of imagining our familiar world jolted out of its normal apprehension, where perceptions are either utterly heightened or powerfully diminished and altered, and where our certainties are put into question within the compelling vision of a fully imagined other world. There are ways that such a mode can be rethought as a kind of modernism, perhaps unrecognizable to itself.

If Wells and modernism often seem to face off as rivals, in concluding this short précis, I want to return to the more dialectical, intricate interactions that, like the two essays on modern fiction with which this introduction began, can be as allied and entangled as they are discrete and antagonistic. Let us consider Joyce and Wells: slender as it is, their interaction nicely captures the accordion-like flow into and out of texts, into and out of agreement, that characterizes Wells and modernism as a pairing. The two were cordial, with letters exchanged as early as 1915, Wells taking an interest in the younger writer, and at least one meeting in 1928, as documented by Joyce's biographer Richard Ellmann. (There is also a tantalizingly unfinished limerick that begins, "There once was an author named Wells . . .").[57] Wells wrote a review of *A Portrait of the Artist as a Young Man* in 1917 for the *Nation* (reprinted in the *New Republic*), in which he praised the novel for its characterization of Stephen's coming of age: "it is," he wrote, "by far the most living and convincing picture that exists of an Irish Catholic upbringing. It is a mosaic of jagged fragments that does altogether render with extreme completeness the growth of a rather secretive, imaginative boy in Dublin."[58] There is some mild critique, as when Wells writes (rather like Woolf in her assessment of *Ulysses* in "Mr. Bennett and Mrs. Brown") that Joyce "would bring back into the general picture of life aspects which modern drainage and modern decorum have taken out of ordinary intercourse and conversation." He calls it a "cloacal obsession," a phrase Joyce liked so much as to drop it right into *Ulysses*, in the Aeolus episode, adding a few twists and some irony.[59] All of these interactions seem to have been friendly, and Wells was solicited by Pound to help Joyce when he was in difficulties with the consular authorities in Zurich in 1919. One letter in particular captures a sense of the potential for alliance, though succeeded by ultimate distance, in a moment of uneasy almost-fellowship between these two diametrically unlike writers:

> Now with regard to this literary experiment of yours [*Finnegans Wake*]. It's a considerable thing because you are a very considerable man and you have in your crowded composition a mighty genius for expression which has escaped discipline. But I don't think it gets anywhere. You have turned your back on common men, on their elementary needs and their restricted time and intelligence and you have elaborated. What is the result? Vast riddles. . . .
>
> All this from my point of view. Perhaps you are right and I am all wrong. Your work is an extraordinary experiment and I would go out of my way to save it from destruction or restrictive interruption. It has its believers and its following. Let them rejoice in it. To me it is a dead end.
>
> My warmest good wishes to you Joyce. I can't follow your banner any more than you can follow mine. But the world is wide and there is room for both of us to be wrong.[60]

The letter is poignant, redolent of missed opportunities. There is a sense of a literary and literary-critical road not taken. I wonder if it was always necessary, as now seems axiomatic, that Wells's and Joyce's directions could not both have been followed. Considering these varied and complex interactions, we might picture it this way: modernism is talking on the phone and literary criticism is in the room with it, only able to hear an occasional intonation from the other end—but who and what is on the other side, and why is that invisible speaker making our modernist friend so agitated and adamant? What is that muffled voice actually saying?

## V. WRITING FOR THE WORLD

One area where Wells staked his ground in starkly unique ways involves his project of totality. There is probably nothing that makes students of the twentieth century more uncomfortable than the idea of the total. It signifies too much that has been ruinous in the century's history, and its place at the root of two of the most atrocious realities of the past hundred years, total war and totalitarianism, tells that story all too clearly. With a history, first, of totalitarian regimes and the wars and genocides they brought and, then, of multinational capitalism, with its devastation of the planet and its cementing of egregious, worldwide inequalities, the twentieth century has furnished us with good reason to be skeptical of the total. Indeed, since modernism, I think we can say that a suspicion of the total has become fully ingrained in literary (and other intellectual and progressive) standards. We will have our epics, but only if they take place over one day, in a small city, and with a marginalized protagonist who seems, in truth, unlikely to redeem the nation. "I do not believe in Belief," wrote Forster in 1940, articulating the situation for modernists; instead, he puts his trust in "personal relationships. Here is something comparatively solid in a world of full of cruelty and violence."[61] Or Lily Briscoe: "The great revelation perhaps never did come. Instead there were little daily miracles, illuminations, matches struck unexpectedly in the dark."[62] Or Eliot's modern Fisher King: "These fragments I have shored against my ruins." The modest, small-scale, fragmentary: even in a literature that could have encyclopedic hunger or could seek the universalism of, say, Eliot's "tradition," into which the fragments may fall, it took to heart the subjectivist creed that all stories are only partial, all perspectives only singular, all triumphs humble.[63] Even the most flexible definitions of the term "modernism," such as Mark Wollaeger's in defining global modernism, recognize that "fragmentation as the marker of modernism is not likely to go away any time soon."[64] As Paul Saint-Amour sums up the state both of modernism and of modernist studies circa 2017 in terms of what he labels "weak theory": "What . . . theorists of weakness share is not a vehement, dialectical negation of strength but an interest in the work accomplished by the proximate, the provisional, and the probabilistic."[65]

But Wells was a totalizer. His vision and most ardent desire, toward which he bent his writing and activism for most of his fifty-year career, were for a world state. Nations are the source of untold evil in the modern world; this became and remained his mantra. A cosmopolitan to the root, Wells wanted to eradicate nations, replacing patriotism with loyalty to the whole human race. In this sense, Wells was a Kantian, hewing to the Enlightenment ideal of universal principles of human ethics and aiming at a common humanity as a uniting, universalizing, and pacifying concept. Critics of the last three decades have, as we know, shown how such universals were in fact founded on essential, worldwide inequities, derived from and favoring particular groups. Such a critique can remain as a given even as we productively assess the meaning and value of Wells's universalist aspirations. Wells sometimes called this cosmopolitan view his "religion," as in his manifesto for the gradual creation of the world state, *The Open Conspiracy: Blue Prints for a World Revolution* (1928), where it is quite simple: "The modernisation of the religious impulse leads us straight to the effort for the establishment of the world state as a duty."[66] As a futurist as well as historian, Wells was certain that the next stage in human history must be one in which all people recognize our mutual dependence and agree to join together as a world polity. It was vividly clear to Wells as early as the turn of the century that the human race was connected by technology and by geopolitical trends, by the reality that those with power were poised to—and, he felt, unless the direction of solidarity was followed, certainly would—destroy the edifices of human life, even ourselves as a species and the planet that sustains us. It was time, he fervently believed, to recognize humanity as a whole, to take the human community as one unit, which must work and live together under a single political and cultural system. People would speak one language (or at least communicate freely in a single language), share a common goal in the ongoing betterment of humanity, and be governed by those who could see past rivalry or patriotism, in a spirit of servitude to the species and to the planet. This is the essential, driving idea sustaining his enormous and diverse output, from around the turn of the century until his death. In its simplest terms, he can write that "peace and national independence are incompatible" and that

> in flat contrast to [the] international school of pacifism is the cosmopolitan school . . . of which I declare myself entirely a disciple. This school thinks not in terms of states and nations but in terms of cosmopolis, the city of mankind. Cosmopolitanism is something entirely different from internationalism, it is antagonistic to internationalism. It does not see world peace as an arrangement of states but as a greater human solidarity overriding states.[67]

This from an address to the German Reichstag in 1929. One can open nearly any work by Wells written after about 1905 and find these views expressed in some form, that humanity is hurtling toward destruction and that its only hope—a real one, not utopian, as he repeatedly insisted—is to create a world state led by a government of the devoted and the skilled. It would not be a democracy; instead, its rulers would come from a class of leaders willing to devote themselves to this new unified community. The rewards for making this revolution, in Wells's view, would be nearly limitless, "a life of liberations.... A graver humanity, stronger, more lovely, longer lived, will learn and develop the ever-enlarging possibilities of its destiny. For the first time, the full beauty of this world will be revealed to its unhurried eyes ... [it] is the awaking of mankind from a nightmare of the struggle for existence and the inevitability of war" (*OC*, 151–52).

For most contemporary critics, these views will be registered along the spectrum from naïve to sinister, and one of the largest obstacles in evaluating Wells and his place in twentieth-century intellectual, aesthetic, and political life will be to return to first principles on the idea of a world state. Strong skepticism was often manifested by his contemporaries and followers, such as George Orwell and Aldous Huxley, both of whose most famous texts, *1984* and *Brave New World*, are, among other things, direct responses to Wells's utopianism about a world government (for Orwell, of course, also the actual totalitarian states of the 1940s). For most critics today, his hopes for a world state would seem irreparably imperialist and the method of governance he envisions overly elitist. This is a legitimate response, but it need not be an automatic one. To be clear, it is not my aim in this book to advocate for Wells's position on the world state or on anything else, for that matter, nor is such necessary. It is my goal, rather, to have us consider the major principle of world unification, which takes many forms across Wells's oeuvre, as a rich, important, and, at this point counterintuitive ideal that gives a different shape to the consideration of many topics, from politics to biology, and helps us think along new lines about Wells's time and about our own.

Wells's totalizing energies took a variety of forms, running from the explicitly political to the formal, thematic, and generic, and to a more amorphous category amounting to a sensibility or *geist*. But the crucial feature to isolate up front, cutting across these rubrics, is an orientation to think at the largest scales. Take history: as we will discuss in chapter 3, "Time," *The Outline of History* can justifiably be named a pioneer in the field recently named "Big History," with its attempt to tell a planetary story, in marked and deliberate contradistinction to national history, by far the dominant mode in Wells's day (and ours), which *The Outline* holds responsible for the First World War. In this sense, reading Wells intersects with the project of world-system analysis, an influential area of political theory, with Immanuel Wallerstein's work helping to catalyze a shift toward larger units of analysis, beyond nation or region. What this bigness means for *The Outline* is (a) beginning with the scale of the cosmos and the origin of the earth; (b) continuing along decreasing (but still vast) temporal and spatial scales, to dilate at length not only on events of the far past but on the nature of these spans of time themselves; and (c) attempting to write the history of all parts and peoples of the world, as distinct from one region or continent, much less a single nation. That Wells is in some ways unsuccessful when it comes to this last effort, his book becoming more Eurocentric as it draws closer to the present, suggests the challenges in his undertaking and his own residual European biases. But the principle remains a potent and distinctive one, and it goaded historians to respond, in most cases with umbrage, to the power of his provocation and to the success of his book. Writing history at such a scale simply had no place in the profession. In *The Outline*, the guiding idea and the method become identical: to insist that the world has a common history means developing schemes to write that singular story.

*The Outline* is only one example; Wells's writing is replete with attempts to think outward from the individual to the species, or from the present to the far past and future, or from the local to the planetary.[68] For Wells, the mandate to extend one's cognition into larger spans of space and time extends from technology, as he took stock of how new means of communication, transportation, and scientific understanding were bringing the world closer together, creating intricate and indelible forms of global interdependence, epitomized in the matrix of complex financial ties across the world. In the Wells universe, such imbrications often work themselves into war. His novel *The War in the Air*, to be discussed in chapter 2, "Civilian," represents his most elaborate dramatization of the meaning and consequences of worldwide connectivity, there played out as the enabling condition for the world's self-destruction. The nature of connectedness is intricately, for Wells, entwined with its waging of ever-more-total wars, yet it is also simply the condition of modernity, for better and for worse. Much of his career was thus dedicated to redirecting the reality of world unity from its destructive to its productive capacities. As he put it in the 1930s,

> There has in fact been a complete revolution in our relation to distances. . . . Everybody knows these facts now, but round about 1900 we were only beginning to take notice of this abolition of distance. Even in 1919 the good gentlemen who settled the world for ever at Versailles had not observed . . . that it was no longer possible to live in little horse-and-foot communities because of this change of scale. We know better now. Now the consequences of this change of scale force themselves upon our attention everywhere. Often in the rudest fashion. Our interests and our activities interpenetrate more and more. We are all consciously or unconsciously adapting ourselves to a single common world.[69]

The abolition of distance, the reality of a shrinking world, the desperate urge to transmute these potentially catastrophic situations into the basis for world peace: these are the underlying principles of Wells's writing.

Another strand of Wells's world thinking involves his version of what Carl Jung in the same period called the "collective unconscious." *The World of William Clissold* (1926), a novel-cum-meditation that contemplates the state of England and the world after the war, puts forth the idea of a "common mental being of our race" (noting that "race" here, as is almost always the case with Wells, refers to the human race, not to any specific racial group).[70] Here is how the narrator-protagonist Clissold describes the idea:

> For imposed upon our minds appears a mind. This is the mind in which exist science, history, and thought. It has the same sort of relation to our individual activities that a regiment or army has to its constituent men. It is a collective human person in whom we all participate and which invades all our personalities. It is no longer mortal as we are mortal. It is life awakening, breaking through the limitations of individuality and growing conscious of itself. We are all presented as contributory units to a Titanic being which becomes conscious and takes hold of this planet. . . .
>
> In the last million years or so our breed has changed from the most solitary habits to habits more social and co-operative than those of any other animal. The fierce, lonely, egoistic ape-soul has been modified and qualified, and had superimposed upon it an intricate fabric of mitigating and restraining dispositions. . . . There is now in man a desire to serve. There is a pleasure in and a craving for co-operation and associated action.[71]

Thinking about collectivity at the level of the mind, Wells attempts to blend evolution with his goal for a peaceful and united world. Ten years earlier, in *Boon* (the novel where he parodied James), Wells tested out the term "mind of the race," wondering what it might entail for literature to be a vehicle for consolidating and expressing a common consciousness. Devotion to the cause of world harmony acts as a kind of faith and as such is enlisted to serve him and others, apportioning value to one's own existence:

> So long as one lives as an individual, vanities, lassitudes, lapses, and inconsistencies will hover about and creep back into the picture, but I find nevertheless that this faith and service of constructive world revolution does hold together my mind and will in a prevailing unity, that it makes life continually worth living, transcends and minimizes all momentary and incidental frustrations and

takes the sting out of the thought of death. The stream of life out of which we rise and to which we return has been restored to dominance in my consciousness, and though the part I play is, I believe, essential, it is significant only through the whole.

(EA, 705)

One might recall, reading these lines, Eliot's strange musings in "Tradition and the Individual Talent": "The poet . . . must be aware that the mind of Europe—the mind of his own country—a mind which he learns in time to be much more important than his own private mind—is a mind which changes," or the way Yeats finds in visions "the power of many minds to become one, overpowering one another by spoken words and by unspoken thought till they have become a single, intense, unhesitating energy."[72] Each is tapping into a shared vein of anti-individualism, with Wells unabashedly claiming the political ambition of world unity as the realization of such potentialities.

To give just one further way in which Wells thought about a common intelligence and objective in the world, in the mid-1930s he became convinced that the answer lay in the development of a huge encyclopedia that would bring together, circulate, and constantly update world knowledge. It was a plan for the mass democratization of knowledge, and for several years he propagated its message in addresses, essays, broadcasts, and conversations with publishers whom he hoped to interest in the massive project. Here is one of his formulations for this world brain (1937):

> A World Encyclopedia no longer presents itself to a modern imagination as a row of volumes printed and published once for all, but as a sort of mental clearing house for the mind, a depot where knowledge and ideas are received, sorted, summarized, digested, clarified and compared. It would be in continual correspondence with every university, every research institution, every competent discussion, every survey, every statistical bureau in the world. . . . This Encyclopaedic organization need not be concentrated now in one place; it might have the form of a network. Quite possibly it might to a large extent be duplicated. . . . It would constitute the material beginning of a real World Brain. . . . It would be undergoing continual revision.

(WB, 69–70)

Even in a first glance, the passage reflects Wells's attraction to language forms that are simultaneously engaged with the world and replaceable, utilitarian, and impermanent. As with The Outline of History, his largest goal for such globally minded projects is to eliminate war by reconstructing the mental workings of the population on worldwide lines of commonalty. The democratization of knowledge envisioned here represents an anomalous project in the 1930s, but it has a great deal in common with contemporary platforms of knowledge dissemination such as Wikipedia. There are differences, of course, with Wells proffering ideas that likely would make contemporary readers uncomfortable—such as his love of "a directorate and a staff of men of its own type, specialized editors and summarists," the particular bureaucrats with which his utopias typically swarm, or his unflinching claim that the mind of humanity needs to be reorganized (*WB*, 69). But what is shared between the world brain and the internet is stunning enough to open new channels of connection between him and us, as well as to show some of the dynamic ways in which totality could be imagined outside of either/or scenarios.

These projects and aspirations give texture and specific credence to the large scope of Wells's imagination; too, some of the greatest pleasure in reading his work derives from his effort to represent the cosmos in its broad dimensions. At ease in scales that dwarf our normal, human perception, Wells set his measure at the cosmic, geological, evolutionary levels, at times in the far future or past, and these transpositions can be especially haunting and rich. One thinks of late sequences in *The Time Machine*, when the Traveller moves ever further into the planet's waning existence, "drawn on by the mystery of the earth's fate, watching with a strange fascination the sun grow larger and duller in the westward sky, and the life of the old earth ebb away."[73] Early passages in *The Outline*, when Wells conveys the earth's place within the universe, share this evocative reach:

> It is well to understand how empty space is. If, as we have said, the sun were a ball of nine feet across, our earth would, in proportion, be the size of a one-inch ball, and at a distance of 322 yards from the sun. . . . *All the rest of space about us and around us and for unfathomable distances beyond is cold, lifeless, and void.* The nearest fixed star to us, *on this minute scale . . .* would be over 40,000 miles away.[74]

Wells's italicized passages stand out lexicographically and also for their power to arrest the reader in wonder, a pause from our work of envisioning these scales and ratios. Many other examples could be cited from across his canon. In an influential analysis, Frederic Jameson has written that modernism emerged as a specific formal response to the epistemological and cognitive disjuncture of imperialism, where the metropolitan writer experiences the gap between what he can know and what in fact imperialism and global capitalism are effecting.

Jameson gives as the defining example *Ulysses*, with its view from the ground in the midsized colonial metropolis of Dublin.[75] Wells offers up another approach to what is fathomable, birthed by training in biology, physics, geology, and chemistry, in which the cognitive disruptions of modernity begin not with a dramatization of partial vision brought on by political and economic forces but instead with the attempted view of the whole, a project of totalizing vision that might be suggestive of an entirely alternative set of literary responses. These responses will continually emerge in this book, as I attempt to develop a specifically Wellsian form of modern literary engagement with the world, as it can be comprehended according not only to the political but also to the cognitive and scalar status of Western thought in the first half of the twentieth century.[76]

Wells may have been at ease in stretching the imagination over space and time, but he also registered in his writing the profound obstacles and contradictions that these scales incur. Uniting them is—axiomatically—the problem of the viewer. Right from the beginning of his career in the late 1880s, Wells recognized that to think at enormous scale is to bump up against the meaning and experience of one's own individuality and perceptual apparatus. One of his widely reprinted essays, "Skepticism of the Instrument," originally delivered as an address to the Oxford Philosophical Society in 1903, offers Wells's view of where the human mind falls short, how, for instance, its instinct to group (rather than to particularize) each object or being leads to false philosophical premises. A very early piece, "A Talk with Gryllotalpa" (1887), makes the point succinctly, with the narrator noting to his friend, a representative of the "new sciences" that "A sun may be a big thing millions of miles away, but, surely, here it is not so big as the eye that sees it. Your duty to aid in the developing of humanity is a vast thing, doubtless, but nearer, and every day before you, is your duty to serve your neighbor."[77] These scalar inconsistencies are always present as a problem in Wells's work, a basic contradiction in the knowledge system. As we will see in chapter 3, "Time," the intransigent conflict between the scale at which one thinks and the kind of work one can accomplish in the world deeply confounds Wells's writing, driving a wedge between two different levels at which he always operated, the cosmic or biological, on the one hand, and the activist-political, on the other. Or, better, we might begin to ascertain a particular literary dimension to this contrast of incompatible scales, a structuring disjunction central to his work.

Yet for all the contradictoriness embedded in the effort to think at divergent scales or to grasp at totality, Wells insisted that it was possible, even necessary to do so, and in this conviction he was, if not unique, at least highly idiosyncratic. "Since the subject of this book is the whole destiny of man, and the whole duty of man," he writes at the outset of *The Open Conspiracy*, "it will certainly be called a pretentious book.... But it is no more pretentious to work upon the whole of life than upon parts and aspects of life; it is a question of scale and method" (*OC*, 7). A question of scale and method: this is true. We might take as an interlocutor to Wells's bold undertaking Paul Saint-Amour's groundbreaking argument in *Tense Future: Modernism, Total War, Encyclopedic Form* that the great books of interwar modernism foreswear totality. Even in those works that seem omnivorous, whose method derives from and radically pursues comprehensiveness, they nevertheless reject totality, insofar as the total is affiliated with a certain sweep of extreme violence. Texts of interwar modernism like *Ulysses* and *Parade's End* may comprise a great deal of material, words, and data and may be driven by the impulse to catalogue, but they nevertheless resist, in Saint-Amour's claim, doing so in a totalizing spirit. For these works, which thwart epic aspirations, the dream is more to archive and to protect than to own in totality and in perpetuity.[78] Saint-Amour's convincing account of modernism's relation to totality—or, more narrowly, the relation of the long works of interwar modernism to a totality perceived in the context of war—as a matter of sensibility, form, and deep attunement to the unequal and threatening realities of power would seem to make little room for Wells's efforts to create new universals and wholes. Rather, it points to another aspect of the modernism/Wells dialectic, in which both take the question of totality as a central problem in the world (total war, global interconnectedness via technology and economics, and, for Wells, also the interdependence among ecosystems at the planetary level) yet depart separately from shared ground—they to the elliptical, partial, and, in Saint-Amour's term, "encyclopedic," he to the world scale and to an unashamed effort to write not just of but *for* the world.

There is one final dimension of scale to be mentioned here, and that is the scope of Wells's own canon and archive. I have already noted that Wells published a great number of books (around one hundred), as well as countless other shorter texts, including essays, newspaper articles, book introductions, and addresses of all kinds, including radio broadcasts (his bibliography contains some six thousand items). His prolixity was legendary. Returning to the earlier discussion of why Wells has fallen foul of literary history, this unstoppable productivity plays a contributing part. Even within a given work, the words often come at a flood. *The World of William Clissold* is eight hundred pages long; *Joan and Peter*, another novel that was extremely widely read when it was published in 1918, clocks in at over five hundred pages, with small font; *The Outline of History* ran to twelve hundred. The economy of Wells's early science fiction, along with his brilliant short stories, makes for a much more amenable reading experience for literary historians. Indeed, the assumption in all quarters is that, with such a vast number of works (and words), many of them must be of questionable quality. More—to name an even larger obstacle—close reading is not the appropriate method as a primary route into the depth of his textual undertakings and the complex meaning of his work, even if there are passages all throughout his work that reward close reading.

Given the size of his corpus and the fact that close reading falls short as an anchoring methodology, what a Wellsian reading strategy entails is, instead, to read *at large*. Three primary elements will be marshaled: to read across texts, to resist the habit of categorizing narrowly by genre, and to reengage the literary work in its dialogue with a reading public. One way to amalgamate these various elements that constitute an at-large reading practice is to think carefully and creatively about the presence of Wells in his writings. Wells was always highly visible in his works, and his writing functions at times as an ongoing written embodiment of the Wellsian idea, of his interests, and even, to some degree, of himself. Importantly, in reading Wells at a larger scale than the autonomous, individual work, we inch closer to his reading public, which emphatically read and responded to him in such terms. As Christopher Frayling reports, "It had . . . been said of him that he wrote a new book in the time it took most people to read his last one."[79] As remarked earlier, there is often a notable vagueness in referencing him among his contemporaries, as if, again, he is more of a force or center of meaning than a writer primarily of specific texts. Individual texts, scenarios, genres, ideas, settings, and forms rise and fall in a more general Wellsian sea, as it surges and flows without shaping itself around a singular, distinguishing object. Reading Wells, then, means not only reading at an expanded scale (ten books, say, for any single one by another author) but also taking a different approach altogether, seeing the text as an instance of something that supersedes it, being willing to engage in the kind of depth-based close reading and textual analysis that stands at the basis of most literary criticism, but also to create dialogue and texture between and among texts, and to place all of them in the rich flow of a broader discourse, the politics of his ideas, the force field of his thought, understood always in an ongoing, endless conversation with his massive public. Such a practice does not suit a normal course syllabus, where each text must be representative, and so the habit of missing Wells's contributions has pedagogical implications, too. Nor is this Franco Moretti's distant reading, as important as that has been in dislodging some of literary criticism's unquestioned assumptions about scale, because it remains author focused, with an archive that rewards traditional reading rather than data analysis. But it learns from Moretti and other data-driven approaches that, in undertaking new reading methodologies at a broader scale, one can find a wholly renewed view not only of those who have been in the shadows—here Wells—but also of a familiar textual corpus, modernism. Digital humanities presses us to ask, "What is our object of analysis?" And for Wells, the answer is rarely, "the individual work of art, autonomous and whole." We need a different approach.

## VI. MEDIA, GENRE, TEXTS

One of the essential insights of media studies has been to recognize how fully the literature of different historical periods—here the decades between 1890 and 1950—is formed around its media ecologies. In the case of Wells, such an insight is inescapable. Wells was a media and technology guru: one of the few aspects of his work that has persisted in the public imagination is his prescience about the direction technology would go. Wells had his eye on the future, predicting everything from moving walkways to air conditioners, electric doors, televisions, and the internet, and he always had a special, uncanny accuracy when it came to weapons. He might be said to have invented both the tank and the atomic bomb, the first in a 1903 short story, "The Land Ironclads," for which Churchill gave him credit in the middle of the First World War ("You will have been interested to see the success with which your land battleship idea was at last—after many uneasy efforts—put into practice," he wrote to Wells in 1916), the second in his prewar 1914 novel *The World Set Free*, in which he provided the first envisioning of nuclear explosion.[80] Wells's understanding of the world's greatest dangers and highest ambitions turned on the abolition of distance brought on by communications technology; these were the basis and the grounds of modernity. As he wrote in *The War in the Air*, "The development of Science had altered the scale of human affairs. By means of rapid mechanical traction it had brought men nearer together, so much nearer socially, economically, physically, that the old separations into nations and kingdoms were no longer possible, a newer, wider synthesis was not only needed but imperatively demanded."[81]

But it was not all about destructive potential and threat. Wells loved new technologies; it was one of his trademarks. Catching the moment, the writers of *Downton Abbey* give the dowager (Maggie Smith) a characteristically clever line, in an episode set just before the war, "First electricity, now a telephone; sometimes I feel like I am living in an H. G. Wells novel." Or, in more academic terms, Keith Williams writes that "Wells made a crucial contribution to understanding and advancing not just the possibilities of cinematic narrative, but also the impact of other forms of recording technologies . . . his interaction with cinema's wider context makes him a principal pioneer of the media-determined parameters of modern subjectivity."[82] Along with such visual and audio technologies, Wells was always enthusiastic about more mundane innovations, such as those of modern plumbing and cleaning, with his utopias figuring arrangements such as the curved rooms in *A Modern Utopia* (1905), where no dust can gather, or hot and cold running water coming conveniently out of a tap in each flat. Critics have attached Wells's affinity for such cleanliness to his young childhood, when, by his own admission, most of his home time was spent in the basement of a narrow house in Bromley, where dust seemed to Wells to collect and collect in a kind of vortex, or out in the back area amid the garbage piles. One of his most famous socialist essays, "The Misery of Boots," opens with a view of people's feet moving past the writer/viewer, who watches the street from a ground-level flat. If such beginnings haunted him, they also catapulted his imagination into startling visions of a bright, self-cleaning world.[83]

Technology and the future: linked then as now, Wells was fully ensconced in both. His inhabitation of the future as the key temporality has wide ramifications. The future meant many different things for Wells, but, most pervasively, his conviction was that we need to do more than forecast: we need to plan, to design. One of Wells's most unrecognized doubles in the period, in this sense, is Le Corbusier. The two never met in person, though in 1932, when Wells proposed on the BBC that the world create a new cohort of "Professors of Prediction," Le Corbusier responded in print to the gambit. Though he rejected the idea of professors (of anything), Le Corbusier aligned himself resolutely with Wells in his essay, seeing both of them as plan makers, or, as he puts it in distinctly Wellsian language, "Discoverers of Men." As he writes, "Well, I think Mr. Wells will agree that *a man who makes a true plan* for the modern age is *doing something new*. He and I agree that such a thing could be prodigious."[84] In another near miss between the two, Wells approached Le Corbusier to design the sets of *Things to Come*, his major film of several years later.[85] Most generally, the names of Wells and Le Corbusier each came to be associated around the world with a phalanx of intertwined principles: the embracing of technology and the future, the broad scale of their vision, the belief that a better human world can be planned and built, their utopianism (Le Corbusier rejected that term; Wells embraced it), and, of course, the strenuous rejection of their sweeping ideas by later generations. During the World's Fair in New York in 1939, with its landmark focus on the future (it was named the "World of Tomorrow"), Wells wrote the cover story for the *New York Times Magazine*, reminding us of how closely he was allied to ideas of radical futures, including those involving cities, homes, transportation, entertainment, and living. Like other missed pairs suggested in this introduction (Wells and Woolf, Wells and Joyce), Wells and Le Corbusier together give a glimpse of a rich partnership of literary and architectural imaginations, a modernism we have not fully registered.[86]

Wells saw the darkest repercussions of technological advance along with a limitless potential for humanity to appropriate innovation toward its own salvation. He thus welcomed the technologies that often provoked his peers, most notably film and the many other new kinds of communications and entertainment technology that inevitably shadow modernism (telephone, telegraph, radio, gramophone).[87] It has been a commonplace since Friedrich Kittler's *Gramophone, Film, Typewriter* (1999) that writers in the early twentieth century felt besieged by film and the other new media forms. Faced with such formidable, even obliterative technologies, literature responded to the onslaught, either adapting itself formally to the sensibility created by the new language/sonic environment or taking rearguard action against these threatening agents, which, in this account, were siphoning readers, making art into commodity, deadening attention, and generally stupefying the modern imagination, leaving writers with a shrunken and unreceptive reading public.[88] For Wells, the problem with technology is not that it threatens literature but that the culture is always responding to it after the fact rather than thinking cohesively and creatively about how it can be marshaled in the direction of what is unifying, peaceful, and constructive. This is an essential point in text after text: Western culture needs to take social science seriously and do it better, assuming control of our technological futures in a way that attends to the nature of psychology, cognition, economic and class formations, and the realities of desire in a complex, global capitalist system.[89] "Mechanical invention had gone faster than intellectual and social organization," he diagnosed in *The War in the Air*, a view he articulated throughout his writings (*WA*, 179). The general principle of a modernity defined by its belatedness in relation to its own technological potential is one that powerfully motivated Wells to explain, think, write, and innovate.

Film, in particular, Wells believed, had a vast capacity as a medium for many kinds of expression. By the mid-1920s, he saw clearly how certain dominant forms, which he felt were designed to placate rather than challenge the visual culture and primary ideas of film audiences, were becoming naturalized as inevitable, and he mused:

> Plainly we have something here that can be raised to parallelism with the greatest musical compositions; we have possibilities of a Spectacle equal to any music that has been or can be written, comprehending indeed the completest music as

one of its factors. Behind the first cheap triumphs of the film to-day rises the possibility of a spectacle-music-drama, greater, more beautiful and intellectually deeper and richer than any artistic form humanity has hitherto achieved.[90]

Here Wells aligns interestingly with the avant-garde embracing of film and other modern technologies as inseparable from literary consciousness (Dada and Futurism, especially). When making *Things to Come* in 1936, he insisted on having the musical score be composed as part of the film's creation; film was a medium that incorporated the arts as part of itself. His comfort with film, his enthusiasm for new genres and technologies, and his welcoming of a thick imbrication of literature with cinema are consonant with his view of his own work as part of a fluid movement of individual ideas and texts into and out of the cultural stream, contributing to the larger story of the world's mind but also submerged, as the future will dictate. His willingness to be eclipsed was generic as well as personal; if the future moves on from the novel, as he was certain it would, this would be no calamity. Then again, the bookless futures of both *The Time Machine* and *The War in the Air* are deeply dystopic scenes of loss. If the book is to disappear, let it be surpassed, Wells would say, not by regression into illiteracy but by newer iterations that even better express our collective ideas and aspirations.

From the beginning, well before he wrote and helped produce movies, Wells's work evinced a particularly close affiliation with film. As several critics have shown, his writing is integral to some of the formative conceptions of cinema in the last years of the nineteenth century and into the twentieth, beginning with *The Time Machine*. The tantalizing historical story, told recently by Keith Williams and by Laura Marcus, is as follows:

> The early British film-maker R. W. (Robert William) Paul's 24 October 1895 patent application for a film exhibit that would simulate a time journey from present to future and back into the past was inspired by Wells's quasi-cinematic concept and was probably developed in consultation with Wells himself.... Paul was drawn to Wells's text not just for its anticipation of visual effects, but by an instinct that they could be adapted by the camera for "a new and perhaps especially effective method of narration" [quoting from the modernist-era film historian Terry Ramsaye].
>
> (Williams, *Wells, Modernity, and the Movies*, 28)

And the language from Paul's patent application: "My invention consists of a novel form of exhibition whereby the spectators have presented to their view scenes which are supposed to occur in the future or past, while they are given the sensation of voyaging upon a machine through time, and means for presenting these scenes simultaneously and in conjunction with the production of the sensations by the mechanism."[91] It is not only the play of time but the experiment with visuality—the way technology mediates effects of existence and consciousness, drawing scenes of other worlds and of the future, and the large perceptual meanings of modernity—that constitute Wells's contributions to film and to a filmic imaginary in this period of cinema's founding.

Wells's acute sense that film would be the future and his texts' cognitive orientation toward states and narratives twinned with film's techniques form part of a larger engagement with media. Radio is another form. The BBC courted Wells assiduously. After a great deal of refusal (probably stemming from his self-consciousness about his high-pitched voice and his resistance to the BBC's control of the content it would air), Wells eventually agreed, and from the summer of 1929, he became a regular on the BBC, all the way through the 1940s.[92] The BBC recognized Wells as a natural figure for its airwaves, with hundreds upon hundreds of broadcasts of his literary works, some read straight and others rewritten as radio plays, along with his own delivered broadcasts. Letters preserved in the BBC archive relay the director of talks, Hilda Mattheson, exhorting Wells in 1929 to consider a broadcast and entreating him, in particular, to present on the radio a version of the address he had given earlier that year at the German Reichstag on the necessity to suppress nationalism in the name of peace. "I have always felt it to be pretty devastating," she wrote to Wells, "that an internationalist like yourself—perhaps you are the only real internationalist?—shouldn't be making use of the most international means of communication there is."[93] Wells did, in fact, recognize the reach and power of radio and film as means of spreading ideas more effectively than print. But his affiliation with media technology is not only utilitarian. It is, rather, inherent. Wells was always probing those forms of connectivity and communication that belie our ordinary sensations and experiences, thinking about how different planes of existence might converge and how these uncanny scenarios register in human consciousness. He had an acute awareness of the power of media to create and express new realities. It is inconceivable that Wells could have written and thought what he did outside of the elaborate media ecology in which he saw himself and his culture enmeshed. I think we can also say that the twentieth century might never have apprehended its own constitution as a product of technological and medial change, as part of both machinic and biological processes, without Wells's penetrating contributions to our imaginative life.

What this technological view helps showcase is the breadth and vigor of Wells as, specifically, an inventor—an inventor and one who believed whole-heartedly in invention. (It was Jules Verne who lamented vis-à-vis Wells's science fiction, "*il invente!*")[94] Airplanes and aeronautical engineers, time machines and their makers, biology and biologists, scientific advances and their propagators: these are the Wellsian ripostes to the artist in his studio or the writer at her desk. His writing figures invention as its creed, the restlessness of his own experimentation exemplifying what might be cast as one of the period's signal instances of literary experiment. Several primary modes across Wells's writings stand out for the import and reach of their experiment. First, and most invisible today, is the hybrid novel/essay, which Wells ambitiously took as a congenial form, to be molded and honed in so many iterations and examples as to constitute a genre of its own. Nearly all of his longer fiction, including speculative texts, utopias, and more traditional realist novels, feature interludes of discussion, sometimes didactic or polemical, often historical. As he wrote in one defense of such tendencies, "At the present time a profounder change in human thought and human outlook is going on than has ever occurred before. The great literary tradition I follow demands that this be rendered in terms of living human beings. It must be shown in both word and act."[95] The discussion novel was a prized form for Wells, and he gave it different shapes, including several novels written as dialogue and others that deeply challenge expectations of plot and form. On one hand, these works may seem to have led precisely nowhere in literary history, so lost are they to criticism, yet, with Wells in mind, Lawrence's writings, for instance, jump into view as, fundamentally, in this line of essayist, often didactic, fiction, with a piercing authorial voice transcending character and even individual text. Orwell is another, more overt heir, but it is not only thematic with Orwell; how might we now approach "the book" at the center of *1984* once we recognize the didactic or future-historical interlude as a common Wellsian scheme? Or, moving into the late-twentieth- and twenty-first-century novel, which has normalized all manner of authorial commentary, Wells's novels of discussion might be seen as quiet precursors whose immense readerships in the first half of the century have never been fully reconstituted.

Analysts of reading in the period tend not to focus on how or why (or even that) Wells engendered his particular body of readers, though in parsing these discussions we can reconstruct a sense of its heterogeneity and breadth. In Jonathan Rose's important study of reading habits among working people in England in the first half of the twentieth century, *The Intellectual Life of the British Working Classes*, Wells makes many appearances, though with no consistent pattern. What is most interesting is how eclectic Wells's placement often is among the authors these working-class readers named as important to them: most often he appears along with Shaw (and frequently other Fabian socialists); at times with those Woolf dubs his fellow "materialists," Bennett and Galsworthy; frequently, too, with James and Conrad; at times with historians like Gibbon, Toynbee, and Macaulay; and frequently he appears with the most revered writers documented by these readers, such as Shakespeare and Dickens. In *Fiction and the Reading Public*, Q. D. Leavis's tendentious work of 1932, to take a contemporaneous example, Leavis, too, seems uncertain about where to place Wells. In her scheme for categorizing authors on a popularity scale from A to D (A for the highbrow of whom she approves, D for "absolute bestsellers" to whom she accords no value whatsoever), Wells would seem to fall somewhere around a level B. In another sense, though, Leavis treats Wells as outside of these categories, more like a translator across the realms of high- and middlebrow. Rather than place Wells in any recognizable category, these studies point to his idiosyncratic place in the reading cultures of his era.

A final area of generic innovation to note up front, closely related to the question of his readership, involves Wells's appropriation and reinvention of the popular disciplines. Taking the disciplines to a mass audience was not new when Wells embraced the principle after the war, with *The Outline of History*. In England, such work had strong connections to the extensive, decades-long effort to spread education to parts of the populace previously disenfranchised, a major aspect of late-nineteenth- and early-twentieth-century liberal culture, while in the United States the mantra of "self-help" gives character to the spread of autodidacticism across a wide public.[96] All of these movements had textual components: Wells's first book (1893) was a biology textbook for the self-educating populace, and his biographers Jeanne and Norman MacKenzie see Wells's childhood reading of "'popular educators' then in vogue—compact encyclopaedias which summarized philosophical doctrines, scientific ideas and historical events"—as formative for his own later projects.[97] These were significant trends: eminent scientists like the physicist James Jeans and the astronomer A. S. Eddington, both of Cambridge, wrote substantive, well-read books for a lay audience in the late 1920s and '30s. Other popular science writers included J. B. S. Haldane, Julian Huxley, and J. Arthur Thompson.[98] Such works formed part of the large expansion of adult education that characterized the end of the Victorian era and the first three decades of the twentieth century. Wells's role in all of this was catalytic: he created a center of gravity around himself and his works, and his high visibility helped spotlight these expanding literary directions. *The Outline of History* in particular was exemplary in its readership and reach, catapulting not only Wells but popular history into a new category of influence. Wells followed *The Outline* with a massive work of popular science, *The Science of Life* (1929, coauthored with Julian Huxley, grandson of Thomas, and his son G. P. Wells), and, less successfully, another two-volume work, on economics, *The Wealth, Work, and Happiness of Mankind* (1931).[99]

More generally, Wells was always and openly *educating* in his writing, and these books in the disciplines, meant to reshape thought across a mass public, hold a conspicuous and logical place within his corpus. At the same time, they stand out and help recharacterize the specifically experimental nature of his achievement, in which the project of blending literature with nonfictional and didactic genres, to create the conditions for world harmony and peace, was as self-conscious as it was ambitious.

Approaching these richly diverse genres makes scholarship on Wells particularly open-ended and inviting. My approach to genre is fully agnostic: throughout this book, I use the term "novel" to refer to all of his fiction beyond the short stories, including the science fiction, often named (including by Wells) romance or fantasy, and normally distinguished explicitly from the novel. There is much to be mined from these works in their guise as fantasies or romance—in that sense as *others* to the novel—even as they bring into their fold the naturalism that contemporaries such as Hardy were perfecting. Nevertheless and emphatically, I believe that Wells's corpus needs to be taken as one. My organization of this book is thus by idea and theme, not by genre or chronology. In all of my chapters, I will read across his works in a spirit of inclusiveness and discovery, allowing their particular mixtures—internal to a given text or multiplying across his huge canon—to accrue interest and meaning.

My readings of Wells's full corpus intend to be lavish, then; when it comes to biography, by contrast, *Inventing Tomorrow* leans toward silence. This is not a biography or a biographical literary study or an appreciation of Wells. The goal of this book is to reinfuse Wells's writings into the period and into our literary consciousness. To the extent that Wells as persona inhabits his works, he is fully present and active throughout these pages, as he was in the culture of the first half of the twentieth century. Wells's life was always on view; he held a staggeringly large place in his culture for four decades. Understanding how this figured in the full zeitgeist of the period is a major goal of this book, though my approach is less about the details of his life than about allowing his restless energy and driving ideas to provide a new entry into twentieth-century thought and culture. Wells lived a long, enormously active, diverse life and, through it all, he wrote and wrote and wrote. His personal story stimulates interest across many categories (class, sex, work, politics, fame, travel, scandal . . .), and because this story has not yet been told to modernist scholars, it beckons full biographical treatment. That is not the work of this book. There are quite a few extant biographies of Wells, mostly lively, readable works that give a feel for him in his many worlds. The most extensive and scholarly is David C. Smith, *H. G. Wells: Desperately Mortal*, which aims to deliver Wells as a progressive and socialist, someone whose intellectual projects were genuine, consistent, and powerfully motivated by his ideals. Norman and Jeanne MacKenzie have written a detailed and wonderfully contextualized account, in which they set Wells firmly in the stream of his era's social, economic, and cultural ferment. One senses that they do not much like their subject—their readings of his literature in particular are often dismissive—but the work is comprehensive and gives a compelling portrait of a difficult man. A more recent biography, interested in how Wells elucidates today's intellectual climate, is Michael Sherborne, *H. G. Wells: Another Kind of Life.* We also have a disgruntled biography from his son with Rebecca West.[100] Nevertheless, Wells awaits the magisterial treatment, germinating around a profound understanding of his literary achievement, that modernists such as Joyce, Woolf, Eliot, Auden, Yeats, and others have invited.

Similarly, textual scholarship could be an industry itself. Wells was unbelievably prolific, and his works were often reprinted, sometimes with changes approved by him. Many of his works, moreover, were initially put out serially, to be followed by book publication. His works were often published simultaneously in the United States and in England and, as already noted, often quickly in translation around the world (*The Outline*, for example, was immediately translated in 1920 into many languages, starting with Japanese and Swedish). In 1924 through 1927, the Atlantic Edition of Wells's works was published by Scribner's, a twenty-eight-volume compendium typically considered the most reliable source for reproducing his works today. Wells wrote brief prefaces to the Atlantic Edition, too, and these provide timely insights into his texts, including those that had been written thirty years earlier. Yet the Atlantic Edition is far from complete even up to 1927. It does not contain the massive works in the disciplines, among other missing pieces, and it was completed twenty years before the end of his writing career. In addition to all of this, there are hundreds of short pieces published initially in newspapers that have not been reprinted, and these invite archival investigation. Similarly, book introductions, reviews, and occasional pieces of all sorts appeared in large numbers over his life. The four volumes of his published letters represent a small fraction of his correspondence, much of which has disappeared. The primary Wells archive, to be found at the University of Illinois Rare Book and Manuscript library, teems with understudied material, including, along with manuscripts of the majority of his books, 65,000 letters. His published corpus is equally ripe for scholarship, about 90 percent of it being out of print.

My approach in working through this material is to aim for the widest story. Most of the material discussed in *Inventing Tomorrow* is from published sources, read in a spirit of ongoing discovery, with the aim of introducing my readers (as I am introducing myself) to the vast trove that is Wells's writing. Wells's body of work is huge because Wells was a writing, speaking, publishing, and disseminating phenomenon; this is the chief point about textual variance and multiplicity in his works. Rather than face this essential fact as an obstacle, I have taken it as a source of inspiration.

## VII. WHY NOT WELLS?

This introduction has given, I hope, an intimation of how reading Wells might reveal new aspects of the twentieth century's imagination, opening up vistas for scholarly exploration and reawakening the era in striking ways, but in closing, the question swerves to ask, are there reasons not to read him? Wells was no saint. Some of the views that occur periodically throughout his writings, particularly distressing for a twenty-first-century reader, include anti-Semitism and anti-Catholicism, racism and racialism, dismissiveness of Irish claims to nationality and a generally pejorative view of Irish culture, a tendency to set women in the light of men or of reproduction, a belief in elite rather than democratic governance of the imagined world state, and a willingness to consider violent, inhuman principles of perfecting the polity. During World War II, he wrote in the *Times* that the Allies should not hold back from bombing Rome, unsympathetic to the value of its treasures and eager for revenge against the Vatican, a particularly troubling opinion to encounter today, in the wake of the deliberate destruction of world heritage sites and art objects by groups such as the Taliban and ISIS. *Anticipations* (1901), Wells's first extended look into the human future (a bestseller at the time, whose contents he never repudiated) forecasts with seeming equanimity that

> the men of the new republic ... will hold ... that a certain portion of the
> population—the small minority, for example, afflicted with indisputably trans-
> missible diseases, with transmissible mental disorders, with such hideous

incurable habits of mind as the craving of intoxication—exists only on sufferance, out of pity and patience, and on the understanding that they do not propagate; and I do not foresee any reason to suppose that they will hesitate to kill
when that sufferance is abused.[101]

Some of these articulations relate to Wells's stated views and thus have a certain
logic internal to his thinking. In that sense, an analysis of Wells that recognizes
the profoundly contradictory nature of his thought will find that these illiberal,
intolerant, racist, or misogynist threads are woven into the whole. To take an
important instance, in the case of Wells's tendency, especially in his utopias, to
relegate women to the realm of biology, we see the limits of his radicalism. Texts
like *A Modern Utopia* are conflicted, however; they envision women as equal
partners with men and unsettled his readers as such, yet the discussion of
"Women in a Modern Utopia" nevertheless dwells almost exclusively on questions surrounding reproduction and motherhood. Such works showcase the
enmeshment of incompatible positions and impulses within a mind of exceptional activity, whose limitations and biases can be visible in the most troubling
way.

If Wells's unpalatable statements and scenarios often function as the dark
yang to the progressive and prohuman yin of his beliefs, others simply stand as
they are, ugly sentiments, common to his era. One is reminded of a quip of Conrad's, in which he told Wells, "The difference between us, Wells, is fundamental.
You don't care for humanity but think they are to be improved. I love humanity
but know they are not."[102] Given Wells's willingness to abjure his own humanity
in thrall to a vision of a perfected future, such may at times ring true. Thus, in
*Tono-Bungay*, the novel most admired by both modernists and today's literary
critics, the stereotyped figure of the Jew persistently breaks into the narrator's
analysis of the social system. An outsider and insider, the Jew's status in the
world the novel seeks obsessively to catalogue, characterize, and influence seems
gratuitously aggrieving to Wells and his narrator. There are other examples of
anti-Semitism and racism throughout his writings; they form part of the Wells
imaginary. In the pages that follow, I will make no effort to apologize for the
despicable ideas that occur at times throughout Wells's writings, nor to will
them away, nor to assume them merely incidental.

At the same time, my underlying conviction in writing *Inventing Tomorrow*
is that the goal is not, per standard critical practice, to find incriminating lines
and sentiments and to assume they provide the key to unlock the essential content of these works. By contrast, I go forward in my analysis of Wells on the
assumption that the mix of attractive and repellant in his textual world has

something to teach us about the nature of progressivism in the period and about the limitations of a mind that grasped ambitiously toward an ideal, if a flawed one. In the context of his contemporaries, Wells was almost universally viewed as radical: a socialist, a Darwinian, an advocate for feminist and liberatory causes, antinational and antireligious. His unconventional life and his powerfully unsettling ideas made him someone who upset rather than confirmed the deep prejudices of his time. The aim of reading Wells is to engage a body of material that sheds new and unfamiliar light on modernity, refracting and reframing the literary world of the twentieth century, and to discover a mind that surprises, intrigues, and at times shocks or dismays. Where Wells disappoints, he disappoints. But he does so not because he was always already primed to tell the story of race, class, sex, and power we have heard so many times before, but rather because when we absorb ourselves in his textual universe, we can almost forget that such predictable responses persevere. In the end, I would like to think that Wells distresses me so deeply at these times because he has convinced me that such old and unwanted sentiments really have no place in his cosmos. Then again, the Wellsian injunction is always this: when you see the world around you with all of its ugliness, inequity, and complacency, try to imagine a better one. Imagine it, and make it.

# I

# Voice

One thing can be said with absolute certainty about H. G. Wells: he was read. He was read by men and women of different ages, classes, and political affiliations. He had many readers among working people, coming in second in the list of favorite novelists polled by the Workers Education Association (WEA) in 1936.[1] He appealed to politicians and others in public life. Winston Churchill quoted regularly from him, and he met one-on-one with leaders including Teddy Roosevelt, Franklin Roosevelt, Vladimir Lenin, and Joseph Stalin and with many other luminaries in the arts, industry, and politics.[2] From the early success of the 1890s scientific romances; to the social-issue novels of the first decade of the twentieth century, which entered forcefully into the fray of cultural debate and incited often passionate responses; into the war-related works (fiction and nonfiction) of the 1914–1919 years; and in his history, science, and political writings of the 1920s and '30s, he remained a consistent force in the world of books and reading, *The Outline of History*'s massive sales of two million representing his most extensive reach.[3] Wells's books were translated copiously; in Europe alone, he was translated into twenty-six languages between 1895 and his death in 1946, including Irish, Serbo-Croat, Latvian, Estonian, Yiddish, and even Esperanto.[4] With his works being produced very quickly in the major European and Asian languages—sometimes within months of their initial English publication—and an especially large body of readers in France and Russia, as well as in America, Wells was a genuinely global author, even by our contemporary standards of worldwide exposure.[5] Taken as such, it would be accurate to say that Wells embodied what Rebecca Walkowitz has theorized as being "born translated," a kind of readiness for the world market that she deems central to our own moment of world literature.[6]

More than numbers, it is the breadth and recalcitrance of this role in the reading public that distinguishes Wells. In England, the same WEA poll that had Wells in the top rank in 1936 still held him there in 1944, though nearly all others from his generation, esteemed a decade earlier, were no longer being read so widely. George Orwell's 1941 assessment was that "thinking people who were born about the beginning of this century are in some sense Wells's own creation," a startling statement.[7] Orwell's point is less about the numbers of Wells's readers than about how his writing had mattered to them; his was a transformational voice, shaping people's ideas, providing a model of activist writing and a set of key texts that powerfully motivated young intellectuals like Orwell and others of his generation. Tributes like these are not always flattering—Orwell was mostly concerned to attack Wells for, in his view, remaining an inveterate Edwardian—but they point to the unusual penetration of Wells's voice in relation to his diverse public, all of which made for a remarkable authorial phenomenon. The goal of this chapter is to show, from a stylistic point of view, what he offered to these many readers, and to excavate from his vast body of work a distinctive Wellsian set of writerly techniques and attitudes. What emerges is a recognizable voice, with implications for how we understand not just Wells but the period's literary innovations more broadly.

To state it clearly, Wells was read because, despite the great variety of his corpus, he wrote in a certain style. He developed his own distinctive techniques across his body of writing, and these, we may surmise, drew together his array of readers. Discovering his voice will expand the range of what we understand as modernist experiment.[8] While later chapters will focus largely on thematic topics, my aim here is to underscore some of the key stylistic and tonal features of his work, in part to construe how he was able to reach such an abundance of readers and, more broadly, as an inauguration into a study of his literary works. These signatures fall into six categories: Wells's complex and pervasive habits for placing himself in his writings; his unusual uses of figurative language (in particular, his penchant for both employing and explaining his metaphors); his development of a mode of fiction-as-argument that stretches his themes across multiple texts; his idiosyncratic use of specialized language; his construction of an ongoing tonal dialectic, where violent, destructive visions are countered by an essential optimism; and his powerful visual imagination, linking his works up with literary modes like impressionism and with the aesthetics of film. Cutting across all of these categories, what is most striking is the profuse energy and indefatigable spirit of Wells's voice. No matter how diverse and voluminous the output, it always belongs unmistakably to this author of ferocious, unappeasable drive. Therein lies one of the great contradictions surrounding his work: in endlessly writing himself, he spoke to a massive public; in playing out his private preoccupations, he created a literature of universal dilemmas.

## I. THE AUTHOR

It was Wells's first novel, and it launched his career with a bombshell. *The Time Machine* has, as its center and climax, a sensational discovery: the sweet, soft, carefree people of the year 802,701 are not alone in the future. Something else is there too, which slinks out menacingly only after dark to terrorize the seemingly joyful Eloi and which, as we soon learn, turns out to be our cannibalistic other half down the evolutionary line, the Morlocks. Everything about the Morlocks is interesting: the primal horror they conjure up (when they paw at the Time Traveller, with tentacle-like touch, they provoke a kind of instinctual terror); the idea of them as the descendants of the working classes, with class transposing into species in the evolutionary scheme; the quality of their subterranean world, part sewer, part factory, part underworld/otherworld; the sense of awful revenge against the complacent well-to-do in Wells's era—or our own—taken against our children hundreds of thousands of years into the future. And how do we get to these Morlocks—what is their point of emergence and contact with the world? Wells.

As the Traveller first notes of these apertures, "A peculiar feature, which presently attracted my attention, was the presence of certain circular wells."[9] It is easy to overlook the resonance of wells with Wells (a decidedly unscientific poll of students in several lecture courses yielded a 0 percent rate in noticing this conjunction), yet, in another sense, it could not be more blunt. "I sat upon the edge of the well," says the Traveller, having had his first confrontation with a Morlock, who looks, he thinks, like a "human spider," "telling myself that, at any rate, there was nothing to fear" (*TM*, 46). The edge of the well is not deep enough; the Traveller, and we, can only penetrate the truths of the future, and hence of the present, if we actually descend into the wells, experiencing their interior contents. It is a wonderfully rich beginning in many senses: Wells setting up the key to the future of mankind, its dark and awful comeuppance, in a journey into his own psyche, a trip into the wells. Of course, he is having fun with this idea, and his tendency to utilize multiple narrators in his works often functions less to isolate himself from his story than to place himself comfortably within it. In this respect *The Time Machine* inaugurates Wells's career very appropriately as a joint venture into the social life, history, and future of mankind and into the always capacious mind of Wells himself.[10] He is, in his own specific way, one of the most self-revelatory of all the writers of the modernist era.

It is a competitive field. Critics have long observed what seems like a contradiction between, on one hand, modernism's poetics of impersonality, to use Maud Ellman's important phrase, and the powerfully autobiographical elements that suffuse many of the most important modernist novels in English.[11] Joyce naturally commands the terrain, with his creation of Stephen Dedalus as one of the greatest alter-egos in twentieth-century fiction. There is something enormously brave and moving about how fully Joyce pours himself into Stephen, not least because his young self can be so unlikable. Lawrence, too, when scripting himself as Paul Morel in *Sons and Lovers* (or as Birkin in *Women in Love*, or Somers in *Kangaroo*, or any of the narrators in his travel writings), forges a voice and persona that combines receptivity to the world with solipsism, in a series of portraits that become recognizable versions of himself. That one can always find the Lawrentian persona in his male protagonists, shouting at the world from their often frail bodies, is one feature that constitutes his canon most distinctively. We can add many others into the list: Woolf, Stein, Hemingway, Richardson, Bowen, to name a few. In a general sense, the modernist novel reads as a moving portrait gallery of its extraordinary authors, and of course the culture of fame and fetishism characterizing these writers shows no sign of diminishing.

Even within this company, Wells stands out for the extent, variety, and sheer gusto of his self-representation across his works, beginning with those intriguing wells. Wells's works are so thoroughly permeated by their author, in fact, that we need to establish some distinctions and categories.[12] There are, first, a host of works whose protagonists are partially modeled on Wells the historical person; these include *Kipps* (1905), *The History of Mr. Polly* (1910), *Love and Mr. Lewisham* (1904), *In the Days of the Comet* (1906), *Tono-Bungay* (1909), and *Ann Veronica* (1909, in the person of Capes), and all of them picture Wells as a young man, forging a way in the world from a position of vulnerability and uncertainty. Other works that closely abut this type of autobiographical novel in the bildungsroman family feature a Wells-like protagonist, even though important enough aspects are changed that one sees both similarity and fairly radical dissonance in the self-portrait; these include *The New Machiavelli* (1911, where the protagonist Remington is a Tory!), *The World of William Clissold* (1926, in which Clissold is a rich businessman with a global empire), and even *The Holy Terror* (1939, where the sulky, angry boy who becomes a world dictator shares some of Wells's most questionable personal traits). Wells was at times very testy about his role in his works, declaring himself entirely bored by the whole phenomenon of the roman à clef in all its forms.[13] In the preface to *The World of William Clissold*, feeling defensive about having lampooned Churchill several years earlier in the novel *Men Like Gods* (1923), Wells grumpily asks, "Cannot those who criticise books and write about books cease to pander to that favourite amusement of vulgar, half-educated, curious, but ill-informed people, the hunt for imaginary 'originals' of every fictitious character . . .?" and declares moreover that "if the author had wanted to write a mental autobiography instead of a novel, there is no conceivable reason why he should not have done so" (*WC*, iv, iii.).

At the same time, he was often explicit about how much of himself and his world he infused into all of his writings and accordingly wrote works of very open self-scrutiny and autobiography. These include the wonderful and widely read *Experiment in Autobiography* (1934) and, more salaciously, an addendum he waited to have published posthumously, which details his vigorous love/sex life, eventually published as *H. G. Wells in Love*.[14] Throughout his life he documented his own mental and intellectual progress, with characters playing out his ambivalences and dilemmas, and his body of writing a space for testing his ideas as he forged, them, all the way up to the very late and depressed work, *Mind at the End of Its Tether* (1945) which sees the end of the world and the end of its author as paired events. It is a subject his biographers and critics have considered, with Jeanne and Norman MacKenzie, as well as Peter Kemp, seeing these tendencies as a sign of obsessional personality and an overwhelming egomania. Perhaps. But the relation of book to self becomes much more revealing and productive when viewed as a praxis, a form of modern self-textualizing that opens up new directions for novelistic exploration.

All of these efforts remain within recognizable rubrics in terms of the author's relation to his writing, but Wells's most pointed innovation around these issues falls elsewhere. These are works—and they could almost be said to include all of Wells's writings, at least after 1900—that centrally include swaths of discussion around his key ideas and primary themes, most prominently world unity, education, innovation, science, and the need to be driven by an interest in the future rather than by the strictures and blind spots of the past. Thematic unity is a central principle in the Wells canon, and that unity is forged in part by the inevitable, recognizable voice of the author, declaiming about the world. It is not, in other words, possible to separate Wells's development of a new type of essay-novel from his development of an expansive authorial persona, roving through his works across every genre. And then, to add an extra dimension, all of this gets thematized in his books, as, for instance, in his 1937 novella *The Camford Visitation*, where a "Voice" makes a series of strange intrusions into a small university town, exhorting its inhabitants to rethink their entire approach to education, in essence to follow all of the precepts Wells had been preaching in the preceding decades. Of course, no one listens. The Voice is Wells, as his multitude of readers by then would easily recognize.

Such self-referencing begins with his younger being, breaking out into the world. The image of the young Lewisham in his attic room, with his "*schema*" pinned to the wall (one list for the day's schedule, one for the life plan), might stand as the quintessential image of the young Wells, at the outset of his professional career, the student/teacher already impressively advanced from where anyone would have imagined of this son of a grocer and lady's maid—inspired, struggling, pretentious. Lewisham's career plan reads as follows: "In this scheme, 1892 was indicated as the year in which Mr Lewisham proposed to take his B. A. degree at the London University with 'hons. in all subjects,' and 1895 as the date of his 'gold medal.' . . . and such like things duly dated." And for the individual day plan, his "Time-table" is even more chronologically demanding: "Mr Lewisham was to rise at five . . . 'French until eight,' said the time-table curtly. Breakfast was to be eaten in twenty minutes; then twenty-five minutes of 'literature' to be precise, learning abstracts (preferably pompous) from the plays of William Shakespeare," and so on for the day.[15] "But just think of the admirable quality of such a scheme!" the narrator notes with a wink, and indeed this sense of detachment, irony, but also real pleasure in the figure of Lewisham characterizes the early scenes of the novel (*LL*, 2). These charming sequences, in which Lewisham begins to fall behind on his schedules, distracted by the lovely Ethel—just too attractive as she walks on the path in the suburban town where Lewisham is a tutor—have about them a poignancy-in-comedy that bespeaks the genuine empathy of one's personal story. As Lewisham slides from his aspirations, makes fatal mistakes, and acquires only partial compensation in the novel's concluding focus on the next generation ("it is all the Child. The future is the Child"), the novel evinces a certain severity toward him, yet there remains a sense of empathy and loss in these disappointments (*LL*, 191).

In portraits like this one—and here too we find Kipps and later Mr. Polly, two of his most famous and beloved protagonists in the years around their publication—Wells creates these appealing men on the border of working and middle class, as they strive and push out of their inherited class positions, each with some distinct quality of speech or thought or aspiration, without idealizing them and without giving them much more than a bump up the ladder. Lewisham succumbs all too easily to the combined desires and restraints that define bourgeois values, and of course that schema, like the one Wells had pinned to his wall at that same age, is ridiculous.

Kipps, too, an enormously attractive character, who like Wells escapes the dreary life of a draper's assistant, remains always a little underdrawn, mostly responding to his environment rather than driving his own story. Kipps's rise, unlike Wells's, comes from a surprise inheritance, not from the precocious genius that let his author pry his way through the restraints of the class system. Even Kipps's great moment, when he abandons his middle-class fiancée and returns to simple Ann, his original girlfriend and a servant for one of the families with whom he now associates, falls flat of romantic expectations and yields a marriage that is in many ways a disappointment. Kipps's Pip-like story of unexpected inheritance promises a universe going right, yet the fortune is lost as quickly as it was won, and when he ends not as an affluent man but as a just-comfortable bookseller, we feel how fully Wells has withheld those riches from his fictional self, giving him instead a very worthy and unimpeachable class position and chosen profession but no great joy and certainly no luxury.

As for Mr. Polly, what is unforgettable are his hilarious malapropisms—they deserve their own title, perhaps Pollyisms—which are simultaneously bewildering and true. From the pleasantness of "oscoolatory exercises" (kissing) to the ugliness of Mr. Polly's violent adversary's "alcolaceous frenzy," he always has his very own mot juste.[16] As John Sutherland, writing in the Penguin introduction, puts it, "to get them to express what Mr Polly means, his words must be pummeled into idiosyncratic eloquence" (MP, xiii). These linguistic convections have something of Shakespeare about them, and a great deal of Dickens, and they prove Polly a character of imaginative power and superb comedy. The narrator agrees, noting that "Deep in the being of Mr Polly, deep in that darkness, like a creature which has been beaten about on the head and left for dead but still lives, crawled a persuasion that over and above the things that are jolly and 'bits of all right', there was beauty, there was delight" (MP, 14). And Polly does fairly well, escaping the indigestion of his early life (literal and figurative), ending up in something like a pastoral pleasure spot, the Potwell Inn, where he lives out his old age as caretaker and all-round man of the house.[17] The fact that he burned down his neighborhood to get there and abandoned his first wife does not bother this novel, and indeed there is an undercurrent of violence in the story of Polly that cuts against what might otherwise seem a fairly simple portrait of a harmless clerk with a quirky sense of language, whose dreams of walking in the country miraculously yield a future. Too, Polly's erotic life is cut off; he is never given a new wife or family, residing instead in a kind of permanent friendship/partnership with the ever-stouter Old Flo, in some sense potted at the Potwell. Even George of *Tono-Bungay*, who is drawn on the realist rather than comic model and hence granted a greater measure of interiority and imaginative complexity, nevertheless cannot, like Dante, have his Beatrice. Another way to describe these mixed outcomes is to say that on one hand, Wells creates a uniquely complex and wonderful gallery of characters who operate, as he did, along the lines delineating the microdifferences among the lower middle classes or those hovering right on the precarious line above real poverty, and, on the other hand, he never lets them catch up to him. Richard Higgins is astute when he notes in his essay "Feeling Like a Clerk in H. G. Wells" that in works like *Lewisham* and *Mr. Polly* Wells is drawing on his own class experience to portray, above all, a structure of feeling—complex and ambiguous—about social position, mobility, and desire.[18] And these connections and distinctions only multiply when one includes works like *The New Machiavelli* that inject an added level of metatextual commentary to this pattern of creating literary likenesses.

The key point to note—avoiding the endless tangle of how exactly the author is and is not revealed in his characters—is that Wells is experimenting with a series of what-ifs with these characters, in relation precisely to himself. Given how public and notorious Wells's affairs often were, this exploration represents a daring and unique strategy for articulating the relationship between fiction and life. Even the opening analogy with Machiavelli (and the novel's title) presses the issue of what it means to see oneself as a historical personage and to write in the allegorical or analogical styles such parallels invite. The flex and agility with which Wells moves in and out of his protagonists, the sense of missed opportunity and personal shortcoming these parallels represent, the combination of self-aggrandizement and self-laceration they register, and the ongoing proposition that the relationships between author and creation are at the very heart of all these novels adds up to a configuration of substance and significance. If we think of transparency as the primary operation—we see through character to the author—we miss an intensely interesting and varied principle that structures (or unstructures) many of Wells's novels.

Taking into consideration the combined depth and diffusion of the autobiographical strain in Wells's writing, it may seem redundant that he also wrote an autobiography. Nevertheless, his *Experiment in Autobiography* is a complex and surprising text, bringing together many of Wells's primary interests in a new and arresting combination. It features disquisition on everything from the state of science education to the character of the great newspaper moguls of the early twentieth century, commentary on the fictional aspirations and achievements of friends like James and Conrad, and a long, culminating section on Wells's efforts toward a world state. In fact, its most notable quality (what accounts, perhaps, for the *Experiment* in its title) is how comparatively little it tells of Wells's own life story, especially after about the age of forty, instead presenting a panorama of his world, mingling anecdotes with historical analysis. This finessing of the personal in the *Autobiography* has led Robert Caserio to include it among a cadre of modernist autobiographies that stand out for their *impersonality*; in their pages, the self dissolves, is abstracted, mutates.[19] As I will discuss more fully in chapter 4, one of Wells's primary aims in his fiction was to create characters who would act as representatives of larger groups, aspirations, struggles, or, as he considered it, the species and to find forms that would depict the narrative of humanity as such.

In the *Autobiography*, the effort to see individuals as lenses onto something broad and shared takes the form of Wells presenting himself as the representative figure. "I am being my own rabbit," he writes, "because I find no other specimen so convenient for study" (*EA*, 347). As a scientist of himself, naturally he looks for trends, themes, forces at work; these he details with characteristic forthrightness, often referring within the *Autobiography* to its motifs, or its narrative arc, or its primary meaning and import. These observations, moreover, feed into the larger questions of history that very often stand at the back of Wells's writing. "I have tried," he writes at one juncture in the *Autobiography*, "to put my personal origins into the frame of human history and show how the phases and forces of the education that shaped me . . . were related to the great change in human conditions that gathered force throughout the seventeenth, eighteenth, and nineteenth centuries" (*EA*, 196). Ever the (popular/general) historian, he undertakes to historicize himself. He provides, in fact, something like a New Historical reading of himself and his moment, reading the individual artist and his output in dialectical relation with the big events of history and with the nitty-gritty of the social, economic, and political contexts around him. As a necessary corollary, if Wells is going to emphasize "world forces," he needs to deemphasize his own remarkableness, and this he attempts from first to last. Most frequent (and a little disingenuous, one feels) are the disclaimers that "the brain upon which my experiences have been written is not a particularly good one" or, in the subtitle of the *Autobiography*, that these will be "Discoveries and Conclusions of a Very Ordinary Brain (since 1866)" (*EA*, 13). In detailing the all-important question of how he got his start in writing, just to take one example, Wells enmeshes his own story in a complex of social factors and cultural currents, and to these he attributes much of his success:

The last decade of the nineteenth century was an extraordinarily favourable time for new writers and my individual good luck was set in the luck of a whole generation of aspirants. Quite a lot of us from nowhere were "getting on." The predominance of Dickens and Thackeray and the successors and imitators they had inspired was passing. . . . For a generation the prestige of the great Victorians remained like the shadow of vast trees in a forest, but now that it was lifting, every weed and sapling had its chance, provided only that it was of a different species from its predecessors. When woods are burnt, it is a different tree which reconstitutes the forest. The habit of reading was spreading to new classes with distinctive needs and curiosities.

(*EA*, 426)

Here is Wells, one among a host of resourceful, hungry young men who happened to be in the right place at the right time, ready to take advantage of the great demands opening in the journalistic and literary marketplace.

It is a portrait, again, of a person whose story is dynamically and intricately bound up with the social—and here textual—forces of his culture. The metaphor of tree growth furthers the idea of organicism over agency; the force here is of basic biology/ecology rather than of genius or any other personal quality. False modesty aside, the text's mantra that Wells is not exceptional so much as exemplary runs deep in his understanding of what imaginative writing is about, why we do it, and where its ultimate import lies. And all of this indicates Wells's powerful affinity with Montaigne, for whom the interplay between the author and the forces of the world provided the friction for almost infinite thought. In Montaigne's preface to the *Essays*, he wrote that "je suis moi-même la matière de mon livre" (I am, myself, the substance of my book).[20] Providing an example for Wells three and a half centuries later, Montaigne exquisitely set out to make himself a prism for analysis of all aspects of private and public life, the human body and the body politic, and to do so via a form he all but invented, the essay.

What becomes clear, as we look at the different forms of autobiographical inquiry in Wells's works, is that these are tightly bound up with his primary emphases and convictions, which is why the dominant feature of his self-writing, encompassing the various modes we have considered so far, is argument. Leaping from text to text comes Wells's voice discussing the problems of our world and offering solutions. Topics return and recur over the years and across the genres. Questions, large and small, get asked, answered, and reasked. On science, for instance, Wells will never stop wondering, is humanity up to it? With all the discoveries and great advances, do we as a people (or, he would say, as a "race") have the ethical and intellectual stature to match our scientific and technological brilliance? The laboratory, to take a neat metonym for the scientific world, is an ideal for Wells. With its commitment to disinterested inquiry, its fostering of equality in relation to class and even gender, its intellectual purity, its fundamental alliance with the betterment of humankind, its aesthetics of cleanliness and transparency (all subject to critique, of course), the laboratory embodies what Wells deems most promising and progressive in the human enterprise. Ann Veronica and Capes meet and meld in such a space; in the film *Things to Come* (1936) it is the decimation of the laboratory that signals the final end of the old, rotted world order. Or in *The World Set Free* (1914), after the global catastrophe of nuclear destruction has ushered in a bright new future, the setting shifts to a beautiful laboratory in the crisp, pure Himalayan Mountains.

But another refrain also sounds throughout Wells's writing. *The Island of Dr. Moreau* (1896) gives an early and powerful view of science gone horribly wrong, the laboratory the site of megalomaniacal torture, where experimental endeavor is ripped clean of morality, a place splashed with blood and rent by screams. And this prospect of science channeled into misery is a frequent lament. Cavor, the brilliant (if naïve) scientist in *The First Men in the Moon* (1901) who engineers the necessary materials to send a rocket to the moon, concludes that mankind is not ready:

> "If I take my secret back to earth what will happen?. . . Governments and powers will struggle to get hither, they will fight against one another and against these moon people. It will only spread warfare and multiply the occasions of war. In a little while, in a very little while if I tell my secret, this planet to its deepest galleries will be strewn with human dead. Other things are doubtful, but that is certain . . ."[21]

Cavor's concern is a very real one, and it presents a serious challenge to some of Wells's most deeply held beliefs. But the key point for us to note here is the formal construction: the textual agora becomes a space for Wells to air his beliefs and ideas as they develop, mutate, self-correct, and loop back over the years and across his works.

And it is this that particularly incensed some of Wells's contemporaries. In her 1918 review of *Joan and Peter*, Woolf makes it clear that Wells's penchant for exuberant argumentation fatally detracts from the novel-cum-novel, committed as fiction must be, in her view, to character. If she admires the passion, energy, and creative zeal of Wells at his most incensed, such blasts are not to overwhelm the novel, which must stay true to its central concern, which is character:

This [following a quote from the novel] is a mere thimbleful from the Niagara which Mr Wells pours out when his blood is up. He throws off the trammels of fiction as lightly as he would throw off a coat in running a race. The ideas come pouring in whether he speaks them in his own person or lets Oswald have them, or quotes them from real books and living authorities, or invents and derides some who are not altogether imaginary.... Fiction, you can imagine him saying, must take care of itself; and to some extent fiction does take care of itself. No one, at any rate, can make an inquiry of this sort so vivid, so pressing, so teeming and sprouting with suggestions and ideas and possibilities as he does; indeed, when he checks himself and exclaims, "But it is high time that Joan and Peter came back into the narrative," we want to cry out, "Don't bother about Joan and Peter. Go on talking about education."[22]

For all the amusement and derision reflected here about Wells's fictional craft, Woolf is not being only facetious in wanting Wells to continue with his discourse on education, meaning either that he would dispense with novel writing or, more subversively, would reshape the principle of novel writing, to invite the author into the novel via conviction and voice. There is, in other words, something in this analysis that hints at Wells's own deepest convictions and aspirations.

## II. FIGURATIVE LANGUAGE

As with the presence of the author and her ideas, Wells's writing poses major questions about fiction's creeds. Here is another one: can you show *and* tell? The answer is emphatically yes, and his methods for simultaneously employing and explaining his figures are deeply intertwined in the dynamics and primary questions of his texts. These habits are to be found across Wells's writings, and they represent his most stark divergence from a literary culture that prides itself on separating out literature from many of its others (politics, journalism, education). Three works open up these complex patterns in all of their layered multidimensionality, *A Modern Utopia* (1905), *Tono-Bungay* (1909), and *Mr. Britling Sees It Through* (1916), displaying expansive forms of metatextual consciousness and forcing the question of Wellsian style as a challenge to literary assumptions.

*A Modern Utopia*, Wells's first full utopian statement, is often taken as a direct, transparent recitation of his political views and aspirations around the turn of the century; in fact, it is a work of fiction, and its primary formal drama involves the clash between the two dominant modes of fictionality that spar in its pages, the novelistic and the utopian. Harvey N. Quamen rightly notes that *A Modern Utopia* is "one instance of a Wellsian generic hybrid" that itself marks a "pronounced skepticism that he held towards taxonomic categories."[23] It is a text, indeed, that constantly tests its own condition of being: if it is a utopia, it is one whose novelistic qualities continually threaten the status as utopia; if it is a novel, it is one whose storyline is drowned out by its utopian imperative to discourse in detail about the envisioned world. These contrasts and tensions rule the novel from its opening pages (and later from an author's preface of 1925, where Wells begins to offer a reading of the novel as well as a justification of its strange form); they account for the stretched and uncomfortable character of the central narrative; and they remain unresolved at the close, when the frame narrator, awkwardly named "the Owner of the Voice," returns to shut down the mechanism as best he can. "*But this utopia began upon a philosophy of fragmentation,*" the Owner of the Voice explains remorsefully, "*and ends, confusedly, amidst a gross tumult of immediate realities, in dust and doubt, with at the best one individual's aspiration. Utopias were once in good faith projects for a fresh creation of the world and of a most unworldly completeness; this so-called Modern Utopia is a mere story of personal adventures among Utopian philosophies.*"[24] We know about those earlier utopias, since a swath of the novel's first chapter had been devoted to a concise discourse on utopian literary history, and it carries forward this analysis especially in its many direct references to its most enamored forerunner, Plato's *Republic*.[25]

The frame narrator's words of exculpation are entirely characteristic of the novel, in one key sense: they seem to do the reader's work for her, providing a gloss and critique of the work as we are reading it. It is we who ought, perhaps, to be making the judgment of whether and how this work stands up to the utopian tradition, especially since Wells has neatly summarized it for us, whether and how it has balanced its representative with individual stories, whether and how it has transcended or fused its twin genres of novel and utopia. Yet Wells is not leaving it up to the reader. At an earlier moment within the story, the internal narrator, in questioning one of the Samurai (the ruling elite of the Utopia), makes a similar move to what the Owner of the Voice performs in his frame narration: "Tell me about these samurai," the speaker invites his host, "who remind me of Plato's guardians, who look like Knights Templars, who bear a name that recalls the swordsmen of Japan . . ." (*MU*, 186, ellipsis in the original). An ungenerous critic—or one schooled in modernism's "show-don't-tell" ideology—might think Wells impossibly pedagogical here or insufficiently willing to credit his reader with the tools to unpack the text. Yet these are not incidental or embarrassing, mere flaws; instead, at every turn, *A Modern Utopia* is showcasing and exploring what it means to perform these literary operations, from the point of view of a writer, reader, and narrator. To stand back from within the text and discourse upon its symbolic qualities or literary resonances represents a recurrent stylistic experiment, one that can be found throughout Wells's canon. These moments of textual self-explanation, in other words, when a Wellsian literary critic seems to reach into the novel and reflect upon it, are at the crux of what this novel embodies and unearths all along, namely the impurity of both its literary and political conceits.

There is a broad literary convention at stake in these moves—those pivotal moments in any work when the nature of its symbolic language becomes overt—and Wells is cutting his own swath through the terrain. Many quintessential instances in modernism jump to mind, such as Joyce's famous plays of textual self-consciousness (Gabriel Conroy seeing himself in the mirror, Stephen Dedalus's reckoning with his name), and these can involve a knowing authorial presence or a tense intimacy between reader and author (Eliot: "hypocrite lecteur!—mon semblable—mon frère!"). In general, the metatextual mood that courses through modernism (and even more in postmodernism) has its own iteration in Wells's writings, which, for one thing, can never resist direct self-quotation and self-parody.[26] In terms of literary tropes, however, the convention we need to isolate is a distinctively Wellsian one: the urge to comment within a text upon its primary literary figures. In *A Modern Utopia*, and in many other works as well, Wells enables such commentary in several ways. First, his layering of several narrators into the text, so that there seem to be multiple authorities standing behind any given speaker, has curious effects of internal discussion and at times ratification of his ideas. Rather than employ multiple narrators in the way Conrad does, to loosen and fundamentally mystify the idea of authorial stability, Wells's many voices have a tendency to come together at key moments in a kind of chorus. When the Owner of the Voice provides critique and literary reference points for the novel, he stands inside and outside of the narrative, and he reaches out to the reader too, inviting us into the authorial community. That is, in aligning himself with the reader as a critic, the Voice also invokes Wells (and the internal narrator), suggesting that, in the end, we might all read the novel in the same way. Of course, such intimations of harmony carry with them the equal possibility of falling out of unison; we as readers know that at moments when texts seem to shore themselves up, they display their fracture points. But Wells is less liable to deconstruction in this respect than contemporaries like Conrad, whose sensibility set the course for later theorists of literary instability. In Wells's works, the metatextual breakpoints often hold together a sense of community among reader, narrator(s), and author.

These sequences when the text analyzes itself directly, providing its own literary-critical and didactic apparatus and instructing the reader precisely how to read the text moment by moment, have been assumed by contemporary readers to be unwarranted and heavy-handed, but in fact they are woven into an intricate pattern of textual self-scrutiny. An elaborate dance of authorial commentary across different styles represents a fundamental and unique style in nearly all of Wells's works, carrying over even from text to text. His first novel sets it all in motion, *The Time Machine* taking a moment to express exasperation with contemporary utopias, as the Traveller declares that readers really don't want to know about the sewage system in the alternative worlds they are vicariously visiting and thus offering tips for evaluating the success of *The Time Machine* itself. But then, what do we do with *A Modern Utopia*, guilty ten years later of these very lapses? Or, in the last paragraph of *The Island of Dr. Moreau*, the traumatized Prendrick takes refuge from his horror at human beings, with their all-too-biological bodies, by observing outer space, which seems harmless by contrast, the epitome of nonliving peacefulness ("there is," he soothingly thinks, "a sense of infinite peace and protection in the glittering hosts of heaven"), but by the opening paragraph of his next novel, published just two years later, Wells has Martians studying our oblivious, vulnerable humanity in preparation for the most violent invasion, as if in direct commentary on the complacency that had closed out his earlier novel.[27]

Such intrusions, cues, countercues, and textual self-analyses abound within and across Wells's works, with an especially shaping presence in *Tono-Bungay*, a novel that, like *A Modern Utopia*, betrays a fundamental inconsistency about what it even is. Using the conceit of the narrator who looks back years later on his story, trying to make sense of it, standing both inside and outside of its great events, Wells seems to be on solid ground, with a frame narration reminiscent of English novels since Defoe. But that particular framing convention falters quickly. The first oddity is that the narrator George Ponderevo (who overlaps in key ways with the autobiographical Wells) right from the start refers to his story as his "novel" or "my one novel," making comments like, "My ideas of a novel . . . are . . ." or "as this is my first novel . . ."[28] But within the frame, George is not writing a novel; he is writing a memoir, his own life story. Wells is writing the novel, using George as his speaker. It is an elementary distinction, in its way, yet one that has ramifications for the whole text, which tilts from one generic paradigm to another as if it really is unsure of its own textual format within a novel, keeping its structural operation in continual view.

*Tono-Bungay* in fact partakes of a variety of generic types: within the realist tradition, the bildungsroman and the condition-of-England novel;[29] a species of futurist fantasia, occasionally; and the subjectivist modern novel, whose presence might be detected in the metatextual confusions of George's misnaming of his work. In keeping with the opening sense of uncertainty and narrative recursiveness, the novel passes now and then into a mode close to the modernism of Conrad, with whom it is in intimate dialogue. So George muses at the outset, "I suppose what I'm really trying to render is nothing more nor less than Life—as one man has found it. I want to tell—*myself*, and my impressions of the things as a whole" (*TB*, 12). Wells's affinity with modernist intentions is overt here, though, characteristically, he will have George go on with his novelistic plan as follows: "to say things I have come to feel intensely of the laws, traditions, usages and ideas we call society, and how we poor individuals get driven and lured and stranded among these windy, perplexing shoals and channels" (*TB*, 12). As in his essay on the contemporary novel, Wells is constructing his own fictional agenda, which straddles the line between impressionism in the Conradian mode and social critique by—and this is the surprising thing—placing them side by side. Indeed, in this case, they follow one another in a single thought stream.

*Tono-Bungay*, we might say, constructs a middle ground in which metaphors and conceits are deployed and then promptly amplified and considered from different angles as part of a larger scheme of direct commentary and critique. Along with the opening chapters, other segments of the novel exploit this oscillation fruitfully, especially in the last pages, when George returns to consider the panoramic view of the social worlds in which he has moved over the course of the narrative. Shaken by his and his uncle's fall and reflecting on the essential waste that has marked every aspect of this story, George takes a tour down the Thames in a newly built warship and offers his final observations on the condition of England.[30] The trip down the river ends in these terms: "The river passes—London passes, England passes . . .", trailing off inconclusively, indistinct and ambiguous (*TB*, 387). This closing look, with its emphasis on perception and its thoughts on London, embodies a return and complement to the novel's first chapter, which had established the narrative in and around the social structure of the country estate while also stressing the importance of George's impressions. Here again, the novel zigzags between attention to social commentary and a recognition that, after all, what we can know is limited to our subjective view.

This last principle puts Wells in direct contact with Conrad. In his *Autobiography*, Wells gives a vivid description of how the two differ on this front:

> I remember a dispute we [he and Conrad] had one day as we lay on the Sandgate beach and looked out to sea. How, he demanded, would I describe how that boat out there, sat or rode or danced or quivered on the water? I said that in

nineteen cases out of twenty, I would just let the boat be there in the common-
est phrases possible. Unless I wanted the boat to be important I would not give
it an outstanding phrase and if I wanted to make it important then the phrase
to use would depend on the angle at which the boat became significant. But it
was all against Conrad's over-sensitized receptivity that a boat could ever be
just a boat. He wanted to see it with a definite vividness of his own. But I
wanted to see it and to see it only in relation to something else—a story, a thesis.
And I suppose if I had been pressed about it I would have betrayed a disposition
to link that story or thesis to something still more extensive and that to something still more extensive and so ultimately to link it up to my philosophy and
my world outlook.

(*EA*, 528)

We recall that Wells, in his exchange with James, represents himself as the plain
speaker to James's artist; here, too, Wells distinguishes himself on grounds of his
proclivity for common phrases, as against Conrad's "over-sensitized receptivity."
Even more striking is his proud elaboration of how all of his work, down to the
chosen word or metaphor, makes common cause with his largest ambitions and
purposes. In this description, written three decades after the moment on the
beach it commemorates, Wells seems very clear about the status of at least one
class of literary figure, that which describes the perceived object, and he proffers
his own approach to these figures as directed, focused, and quite unconcerned
with the dominance of subjective vision.

And such a position finds expression in *Tono-Bungay*, too, notwithstanding
the text's suggestion that as George writes his "novel," his expression naturally
takes the form of impression, his vision limited and personal. Thus the opening
of the trip down the river, whose conclusion we have noted, had begun as follows: "It is curious how at times one's impressions will all fuse and run together
into a sort of unity and become continuous with things that have hitherto been
utterly alien and remote. That rush down the river became mysteriously connected with this book. As I passed down the Thames I seemed in a new and
parallel manner to be passing all England in review. I saw it then as I wanted my
readers to see it" (*TB*, 382). In these reflections, George wants to encourage a
mode of subjectivist narration and to hint at meanings and perceptions just outside of the visible or comprehensible frame. He also wants to tell us how and why
he is making such efforts. The text becomes metatext in a precise manner, its
explanatory emphasis and its self-consciousness fusing together. Or again, in an
even more blunt instance of this figuration and explanation, what immediately
follows "London passes, England passes" is: "This is the note I have tried to

emphasise. . . . It is a note of crumbling and confusion, of change and seemingly aimless swelling. . . . I have figured it in my last section by the symbol of my destroyer, stark and swift, irrelevant to most human interests. Sometimes I call this reality Science, sometimes I call it Truth. . . . It is a something, a quality, an element, one may find now in colours, now in forms, now in sounds, now in thoughts" (*TB*, 388). Sequences like these, when Wells instructs us in his usages and meanings, might drive a reader today to deplore being given such direct tutelage and to request that the author stay on his side of the fourth novelistic wall; nevertheless, we might more productively take stock of the effects of such double positioning. Such passages offer a certain pleasure, giving an authorial stamp of confirmation to what one had discerned through attentive reading (the significance of the destroyer, the place of science). There is a pattern: the creation of a rich idea clustering around an image, or sequence, or vivid sense, in constant dialogue with commentary, coming from within the text and seeming to have behind it the weight of the author.

Wells's dance with modernism in *Tono-Bungay* is especially overdetermined in the interlude when George takes a desperate trip to Africa to make off with a mysterious and, he hopes, profitable substance (quap) that offers the last chance to revive his uncle's fortunes. The whole sequence is saturated with Conradianism, from its initial gestures ("That expedition to Mordet Island stands apart from all the rest of my life, detached, a piece by itself with an atmosphere of its own" (*TB*, 320), to its descriptions of the journey into the interior ("the darkness brought a thousand swampy things to life and out of the forest came screamings and howlings, screaming and yells that made us glad to be afloat" [*TB*, 325]), to its central moral quandary. Yet Wells wants to give us a form of subjectivism that is, nevertheless, explanatory. As George reflects on the nature of quap, he thinks, "there is something—the only word that comes near it is *cancerous*—and that is not very near, about the whole of quap, something that creeps and lives as a disease lives by destroying; an elemental stirring and disarrangement, incalculably maleficent and strange" (*TB*, 329, italics in the original). So far so good. But the Wellsian impulse to take the arresting metaphor and begin to read it for us is immediately felt: "It is in matter exactly what the decay of our old culture is in society, a loss of traditions and distinctions and assured reactions. When I think of these inexplicable dissolvent centres that have come into being in our globe . . . I am haunted by a grotesque fancy of the ultimate eating away and dry-rotting and dispersal of all our world" (*TB*, 329).

To read such a passage, we must rally against the principles that have dominated literary taste since the 1920s and ask why one cannot explain the meaning of the metaphor as one is using it. Is there a loss of imaginative power in the idea of quap if the author (via his narrator) steps in and begins to elaborate on its meanings? Similarly, does the trip down the Thames become flattened when George isolates and analyzes his choice of metaphor (the destroyer)? On the contrary, Wells's practice points toward a style of fiction in which the essayistic principle of argumentation is brought to bear within and as a feature of the novel, part of its traffic in rich, ambiguous figuration. In a sense, Wells is opening up the prospect that the literary critic forms part of the authorial persona. Or perhaps more accurately, Wells's simultaneous using and explaining of figurative language has a kind of tutorial function for his readers, a way of ensuring that all readers might gain access to the great pleasure and power of literary figuration. At the minimum, it bears stressing that Wells's manner of discussing his figures *is itself* a literary mode, one that, as we will see more fully later, is connected to his ongoing proposition that discussion and argumentation can be fundamental aspects of the novel. It is a mode in which form and content are mutually expressive. In constructing these patterns of symbolic usage linked with exegesis, that is, Wells takes the idea of commentary and analysis and implants them inside the formal architecture of the novel. In novels such as *A Modern Utopia* and *Tono-Bungay*, the question of form is central to the novel's meaning at a thematic level (in the first case, the question is about what a utopia can be, in the second it involves what *Tono-Bungay* can teach, a personal story of characters rising and falling, or a social story of class and capitalism), and thus this pattern of figuration and commentary becomes a formal correlative to the novel's larger dilemmas. The novel's essential question of what kind of moral can be gleaned from the narrative is functioning, too, at the level of its formal experiments, as it shuffles among different formal types to find the right mix of uncertain and subjective versus explanatory and pedagogic.

One final variation and intensification of this scheme is exemplified in Wells's major war novel, *Mr. Britling Sees It Through* (1916). *Mr. Britling* marks the cornerstone of Wells's decades-long effort to figure the experience of the civilian in war; it will therefore be central to chapter 2, "Civilian." Of importance here is how thoroughly it depicts the dilemmas of civilian life in terms of style. What is the proper form for expressing one's ideas, emotions, and ultimate psychic devastation in relation to the war, as the great historical catastrophe approaches, sets in, and ultimately engulfs us all? This is the novel's key question. It thereby joins works like *A Modern Utopia* and *Tono-Bungay* in making a formal problem (the proper expressive mode) into a thematic one (the effects of war on civilians) and back again. Similar to those earlier novels, *Mr. Britling* operates along the line between developing and commenting on its key tropes. In this case, the pattern emerges primarily through the mental tribulations of Mr. Britling, the novel's enormously verbal, transparently autobiographical protagonist.

Written in free indirect discourse rather than in the first person in the manner of *A Modern Utopia* and *Tono-Bungay*, *Mr. Britling* shares with them the overriding suggestion that there is no clear formal key appropriate to the matter at hand, that is, the war. Mr. Britling authors an early screed in support of the war (a fictionalization of Wells's "The War That Will End War"), to be followed in the novel by other productions, including essays that mark the stages of Mr. Britling's ideas about the war, late-night agonized meditations, and many conversations with the assembled community at his home, including an epistolary conversation with his beloved son Hugh, soon to die in combat. The conclusion of all these written efforts is a letter Mr. Britling attempts to compose for his German counterparts, the parents of young Karl Heinrich, also killed in the war. Herr Heinrich has been a tutor in the summer of 1914 with the Britlings and in himself represents an aspect of Wells's own aspirations for world community; he is a philology student, and his research centers on universal languages. When Heinrich leaves in a hurry to fight in the war, abandoning his room, he leaves behind his violin, which it will be Mr. Britling's ultimate task to return to his parents. In returning his violin to the bereaved parents, Mr. Britling plans to append a note that will express . . . what exactly? This is the question that occupies many pages of the novel's conclusion and that pulls the novel toward a self-reflexivity of its own particular stamp.

Mr. Britling will write many drafts of this note; over and over, compulsively and with less and less surety, he attempts to find an idiom to express the idea of universal grief, shared (but also unequal) responsibility for the war, and the mixture of devastation and dedication that falls upon the parents of dead sons. Wells includes in the novel draft after draft of the letter, from short, heartfelt notes to long discourses about the causes of the war. In one case, he has Mr. Britling test three different sentence forms to capture one idea:

> He took a fresh sheet and made three trial beginnings.
> "*War is like a black fabric*" . . .
> "*War is a curtain of black fabric across the pathway.*"
> "*War is a curtain of dense fabric across all the hopes and kindliness of mankind. Yet always it has let through some gleams of light, and now—I am not dreaming—it grows threadbare, and here and there and at a thousand points the light is breaking through. We owe it all to these dear youths—*"
> His pen stopped again.[31]

In these repeat formations, Mr. Britling exposes the writerly process, the drafts, corrections, and enlargements that constitute his own often frustrated efforts. Clearly, in this respect, he is channeling Wells, and the sequence joins those other passages from *A Modern Utopia* and *Tono-Bungay* where there is a commingling of metatextual energy at the moments when the novel's most pressing themes and stresses are being worked out. In *Mr. Britling*, it is precisely the content of this tripartite sequence—the challenge of deducing what "War is" for those not in the trenches—that constitutes the intellectual and even dramatic center of the novel. In fact, one might divine in the movement from the first to second to third of these fragments something like Wells's authorial tribulations, to begin in a style that shares something with the aesthetic habits of his peers (the first two clauses) and then glide into his own distinctive formation, where the symbol/metaphor is used (war as fabric) but also attached to a wider discourse that amplifies its meaning and dilates out to the expanded political and emotional situation. In keeping with this gesture, moreover, Mr. Britling as a character and central consciousness has, at the same time, been unpacking these very issues for the reader: "He fell into an extraordinary quarrel with his style. He forgot about these Pomeranian parents altogether in his exasperation at his own inexpressiveness, at his incomplete control of these rebel words and phrases that came trailing each its own associations and suggestions to hamper his purpose with it" (*MB*, 428). In this move, quintessential to his method, Wells provides a critical language for thinking about his writing amid the text at hand. This signature trope, again, comprises a confluence of several features: the exhuming of the writing practice from an authorial or metatextual perspective; the heightening of a critical or didactic voice, which provides a form of readerly training in the moment; and the wrapping of these kinds of language around the novel's key questions, which in all of the cases we have examined are, at least partly, about the efficacy or stability of language forms.

In *Mr. Britling*, this pattern culminates in the most extraordinary segment of the novel, another letter, this one to Hugh. "The last sheet of Mr. Britling's manuscript may be more conveniently given in fac-simile than described," the narrator explains, after which Wells includes a partially illegible transcription of a letter to "Hugh, Hugh, My dear Hugh." The letter, appearing in what we are to take as Mr. Britling's handwriting, gives a visual picture of an unhinged mind, a devastation. The text of the letter is something like "Lawyers Princes Dealers in contention . . . *Honesty* . . .'Blood Blood'" (*MB*, 441). These repeated words (Mr. Britling's version of "The horror! The horror," perhaps) are followed by a scribble for emphasis and then four or five essentially illegible words.[32] This visual testament to Mr. Britling's desperation as both writer and father (and also, as we shall see in a later chapter, as a civilian) is moving and highly expressive, recalling such divergent literary examples as the pages of Richardson's *Clarissa* that follow her rape and the many avant-garde efforts to formalize the textuality and visuality of literature that arose in this same period. Mr. Britling's letter to Hugh might also be imagined as an addendum to his difficulties in composing the epistle to Karl Heinrich's parents; having followed the course of that composition process, we can see here just how closely the matter of style is to the mind of the person composing and to the intransigence of the idea being expressed. War is a fabric . . . war is a black fabric . . . here we see a page scribbled in black ink, unfinished and unfinishable. In these late lines in *Mr. Britling*, the language of commentary has preceded the literary instance (where usually we have found the two enmeshed or one quickly following the other), but the principle remains. Wells can provide a form of visual subjectivism because he has already told us how to read it.

There is one further aspect of Wells's pressuring of literary figures to isolate, taking us in a different direction, and that is his penchant for literalization. With alarming regularity, Wells erases the line separating metaphor from the actual, and these transgressions play out largely as nightmare or as the overturning of a world order. *The Time Machine* makes literal the reiterated nineteenth-century trope of intractable, binary class division (two classes, two peoples, two Londons); *The Food of the Gods* (1904) literalizes the idea of progress in human life and society as *growth*; both *The Island of Doctor Moreau* and the second half of *The First Men in the Moon* provide actual depictions of the forging of beings; "The Country of the Blind" (1904) takes the metaphor of communal blindness quite truthfully; *The Invisible Man* (1897) imagines the dream of being able to wield power invisibly as an actual plan; and the list could continue. In each of these cases, Wells makes his trademark move of surrounding the supernatural or fantastic element in the story with recognizable, ordinary settings and/or characters. "The realist of the fantastic," we recall, is what Conrad named him in 1898, capturing the way his works take the logic of normal life into a setting or situation manifestly nonreal. Yet there remains something uniquely disturbing about these visions, precisely because they show so exactly what the consequence or outcome would be if our habitual figures of thought and language were actualized. This is what it looks like to break up the world by a strict class division. This is what would actually entail if a culture were blind. Here is a real vision of a later generation growing beyond their ancestors. To make a human being looks like this. Wells's literalizations can be violent and confrontational, and hold a powerful trenchancy; they are among the most memorable and haunting effects in his writing.

It is especially in those works that center on life processes and the biological order that Wells stages his most explicit literalizing of the culture's organizing metaphors. It would be hard to overstate how literal this could become, and how disturbing for that very reason. Ordinarily, if we speak of "making men," we don't mean for a scientist to take an animal, strap it to a gurney, and over the course of a brutal operation turn it into a man. Literalization in such a scenario enacts a spectacular violence, and it is one, moreover, that may be endemic to the boundary crossing it represents. There is, in other words, always something profoundly challenging, even aggressive, in the Wellsian insistence on making literal the norms of culture through its figures of language. Historically, literalization has often been the basis of satire, in the Swiftian tradition, and more widely of comedy. But literalization is also a deeply disruptive, even insidious, premise in literature; it seems to interrupt and disrupt the principle of reading and of language use in general. As Branka Arsić writes, in her magisterial account of Henry Thoreau's startling literalizing of so many aspects of experience, "To maintain the very being of the literary, its own generic specificity, literature must interrupt the flow of the particular. Literary forms thus do for literature what concepts do for philosophy: they classify, segregate, bind, and regulate. . . . Thoreau's effort at literalization should therefore be registered as his resistance to the literary, as a subversion of literary forms."[33] Wells's literalizing moves, too, are intricately connected to his probing of the essence of life, as we will see further in chapter 4, "Biology." As readers, we are obliged to accept the interior completeness of the text's world structure, our willing suspension of disbelief; as language users of any kind, we subscribe to the ordinary patterns and usage of figuration. Yet in return, we might expect figurative language to abide by its rules. Metaphors are metaphors. Except, of course, when they reveal their shocking corporeality. These tableaus bring an especially vivid, even garish, life to what might seem merely commonplace assumptions, long overlooked in their familiar linguistic surround. But for Wells, no figure can be left on its own for long, before a true frightfulness—or beauty, or interest, or social meaning—will be invested there.

## III. ARGUMENT

Indeed, one of the great imperatives of fiction, in Wells's view, is to breach the walls of topical restraint and discuss . . . everything. As noted in the introduction, Wells's aim for the modern novel was that it be "the social mediator, the vehicle of understanding, the instrument of self-examination, the parade of morals and the exchange of manners, the factory of customs, the criticism of laws and institutions and of social dogmas and ideas," and he proudly asserts that novelists of his era "are going to write . . . about the whole of human life."[34] One of the shaping features of Wells's work, emphatically, is the conviction that fiction is a crucial forum for argument about social issues, often occupying the central position and nudging out action and character development. Discussion is one of the driving principles of Wells's writing, the blending of fiction into essay and essay into fiction, with novels that work through ideas on a particular topic—*Ann Veronica* with women's sexual liberation, *Joan and Peter* (1918) with education, *The War in the Air* (1908) with militarism, *The Sleeper Awakes* (1899/1910) with capitalism, to name a few. As Caserio has argued, Wells set new standards for the essay-novel, pushing its bounds and developing it in his own direction. Caserio calls it "the Wellsian New Essay," a mixed form he argues "intended to execute a revolution in generic history."[35]

*The World of William Clissold*, which begins with the narrator reflecting on aging (he happens to be the very age of Wells himself at the time of composition), is an especially compelling case, a three-volume consideration of the state of England after the war, the state of the world at any time, and the state of its protagonist at something like a midlife pause, written through the prism of Clissold's vacillations and theorizations. These are meditations, to some degree, and like *Tono-Bungay*, the novel gestures toward impression as a methodology, but more it tends toward the construction of a theory of the contemporary world; it intends to build more than dissolve and to see outside the self rather than remain within the subjective orbit. The ideas in this packed novel run according to a variety of Wellsian tracks. "Every great religion and every philosophy of life throughout the world seemed to have been feeling its way, often in spite of enormous initial difficulties of creed and training, towards this same process, the process of subordinating the egoism to a broader generalised being, the being of communion," Clissold thinks, very much in keeping with the Wellsian reach toward human unification. He also seems to have been reading *The Outline of History* when he muses how in Provence "the soil everywhere is rich with human traces," a theme of deep historicity on which he expands (*WC*, 96, 106). Perhaps above all, the novel wonders about the status of temporality, positing "flux universal" as its key observation: "Of one thing only can I be sure," thinks Clissold, "that all this goes. . . . Could my moment be enlarged to the scale of a thousand years, my world would seem less lasting than a sunset and the entire tragedy of this age the unimportant incident of an afternoon" (*WC*, 116). *William Clissold* is an exceptionally engaging and unique novel of ideas, and it brings the generic dynamism of Wells's fiction/nonfiction experiment into bold relief.

Once we come to recognize the essay-novel as a force in twentieth-century fiction, we can appreciate its pertinence for writers like Lawrence, Orwell, and Huxley, all of whom followed Wells in writing fiction saturated with discussion and also in experimenting with other genres of nonfiction prose. In fact, to push at the edges of this argument, we might think of modernism itself as making a large-scale effort to renovate and recast the novel of ideas. What else is *Ulysses*, really, or *Mrs. Dalloway*? When Woolf wrote *Jacob's Room*, the novel that inaugurated her formal innovations, she had been thinking very hard about what kind of experiment she and her peers were undertaking, and what she created in *Jacob's Room* was a novel based around a radical idea—that we can have a novel about the absence of its protagonist. In a certain way, a move like this is of a piece with exactly the kind of idea-driven fiction that Wells practiced and promoted, even if both Woolf and Wells would disagree that they were embarked on a shared mission (and for the same reason: overt explanation is outcast from modernism as its condition of existence, while such discussion is essential to Wells's goal of writing to improve the world). Still, the notion that Wells helped take the modern novel into a place where the author can be free to do things like investigate a primary, metaphysical problem as the centerpiece of a novel sounds radical, but perhaps it is only a different angle on a familiar point about modernism. At the same time, as with the larger argument of this study, when we consider the directions Wells took the novel, we notice not only how much has been hiding in plain sight (here the predominance of the novel of ideas) but also how many roads seem not to have been followed, both critically and creatively, such that, for instance, the politically engaged discussion novel, understood as such, has never had anything like the prestige of the modernist and postmodernist novel of subjectivity.

For Wells, unquestionably, the novel is the site of inquiry into many possible topics, and one of the most recognizable and distinctive features of his fiction is its preponderance of discussion. In so many cases, Wells's works extend an ongoing conversation from one to another, one text picking up where the last left off, as we have seen in several contexts already. I have noted how *The War of the Worlds* begins by undercutting the complacency about our human place in the universe that had concluded *The Island of Dr. Moreau*. In later novels, these continuities are discursive rather than suggestive, as the case of science indicates. And these conversations can be elaborate and extensive. With *Joan and Peter*, for instance, it would seem that Wells had exhausted his thoughts on the state of education, in terms of his diagnoses of what he felt to be missing from the

British schools, in his consideration of what it means to educate at all, and in pressing to understand the relationship between schooling and empire or between the individual, private person as she matures and the broader, political world over which she will soon be expected to exert some control. "After all," Oswald thinks, "the empire, indeed the whole world of mankind, is made up of Joans and Peters. What the empire is, what mankind becomes, is nothing but the sum of what we have made of the Joans and Peters," and then, after the cataclysm of the war, as Oswald prepares a final dissertation to Joan and Peter, "he had to show that all this vast disaster to the world was no more and no less than an educational failure" (*JP*, 254, 550).

Despite these summations and the intensely full rendering of the theme of education in *Joan and Peter*, one year later Wells published *The Undying Fire* (1919), taking up the subject again. He provides the seemingly exhausted topic with a little shock, however, in the form of the novel's unusual formal construction. *The Undying Fire* is a rewriting of the story of Job, and like its biblical predecessor, it takes the form of dialogue. As with the original, Wells's story begins with a council in heaven, but is centered mostly here on earth, in the midst of the war, where among Job Huss's many grave and escalating misfortunes is that his only son disappears in combat and is presumed dead. Job is a schoolmaster, and, as we know from the Bible's story of Job, he is a righteous man. The novel takes a high moral tone; it is dedicated "To All Schoolmasters and Schoolmistresses and every Teacher in the World," and Job's fall and eventual re-rise provides Wells the opportunity to detail just what kind of heroism great teaching can constitute. The tone is elevated, as Job makes an impassioned case for continuing to believe in the "undying fire" that he sees sustaining the human enterprise at its best: " 'What . . . is the task of the teacher in the world?' " Job asks and answers, " 'It is the greatest of all human tasks. It is to ensure that Man, Man the Divine, grows in the souls of men. For what is a man without instruction? He is born as the beasts are born, a greedy egotism, a clutching desire, a thing of lusts and fears. . . . We teachers . . . We can release him into a wider circle of ideas beyond himself.' "[36] *The Undying Fire* is more successful than one would imagine, thanks to the gripping quality of Job's convictions and the deft affordance made of the biblical parallel, and in connection with *Joan and Peter*, it provides a neat example of how Wells created thematic canons across his body of work linked not only by topic but by conviction, enabling a sense of ongoing enterprise despite wide stylistic variation.

*The Undying Fire* is unusual in taking the form of dialogue, but this structure also highlights a common feature of Wells's works, crucial to the way he builds up the mode of argumentation: the presence of an adversary or countervoice within the texts. In *The Undying Fire*, the concept is literalized. Following the biblical model, in which Job's four interlocutors function as adversaries, blaming him for his fall and pressing him to renounce his faith, Wells gives a great deal of his narrative to Job's opponents and, significantly, to the most appealing and attractive of them, the doctor (who has come to operate on Job's cancer, one of his long list of woes). Dr. Barrack is the last to arrive, and he responds to Job according to his character: as a person of science, a secularist, and a skeptic. He is also a believer in ongoing evolution, what he calls "The Process," and has this to say about his attitude: " 'Now my gospel is this:—face facts. Take the world as it is and take yourself as you are. And the fundamental fact we all have to face is this, that this Process takes no account of our desires or fears or moral ideas or anything of the sort. It puts us up, it tries us over, and if we don't stand the tests it knocks us down and ends us. That may not be right as you test it by your little human standards, but it is right by the atoms and the stars" (*UF*, 143–144). Barrack sounds quite a bit like Wells—or Wells shorn of his social vision—as he voices the kind of clear-thinking, scientifically driven modern ideas Wells always encouraged. The move, then, is a complicated one. What novels like *The Undying Fire* do is to spread Wells's ideas and sympathy around; where he seems at first to be declaiming in the voice of one character (Job), in fact, he is also arguing on the other side, diluting the sense of his personal stakes in one character or position but deepening the force of the issues overall, which are treated as multifarious and fluctuating. In *William Clissold*, an alternative viewpoint manifests in the voice of William's brother Dickon, an enormously successful advertising mogul who sees the future as a vista for limitless commercialism.[37] He acts as a foil to his brother, his muscular optimism about how advertising represents progress contrasting jarringly against the Montaignian scene of reflection that is the center of the novel, as William puzzles out questions about the nature of the contemporary world, the longest passages of history, and the destiny of mankind. Or again, in the late novel *The Holy Terror* (1939), in which Wells provides the anatomy of world revolution and the rise of a dictator in England, the work of isolating and delineating the political positions that accord with Wells's own from those he abhors becomes almost impossibly difficult. The rub in *The Holy Terror* involves the protagonist himself, whom Wells makes utterly unlikable, from his beginnings as a spoiled and sadistic child to his conclusion as a paranoid tyrant, yet it is he who becomes the catalyst to unleash the world revolution that, one is asked to assume, dramatically finishes off humanity's story of war, inequality, hunger, and hopelessness and therefore realizes Wells's dreams.

In *A Modern Utopia*, where, as we have seen, the novel is structured around a central generic division (novel/utopia), Wells also figures several alter-egos for the internal narrator, both of whom are meant to be dismissed, yet both of whom raise alternative possibilities that cut against the grain of the novel's overarching message. The man of nature, whom the travelers meet early on, articulates many concerns that the reader of today might also raise: the overbearing quality of this world state, where every movement of every citizen is tracked continuously and recorded; the emphasis on indoor life and comfort, when he prefers to roam in the mountains and sleep under the stars; the necessary conformity, even of dress. Including the man of nature in the story at the outset, Wells would seem to co-opt and neutralize his critique, and the man's behavior is erratic, but his words and persona nevertheless provide a crucial reminder in the novel that the desire for personal liberty and difference, as well as the very principle of opposition to the state, are positive requirements and political goods that have been essentially banished in the generally happy new world.[38]

The most serious threat to *A Modern Utopia*'s apparent aims, however, comes in the person of the botanist who accompanies the narrator on the tour of Utopia. His problem is that he can never concentrate on the details of this marvelous new world, so caught up is he in his own personal life. (The personal dimension follows from the novel's organizational conceit, whereby everyone from the old world has an exact double in the new, affording the botanist a chance to reunite in Utopia with his estranged lover from England.) The narrator, seemingly with his author's approval, expresses nonstop disdain for his companion's myopic focus on his own love life, and many readers no doubt will take this alignment as fixed. Yet the botanist's interest in the individual, erotic, and domestic aspects of life tallies with the concerns of the novel as genre. To ask novel readers not only to dispense with but in fact to decry an interest in the individual story is an act of internal sabotage. And the narrator too, to his shame, becomes consumed with his own storyline, as he comes closer and closer to meeting his double in the new world. Thus, the novel's culmination and crescendo take shape in this face-to-face, a situation that would seem entirely to conform not to the narrator, nor one might think to Wells, but to the botanist's predilections. If the problem of where narrative fits within the Utopian tradition is a longstanding one, here it finds robust figuration as the text's essential crux. Meeting with his double becomes a reckoning, moreover, with the narrator's past, something that this novel has studiously left unmentioned; the narrator, it has wanted to insist, is supposed to be a simple guide to Utopia, not to be interesting as a character in himself. In implanting a principle of opposition at both the characterological and structural levels, *A Modern Utopia* does two things at once: it deepens and complicates its overall idea (that the pleasure and excellence of this new world outweighs the interest in any single person), and it also finds a renewed conviction that the novel, with its contradictions and multiplicities, can be the forum for embodying and giving life to the biggest ideas about our future and our present.

Wells's novels of ideas are unabashed in their efforts, radiating an urgency and ownership in relation to their subject matter. Wells felt no compunction about turning over swaths of his fiction to the exposition of a problem or idea, where his peers were more likely to disperse such conversation in favor of partiality, suggestion, and dramatization. Yet in many cases, it is a difference of degree rather than of kind. A second strand we can now isolate powerfully in Wells and among contemporaries and followers is that in his works the force of argumentation, though markedly attached to the author, is not always centered on a primary character or consciousness, and it is not always consistent. The closest modernist to Wells, in both of these ways, is Lawrence, who was willing, in many of his writings, to allow an idea to dominate segments of the novel and to have some life outside of a central character. (Proust, too, gives over segments of *A la recherche* to Marcel's views on, say, photography.) But in comparison to Wells, this leeway is restricted; the dominant strand in Lawrence's fiction is to have his topics ferment in and through the free indirect discourse of his protagonists; any change in outlook corresponds to characters' shifts in view or mood. In the end, we might say that Lawrence falls somewhere between Wells, who forcefully pushed ideas and argument through the novel form, and other modernists, who aimed to display the world of ideas instead through consciousness and character experience. To recognize that such a spectrum exists and is a meaningful fulcrum for (re)framing literary works of the period makes a new space for Wells and perhaps for others who might have wished to open up the field of fiction to new forces of discussion and debate.

## IV. DARK AND LIGHT

Argument, then, does not come as a consistent font of authorial declamation but in points and counterpoints, and something akin can be said about Wells's tone: it is fundamentally divided in spirit.[39] The pendular swing between optimism and pessimism is one of the signature features of his canon, as we will encounter throughout this study, in relation to the primary themes that structure his thought and play out in his works. A passage from *William Clissold* offers a concise example, as Clissold "see[s] as plainly as I see that those stars are rising and setting, our waste and disorder, our petty, distressful, and dispersed life, so intelligent and eager, so hasty and undisciplined and tragically silly, giving place to the advent of a conscious, coherent being of mankind, possessing and ruling the earth" (*WC*, 119). Even in this short passage one can hear a resonance that sounds throughout Wells's writings, an intense vision of catastrophe countered and ultimately superseded by a resilient optimism. Importantly, these almost always occur together. Those contemporaries (like Forster) who responded to Wells as a hopeless optimist had to overlook the very dark, depressive swaths of his writing, and those today who remember above all the landscapes of destruction have to stop reading one chapter before the end.

Surprisingly for its genre of history, even *The Outline of History* is organized according to a logic of violence and chaos funneling into peace and harmony. On one hand, the story Wells tells in *The Outline* is one of unremitting tragedies, missed opportunities, failures, energies blossoming only to be destroyed, power abused, and absolutely limitless killing. On the other hand, the very plan of *The Outline*—to use the writing of world history as a counter to national hatred and war—indicates how fully *The Outline* is meant to proceed with a guiding principle, a moral, and an upshot: peace and unity. And this is how it ends, too, with a last swing through misery and out toward hope. The historical narrative culminates in the slaughter and insanity of the First World War and its disastrous peace arrangements. Wells devotes less space in *The Outline* to the material cataclysm of the war, such as the experience of the trenches or the precise way gas attacks the lungs and body than he does in other works, where he comes back over and over to the obscene carnage of those years. Here, by contrast, he takes the tale of horrendous violence and reimagines it as the first phase in a new history, which he is ready to envision. Even in writing his *history*, that is, he begins a *future history* (a mode or genre that he explores more fully in other works), and he can then portray the war, in a sense, as actually functioning in the way he had blithely and influentially hoped in 1914—to end war (to be discussed in chapter 2, "Civilian"). Thus the World War I segment gives way to *The Outline*'s culminating discussion of the possibility of a humane world state.

In these last pages, historical observation and analysis morph into speculation and hope, and even the last dregs of Versailles are cleared away in the name of a better future. In concluding his great work, Wells writes:

History is and must always be no more than an account of beginnings. We can venture to prophesy that the next chapters to be written will tell, though perhaps with long interludes of setback and disaster, of the final achievement of world-wide political and social unity. But when that is attained, it will mean no resting stage, nor even a breathing stage, before the development of a new struggle and of new and vaster social efforts. Men will unify only to intensify the search for knowledge and power, and live as ever for new occasions. Animal and vegetable life, the obscure processes of psychology, the intimate structure of matter and the interior of our earth, will yield their secrets and endow their conqueror. Life begins perpetually. Gathered together at last under the leadership of man, the student-teacher of the universe, unified, disciplined, armed with the secret powers of the atom and with knowledge as yet beyond dreaming, Life, for ever dying to be born afresh, for ever young and eager, will presently stand upon this earth as upon a footstool, and stretch out its realm amidst the stars.[40]

There is something deeply moving in the leap of faith needed to credit humanity with such a vital, bright future after all that has come before in *The Outline*, yet that little phrase "with long interludes of setback and disaster" reminds us of the historian and realist who always stands shoulder to shoulder with the visionary. The story of human life, Wells wants to say, is one of gradual unification, from the smallest units of individual and family (back in the Paleolithic days) to clan, nation, and ultimately to the broad human community sharing one globe. In that sense, it is a fully progressive history. But the shadows always hang over this vision.

These lines also remind us of Wells's ongoing exploration of flux and temporality, in a spirit that dovetails with many modernist works. In particular, these last pages are suggestive of Woolf, especially the Woolf of *Between the Acts*, which employs *The Outline* as a mirror and foil. Take this passage, for instance, which opens *The Outline*'s final chapter on the future: "We have brought this *Outline of History* up to our own times, but we have brought it to no conclusion. It breaks off at a dramatic phase of expectation. The story of life which began inestimable millions of years ago, the adventure of mankind which was already afoot half a million years ago, rises to a crisis in the immense interrogation of to-day. The drama becomes ourselves" (*OH*, 2:579). It is a moment that melds the vast historical ambition of *The Outline* to the self-reflexive orientation of his literary era and of Wells himself.

Many of Wells's more modest works also operate according to this structure of hope bursting (improbably) out of ruin. One might read this tendency as a secularization of the salvational narratives of his childhood, outwardly rejected, figuratively repurposed. Certainly, the archetypal principles of destruction and rebirth, or punishment and redemption, fuel Wells's imagination and help shape his binary world orientation. If we return to *The Undying Fire*, with its soaring oratory of the "What is the task of the teacher" variety and its tale of faith ultimately rewarded (no surprise, Job's son turns out to be a POW, his tumor was benign after all, and he gets his teaching position back), the novel is nevertheless equally engrossing for its long passages that tell of violence, the indignity of the body, and the futility of life. This is a point we need to emphasize, since so much of Wells's most haunting, rich, and memorable writing comes from the dark side of his divided idiom. In *The Undying Fire*, moreover, what is striking is how close these emphases are to the disillusioned combatant writers who would be canonized a decade later. Job, feeling dark and savage, enters into a long narrative of how life itself, the very animal reality we share with rabbits and dogs, can be a cruel joke (here we catch echoes, too, of one of Wells's most frightening works, *The Island of Dr. Moreau*). Job has a long excursus, even before he gets to the war and humankind more generally, on the raw miseries that constitute existence in the animal kingdom, which begins with his seeing a tiny rabbit having been mauled by some predator, "The back of its head had been bitten open and was torn and bloody, and the flies rose from its oozing wounds to my face like a cloud of witnesses," then some dead insects, soon a rat, later a half-dead bird, which he puts out of its misery: " 'And this,' I cried, 'this hell revealed, is God's creation!' " (*UF*, 83, 84). Out of such observations Job will say, "And now that my heavens are darkened, now that my eyes have been opened to the wretchedness, futility and horror in the texture of life, I still cling, I cling more than ever, to the spirit of righteousness within me" (*UF*, 105). And certainly Job embodies that spirit, essentially Wellsian. But Job is Job after all. Would the rest of us—or any one of us in fact—facing the universe revealed for its cruelty and randomness believe all the stronger in our undying flames? The novel *says* yes, but it shows its counterforce as powerfully. Job traces a compelling picture of life as decay and loss, beginning "a mere stir amidst the mud, creeping along the littoral or warm and shallow season the brief nights and days of a swiftly rotating earth," until it is all extinguished: "Steadily the earth cools and the day lengthens" (*UF*, 107).

The stress throughout is on what Wilfred Owen saw as "Futility" in the largest sense—"Was it for this the clay grew tall?"—and Job, too, will come to dwell on some of the great ironies of the war as the very epitome of the most meaningless, assaultive world forces. Thus from these dismal reckonings he moves into a lengthy segment in which he proposes one war object, the submarine, as an emblem of the corruption of our energies—such a marvel of engineering and ingenuity turned into the engine of uniquely modern war horror not only for the innocent victims on the surface but also for the young German men inside, whose story he imagines with empathy.[41] Above all, what the war exemplifies for Job is waste: " 'The supreme fact' " of the war, he laments, " 'is exhaustion' " (*UF*,

153). Many of his novels struggle with the specter of waste. As early as *The Time Machine*, the question had loomed: is this the endpoint of humanity, these two species, mutually dependent on yet at war with each other, a grotesque legacy of the modern world's stratifications? And it was *The Time Machine* that had starkly imagined the earth at its final twilight, millions of years in the future, just about to yield its last breath of life.

Waste may be the condition of our existence—an entropic universe, as scientists thought at the turn of the century—but Wells also took a livelier approach to the destructive energies of humanity. Henry James once described himself as having the "imagination of disaster"; his friend expanded that habit into a full-blown cosmos.[42] Some of his most remarkable writings are those that figure the destruction of the world in graphic terms (*The War of the Worlds*, *The War in the Air*, *The World Set Free*, *The Shape of Things to Come*, and the film *Things to Come*). I will discuss these works more fully in chapter 2, "Civilian"; here I want to note two things about Wells's scorching of the world, its people, and ultimately its civilizations. One is a certain satisfaction in these visions—for the writer, who reminisced in the *Autobiography* about cheerfully bicycling around Woking in 1897, looking for sites his Martians might destroy, and for readers who, as we know, seem unable a century later to be satiated by images of our favorite cities being obliterated. But the second point to stress is how elaborate and serious these destructive scenarios are in Wells's texts. In *The World Set Free*, Wells gives vivid, fully drawn, and strangely aesthetic depictions of atomic explosion; some of the sequences in this forgotten novel of 1914 (published before the outbreak of the First World War) are among the most moving in the period in displaying how the annihilation of the world will look, feel, and be experienced. " 'I saw the bombs fall,' " says one of the novel's several internal narrators, who has an unusually formal eye for the apocalypse around him, " 'and then watched a great crimson flare leap responsive to each impact, and mountainous masses of red-lit steam and flying fragments clamber up toward the zenith. Against the glare I saw the countryside for miles standing black and clear, churches, trees, chimneys. And suddenly I understood.' "[43]

Wells's writings of all sorts are washed by waves of violence and decimation that simply are there, part of the universal story, notwithstanding his will to recruit them into a happier narrative. And late in his life, as his frustrations grew and grew, this extinctive orientation threatened entirely to triumph over hope. Dr. Moreau may disdain our moral concerns about horrible bodily violation as so much inferiority—" 'This store men and women set on pleasure and pain,' " he says, " 'is the mark of the beast upon them, the mark of the beast from which they came. Pain! Pain and pleasure—they are for us, only so long as we wriggle in the dust' "—but Wells's works come back over and over to these primal scenes of massacre, waste, endurance, physical suffering, and failure (*IDM*, 74–75).

## V. SPECIALIZED LANGUAGE

What does it mean to be challenged by a text? This is a question Wells insistently brings to the fore. He challenged his readers ferociously—with his ideas, his aggressive presence, his unflinching discussion of topics that push against convention or that terrify a reader, his wild generic twists, and his constant, nagging insistence that we can do better. He also challenged with his words, literally his choice of individual words. Often these derive from science, which, as we know, had been Wells's training ground. What comes as a surprise is how estranging and richly transformative these can be. Wells will often create disorienting effects with the inclusion of a single word, and he takes inspiration, too, from the terminology belonging to whatever system a given text may be plumbing—such as biological, physical, financial, or military. If one of Wells's aims was to educate the world, his utilization of specialized language, counterintuitively, can have the opposite effect, distancing the reader or making her pause uncomfortably. This penchant to instruct and disrupt, then, forms part of Wells's larger dualistic style, where counterpointing impulses structure his large project.

But it starts small. Here is the opening of *The War of the Worlds*:

> No one would have believed, in the last years of the nineteenth century, that this world was being watched keenly and closely by intelligences greater than man's and yet as mortal as his own; that as men busied themselves about their various concerns they were scrutinized and studied, perhaps almost as narrowly as a man with a microscope might scrutinize the transient creatures that swarm and multiply in a drop of water. With infinite complacency men went to and fro over this globe about their little affairs, serene in their assurance of their empire over matter. It is possible that the infusoria under the microscope do the same. No one gave a thought to the older worlds of space as sources of human danger, or thought of them only to dismiss the idea.[44]

A reader today might hear the reverberations, in these opening sentences, of various familiar voices, such as Orson Welles, reading these lines in the famous radio broadcast of 1938, or Paul Frees in the 1953 film, or Morgan Freeman at the opening of Stephen Spielberg's 2005 remake. The allegorical suggestions established in these lines are many and rippling. It is an opening that invites the reader immediately into its fraught universe, where anxieties of the here and now are displaced and allegorized onto the cosmic scale, and the story that will follow likewise manages to condense a whole range of social nightmares into a sensational tale that can be read almost in one sitting. But there is one word that stands out from all of this: "infusoria." That word does not sound quite right in this opening segment, and in fact all of the radio or film openings just named omit or rewrite that line, excluding its problematic word. This is a hitch in an overture that otherwise is about infinite complacency and allows us to relax into the readerly security of a narrator who, as Jed Esty has argued, may not person-ally be able to do anything to combat the Martians but, in radiating a kind of easy, nontechnical British expertise, is a deeply reassuring voice to its 1898 (or perhaps any) audience.[45] But the inclusion of the clunky scientific term disrupts the flow, sending us to the dictionary (its definition is as follows: "protozoans of the class ciliophora," or, "any of various microscopic organisms found in infu-sions of decaying organic matter"). The *OED* lists the first usage in the 1750s in the scientific literature, and one might go out on a limb and credit Wells with its first literary usage.[46] This momentary shift in vocabulary gives a jolt, of a kind in fact we might recognize, as in this more familiar modernist swerve:

> April is the cruelest month, breeding
> Lilacs out of the dead land, mixing
> Memory and desire, stirring
> Dull roots with spring rain.
> Winter kept us warm, covering
> Earth in forgetful snow, feeding
> A little life with dried tubers.
> Summer surprised us, coming over the Starnbergersee
> With a shower of rain; we stopped in the colonnade,
> And went on in sunlight, into the Hofgarten,
> And drank coffee, and talked for an hour.
> *Bin gar keine Russin, stamm' aus Litauen, echt deutch.*[47]

Wells's infusions (or, shall we say, infusoria) of specialized vocabulary, like Eliot's untranslated languages, can be found throughout his writings, where a key sequence will suddenly be invaded (so to speak) by an alien idiom. They are quieter and less demanding than Eliot's variety, but they are working on and in the text (interestingly both of these examples involve the question of compla-cency and comfort disrupted, as signaled by a startling form of language).

Here is another such moment toward the end of *The War in the Air*, when destruction by air, financial collapse, pestilence, and general human failure have finally finished off civilization, and the narrator writes:

> Everywhere there are ruins and unburied dead, and shrunken, yellow-faced survivors, in a mortal apathy. Here there are robbers, here vigilance committees, and here guerilla bands ruling patches of exhausted territory, strange federations and brotherhoods form and dissolve, and religious fanaticisms begotten of despair gleam in famine-bright eyes. It is a universal dissolution. The fine order and welfare of the earth have crumpled like an exploded bladder. In five short years the world and the scope of human life have undergone a retrogressive change as great as that between the age of the Antonines and the Europe of the ninth century.
>
> (*WA*, 253–54)

The Antonines? Who and when are they? Why would that be the right reference to clarify things? The Antonine period was a prosperous one in the Roman Empire starting circa 100 CE, but the point is, who among Wells's readers is expected to know this? As with the infusoria, these specialized terms and obscure reference points have an effect on the surrounding text, the choice bearing on the form of writerly interruption the lexical trip forces (here in layering the novel's imagined history with actual historical trends in the European past, say). Even if some of Wells's readers would have recognized the Antonines from Gibbon's hugely influential *Decline and Fall of the Roman Empire*, the broad readership to whom Wells geared his writing would likely need a refresher. Moreover, in this passage the historical analogy needs to be set in the figural context of the simile Wells has just used, "like an exploded bladder," to characterize the total cultural destruction he has just named. This one, too, is a little uncomfortable, insofar as he is straddling a somewhat homely image, bladder as a kind of rustic bag for containing water, with the more biological resonance of a human or animal bladder, whose explosion would be anything but palatable to view. The point is to see these moments of lexical disruption—to see them in the first place—and to begin to ascertain the kind of work they are doing.

These examples are two of an almost endless sequence across Wells's works, and always they push forth questions of what kind of challenge Wells wants to afford, how he allows the smoothness of his textual surfaces to be disrupted, and what kind of reading experience he is willing to make and undo. Take *The Island of Doctor Moreau*, which is, among other things, a masterpiece in suspense, the thrill and horror of Prendick's discoveries experienced in real time by the reader.

There is much to confuse Prendick in this text, which takes place in a classic otherworld (an island of indeterminate location, drenched in symbolic value, itself the third setting amid a host of estranging locations that seem to wrench us out from our social moorings) and involves experiences in which the senses and mind are powerfully disturbed. For the reader, moreover, we have passages such as these, both of which transpire as key moments along Prendick's learning curve:

> I was startled by a great patch of vivid scarlet on the ground, and going up to it found it to be a peculiar fungus branched and corrugated like a foliaceous lichen, but deliquescing into slime at the touch. And then in the shadow of some luxuriant ferns I came upon an unpleasant thing, the dead body of a rabbit, covered with shining flies but still warm, and with its head torn off. I stopped aghast at the sight of the scattered blood.
>
> (*IDM*, 41)

And:

> The path coiled down abruptly into a narrow ravine between two tumbled and knotty masses of blackish scoriae. Into this we plunged.
>
> It was extremely dark, this passage, after the blinding sunlight reflected from the sulphurous ground. Its walls grew steep, and approached one another. Blotches of green and crimson drifted across my eyes. My conductor stopped suddenly. "Home," said he.
>
> (*IDM*, 56)

And thus the lair of the beast people is revealed. In each of these passages, which transpire as part of the text's nearly nonstop hunt/chase/discover action, Wells's inclusion of a startling, distracting Latinate phrase ("foliaceous lichen . . . deliquescing," "scoriae") offers a strange braking or stumble before, in each case, a truly sensational discovery. Readers will no doubt remember, after the novel has been completed, that bloody, decapitated rabbit, the first dead creature we meet on the island (and then, when Prendick eats an "ill-cooked rabbit" for breakfast the next morning, we may well feel distinctly queasy), and of course the world of the beast people is one of the novel's great inventions. Yet we should not jump too quickly over Wells's unsettling insertions of specialized language, which run counter to the rapid, page-turning style of the novel. How does one "plunge" into these "scoriae," if one cannot visualize them? Before I can figure out what "foliaceous" is likely to mean, I am staring at that liquefying rabbit. In a sense, the frequent placement of scientific terminology, though in theory offering an exactitude to allow more perfect visual acumen, works against the sensory intensity of this novel, one of its key attributes. It also creates a verbal surround for the novel's different locations, each such linguistic context derived from the specific atmosphere. Here on the island, terms of botanical and geological specificity appear, while in the earlier, nautical scenes that precede arrival on the island, Wells loads his prose with maritime vocabulary. If there is a logic, then, behind such usage, there is equally a qualification; the reader cannot quite plunge into Wells's brilliant otherworlds if she is hesitating around a specialized term and wondering if she should, in fact, know what it means.

Difficulty then, of a very specific sort, and there can be no stricter criterion for entry into the modernist party, as we know, than difficulty. Eliot, in his famous phrase, taught that poetry today "must be *difficult*. . . . The poet must become more and more comprehensive, more allusive, more indirect, in order to force, to dislocate if necessary, language into his meaning."[48] Formal experimentation as confusion, illegibility, erudition, streams and strands of consciousness, a basic decentering of the reader, an immersion into multiple sensory worlds, a surrendering of mastery: these are some of the hallmarks and the joys of reading modernism. Wells had his own forms, and his use of language from medical, scientific, or other professional spheres, sprinkled into the text at the very moment when it is otherwise at its most inviting, adds a new entrant into the cohort of destabilizing modernist methods. As is so often the case with Wells, these moments reintroduce the author—with his scientific training and interests—yet here his learning is less a summons to engage directly in an ongoing conversation about recurrent topics than a reminder of how fully the worlds we might think separable (fiction from biology, say) are always enmeshed. No word ever drops in entirely from nowhere. Wells, with his famous prolixity, had his own version of le mot juste.

## VI. THE VISUAL

A passage from *The War in the Air*:

Steadily the *Vaterland* [airship] soared, and the air-fleet soared with her and came round to head for New York, and the battle became a little thing far away, an incident before breakfast. It dwindled to a string of dark shapes and one smoking yellow flare that presently became a more indistinct smear upon the vast horizon and the bright new day, that was at last altogether lost to sight . . .

(*WA*, 121, ellipses in original)

And one from *The War of the Worlds*:

> Dense black smoke was leaping to mingle with the steam from the river, and as
> the Heat-Ray went to and fro over Weybridge its impact was marked by flashes
> of incandescent white, that gave place at once to a smoky dance of lurid flames.
> The nearer houses still stood intact, awaiting their fate, shadowy, faint, and pal-
> lid in the steam, with the fire behind them going to and fro.
>
> (WW, 65)

In these two works of feverish, destructive imagining, one feature stands out:
the visual intensity of Wells's writing. Passages like these could be selected
almost at random from these two novels, which construct elaborate visual patterns, *The War in the Air* in the panorama from above, before, during, and after
attack, *The War of the Worlds* in the projecting of flames against darkness.
Often, too, such scenes have a specifically filmic encasing, as when Bert watches
from his porthole in the airship, the window literally framing the scenes of carnage and burning below, safe from his post in the sky,[49] or in passages like this
one at the opening of *A Modern Utopia*:

> *The image of a cinematograph entertainment is the one to grasp. There will be an*
> *effect of these two people going to and fro in front of the circle of a rather defective*
> *lantern, which sometimes jams and sometimes gets out of focus, but which does*
> *occasionally succeed in displaying on the screen a momentary moving picture of*
> *Utopian conditions. Occasionally the picture goes out altogether . . .*
>
> (MU, 8, italics in original)

The picture will go out; this is part of Wells's basic understanding about the way
our visual imagination operates (in life, in the novel). His is a visual universe
that impresses us in vivid ways, then goes dark, a world in which old and new
modes of technology and perception must live side by side. In the new mode,
there is the film camera (or its early equivalents), along with a variety of other
technological inventions, but these can fail, leaving us again with the man at his
desk with pen and paper, an older method for creating the illusion of reality.

Always, the impulse to convey in distinctive pictorial terms is countered by
the problem of blurred vision. In *The Time Machine*, the first thing the Traveller
meets when he gets to the Golden Age is his own perceptual limitation; when he
arrives, it is hailing. Despite all the wonderful effects of slow and fast motion, of
time warps and fourth dimensions, the Traveller's actual, human vision falters
in the organic materiality of the atmosphere. And the sphinx, the monument

that will be his landmark throughout his stay, is hardly visible through the mist: "A colossal figure, carved apparently in some white stone, loomed indistinctly beyond the rhododendrons through the hazy downpour. But all else of the world was invisible" (*TM*, 21). Such visual impediments remain throughout the novel, despite many moments when curtains seem to rise—when the literal clearing of the air or a visual revelation of some other kind signals an important new insight about the condition of life in the future. "I felt naked in a strange world," says the Traveller of the moment when he first really sees the future landscape, and there is always such reciprocity in *The Time Machine* between being able to view/understand and being vulnerable to what one now sees and knows (*TM*, 22).

In 1895, such reflections contributed to the generating of filmic consciousness. I noted in the introduction how closely and curiously *The Time Machine* overlaps with film history in its early stages, a story that several recent critics have expounded. Keith Williams, who describes Wells as "a principal pioneer of the media-determined parameters of modern subjectivity," credits Wells with a whole range of accomplishments related to the modern film era, including the particular visuality encoded in the science fiction Wells helped invent; his extraordinary understanding of mediation and the interpenetration of visual forms with their modes of transmission; his emphasis on science and technology as integral with perception's cognitive, social, and libidinal qualities; his rendering of imagined future cities and landscapes; his promiscuity across popular and elite styles; and, most famously, his manipulation of time. As Williams writes of this last, "Wells's early writing and the birth of cinema were leading and interrelated manifestations of the 'chronotope' of late nineteenth- and early twentieth-century consciousness in its transition to modernity."[50] Laura Marcus, too, has argued for Wells's importance in early cinema, demonstrating how "in many ways his writing career ran parallel to the 'evolution' of cinema." Marcus describes Wells as outstripping the era's technology, in terms of how his ideas could be translated into visual effects (this is a point Williams makes as well), such that "The moving image, with its power to make manifest the speculative and the impossible, was such a powerful dimension of Wells's imaginative world that the [early] 'adaptations' of his work could hardly be other than disappointments."[51] What both of these critics affirm is how richly Wells's writings anticipate and give depth, texture, vividness, drama, and figuration to a range of visual possibilities that, over many decades, would become realized in film and recognized as central to our media-driven universe.

Even aside from its cinematic significance, Wells's approach to the visual world is complex and absorbing, as he teases out a range of biological, social/

sociological, and psychological issues in terms of how and what we see. The works that focus most tightly on this conjunction tend to be his stories, or in some cases short novels, and often it is the technology or science of seeing itself that structures these tales. A whole cluster of stories investigate mutations in perception and probe the possible consequences—whether psychic or more broadly social—of such shifts. One thing to note about these works, in considering the genre of the short story in the period, is that they tend not to be oriented around the epiphany (a form of inner vision), and this differentiates them from the modernist story, as critics have canonized it. Instead, the key turn or crux involves the perceptual situation itself. "The Remarkable Case of Davidson's Eyes" (1895), to take one example, features a protagonist who finds himself one day overcome by a strange vision that eclipses the actual world around him, so that he is, in effect, blind. Instead of being locked in blackness, however, his mind's eye is focused on a scene involving a ship, island, and even a colony of penguins. The incongruity and seeming meaninglessness of the vision gets explained at the end of the story, when we learn that there really was a ship in this position and that Davidson, working near an electromagnet, "had some extraordinary twist given to his retinal elements through the sudden change in the field of force," such that he spent several weeks watching a scene eight thousand miles away. The event is also explained as having to do with the fourth dimension and a "kink of space."[52] Notwithstanding the murkiness of the physics here, the overlapping of visions yields engrossing sequences, as when Davidson begins to get his real sight back; he experiences the return of the actual, present world like a tear in the canvas of his vision. " 'It's very dim and broken in places, but I see it all the same, like a faint spectre of itself,' " Davidson says of this first reemergence of the real, " 'It's like a hole in this infernal phantom world.' " A few days later, the narrator reports, "At first it was very confusing to him to have these two pictures overlapping each other like the changing views of a lantern, but in a little while he began to distinguish the real from the illusory" (*Stories*, 280, 281).

It is this line between real and illusory that stands at the center of many of these stories. In "Davidson's Eyes," as the actual setting nudges the vision further and further to the edges and then out altogether, Davidson is restored to normalcy and can resume life—but of course, there is a catch. Now that the "infernal phantom" has been extinguished, a sense of melancholy or loss washes in. An undercurrent of heaviness lingers in many of these stories once the vision or supernatural effect ceases. This undercurrent is not really addressed in this story, but Wells is hinting at what kinds of desires and impulses such shifts in view might be channeling. "Under the Knife" (1896), too, is a story about the coexistence and commingling of vision and reality, in this case as the narrator details an elaborate account of himself leaving his body and extending into outer space while his physical self undergoes a risky surgical procedure. The twist is that we as readers do not know, over the course of the vision, whether the narrator is actually dead—this then being an experiment in writing the after-life—or having a hallucination brought on by chloroform. There is a conscious-ness of artistry in the story, a kind of virtuosity effect, accompanying the sense of exhilaration as the body is left behind. The body to which the speaker does in fact return (he was not dead after all) is as physical an object as could be, having been severed open by the doctor's lancet and operated on, now terribly weak, in a room of bloodied sheets and instruments. All of these stories revolve around some kind of dichotomy, where on one side is a narrative of intensified or altered sensory experience and, on the other, an eventual grounding in material neces-sity. Often, too, it is science itself that demands the return. Scientific invention turns out to be double edged; it generates the story's visionary activity, and, at the same time, it calls us back from imaginative flight.

Most remarkable among all of these stories of vision and its complex disman-tling is "The Door in the Wall" (1906), which, in a sense, comments on the mode itself, insofar as it gives us an actual door and an overtly visionary experience on its far side. Like many of Wells's stories, "The Door in the Wall" is a frame nar-rative, and it is the internal narrator who tells of his on-again-off-again relation-ship to the magical door. The door, which the protagonist sees periodically over the course of his life, though opens only once, remains as a kind of other for him, a space of alterity to his increasingly busy, conventional life, with all its markers of worldly (and, one must read, empty) success.[53] With its suggestion of haunting and alluring promise, the door tends to appear at moments in his story when the continuity of life is being assured (when he is on the brink of receiving a scholarship, say, or heading for a cabinet post). The door, which he never opens after his initial foray as a child, raises insistent questions about what the world on its other side signifies. Is it art? Beauty? Play (that is, not work)? Is it a queer world, where ordinary expectations can be skewed? Is it a world of love and sexu-ality? Is it a place of reading? All of these are essentially true, with its dominant suggestion being its sensory intensification, its beauty and kindness. After all, the protagonist only enters when a child, a lonely boy, bereft of affection, and there he finds a most exquisite dramatization of childhood fantasy (complete with tame leopards and magical books). The door that he won't open again func-tions like a metaphor for so many chances not taken, a Romantic story, with Wordsworthian overtones in the lost possibilities of childhood, the closed doors of maturation.

These stories are thus less lighthearted than they initially appear; others of Wells's most visual narratives have no such uncertainty and mutate quickly into portraits of brute domination. The most memorable, such as *The Invisible Man* (1897) and "The Country of the Blind" (1904), are parables of power. They circulate around the dialectic of vantage and supremacy, undoing any simple scheme between the two and upending inherited wisdom. In fact, the link between seeing and controlling is anything but straightforward in Wells's stories and novellas, which portray the relation between these old partners not as known and fixed but as suggestive, ambiguous, and unpredictable. They thus help give concrete expression to Wells's lifelong interest in the unpredictable relation of knowledge to time, where seeing the future may become a paradoxical strategy to understand the present or may yield instead only ambiguity.

In *The Invisible Man*, there is much that overlaps with stories like "Davidson's Eyes" in having at its center the slippage of material into immaterial, reality into specter. The early sequences at the inn, when the shocking discovery is made that Griffin's covering in fact covers nothing, are delightfully sensational, as we circle around the idea or image of the man's body, there and not there. Throughout the story, and more generally in these visual tales, Wells is thinking, again, about the nature of impression, often quite literally, as with the problem of snow or mud. When Griffin walks in it, his feet leave impressions, revealing his presence; likewise the dust of London sticks on his feet and body. Riveting, too, are the details of Griffin's experiments, as we watch these material bodies disappearing under the action of the machine, first a cat as a test, then the man. There is something haunting (almost literally) about that invisible cat, whose fate assuredly will be grim. In *The Invisible Man*, these spectacular visuals—with the attendant questions they trail about dualism, materiality, and the powers and limitations of scientific advance—provide readerly pleasure and interest, but within the story, things rapidly degenerate into escalating violence. Griffin's terroristic plan chimes in with larger fantasies and fears of political violence in the period, as Griffin imagines a "Reign of Terror" whose ruthless leader will "take some towns like your Burdock and terrify and dominate it. . . . And all who disobey his orders he must kill, and kill all who would defend them."[54] This seems serious, and the towns eventually do rally to defeat their foe, but here is the strange thing: *The Invisible Man* is characterized, in this respect, by a kind of pettiness. Its scale is small, its personages drawn from the comic tradition, its structure mostly picaresque, and its quintessential device the chase. Scenes in which the invisible Griffin attacks one or more townspeople become repetitive and a little weary. As the novel comes to revolve around Griffin's desire for revenge against Kemp, the bachelor with a science education who functions as the text's eventual protagonist (another Wellsian alter-ego), the high stakes around invisibility are slowly reduced. As in *A Modern Utopia*, the myopic turn to a story about individual rivalries and reprisals depletes the tale of its larger political message or metaphysical significance. With such narrative shifts, Wells reminds us forcefully that these supercharged, spectacular changes in view may not, in the end, radically alter the larger worlds into which they enter. Perhaps, as Wells's writings will so often insist, it is foresight, rather than present sight, that matters.

The work that does most to bring together Wells's concentrated visual apparatus with an analysis of power is "The Country of the Blind," a story that provides an apt conclusion to this chapter on voice, since its theme, above all, is the contingency of any sensory power. "The Country of the Blind," like *The Time Machine* and *The Island of Dr. Moreau*, is one of Wells's fables with especially wide resonance, riffing, for instance, on evolution and the close penetration of biology into culture, and taking blindness seriously, unusual for its historical moment. As Maren Linett writes, "The anti-imperialist thrust of the story leads it into a progressive representation of blindness as something that can not only be lived with, but lived with well. . . . The story exemplifies the social model of disability in its portrayal of a society so well adapted to the needs of blind people that sight, and not blindness, becomes a disability."[55] One aspect of Wells's vision-oriented tales is that they immediately dispense with received wisdom about visual supremacy and power (a lesson Griffin of *The Invisible Man* is never able to learn). "The Country of the Blind" takes the disentangling of sight and power very literally, with its overall message that there is no inherent superiority in one or another physical or genetic condition; there is only adaptation and belief. The village of the blind is perfectly adapted to its citizens, from its roads to its farms to its home design, and its cosmology is equally well suited to the inhabitants' needs, the sky understood as a dome, the cosmos a place of safety and enclosure, whose qualities are tactile rather than visual, an apt realization of the universe as actually experienced here. Nunez, the story's unlikable protagonist, happens in on the mythical valley after a miraculous survival from a mountain fall and a trek into what seemed total wilderness. We do not know much about him except that he is a mountain guide and a good reader, and, after his survival, he also has something of the Last Man about him. Coming upon the valley with its generations of blind inhabitants, he quickly takes to the idea— gathered one imagines from reading Kipling—that he will easily rule over these pathetic simple people; after all, they are blind, he can see. He is the man who would be king (the ditty he takes as his motto runs "in the country of the blind, the one-eyed man is king," an aphorism attributed to Erasmus).[56] Such a principle is easily dispatched, as Nunez finds himself overcome by these citizens of a different world; they have no time for his assumptions of superiority, no fear of his blundering efforts at physical violence, and no interest in his abilities, which they see as the gravest defects. Humbled and in servitude, Nunez drifts toward his own major possibility of adaptation and is on the verge of sacrificing his sight in order to be made a full member of the community (which is to say, to be allowed to marry his master's beautiful daughter Medina-saroté)—when he changes his mind and retreats.[57]

There are a variety of interpretations one might pursue in this impacted little tale. The literal blindness of the valley people might be read as figurative blindness of one sort or another, but what I want to stress here is the story's visual dimension, not so much its parable about sight as its own visual sensibility. Just as Wells's works that figure destruction each have a dominant style (aerial, painterly, cinematic), here the overarching note is impressionist, with an emphasis both on the wonder of color, distance, light, and beauty and on the powerful subjectivism of such effects. Everywhere the story stresses the relativity of vision; this is its key point, really, that what we see and what we think are powerful, reciprocal determinants. When Nunez first sees the village houses, "They were very strange to his eyes, and indeed the whole aspect of that valley became, as he regarded it, queerer and more unfamiliar" (*Stories*, 172). There is a learning curve with the eyes, which must adjust to strangeness as to light or shade. The highly panoramic tale is full of visual display and also features Nunez's unsuccessful attempts to convince his would-be bride of the value of sight. "Nunez had an eye for all beautiful things," the narrator remarks, and Nunez's recollections of the world he has left are decidedly aestheticized and painterly, so that when he agrees to be blinded, he is assailed by "a vision of those further slopes, distance beyond distance, with Bogota, a place of multitudinous stirring beauty, a glory by day, a luminous mystery by night, a place of palaces and fountains and statues and white houses, lying beautifully in the middle distance" (*Stories*, 179, 191). The emphasis is on perspective, on ranges and layers of distance, with the eye attempting to fix some space as the center of vision ("the middle distance") and with the stirring, mysterious beauty of the city entirely a function of how it is seen, by whom, and from what vantage point. The story's emphasis, in stark contrast to the conception of the villagers, is on these kinds of distance views, where color ripples and fluctuates, and the eye is attracted to rolling and shading and the play of light. "And there," concludes Nunez's thought sequence about the world to be left behind, "unpent by mountains, one saw the sky—the sky, not such a disc as one saw it here, but an arch of immeasurable blue, a deep of deeps in which the circling stars were floating . . ." (*Stories*, 191, ellipses in the original). Is the sky "as one saw it here" a disc because of the physical setting in the valley or because the notion of sky here is of a roof? It is an unanswerable question, but Nunez and Wells dwell on these distinctive styles of seeing; even something as seemingly objective as the sky is fully determined by culture.

It seems that Wells had an offer to make a film of "The Country of the Blind" in 1914, and there is a surviving film script; as one might expect, in this iteration, Wells lets his visual imagination run further and faster. The silent film Wells contemplated provides a perfect template for the story's visual style, in part because he appears to have been envisioning production in color! In one notable shift in the drafting of the script, the first time we see Nunez with Medina, as she is now called, he is leaning in to her, relaying the joys of sight; then "the scene dissolves into a richly coloured view of a bed of beautiful tropical flowers waving in the wind," and a line or two later, the "scene re-dissolves, this time into a stretch of blue ocean with sunlit wave, or rich green vegetation with brightly coloured birds flittering about."[58] One can see how shifting from black and white to color, with the emphasis on scenes dissolving into one another in superb new palettes, would give visual force to what the written story is constructing as a basic division in worldviews ("views" understood in both senses). The film was not made, but its conception demonstrates how fluidly Wells's thinking moved along painterly, cinematic, and subjectivist lines and how a story that takes as its central idea the relation of sight to culture is rich ground formally to play out those dynamics.

This is Wells's hallmark, the restlessness of his imagination adjusting itself to new ideas and technologies and bending those ideas and technologies to his own powerful determinants. *The Outline of History* was remarkable, among many other things, for the fact that in its initial serial publication it employed color photographs, creative large format, and other visual additions to bring out, complement, and in some cases play off against the text. Let me conclude, though, with what we might take as a quintessential scene of viewing in Wells's writing, a passage from *Tono-Bungay*. Here is George, looking in the gates of one of the great country estates that stand at the center of the novel's social analysis:

> Eastry House is so close that it dominates the whole; one goes across the marketplace (with its old lock-up and stocks), past the great pre-Reformation church, a fine grey shell, like some empty skull from which the life has fled, and there at once are the huge wrought-iron gates, and one peeps through them to see the façade of this place, very white and large and fine, down a long avenue of yews.
>
> (*TB*, 67)

There is much one might say about this sequence, where George—and no doubt his author Herbert George—can stand outside and critique the social system embodied by the country estate, can feel the pull and magnetism of that view, can recognize how the line of yew trees draws in one's eye—yet the view is always framed by heavy gates.[59] That is what produces the *frisson*, the energy: to recognize a social and also aesthetic principle that is made from distance, framed and limited by the social structure. Wells was always fundamentally the protagonist of his writing, but he was also the person just outside, looking in, observing, scripting. Perhaps he plays that role in modernism, too, if only we could gain just the right vantage to see the picture anew.

# 2

# Civilian

"**I** seen too much smashing and killing today,'" reports Bert Small-ways, nauseated and horrified as he watches the beginnings of what will soon become worldwide aerial war, "'I don't like it. I didn't know war was this sort of thing. I'm a civilian.'"[1] In a literary era crowded with wonderful everymen, from Leopold Bloom to Hans Castorp to J. Alfred Prufrock to Ellison's Invisible Man to Mary Seton/Beton/Carmichael, Bert Smallways holds a unique and crucial place: he is the civilian. What that will mean—for *The War in the Air*, Wells's 1908 prophecy of world destruction, for Wells more generally, and most importantly, for literary culture throughout the twentieth century—is an intensely important question, as writers, artists, film-makers, journalists, political leaders, scholars, and human rights advocates have recognized since the First World War. A civilian qua civilian is constituted by two primary, interconnected facts: that he is not a combatant in war but that his condition is defined in relation to war.[2] As Mary Favret has noted, conceptually, the civilian is known first in reverse; a person is a civilian only because she is not in the military, required to take up the combatant role, and because there are others—in the twentieth century millions of others—who are.[3] That there is something normative, or even definitive, about this configuration as a feature of life in the twentieth century has become more and more inescapable, beginning with the world wars of the first half of the century followed by the Cold War, colonial and anticolonial conflicts, and into our own era of terrorism and drone airstrikes. All of these, in different ways, have revealed the prevalence and fragil-ity of the civilian in the cauldron of world experience. It could be said, in truth, that any person who has ever lived in a walled city has, at some level, this quality of existing in relation to the possibility of war, even if she is not asked directly to fight in it.

In the twentieth century, with the two world wars establishing the stark realities of how civilians can be targeted, or even annihilated, the idea that one might be simultaneously subject to war yet defined outside its immediate purview has cut close to the bone for untold numbers of people. Since the end of World War I, international law has worked to acknowledge and attempt to address this disastrous reweighting of civilian vulnerability to warfare, often with only meager results; historians today estimate that an astonishing 75 to 90 percent of casualties in a variety of ongoing conflicts are civilians. Another way to frame this is to say that modernity has defined its claim to "civilization" in part on the presumption of civilian immunity in war, at the same time that it has, in equal measure, reneged on that promise.[4] This much seems straightforward, if deeply troubling: what is unknown today is that Wells was a generative thinker—arguably *the* generative thinker in the English language—in bringing this premise, as an imaginative principle, into the mainstream.

For Wells, there was something absolutely basic about how the civilian becomes representative, since he was constantly advancing two lines of inquiry that came together in the form of the nonsoldier caught up in war: the modern thrust of industry, global connectedness, and, in his view, political and moral inadequacy in relation to the new forces plunging world conflict into ever greater extremes, and his interest in the ordinary person. As we have seen, Wells wrestled in his writing with the contradictory urges to tell individual stories, in the tradition of the novel, and to tell his own brand of species story. "It is not the individual that reproduces himself," he wrote in 1908, "it is the species that reproduces through the individual and often in spite of his characteristics. The race flows through us, the race is the drama and we are the incidents."[5] At the same time, it was his philosophical creed that there are no identical units in the world as revealed by science, only unique individuals. Straddling such contraries, his primary unit of attention in fiction was meant to be the representative character—all these different everymen, foraying into the future, surveying utopia, taking cover from bombs, or simply struggling along in the ambiguous spaces of class ascendency. Characters like Kipps, Polly, or Lewisham offer compelling instances of how the representative story keeps giving way to the richness of individuality—the tale of all of us into the bildungsroman, perhaps—and then back again. But the point here is to note how, with the jolt in scale that mass war entails, Wells's effort to chart the narrative of humanity finds new meaning and gravity. Perhaps Yeats would say that a terrible beauty is born.

Indeed, to consider how Wells came to envision the civilian as a normative figure for the twentieth century is to see him interacting powerfully with modernism, which had its own stake in these outcomes. Woolf and Joyce, to name two especially compelling comparisons, were operating in tandem with Wells in refracting the modern world through a lens more and more darkened and distorted by war. All three recognized disproportion as the defining quality in the way people are related to mechanized warfare and evolved writing styles that carved out a space of prominence for the civilian. Wells blazes off in his own direction, however, in part because of the reach of his writings on this subject and also because his configuring of civilian experience mapped so closely to his stated goal of world harmony. Throughout the many works in this canon, Wells set his feverish imagination on the full panoply of consequences that ensue when the forces of warfare overtake all of the culture's constraints—constraints that look in Wells's writings absurdly flimsy in relation to the powers catapulting the world into warfare—and claimed, or rather insisted, that in the confrontation of people with war lay the seeds of future peace. It was the civilian who would be both the victim of history's brutal onslaughts and the agent of its ultimate pacification. As he wrote in one of his articles covering the Washington disarmament conference of 1921,

> there is an immense task before teachers and writers, before parents and talkers and all who instruct and make and change opinion [i.e., civilians], and that is the task of building up a new spirit in the hearts of men and a new dream in their minds, the spirit of fellowship to all men, the dream of a great world released for ever from the obsession of warfare and international struggle.[6]

Wells took up the idea of civilian exemplarity at several different levels, and in each of these areas, his writings have far-reaching implications. First, and most spectacularly, he figured the panorama and experience of worldwide destruction, or total war. *The War in the Air* is one of a spate of works that, in different contexts and produced over the course of three decades, gave expression to the central question of what it would feel and look like to behold the obliteration of cities, nations, and ultimately civilization itself. The connection between "civilian" and "civilization," it should be stressed, was more than coincidental in this era, when the survival of the latter, understood as perhaps the final Western accomplishment, came to be figured in accordance with the fate of the former. Christine Froula, in *Virginia Woolf and the Bloomsbury Avant-Garde*, has made a strong case for reading Bloomsbury as deeply engaged with the meaning and value of civilization as such, defined in the context of war.

Wells, for his part, wrote a book with the title *The Salvaging of Civilization* in 1921, in which he presented the case for international unity as the way out of the world's staggering ills, figured by Wells as complete social and economic collapse, under the shadow of total war.

In Wells's total-war fictions, some of the expected features, such as his famous prescience about the future of war and its technologies, are yoked to larger, deeper meditations on the way one *becomes* a civilian by virtue of the unstoppable, sweeping qualities of warfare in the modern era, defined for Wells as much by the way the globe has become interlocked as by its destructive capacities. That so much of Wells's writing on the quality of total warfare was formulated before the First World War is testament to his far-reaching insights and to the second register at issue here: that in Wells's works, to be a noncombatant is, in a certain sense, a matter of and for the imagination. The initiating act of the civilian in relation to war is to send the mind to war, to reach out toward the sensory and psychic experience of those in combat. Wells's sensibility around violence was always intensely physical, his lifetime of writings expressing what I have elsewhere called "disenchanted violence," the decimated flesh thrust before the reader, uncompromising and impossible to idealize.[7] In the case of war, to be able to imagine the horrors and other material aspects of warfare is, in essence, the first duty of the noncombatant. It is a gesture of empathy or—better—what recent critics have begun to theorize as shared vulnerability, and this effort accounts, I believe, for the stunning success of his 1916 war novel *Mr. Britling Sees It Through*. That novel was a watershed in civilian war writing, and its resonance with readers around the world indicates the power of this construct—the imagining civilian whose mental torments track the downward spiral of war.

For Wells, moreover, the ethics of imagining reorient us, almost invisibly, to the future, and this is a third aspect of his construction of the civilian, the emphasis on *what is to come*. In part, Wells borrows his future temporality from the popular category of next-war fiction, a minigenre that had flourished since the 1871 defeat of France by Germany.[8] The commitment to thinking ahead represents a major aspect of Wells's writing trajectory, which began so dramatically with a look into the long future. Looking, thinking, and imagining ahead: these are deeply embedded in the larger ethical principle of writing about war's effects on ordinary people and the world at large.

Finally, then, the culminating feature of Wells's establishment of civilian expression is his development of a mode of writing that positions the noncombatant to take responsibility for peace.[9] As early as August 1914, Wells began to write pamphlets about the war, inaugurated in his famous collection *The War That Will End War*. In what we might deem a speech act of self-empowerment, the pamphlet form as Wells adapted it accorded voice to those at home who were not only noncombatant but nonanything—not politicians, established journalists, military strategists, civil servants, or members of the ruling elite. In the name of peace, Wells argued, the civilian is thrust into activation. He never let go of that conviction, his work on the Declaration of the Rights of Man providing a new idiom and concept geared, by World War II when it was written, to the times. Like Woolf, with whom he powerfully converges in this respect, Wells decided that when it came to the overwhelming danger of twentieth-century war, it is we—here at home, with no more than our passion for peace to aid us—who must make the world see itself, and then, even more daunting, turn away from its history of nations and their wars.

## I. SWEPT UP: THE NONCOMBATANT
## EXPERIENCE OF WAR

There is nothing that characterizes the twentieth century so fully as the ever-dawning awareness of war's scale and ferocity. How, we have to ask from our basements or shelters, or even in front of our television sets and today our internet platforms, did science, technology, and progress turn against us so fully? Why can't someone stop it? It is a story of lost innocence that, in a certain way, gets replayed for each generation, and it was one that Wells told repeatedly, starting even before the century had turned and with ever-increasing urgency as the decades and body counts piled up. The narrative of total war is one of escalation, with Clausewitz's formula that war always tends to extremes historicized and projected onto the scales of the twentieth century's capacity for mobilization and its military and chemical/atomic technology. The phenomenon of total war, which came of age over the course of Wells's writing life, distinguishes itself from other wars in two primary ways. What makes war total is, first, that it involves a major mobilization of the populace and, second, that it erases the distinction between civilian and combatant. As Trutz von Trotha compactly describes it, total war "tends to involve all members of the society engaging in warfare and at the same time is directed without distinction against all members of the 'hostile' society," such that "the total war of industrialized societies is unlimited. . . . The distinction between soldier and civilian is lost. Everyone becomes a part of the 'war machine.' Everyone becomes a target of absolute violence."[10] Wells wrote, as early as 1901, that the warfare of the near future will become "more and more as a whole a monstrous thrust and pressure of people against people," that "behind the thin firing line on either side a vast multitude of people will be at work," and even that "there will be a very considerable restriction of the rights of the non-combatant."[11] There are, of course, other features we might add to the primacy of noncombatants in defining total war, such as the involvement of many countries, so that the conflict becomes global in both character and implications, or the quality of relative stalemate that catapults the war into ever further escalation, or the intensity of the issues at stake, minimizing the possibility of settlement. Even when defined in the most skeletal, intuitive way, however, and despite an almost universal sense that there is something we can call "total war," epitomized by the two world wars and involving a degree of violence that, as Ian Beckett puts it, "resulted in the destruction of life and property on an unprecedented scale compared with previous wars," the term remains exceptionally unstable.[12]

For all its currency, historians have debated the term "total war"—its meaning, its accuracy, and the consequences of its ubiquitous usage. The military historian Roger Chickering, for one, has taken issue with the way total war has become a "master narrative" by which we read both backward and forward through World Wars I and II, overlooking features that do not conform to this telos and emphasizing above all the escalating scope and intensifying nature of war's violence. In Chickering's terms, the story of total war has become not only dominant but irresistible: "Despite the fact that this narrative portrays increasing levels of violence, death, and destruction," he writes, "its structure is romantic. The narrative subject is war, whose growth and fulfillment provide the central element of the plot."[13] Chickering's critique helps expose what we might think of as the affective underpinnings of total war, the way it has a logic of its own that reinforces some arguments about war as natural and self-perpetuating, while suppressing others that are then relegated to the exceptional or the minor. Both Mary Favret and Paul Saint-Amour, to name two brilliant readers of warfare in the literary context, have taken up the challenge of rethinking the narrative of total war, to see, in Favret's case, how its historical trajectory has distorted our understanding of the civilian experience of war in the Napoleonic era, and in Saint-Amour's, how the idea of total war, with its bias toward the Western powers and metropolises, has occluded the use of force against civilians in other parts of the world, hence what he calls the "partiality of total war."[14]

But what neither Chickering nor anyone else has noticed is that Wells helped write the story of total war exactly as it has come down to us. As with all formulations that make history understandable, the idea of total war is not a simple outgrowth of events; how it came to be imagined, known, felt, and interiorized has significant implications for the broad understanding of war, whether in realms of aesthetics, popular culture, law, human rights, or politics. From a legal and geopolitical point of view, the questions of what total war does and how it might be curtailed are, of course, of enormous importance. It was during the interwar period that these questions began to animate the public widely and pressure political structures. Several international conferences were convened, the first in Washington, DC, in 1921–1922, followed by further deliberations in The Hague in 1923, and then again in Geneva in 1932–1933. The Kellogg-Briand Pact of 1928 represents the most tangible agreement of these years, with its goal of convincing nations to renounce military force. These conventions operated around one principal set of assumptions and concerns: as the First World War had shown, the twentieth century had adopted new forms of warfare, which would most certainly be expanded in future wars. These—poison gas, the targeting of civilians in bombing raids, the sinking of passenger ships—seemed to exceed what many considered legitimate or permissible, at least when Western citizens were the targets. As history has shown, not much was secured from these conventions, particularly with respect to protection from aerial bombardment. Yet they were part of the zeitgeist—and Wells was part of them. He attended the Washington convention as a reporter sponsored by *New York World*, for which he wrote a series of twenty-nine articles (also reprinted in other American, English, and European papers), collected in 1922 as *Washington and the Riddle of Peace* (in the English edition, interestingly, *Washington and the Hope of Peace*).[15] That Wells was invited to comment on the events is not surprising, given his role during the war years as self-appointed civilian designate, his early, passionate work for the League of Nations, and the enormous success of *The Outline of History*, which Wells wrote and promulgated in the name of universal peace.

Yet with total war, it was, first, a matter of representation. Wells envisioned total war across his genres, in novels, speculative essays, hybrid discussion/fiction, and in film. It was a scenario to which he was endlessly drawn and illuminates an especially dynamic set of intersections and distinctions in relation to modernism.[16] Often such meaning can be buried or oblique. In *Ulysses*, the burning city, with its apocalyptic and archetypal associations, also holds in its shadows, implicit and felt, the very real and intimate history of Dublin's own warfare, six years before the publication of the novel (an anachronism within its literal timeframe).[17] Or in Yeats's plays, a smoldering ruin can stand for national and personal violence, a site of trauma where the cycles of history come into view; in some of his more abstract plays, something as schematic as a red square can stand in for long bloody histories (and perhaps futures). And of course, *The Waste Land* gives Anglo-American modernism its canonical panorama of burning cities, tolling bells, waste, and rubble. Moreover, as I have argued in *At the Violet Hour*, the temporality of incipience with respect to violence, that tense period just before the world shatters, was a salient one for modernism, which drew always closer to recognizing its own fatal status as between the wars, a pattern richly elucidated in Saint-Amour's work. As Wells predicted of the new century, "Everybody, everywhere, will be perpetually and constantly looking up, with a sense of loss and insecurity, with a vague stress of painful anticipations" (*Ant*, 213).

For Wells, however, these conditions of incipience and aftermath are placed concretely in their own full histories. Even if, as Jan Mieszkowski has argued, total war by necessity cannot be imagined in totality, Wells took up the task of imagining war as a calling, and to do so from many positions, a kind of ongoing straining of the sensory apparatus in the face of something not only enormously beyond the scope of any viewer but designed precisely to injure the viewer's ability to see or record.[18] In his works, despite such obstacles, we read of the buildup, onset, crescendo, and afterlife of war's devastation, always taking the view of those who, in one way or another, are both in the action and apart from it, civilians caught in the storm. One thinks of Woolf in *Three Guineas*, staring at the Spanish photographs, which carry with them a quality of the absolute, as if to say, this, and only this, is what war means and does. Wells stretches his perspectival and affective reach to find new ways into that story. If his narrators often write from a space of distance (in the future or from a perspective beyond the immediate crises) where the long or wide view is possible, his protagonists and texts find themselves fully enmeshed in the excessively violent tumult of war when it yawns toward totality.

One key feature of all of Wells's articulations of total war is his desire to make these destructive horizons visually potent for the reader. As we have seen, striking visual schemes are typical stylistic features across Wells's writing, and in his texts of military catastrophe they have special prominence. From the ground and the air, the Wellsian observer of total war is like a modern flaneur of extreme violence, exposed in eyes and body, protected just enough to do the telling. Wells's film *Things to Come* (1936), one of the latest works in this canon, is also one of its most stunning in this respect. The film's plot was drawn from his sprawling future history *The Shape of Things to Come*, and it offered a panoramic spectacle of civilian destruction and suffering. The storyline follows Wells's reiterated view that total war tends to feature a particular sequence of events: aerial bombardment; the collapse of commerce, trade, and communication at a world level; panic, famine, pestilence; and then the degeneration into primitive bands ruled by mobster-like bosses. Whether a better world follows (as it does in *The*

*Shape of Things to Come* and in *Things to Come*) is perhaps less interesting to readers and viewers today than the logic of collapse, though Wells's contemporaries not only came to expect mass destruction to yield bright outcomes in his works; they depended upon it. His utopianism was a welcome given, the source for endless critique and parody, but also a reliable voice calling out from the depths that there still remains fulfillment ahead. A strain that runs throughout the correspondence to and about Wells—a kind of leitmotif among commentators on his role in the culture over a half-decade—is this idea that Wells will always find a form for his optimism, however bleak the world adumbrated throughout his writing.

First, though, is the spectacle of obliteration, and this takes the shape of a kind of implacable fate. *Things to Come* offered a great visual tribute to such thinking, rumbling through Wells's writing for three decades before the film was made, to be contextualized in the mid-1930s' acute threat of war posed by fascism. It was an ambitious film, in many respects: its sets for the future and its scenes of destruction were some of the most elaborate ever undertaken, along with its enormous budget of £300,000; its combination of drama and didacticism (Wells's hallmark) represented a risky choice for film and may have contributed to its box-office failure; and the involvement of Wells in writing the script and in production pushed the usual boundaries of these roles (he was billed very centrally as the film's author and was on set regularly during production, in addition to publishing his screenplay in book form even before the movie was released). The result is a film that does, to some degree, match Wells's large ideas about world catastrophe and rehabilitation, even if he was personally disappointed by the outcome. As Jeffrey Richards puts it, *Things to Come* "dazzled" contemporary critics and "remains a classic of science fiction cinema, a visionary work of compelling power, awesome imagination and uplifting optimism."[19]

For all its optimism, *Things to Come* makes visually explicit the implacability that always stands at the base of Wells's world-catastrophe texts. Take, for instance, his decision to have the same actors play characters across the two generations represented in the film (those who experience the initial apocalypse and postwar sufferings return as their descendants in the future utopia), a move that may not have been well received by audiences.[20] The returned actors give force to the idea that the massive events depicted in the film supersede any individual story; these are the circumstances of a world, Wells wants to say, in which any person might be everyperson. The sweep of history is the subject, filtered through people who come, instead, to stand for clusters of ideas. And it is not just the actors—the film is marked by repeated motifs, including shots of children (some of them dead), close-ups of newspapers and of groups of people reading them, the setting of Everytown (meant to convey universality in its name even if its central square looks an awful lot like London), to which we return at each stage in the half-century history the film relays. In a sense, all of this continuity belies the film's ostensible message, which is that the utopian society of the future will be entirely unlike the world of the present. Far from the war-mad, complacent culture of the film's start, not to mention the ruined world of the film's middle, the later setting comprises a social order cleansed of nations, wars, self-interest, and violence, and, of course, of filth, inequality, and disease. There is much of Hollywood grandeur in these future scenes (designed initially by László Moholy-Nagy), with its huge television-like screens and its myriad new technologies, culminating in a giant space gun, and Wells specifies in his detailed instructions about the film's design that, say, the clothes of the future be crisp and practical, to give a kind of realism effect to the scene and to avoid what he felt was the absurdity of *Metropolis*'s costumes and sets.[21] (That said, the apparel of the citizens of the future invited critical ridicule and today look dated and a bit absurd).

But the film never really forgoes the sense that the past and the future are linked. They are united not only by faces (or, we might say, genetics) and reminiscent tableaus but more centrally by the basic conundrums of modernity: what is the ultimate value of science? Should men and women view themselves as coworkers or as sexual partners and/or rivals? What kinds of sacrifice are necessary to push the world forward? Where does selfless commitment to the community end and narcissistic overreach begin? What is the right place for dissent in modern culture? These questions traverse the film's time spans and provide an undertow of resistance to its seeming vision of massive and heroic change. Moreover, the character of Theotocopulos, along with his restive followers, offers a counterforce in the film to Cabal and the other world leaders of the new era. Just as Cabal insists to his security chief that they must and will not stifle the dissent provoked by Theotocopulos—"an end of free expression. That would be the beginning of the end of progress. No. They have to hear him and make what they can of him"—so the film itself gives some leeway to the lingering view that this new world, driven by rationality, science, progress, and humane planning, nevertheless ignores basic truths about human desires, goals, and feelings (*TTC*, 127). "You are a monster," says the beautiful Rowena to her ex-husband Cabal, speaking in the future, as her predecessor had argued in the past, of the limitations in this hyperrational universe, "You and your kind are monsters. Your science and your new orders have taken away your souls and put machines and theories in the place of them" (*TTC*, 120).[22] The soul and all it harbors, cannot, it turns out, be subordinated, and—crucially—it is not clear that the film wants it to be. That said, the final edits of the film cut these and other scenes involving Rowena and her challenge to the rationalist utopian order. Nevertheless, it is a serious misreading (though a common one) to see the film as a clear and unambivalent endorsement of Cabal and his new world. Thematically and visually, *Things to Come* marks a grand futurism, but it is underpinned and undercut by an equally strong indication that forward movement can only take humanity so far, that the past and the future meld into one unit, always expressing the continued human dialectic.

Relatedly, the ultimate visual power of *Things to Come* rests as much on the many moving sequences purveying the world's destruction as on the gleaming new underground Everytown where the film transpires in its final sequences (following a Soviet-style interlude of muscular rebuilding), and in this sense the film shares common ground with others of Wells's destruction texts. For all the sparkle and drama of these sets and the visual spectacle of huge crowds streaming over the space gun (a rocket) toward the end of the film, still something in those earlier scenarios of dismal misery haunt the film. There is an intimacy and poignancy in, say, the sequences around the plague (or "wandering sickness"), as Wells's core values—science, the ability to retain sanity in the face of the geopolitical slide toward war, educating young people for peace—disintegrate on screen. Moreover, the film's visual qualities, pre-utopia, owe something to one of Wells's extraordinary total-war texts of a different sort, *The War of the Worlds*, which, as we have seen, has its own arresting visual scheme involving the silhouette, flames against darkness, and contrasting scales.

Such contrasts take new life in war texts like *The World Set Free*, Wells's most overlooked world-catastrophe novel, written and published in the spring of 1914. As noted in the *OED*, Wells coined the term "atomic bomb" in this novel, and certainly it stands among his more far-seeing works in its envisioning of the great Western cities destroyed by atomic explosion. As scientists have concurred, Wells's prevision of how the unlocking of atomic energy might look was surprisingly on point. Richard Rhodes opens his landmark *The Making of the Atomic Bomb* with the nuclear scientist Leo Szilard having a kind of epiphany as he walks absentmindedly through the wet streets of London in 1933, having just read *The World Set Free*: "As he crossed the street time cracked open before him and he saw a way to the future, death into the world and all our woe, the shape of things to come."[23] Rhodes is not being rhetorical when he begins his story of the bomb by invoking Wells. His suggestion is that Wells's vision of what a nuclear chain reaction could do (based on Wells's reading of the important work *The Interpretation of Radium* [1908], by Frederick Soddy), along with his utopian goals for a world state to be managed by the science-minded in the name of universal peace, unleashed Szilard's own vision of these combined possibilities.[24] More than accuracy, as these works suggest, what Wells's foray into the interior life of the atom accomplished was a powerful depiction of how this new chemical power would react in and on the world; how it would look, sound, feel, even smell; and what its enormous ramifications would be for the global order.

A strange assemblage of multiple voices, with war tales woven together and ultimately superseded by a new world order, free of nations, monarchs, and world conflict, *The World Set Free* comes alive as a novel when the atom bombs are dropped, with their spectacular effects. Here as elsewhere, Wells bundles sound and other sensory perceptions into the visual display, as Barnet (one of the text's internal narrators) describes the first view of the bombs from the Dutch countryside:

> "And then, while I still peered and tried to shade these flames from my eyes with my hand, and while the men about me were beginning to stir, the atomic bombs were thrown at the dykes. They made a mighty thunder in the air, and fell like Lucifer in the picture, leaving a flaring trail in the sky. The night, which had been pellucid and detailed and eventful, seemed to vanish, to be replaced abruptly by a black background to these tremendous pillars of fire ...
>
> "Hard upon the sound of them came a roaring wind, and the sky was filled with flickering lightnings and rushing clouds ...
>
> "There was something discontinuous in this impact. At one moment, I was a lonely watcher in a sleeping world; the next saw everyone about me afoot, the whole world awake and amazed ...
>
> "... I saw the bombs fall, and then watched a great crimson fire leap responsive to each impact, and mountainous masses of red-lit steam and flying fragments clamber up towards the zenith. Against the glare I saw the countryside for miles standing black and clear, churches, trees, chimneys."[25]

As in *The War of the Worlds*, all reflections on the great battles come from the perspective of the spectator, dwarfed by the scale of the events, whose vision itself is inevitably a feature of what he is able to see. In both texts, the speaker is a witness to the violence, himself tangential to the world-changing events. He shares with others around him the stunned quality of being "awake and amazed," yet in translating the immediate impression of exceptional violence into narrative, he naturally assumes importance. To see the bombs firsthand, then, becomes a kind of métier for the witness. Barnet is technically a soldier, but in relation to the engulfing war the novel comes to track, he might as well be a civilian. Not only that, the witness in these works often expresses the awed sense of being alone in the ruined world.

In passages like this one in *The World Set Free*, the aesthetics of the bombing are presented in neutral terms, in an idiom that keeps judgment at bay. Even so, the history (and future) of aesthetics impinges everywhere in Barnet's reportage—the comparison with classical painting, the contrast of the flames with the black background, the filmic fade to black, the pillar of fire. The attempt here to characterize the awesomeness of war at its extreme, without veering into outright enchantment, is one Wells shares with others of his generation, such as Owen, in a poem like "Spring Offensive," which aims to delineate states of wonder, exaltation, and terror. Wells also prefigures later writers like Tim O'Brien, who has this to say about the visual aspect of napalm:

> For all its horror, you can't help but gape at the awful majesty of combat. You stare out at tracer rounds unwinding through the dark like brilliant red ribbons. You crouch in ambush as a cool, impassive moon rises over the nighttime paddies. You admire the fluid symmetries of troops on the move, the harmonies of sound and shape and proportion, the great sheets of metal-fire streaming down from a gunship, the illumination rounds, the white phosphorous, the purply orange glow of napalm, the rocket's red glare. It's not pretty, exactly. It's astonishing. It fills the eye.[26]

O'Brien's spellbinding analysis here keeps close company with Wells's thinking, as *The World Set Free* works its way through the ethical consequences of its attraction to the pure aesthetics of the explosions. What, Wells also asks, is the right balance of recognizing the "awful majesty of combat" while refusing to glorify it? Barnet does have a tendency, at least in passing, to enchant the scene of bombing, as in this moment, not long after he has witnessed the first explosions: "[The eruptions] showed flat and sullen through the mist, like London sunsets. 'They sat upon the sea,' says Barnet, 'like frayed-out water-lilies of flame'" (*WSF*, 143). In this passage, it is the voice within the quotation marks (Barnet) who makes the most consciously artistic comment, though "London sunsets" also suggests stakes in the history of aesthetics. Barnet's voice is generally taken at face value, but in this case, Wells hesitates to admit without qualification this kind of language about the atomic bombs.[27] "For a time in western Europe at least it was indeed as if civilisation had come to a final collapse," the primary narrator notes a little later; "These crowning buds upon the tradition that Napoleon planted and Bismarck watered opened and flared 'like water-lilies of flame' over nations destroyed, over churches smashed or submerged, towns ruined, fields lost to mankind for ever, and a million weltering bodies. Was this lesson enough for mankind, or would the flames of war still burn amidst the ruins?" (*WSF*, 147). The Wellsian frame narrator is here qualifying his witness, framing the violence in disenchanted terms, and allowing Barnet's language to furnish an ironic culmination to the military practice of the previous century, led by men whom Wells deems two of the great villains of history.

*The World Set Free* shares with Wells's other war writings this basic point, that we know total war through the common spectator and victim, that it comes first as a striking new point of view, and that this view draws our eye and our imagination; at the same time, the effects are shown in gruesome detail, unmitigated. Such is the emphatic message of *The War in the Air*, Wells's greatest total-war novel. From Bert Smallways's accidental launch in the balloon off the beach in Dymchurch, which sets him on his sky journey; through his long ride across the Atlantic in the German air fleet, culminating in the bombardment of New York City; and finally back on the ground as the Asiatic planes battle the Germans over his head, the novel is consumed with the idea of watching war. Even before the war begins, in fact, it is a novel of watching. It opens with Bert's brother Tom Smallways surveying the landscape of the town of Bun Hill where the novel's first segment transpires, an old neighborhood on the outskirts of London, now criss-crossed, passed through, and overhung with new technologies like monorails and balloons. And when Bert sails along in his balloon journey, he sees "a spectacle of incredible magnificence," a tableau of awed watching that persists throughout the novel (*WA*, 63). "Essentially," the narrator observes early in Bert's adventures, and it remains true for much of the story, "his state was wonder" (*WA*, 53). Traveling with Bert, we see it all from above and, when the air battle rages, even from within. Always the novel calls special attention to the facts of perspective, as when the narrator drily asserts of the chaotic scene in New York below the bombing airships, "Foreshortened humanity has no dignity" (*WA*, 148). At times, Wells takes his metaphors from fairly homely sources—"the country on both sides of the gorge might have been swept by a colossal broom," or "Houses had an appearance of being flattened down by the pressure of a gigantic finger" (*WA*, 184, 184–85). At other times, the mode is more descriptive, yet always the novel stresses the important, relativizing quality of perspective and complicates the presentation by adding extra layers of distance and embedded points of view:

> The swaying view varied with these changes of altitude. Now they would be low and close, and he would distinguish in that steep, unusual perspective, windows, doors, street and sky signs, people and the minutest details . . . ; then as they soared the details would shrink, the sides of streets draw together, the view

widen, the people cease to be significant. At the highest the effect was that of a concave relief map. . . . Even to Bert's unphilosophical mind the contrast of city below and fleet above pointed an opposition, the opposition of the adventurous American's tradition and character with German order and discipline. . . . In the sky soared the German airships like beings in a different, entirely more orderly, world, all oriented to the same angle of the horizon, uniform in build and appearance, moving accurately with one purpose as a pack of wolves will move, distributed with the most precise and effectual co-operation.

(WA, 142–43)

Clearly, the fact of perspective is as important here as what Bert sees. As the narrator indicates, Bert can recognize that there is a deep connection between view and our ability to understand what we see—even when what we see is our own culture. The British are notably missing from this confrontation of grand, organic, chaotic, doomed America with its overseeing and overmastering Prussian killers, yet there is no doubt where the English would be found, in the jungle, fighting for life. It is a scene that allies the reader strongly with Bert as he rises and drops, giving us the wonder-filled experience of viewing this unfurled map along with him, just at its moment of catastrophe. It also makes the quintessentially Wellsian move of attaching such vision to historical analysis and sociological commentary. Moreover, here as elsewhere, Wells manages a complicated blend of showing us the world from Bert's birds-eye view and also setting an extra line of sight on Bert himself or on the wider scene that Bert would be unable to see, such as his own place within the line of German ships. However wide one's view, the novel reminds us, it turns out that there was something that one did not—could not—see.

Such blindspots take thematic shape in the form of the Asiatic airships, whose dominance comes as a shock to the whole of the Western world—and also to the reader, who has understood herself to be in a story of Germany versus the Anglo-English nations. The Asiatic airships rise, literally and figuratively, over a horizon—the western—where no one was looking (also inviting the ironic comment, "the Yellow Peril was a peril after all!" [WA, 169]). The shock to readers of what we have not been seeing is hard to overstate; the first three-quarters of the novel—the whole narrative development, including the building up of the person of Prince Albert, he who "made the war," and the war itself, whose opening episodes are presented with riveting force—all of this turns out to have been a false lead (WA, 79). Wells both shows and tells the way the war, once begun, quickly overwhelms what any of the initial players had imagined (he shows by blindsiding us within the text, just as the culture was self-deceived; he tells in the discursive interludes). Moreover, such a surprise is in keeping with the visuals of the novel, which seem to present a kind of certainty—that of the witness to historical events, Bert's view—alongside a very deep uncertainty about any single point of view.

Meanwhile, the narrator's own perspective is slightly off, as well. On several occasions, the narrator will suggest in passing that he writes from a time after all these wars, when the lessons, it seems, have been learned. "It is difficult perhaps for the broad-minded and long-perspectived reader," he writes, "to understand how incredible the breaking down of the scientific civilization seemed to those who actually lived at this time," seeming to suggest that his enlightened reader comes from some future time after the events of the novel have passed, in the mode of other future histories (*WA*, 239). This speculative temporality, which figures a narrator in the future looking back and telling the tale up to that future-now, was congenial to Wells—indeed he was one of its pioneers—yet the oddity of *The War in the Air* is that except for these very slight references, there is no reason to believe, within the parameters of the story he tells, that there ever would be such a time.[28] The novel ends in a state of dystopic ruin, where the communities of England (and the world) have returned to conditions of a thousand years prior, mixed in with a yet more primitive state. As Bert recognizes, "They were back already in the barbaric stage when a man must fight for his love," and indeed in shooting the local warlord point-blank in the chest upon his arrival, he shows how well he has adapted to this precivilized way of life (*WA*, 260). Just about everything has disappeared from this world of "universal dissolution," with all the modern achievements, from commerce to science to culture, totally eradicated—"in five short years the world and the scope of human life ha[d] undergone a retrogressive change as great as that between the age of the Antonines and the Europe of the ninth century..." (*WA*, 254, ellipses in the original). But perhaps the most salient fact in this scenario of smashed-up culture is that literacy has completely disappeared; all the books of previous eras, including those of the novel's own time-world, have crumbled to dust, and the children of this new era are never taught to read. How, then, would that later moment, from which the narrator seems to speak, come into being, and how would its history have been written?

In addition to its deconstruction of perspective in various guises, the novel also plots the visual as a matter of how the eye sees—a painterly mode, as discussed in the previous chapter as one of Wells's stylistic signatures. In this first decade of the century, Wells was intrigued by the impressionism of his friend Conrad, as we have seen for instance in *Tono-Bungay*, published one year after *The War in the Air*, and he wondered how the emphasis on impression, with its subjectivist underpinnings, might be squared with his more developed sociological and political objectives. Or perhaps these are not as irreconcilable as they seem; Jesse Matz has argued—persuasively as well as counterintuitively—that modernist impressionism precisely aimed to weld the momentary vision with larger social realities, such that "The demands of receptivity and judgment become functions of experience and retrospection."[29] There is in Matz's account of modernist literary impressionism no great distance between the perceptual emphasis dramatized by the momentary vision and the larger social dynamics that allow such perceptions to have meaning and effect. For Wells in his total-war texts, the experiment with impression and with painterly style more generally toggles in these ways, yet the relation is strained. As we observed in *The World Set Free*, the Wellsian narrator hesitates to adopt a descriptive form that seems to dissolve the bomb's unprecedented destructiveness into familiar aesthetic terms, and here, too, the most painterly moments signal some kind of retreat from the violence. It is only when the *Vaterland* moves off from the battle that the scene of carnage, seen vividly by Bert and the others in the fleet, "dwindled to a string of dark shapes and one smoking yellow flare that presently became a more indistinct smear upon the vast horizon and the bright new day" (*WA*, 121). Such painterly figuration can only find utterance when the battle is out of range. Meanwhile, in the early stages of the fighting, when Bert witnesses the destruction of the great warships in the North Atlantic, Wells emphasizes his position of watching through a porthole, which he grips with intensity. If we are looking for analogies, he seems to be viewing a movie more than looking at a painting, as if to signal that the painterly perspective is one that tends to deny modern violence or amalgamate it into a more comfortable visual scheme.

Or perhaps it is the other way around: the reality of total war means that such aesthetics become obsolete. Thus, it is at the moment just before the Germans begin their bombardment of New York City that its painterly qualities are most pronounced, and both Bert and Wells find the prospect of its destruction unconscionable. The men on the airship gaze down at the glorious city, looking at "its splendid best":

> It was so great, and in its collective effect so pacifically magnificent, that to make war upon it seemed incongruous beyond measure, like laying siege to the National Gallery or attacking respectable people in an hotel dining-room with battleaxe and mail. It was in its entirety so large, so complex, so delicately immense, that to bring it to the issue of warfare was like driving a crowbar into the mechanism of a clock.

> (*WA*, 135)

Wells's three metaphors are themselves incongruous and together give the sense of a mad search for a way to convey the particular revulsion and sheer discordance embodied by this moment of impending violence. His invocation of the National Gallery brings the place of painting, and of the reverence for Western art more generally, into double view; both the signified (the city about to be destroyed) and its signifier (the metaphor of attacking an art gallery) embody something that should be exempt from warfare—art, the beautiful, civilization—at the instant before all such exemptions are canceled once and for all. As Jan Mieszkowski writes, thinking about the essential disjunctions among registers of war experience and expression, "war spectatorship is defined in contradistinction to rather than on the basis of the faculties of human perception. The result is that the spatiotemporal integrity of the military event is shattered."[30]

For his part, Bert shares with everyone else on the airship "the distinctest apprehension of these incompatibilities," yet the bombing begins, thanks to the one person who does not hold this view, the Prince, whose head is filled with "the vapours of romance: he was a conqueror, and this was the enemy's city. The greater the city, the greater the triumph" (WA, 135, 136). It is not only the difference of power and personality that divides the Prince from all others as they apprehend the diminishing separation of civilian life from the realities of war; the truth is, the Prince is really the only person on board who is not a civilian. Bert has obviously stumbled into it all, but in fact all of the Germans aboard are unprepared for war. They are not soldiers in the conventional sense, nor are they the (invisible) scientists who must have designed the machines. They become seasick and confused in the air, and their shock when battle begins is as acute as Bert's. Take the case of Kurt, another Wellsian double, an altogether likable, thoughtful cosmopolitan who plays the role of Bert's (and our) unofficial guide to the German world on board. His insights about the ruin and waste of war channel Wells's own: "Oh! It's all foolishness and haste and violence and cruel folly, stupidity and blundering hate and selfish ambition," that is, everything Wells seeks to counter, and Kurt goes on to articulate the great futility of humanity, "all the things that men have done—all the things they will ever do. Gott! Smallways, what a muddle and confusion life has always been—the battles and massacres and disasters, the hates and harsh acts, the murders and sweatings, the lynchings and cheatings" (WA, 172). Yet of course, it is Kurt and all on board who are in process of wreaking horrific destruction on the innocent world below, and even Bert recognizes his own unwitting and unwanted participation, even before he is required actively to aid the crew, as when he thinks only of himself (rather than his country) in bargaining to sell the plans for the airship that would hand air supremacy to the Germans, or, in more general terms, "So Bert, slightly refreshed by coffee and sleep, resumed his helpless co-operation in the War in the Air" (*WA*, 141). To an important degree, everyone in *The War in the Air* is a civilian, and everyone is also a participant; the boundaries no longer exist, just as this total war has stripped away the recognizable spheres defining warfare (fronts, battlefields, combat zones versus civilian havens, even national frontiers). Bert is representative of representatives. Among the civilians who both prosecute and suffer from the war, he is meant to be the vehicle for transmitting what they see, hear, think, and suffer.

In fact, for all the tremendous appeal of Bert, *The War in the Air* is a novel that seems to want no protagonist at all but instead a receptacle to view the great destruction, and though it gives way—a little reluctantly, one senses—to a Bert Smallways bildungsroman, such character interest is never complete. The novel in fact drifts from Bert whenever the scope of world violence grows beyond what he can experience firsthand, at which point it is the narrator who will recount the larger story of the war as well as dilate on the world conditions that led up to the conflict. A parallel point is that there really are no authority figures in the novel either; with the exception of the Prince, Wells denudes the novel of any sense that there is a center of power or sphere of influence. The war comes because it does, unguided by individuals or even by human institutions. Nor are there inventors, as one might expect of an author for whom invention was such a central principle, and in a novel about the destructive reach of new technology. Despite the large presence in the first half of the novel of a dubious inventor of a key airship (Butteridge), the fantastic technology that sweeps and drones through the novel in fact hails from invisible sources—as if to say, the inventions are here, but do not think that a scientist will appear as deus ex machina, averting the cascading trouble, once begun. The novel's attitude of protagonist-ambivalence thus exceeds Bert, though it is most strained in relation to him. The story begins and ends not with Bert but with Tom, a thoroughly mediocre and fixed personality and in that sense a much more appropriate everyman than the gifted Bert, who quickly becomes the most well traveled of all Englishmen (if vertical travel counts), exceptional among his community and his nation in experience and consequence and finally even triumphant.

In his capacity as everyman protagonist, restricted as that may be, Bert staggers alongside the unfolding world calamity, and his actions fall into several primary categories, none of which affiliate with the traditions of the bildungsroman.[31] Representing the civilian as such, in that sense, runs counter to embodying the full capacities of the individual. Most of what Bert does in the novel can be classified as follows: He watches—gawks, stares, often gripping the sides of his porthole or balloon basket. He clutches—to those windows, to the railings of the tumbling airships, to ropes and lines that he never learns to control. He hears—the novel is striking for its efforts to record the sounds of all these new machines, from the Butteridge airship to the many craft and impressive weaponry being deployed on all sides, total war presented as assault on all the body's senses.[32] He exclaims—most notably and repeatedly, "Gaw!" and "Golly!" And he cowers. "For a time," Wells writes, "Bert gave himself body and soul to cowering" (*WA*, 192). What distinguishes these characterizations is Wells's attempt to distill in Bert's experience something quintessential and absolute, that which is—or rather, will come to be—universal in a world where total war is the norm. In fact, one could go further and suggest that this normativity applies not only to the time of total war but to modernity itself once it has reached the point where such warfare has become an ongoing condition of possibility. Here Favret's notion of "wartime" can be activated, the principle that civilian consciousness is powerfully shaped by the presence, possibility, and distant awareness of war. Wartime, as she writes, "is not just a period of time that can be got over or settled, but rather a persistent mode of daily living and a habit of mind." Or, in Mary Dudziak's terms, writing about the United States in the twentieth century, "wartime has become normal time in America."[33]

For Wells, the correlative to such universality is the need for all of us to see our precarious condition and, in complementary fashion, his own mission to warn. In 1921 and again in 1941, in prefaces to the novel's reprints, he asks of the modern world's endless complacency, "Do we still trust to somebody else?" (1921) and "Again, I ask the reader to note the warnings I gave [in 1921] twenty years ago. Is there anything to add to that preface now? Nothing except my epitaph. That, when the time comes, will manifestly have to be: 'I told you so. You *damned* fools.' (The italics are mine.)" (*WA*, 279). A neat example of what we have seen to be Wells's habit of making, showing, and underlining his points all at once ("The italics are mine"), these warnings hone in on the novel's overall argument—that once you invent weapons, they will bring war, and when the weapons are those of aerial bombardment, that war will quickly and easily overtake society's ability to contain or stop it. Wells drives this point home in several ways, including in the discursive sections, when the narrator surveys the state of the world just before the war and diagnoses its catastrophic fault lines—"So that a universal social collapse followed, as it were a logical consequence, upon worldwide war," and especially at the novel's close, when the young boy (Bert's son) presses the still-surviving Tom to explain why no one stopped the war, to which Tom can only reply, "'It didn't ought ever to 'ave begun'" (*WA*, 251–52, 276).

Wells's prefaces also remind us that, in some simple sense, *The War in the Air* is less a wild fantasia of possibility than a self-portrait. We may not want to see ourselves in Bert, cowering in the airship, or in the victims below, cowering even more helplessly on the ground, foreshortened and undignified, or indeed in the efficient German fighters, bringing on the havoc, but in another way, how can we not?

## II. THE CALL TO IMAGINE

The task, in other words, is to imagine. Along with Wells's elaborate and literal representations of total war is another, entirely forgotten feature of his writing that played a significant part in exposing and expanding the idea of the civilian: his taking up the mantle of the noncombatant as a position of ethical responsibility, where we all are asked to make a mental leap and join those in combat. In Wells's prodigious body of First World War writing, this was the key task for those at home, to force themselves out of mental comfort and into a kind of parallel agony and perceptual dislocation with those serving in the trenches. *Mr. Britling Sees It Through* gives the most elaborate dramatization of what such imagining might be and mean, and its stunning success is testament, I believe, to how deep a chord this desire struck with the wartime public. More generally, Wells's novels in and around the war, including not only *Mr. Britling* but others such as *Joan and Peter* (1918) and *The Undying Fire* (1919), feature a central consciousness whose work, in some basic way, involves the intellectual and affective labor of approaching the war. In *Joan and Peter*, the struggling thinker is Oswald, too old to fight (he's had his wars, in Africa), and in *The Undying Fire* it is the canonically suffering Job Huss, whose testing by Satan might be seen as a parallel to the war raging in the background of the tale.

These efforts to place the civilian in an imaginative attachment to combat were not Wells's alone. As Susan Sontag was one of the first to note, since at least the middle of the nineteenth century, there has been a shared sense that for all the obvious realities of distance, one key component of Western cultural expression during and about war is to elaborate forms of meaningful intimacy between those at war and those at home. World War I, with its gigantic citizen armies, made up overwhelmingly of nonprofessional soldiers, and given all the qualities of "strange proximity" Paul Fussell has documented between experiences of home and front, created exceptional demands on the imagination to traverse (but also to acknowledge) these lines. That was, we might say, its job from 1914 to 1918. During these years and in the decade that followed, the conundrum of civilians thinking and writing about war took its canonical forms, including such 1920s modernist statements about the war as *The Waste Land*, *Mrs. Dalloway*, and *To the Lighthouse*, where direct representation is eschewed. War is off-center in modernism in part because all experience is refracted, yet readers for decades have understood these works to register a deep sense of responsibility to the war, an attempt to forge new language that would keep company with the many derangements the war had produced and to engage richly with an ever-expanding set of memorializing forms.

Such attempts to write the war from a position of calculated distance have more in common than we often recognize with more overt accounts of war. Writings of First World War nurses, for instance, often become especially charged when confronting the barrier that separates these noncombatants from those they treat—despite the strong sense of commonalty and the reality of shared danger and trauma that gives these works their character. Even combatant poets found themselves needing to breach some space of distance to reexperience the war with fresh pain and outrage. Together, these different kinds of writers—the civilian at home, the nurse or doctor working with patients behind the lines, the combatant seeking intense unification with the men still fighting—generated an imperative to extend the mind from safety to struggle. There are also echoes in this mission of Victorian conventions of sympathy, a kind of ethical bedrock that, for the British at any rate, persistently stood beneath the apprehension of experiential (and often class) difference.[34]

But the case of war was particular—not only the situation of war but the actual years of combat—and in Wells's writing of this period, he pursued the imaginative potential of civilian experience with passion. Before we turn to *Mr. Britling*, where he elaborated these motifs in great depth, we might listen to these words from a few years after the war, which pinpoint the aftereffects of such calls to imagine. The passage comes from Aldous Huxley's postwar novel *Crome Yellow* (1921), his brilliant and under-read account of the vitiated spiritual state of England (in this case its upper classes) several years after the armistice, a literary minigenre that includes such works as *The Waste Land*, *Mrs. Dalloway*, *The Sun Also Rises*, and *Heartbreak House*:[35]

> "At this very moment," [Scogan] went on, "the most frightful horrors are taking place in every corner of the world. People are being crushed, slashed, disembowelled, mangled; their dead bodies rot and their eyes decay with the rest. Screams of pain and fear go pulsing through the air at the rate of eleven hundred feet per second. After travelling for three seconds they are perfectly inaudible. These are

distressing facts; but do we enjoy life any the less because of them? Most certainly we do not. We feel sympathy, no doubt; we represent to ourselves imaginatively the sufferings of nations and individuals and we deplore them. But, after all, what are sympathy and the imagination? Precious little.... At the beginning of the war I used to think I really suffered, through imagination and sympathy, with those who physically suffered. But after a month or two I had to admit that, honestly, I didn't."[36]

The passage is lengthy, but worth the pause because Huxley touches so exactly on a little-recognized phenomenon that was central to the work Wells was doing during the war years. Huxley often engaged with Wells (his most famous work, *Brave New World*, being a parody of a Wellsian utopia), and here he makes the imaginative challenges Wells had hoped to muster as genuine cultural transformation into so much fodder for cynicism and parody. But even so, there is something serious and laudable standing behind the soulless Scogan's self-representation, as Huxley slips in between his unlikable intellectual's harangue some remaining germ of an impulse, at least back in 1914, to try to turn the distinctions between civilians and combatants into an opportunity for an almost mystical transformation.

This is the aim and goal of *Mr. Britling Sees It Through*. The novel, as we have noted, was a phenomenal success, and, coming alongside his prolific pamphlets, turned Wells into a preeminent civilian writer of the conflict. In commenting on the novel's reach and effectiveness, Robert Crossley relays the anecdote that the officer and writer "R. L. Henderson wrote Wells on 15 January 1917 while on sick leave at a Swiss Red Cross hospital with 14 other officers, nearly all of them, he said, had just received a copy of *Mr. Britling*." He also notes a warm response from at least one German reader, who wrote to Wells in 1917 from New York to express her gratitude for the novel and, as she put it, to hold "out my hand to you across the ocean."[37] *Mr. Britling* is almost never read today, which is especially unfortunate given how well it holds up, in part for its experimental style (as discussed in chapter 1) and mostly as a great war novel whose particular legacy might be to take the genre in the direction of civilian experience. It thus makes for a rich synchronicity with works of women modernists such as Woolf and Elizabeth Bowen, whose war-themed writings are being reexamined by scholars today as important efforts to engage war from a position outside of combat.[38] It also stands in a more direct relationship to Rebecca West's *The Return of the Soldier* (1918), which offers a response and riposte to *Mr. Britling* (as well as containing biographical passages about West and Wells's relationship).[39]

In characteristic Wellsian form, *Mr. Britling* takes on its problem of writing a civilian novel with fervor, figuring the deep effects of war spread out among the English at home, filtered most directly by Mr. Britling. The novel makes Mr. Britling's twisting and constantly changing relationship to the war its central drama and action. As a novel, it is very close to its protagonist, whose minute reactions to the international situation and then the war it tracks in a day-by-day and later stage-by-stage manner. Ultimately, this relationship of Mr. Britling to the war becomes extremely personal, as his beloved son Hugh is killed in combat. But this intimate and wrenching reckoning with war is something that the novel wants us to consider in more impersonal, worldwide terms, and it casts Mr. Britling, for all his eccentricity, as a representative for millions of others like him in their villages and cities all around the warring nations (his name can be recognized, in this context, as a Germanized "little Brit"). "This story is essentially the history of the opening and of the realisation of the Great War as it happened to one small group of people in Essex," Wells writes, "and more particularly as it happened to one human brain. It came at first to all these people in a spectacular manner, as a thing happening dramatically and internationally, as a show, as something in the newspapers . . . only by slow degrees did it and its consequences invade the common texture of English life" (*MB*, 210–11). Formally and thematically, the novel is built around a constantly diminishing division between, on one hand, the personal, private, and small scale and, on the other, the political, public, and historic. As these two realms collapse into each other, the novel finds itself anguished and awry, its mechanism broken. It is, in essence, a story of Mr. Britling's development, a vicarious coming-of-age for the middle aged who watch helplessly as their sons go off to fight, where the growth in wisdom/experience is essentially negative, a mind coming unhinged, a system that had functioned well to create a comfortable life destroyed. Even the novel's final movement in the direction of a hasty religious conversion cannot salvage what has been decimated. But what is most important about the novel's development is that it is *about development*. We watch and listen as Mr. Britling moves from an initial patriotic rush, through misgivings and dark questionings, to frustrated outrage, to personal loss, and, in the end, to pseudoreligious acceptance, which cannot ward off, at the same time, a threatening blankness. The novel sets up a series of parallels and connections between its civilian protagonist at home, distraught, desperate to understand, grieving, experiencing the kind of disillusionment we have since come to associate with soldiers' narratives, and the war, whose violence constantly impinges, deeper and deeper into the spaces of home.

These home spaces are highly developed in the novel. Mr. Britling and his village of Matching's Easy are together presented as quintessentially English, even more so the Britlings' rambling home of Dower House, still carrying with it traces of an old farmhouse, where an eclectic band of regulars gather for conversation, hockey, and fancy dress and to listen to their always voluble host, in an international and cosmopolitan scene the novel most certainly rues, its own version of "the summer of 1914."[40] But of course war is coming, and Wells structures the first half of the novel around a basic discordance: here in the village, life turns on hockey and flower shows, the social life is dominated by the local gentry, things move according to some comfortable compromise between tradition and welcome change, evidenced, say, by Mr. Britling's ecumenical feelings about race or his modernization of the barn. And yet:

> Now just at that moment there was a loud report. . . . But neither Mr. Britling nor Mr. Manning nor Mr. Direck was interrupted or incommoded in the slightest degree by that report. Because it was too far off over the curve of this round world to be either heard or seen at Matching's Easy. Nevertheless it was a very loud report. . . . It came from a black parcel that the Archduke Francis Ferdinand of Austria, with great presence of mind, had just flung out from the open hood of his automobile. . . . The procession stopped. There was a tremendous commotion amongst that brightly-costumed crowd, a hot excitement in vivid contrast to the Sabbath calm of Matching's Easy.
>
> (*MB*, 78–79)

Needless to say, these distances will eventually be overcome; in fact, the novel's great question is to ask what, exactly, it means for the "hot excitement" of historic violence to define civilian consciousness in England and all across "this round world."[41] In the discursive sequences, Wells considers these disjunctive realities with such ironic comments as "It was quite characteristic of the state of mind of England in the summer of 1914 that Mr. Britling should be mightily concerned about the conflict in Ireland, and almost deliberately negligent of the possibility of a war with Germany" (*MB*, 125). Meanwhile, these gulfs between the quiet obliviousness of home (or its misdirected angst) and the danger brewing in Europe have a powerful correlative in Mr. Britling's mental style, who embodies a double life. During the day, he is ensconced in the social and family world at Dower House, where he also proceeds with his work of cultural criticism; at night he carries on an affair with a widow and, more centrally, struggles with an internal dialogue in which all that is kept at bay during the day comes flooding in to torment him. This parallel between the world and Mr. Britling, both operating by maintaining sharp divisions between realms, continues for the whole novel; as the war comes to invade the confines of Matching's Easy, destroying its illusory peace (as first one then the next young man join the war), so too do Mr. Britling's nightly struggles become more and more gruesome and unbearable.

Yet to talk about the two divided realms collapsing into each other, though accurate as a description of the novel's structural movement, misrepresents a critical fact, which is that Mr. Britling powerfully wills a closer connection to the violent world outside and to the war. This is the crux of the novel and why it should be understood as a generator of a new kind of civilian awareness. As a civilian, Mr. Britling cannot see the bodies of those fighting abroad, nor is he invited to do much of anything to serve (the chapter titled "Onlookers" is a critical one in forging this sense of his own frustrated irrelevance). More and more, as this distance becomes the defining condition of the narrative, the novel in turn works ever harder to *imagine*. It is quite literal; what Mr. Britling does, for most of the novel, is to imagine, or to try to imagine, or try to stop himself from imagining all the various ways in which the war can be thought and encountered. Wells wants to claim a moral calling in these attempts to understand, just as he and Mr. Britling make the case (highly unusual in 1916, or at any time) that it is men in their forties like him, rather than these supple boys with all the promise of their lives ahead of them, who should be sent off to the trenches. All through the war, in fact, Wells surged with fury at his own marginalization and hatched schemes to involve himself and others of his generation in the effort. It is this aching desire to participate, thwarted at the practical level by the military organization, which gets routed into more mental engagements: intellectual, spiritual, and literary. Thus, Mr. Britling will rise from a tormented, sleepless night and begin furiously writing a pamphlet. These texts, fictional versions of Wells's wartime writings (the first of which is here named "To End War"), act as a shadow textual world to what we are reading, an alternative genre born of civilian desire for involvement.

At other times, the internal dialogues themselves are the only outcome, exhausting and miserable, yet allowing Wells to breach decorum and express the dark ideas that were emerging in his own understanding of the war:

> He began to fret and rage. He could not lie in peace in his bed; he got up and prowled about his room, blundering against chairs and tables in the darkness ... We were too stupid to do the most obvious things; we were sending all these boys into hardship and pitiless danger; we were sending them ill-equipped, insufficiently supported, we were sending our children through the fires to

Moloch, because essentially we English were a world of indolent, pampered, sham good-humoured, old and middle-aged men. (So he distributed the intolerable load of self-accusation.) Why was he doing nothing to change things, to get them better?... They were butchering the youth of England. Old men sat out of danger contriving death for the lads in the trenches. That was the reality of the thing.

(*MB*, 324, first ellipsis in original)

It seems a perfect encapsulation of the disillusioned war mentality that has been said to characterize the lost generation, here articulated by the civilian. The only difference in sentiment, perhaps, between "they were butchering the youth of England" and, say, Graves's poem "Goliath and David" (1918) is the agonizing admixture of "self-accusation" and the fact that this one was published in the middle of the war. Another instance has Mr. Britling roaming the countryside at night, wondering whether war and hatred are not, after all, basic to the human condition, raging that perhaps they are preferable to an indolent peace, then falling back into humaneness with a terrible vision:

It seemed to him that suddenly a mine burst under a great ship at sea, that men shouted and women sobbed and cowered, and flares played upon the rain-pitted black waves; and then the picture changed and showed a battle upon land, and searchlights were flickering through the rain and shells flashed luridly, and men darkly seen in silhouette against red flames ran with fixed bayonets and slipped and floundered over the mud, and at last, shouting thinly through the wind, leapt down into the enemy trenches.

(*MB*, 291–92)

Passages like this one represent a growing susceptibility to the engulfing violence of the war, qualities that develop in an almost preconscious way, at night, via dreams, as a matter of visualization. These visions are, of course, mediated—that last one carries overtones, say, of the famous propaganda film of 1916, *The Battle of the Somme*, one of the most widely seen war films of all time—but, crucially, Wells transforms the view, darkening it. The visual archive of the war was only fledgling in 1916, and the novel seeks to depart from the photographic surround of those years. In an important way, it is the drama of finding a way around such mediation that presents Mr. Britling with his great ethical challenge.

As this last passage suggests in grisly terms, what disturbs Mr. Britling above all is the specter of dismembered bodies, of soldiers and also civilians mangled and deranged by the war. If we think of *The War in the Air* as epitomizing Wells's spacious attempt to catch total war in its vast spectacle, here, in the midst of actual war, Wells hones in on a different unit—not the city or the sweeping vista but the person, the body, even the limb. Mr. Britling is haunted by the prospect of bodily harm to others, envisioned in gory detail, and as the war lengthens, this tendency to make a mental reach toward the physical catastrophe of others becomes increasingly urgent and increasingly debilitating. There is an affect of vicariousness in all of this, as Mr. Britling, and in some cases also his fellow civilians, strain to see and feel the hideous carnage accumulating a few hundred miles away. Or, better, as Mr. Britling stretches imaginatively toward combat, its violence also reaches back toward the English at home, so that the gap separating combatant and noncombatant is shrunk from both sides. "Abruptly and shockingly," is how the narrator describes it at one juncture, "this malignity of warfare, which had been so far only a festering cluster of reports and stories and rumours and suspicions, stretched out its arm into Essex and struck a barb of grotesque cruelty into the very heart of Mr. Britling" (*MB*, 292).

Several powerful sequences jolt the novel with their violence, as if a window is opening to admit one small swath of the raging storm outside. One particularly grim sequence features the aftermath of a zeppelin attack, in which Mr. Britling's old Aunt Wilshire (a grand dame out of the Victorian tradition) is killed. Visiting her in the hospital after the raid, Mr. Britling finds her traumatized and insane, and "for the first time, it seemed to Mr. Britling that he really saw the immediate horror of war, the dense, cruel stupidity of the business, plain and close" (*MB*, 297). To recognize that the familiar, slightly absurd and annoying Aunt Wilshire "should be torn to pieces, left in torment like a smashed mouse over which an automobile has passed, brought the whole business to a raw and quivering focus" (*MB*, 297–98). It leaves Mr. Britling reeling, envisioning her at the time of the bombing, "a thing of elemental terror and agony, bleeding wounds and shattered bones, plunging about in the darkness amidst a heap of wreckage" (*MB*, 297). That Aunt Wilshire is an incidental character in the story is important; such visions of unwitnessed violence, in which the body is nevertheless vividly and gruesomely figured in the mind, are repeatedly, almost obsessively, generated.

The novel is replete with such situations; they constitute its essential focus, as when Mr. Britling learns of a local territorial who has been horrifically mangled in the night after being hit by a train, and Mr. Britling's feverish mind will keep coming back, in the deep nights, to "this bloody smear, this thing of red and black" (*MB*, 245). Is this Ivor Gurney's "red wet thing I must somehow forget"? Similarly, a series of stories filter through from Belgium to trouble the local

English families, many of whom are hosting refugees. The Britlings hear, from their displaced Belgian man, of German violence in the family's home town, violence of a sort they cannot recognize or in fact even translate from the French. Particularly shocking, and what will later enter Mr. Britling's and the novel's unrepressible thought stream, is the image of the "shoulder blade of a woman" lying in the street, surrounded by pools of blood (*MB*, 256). Everyone is taken aback by that image, the shoulder blade of a woman in the street; it seems to disturb the universe.[42]

These disparate stories of awful violence and death, brought home to the comfortable English village, might be taken as the precise kind of spur that recent theorists have considered as the ethical incitement of shared vulnerability. Judith Butler's idea that we might take vulnerability as an opportunity to forge alliances where there might otherwise be indifference has energized theorists for the way it produces a positive agenda and a basis for activism, from the stark, violent realities of war and injustice.[43] Considering the significance of Butler's intervention, Marianne Hirsch writes that "an acknowledgment of vulnerability, both shared and produced, can open a space of interconnection as well as a platform for responsiveness and for resistance."[44] For Hirsch, to move from trauma to vulnerability as a guiding rubric turns the stress from the past to the future or, more subtly, from the overwhelming, often disabling past to a sense of possible amelioration in the future. Anna Tsing, thinking about environmental crisis and its forms, writes, "Precarity is a state of acknowledgment of our vulnerability to others. . . . If survival always involves others, it is also necessarily subject to the indeterminacy of self-and-other transformations."[45] This idea of shared vulnerability, a way of transforming precariousness and threat into empowerment and alliance or even intersubjectivity is, I want to suggest, almost exactly like what Wells is proposing in his novel and, as we will see a little later, in his popular wartime polemics. As Hirsch considers: "I have been trying to think about how the retrospective glance of trauma might be expanded and redirected to open alternative temporalities that are more porous and future-oriented and that galvanize a sense of urgency about the need for change now" (337). In the contemporary theorizing of vulnerability, as with Wells's approach to the First World War, there is a real urgency about seizing the moment history has handed to us, the here and now of a violence that seems to have destroyed just enough to leave open the chance for something new to emerge, something better.[46] There are historical junctures, in other words, when it might be possible to effect real changes in understanding, outlook, affiliation, and political climate—as a New Yorker, one thinks of those unforgettable months after 9/11—and these rely on a combination of violence and imagination. Wells was acutely aware that the war presented such a moment (this is the meaning of his always misused phrase, the war that will end war, as I will discuss shortly), and in *Mr. Britling* he experiments with this principle as the novel's central, motivating idea.

All of the instances of violence we have discussed so far in *Mr. Britling* are decidedly civilian: both the victims and those who encounter them are outside the sphere of combat, and the sense of outrage and unreality about these grisly bodily relics stems from the incongruity of facing such spectacles in seemingly peaceful locales. Yet not quite. One key consequence of Wells bringing the reader up close to these smears and bones and torturous episodes is to insist on continuities across the threshold of civilian and combatant, such that we see both conditions as very clearly the product and emanation of war. Or, perhaps most accurately, the novel is based upon the division between home and war that thrusts into existence the category of civilian only to undermine that division in several ways: the willed effort to imagine, the reality of civilian vulnerability (as with the zeppelin raid or the Belgian experiences), the porousness of the village that sends out soldiers, receives refugees, and seems somehow to have crossed a threshold of continuity with its own past. In *Mr. Britling*, the thrust all along has been to bring the blood, terrors, and meaningless loss into closer and closer focus.

Thus as the novel turns its reluctant gaze to the three young men of its family circle who are on active duty in Europe, there is less disjunction than seamlessness in the imaginative structures at work in bringing their bodies into mind. To start with the most devastating for this novel, Mr. Britling's son Hugh is shot through the head. If there always persisted in the First World War an aching fiction that the soldier—or at least one's own son, husband, father—might have died instantly and painlessly, Mr. Britling finds no such consolation in Hugh's quick killing.[47] Instead, he is haunted in the darkness at nighttime by a whole range of horrible specters, which always culminate in "the dead body of Hugh, face downward. At the back of the boy's head, rimmed by blood-stiffened hair— the hair that had once been 'as soft as the down of a bird'—was a big red hole. The hole was always pitilessly distinct" (*MB*, 417–18). There can be no consolation in that big red hole (one thinks, again, of the smear of blood from the man hit by the train and of Gurney's "red wet thing"), and the classical association one might register of Hugh with the Trojan hero Hektor, dragged in the dirt by the rampaging Achilles, his beautiful head and flowing hair defiled in front of the whole city, is particularly stark.

Hugh's death is the novel's heartbreak, yet it is the young German's death that, in many ways, sets the novel on new ground. For the British to mourn their own sons is expected; for them to extend that gesture to their German counterparts is more of a surprise. The novel, recall, was published in 1916, in the middle of the war and more than a decade before the boom in war books of the late 1920s, which made the identification with the enemy one of its regular features—those other "lads" suffering miseries and terrors like our own, all subject to the same inept and cynical leaders, all broken by combat and consigned to a lost generation.[48] This attitude is on full view in *Mr. Britling*. Paul Fussell remarks that soldiers at the front read *Mr. Britling* in great numbers, especially enjoying Wells's harsh criticism of their bungling leaders; perhaps they also caught in Wells's novel a sensibility of commonalty with the enemy that would later help define combatant literature.[49] In works like *All Quiet on the Western Front*, sympathy for German soldiers is generally the matter of strange meetings, to use Owen's term, but in *Mr. Britling*, Karl Heinrich has been established as a member of the community before the novel opens. Stuffy, orderly, a tad humorless, in stereotypical German fashion, Heinrich (as he is called) is nevertheless an appealing young man, with his unusual preference for squirrels as pets, an iconic violin, and, above all, a devotion to the study of universal languages. If, as we know, Wells pours parts of himself into many of his characters, Heinrich is given the gene that expresses the dream of world peace. In this case, he needs no great schemes of a technocratic revolution to get there; global harmony will follow, organically and without fail, from the adoption of a universal language, and this accordingly is his passionate subject of scholarly focus. Of the war when it arrives, Heinrich (who must enlist immediately, rushing home from Matching's Easy to Germany) has this to say: "'I am entirely opposed to the war . . . I am entirely opposed to any war,'" and "'If there was only one language in all the world, none of such things would happen. . . . There would be no English, no Germans, no Russians'" (*MB*, 167–68). Pacifist, unobtrusive, orderly, a believer that all of life might be indexed along with all words, Heinrich is as incongruous a soldier as the novel can figure. Thus when the family learns that he has died as a Russian prisoner of war, the news, bereft of detail, sends Mr. Britling into throes of heated vision:

> Imagination glimpsed a little figure toiling manfully through the slush and snow of the Carpathians; saw it staggering under its first experience of shell fire; set it amidst attacks and flights and fatigue and hunger and a rush perhaps in the darkness; guessed at the wounding blow. Then came the pitiful pilgrimage of the prisoners into captivity, captivity in a land desolated, impoverished and embittered. Came wounds wrapped in filthy rags, pain and want of

occupation, and a poor little bent and broken Heinrich sitting aloof in a crowded compound nursing a mortifying wound . . .

He used always to sit in a particular attitude with his arms crossed on his crossed legs, looking slantingly through his glasses . . .

So he must have sat, and presently he lay on some rough bedding and suffered, untended, in infinite discomfort. . . . Until one day an infinite weakness laid hold of him, and his pain grew faint and all his thoughts and memories grew faint—and still fainter.

(*MB*, 424)

It is crucial to the novel's overall intentions that this narrative of Heinrich's war service and pitiful death are given only in Mr. Britling's imagination (none of these scenarios have a basis in received information). In addition to the novelistic quality of Mr. Britling's thoughts when he envisions Heinrich's war service— the details that give a sense of material truth to the vision, such as the filthy rags or the rough bedding—what is so striking about the passage is the way it blends the known past with the unknowable recent tragedies, which are nevertheless brought into a bracing reality. In the slippage among verb tenses, the passage renders these novelistic moves highly visible. It is a gesture of the mind that acts, perhaps, as homage, a giving back of life.

And then there is Teddy, whose story of war service spreads the production of civilian imagining out beyond Mr. Britling. Teddy's situation is ripe for terrible thoughts and visualizations; he has fallen into that great, unknowable territory of "missing" (later, "missing, since reported killed" [*MB*, 383]), the quintessential crisis to demand a necessary imaginative response. It is no wonder that literature since the First World War and before has been so drawn to the double unknowns of "missing, presumed dead" and the soldier with no memory; both become figures around which imagination, narrative, and desire swirl with fervid intensity. In *Mr. Britling*, Teddy's wife, Letty, becomes, in effect, shell shocked by his disappearance in France, going so far in her madness as to plan something like a multiyear anarchist campaign of terror against the war's leaders, with the aim of preventing future wars (here again, the peace instinct filters through the community, if in psychotic form). Letty's madness shows in stark terms how fully the civilian can inhabit what might seem a combatant position, here shell shock; in fact, she seems to be experiencing Teddy's trauma for him. When Teddy returns home, amazingly alive but missing a hand, we have no sense of how he is responding to his ordeal. He seems mostly relieved to be alive and reunited with his family. Letty and the community have only the barest sense of what he has experienced, which included witnessing a massacre of fellow soldiers and months of terrible pain, and Teddy seems disinclined to relive these grisly scenes. The civilian's response and identification, however, is another story, one the novel has attempted to tell as a universal principle: "But Letty's concern was all with the hand. Inside the sling there was something that hurt the imagination, something bandaged, a stump. She could not think of it. She could not get away from the thought of it" (*MB*, 413). This is the essence of *Mr. Britling* and, beyond that, of the Wellsian civilian as she grasps at the war. The wife (or parent, child, friend, even a stranger) is drawn toward the wound, yet it hurts her imagination, in a process that cannot be halted. She could not think of it. She could not get away from the thought of it. That the wound is in the hand—the place of touch and intimacy, of writing, also that which holds the gun—makes these (not yet) withered stumps of time all the more magnetic for Letty's reeling mind.[50]

Letty's reaction to Teddy's stump, that sense of being caught in the grip of contradictory states of horror, empathy, distance, and identification, aligns her with others of the war generation who found themselves in positions of intimacy with the injured bodies of soldiers. For all of the emphasis on the authentic experience that qualifies the soldier poem, there is also in these texts an urgency to maintain the intensity of war's assault in the mind or memory, in order, as Owen writes, "bleeding-fresh / . . . for speechless sufferers to plain."[51] When we look back and forth across the trench lines and over the Channel, the idea emerges very clearly; there is always that need to jump over the boundary of combat, whose fixity remains a great fiction. The violence of war is never contained by that boundary, and thus to retain what the World War I generation saw as civilization, under conditions of catastrophic war, requires that a person see herself as part of the struggle, from here or there.

We might, indeed, take one of modernism's great attempts at unity in this light, Clarissa Dalloway's experiencing of Septimus Warren Smith's death, which stands as the crescendo of *Mrs. Dalloway*. In feeling his suicide, as if from the inside, Clarissa achieves something akin to the ubiquitous desire for a deep connection to the suffering of soldiers that was so important to Wells and that pervaded the culture of the war years more broadly. Critics will continue to debate the value of Clarissa's gesture, whether to see it as a moment of sublime externality, a kind of gift, where her understanding redeems his sacrifice, or, on the other hand, as yet another way for the upper classes to prosper while the likes of Septimus plunge to a meaningless death. These disparate responses are answerable, perhaps, to the fact that the novel was written and set in a postwar world that no longer sought those continuities. Once the war was over, what would it mean to imagine a connection with the soldier's experience and to derive meaning from someone else's pain? In its backward movement, such impulses—fueled during the war years by urgent desire, by ethics, by necessity—become instances instead of a deep conundrum. If the meaning of civilian life has been drawn around recognizing, honoring, and especially overcoming the gulf between those at war and those at home, such polarities fall away once the troops come home. Yet as Woolf and so many of her generation recognized, war is never really in the past.

## III. WILLING AN END TO WAR

The harvest of this darkness comes now almost as a relief, and it is a grim satisfaction in our discomforts that we can at last look across the roar and torment of battlefields to the possibility of an organised peace.

For this is now a war for peace.

It aims straight at disarmament. It aims at a settlement that shall stop this sort of thing for ever.

\*\*\*

That is why I think we liberal English should draw our new map of Europe now [1914], first of all on paper and then upon the face of the earth.

We ought to draw that map now, and propagate the idea of it, and make it our national purpose, and call the intelligence and consciences of the United States and France and Scandinavia to our help. Openly and plainly we ought to discuss and decide and tell the world what we mean to do. The reign of brutality, cynicism, and secretive treachery is shattered in Europe. Over the ruins of the Prussian War-Lordship, reason, public opinion, justice, international good faith and good intentions will be free to come back and rule the destinies of man. But things will not wait for reason and justice, if just and reasonable men have neither energy nor unity.[52]

*This is now a war for peace.* It was September 1914, just a few weeks into the conflict, and not many English civilians were working feverishly to imagine exactly what the peace might look like, or making a deep inquiry into the nature of this war, or, indeed, taking the measure of how history would be permanently changed in Europe and around the world. Few would have written on August 5 that soldiers would soon "have to march, through pain, through agonies of the spirit worse than pain, through seas of blood and filth," much less taken it upon themselves to insist that such violent events would be the last of their kind; "we face these horrors to make an end of them" (*WEW*, 15). And I believe even fewer would have demanded, in the dizzying days of August, that those at home, civilians with no public authority in the matter of war or peace, should—indeed must—wrest control of these great international matters from leaders and diplomats, to make themselves the new legislators of the society that would follow the fighting. Wells argued for all of this, beginning as early as one day into the war.[53] His form was the pamphlet, which he adopted with gusto for his highly individual purposes, and his most famous one, published in September 1914, was titled *The War That Will End War*, in what became a key phrase of the era. I use the term "pamphlet" loosely, to characterize these essays, short pieces mostly published in newspapers, to be quickly brought out as small books, to convey a tradition of political literature aimed at a wide audience, with roots in the nineteenth-century political commons and a strong sense of urgency in the occasion. If the First World War was the era of state propaganda, when, as Mark Wollaeger puts it, "the evolving British strategy . . . chart[ed] the emergence of what in retrospect looks like a modern media environment," Wells's use of the more traditional pamphlet had its own efficacy.[54] It was a nimble form, allowing for bursts of powerful statement and idea, responding to the news of the day yet looking always into the future. The pamphlet is defined by brevity, not something we associate with Wells, but, as always with him, writerly forms are picked up, shaped, used, and retired according to his sense of the moment and its literary demands. War has its genres—epic, ode, allegory, patriotic hymn, recruiting poster—but peace must always be (re)creating its own.

During the war years, Wells took good advantage of the timely agility of the pamphlet and other short and quick pieces, and his words traveled through English culture and beyond. These dynamics have gone unnoticed by war scholars, much less by critics of modernism. Even more absent from our cultural memory of the war years is what we might think of as the tense of Wells's agenda—namely, the imperative—and the dominant principle of action—namely, the will. The word "will" is right there in the center of his famous formulation, yet its ambiguity has always been read only one way, the simplest: this war naturally will turn out to be the last, in which case Wells was spectacularly wrong. But the phrase also suggests something else, which is that we must will the end of wars. Faced with such a catastrophe, there is only one thing to do, to make this one the final. So a new emphasis: "the war that *will* end war." As he writes at the conclusion of "The War of the Mind," the final essay in *The War That Will End War*:

How are we to gather together the wills and understanding of men for the tremendous necessities and opportunities of this time? Thought, speech, persuasion, an incessant appeal for clear intentions, clear statements for the dispelling of suspicion and the abandonment of secrecy and trickery; there is work for every man who writes or talks and has the slightest influence upon another creature. This monstrous conflict in Europe . . . goes on only because we, who are voices, who suggest, who might elucidate and inspire, are ourselves such little scattered creatures that though we strain to the breaking point, we still have no strength to turn on the light that would save us.

(WEW, 106)

At its core, the pamphlet is sounding an appeal. It calls out to anyone "who writes or talks and has the slightest influence upon another creature," that is, to all of us, and it does so both as a matter of its own volition and in the name of the reader's purported desires. Over and over in these pamphlets Wells reminds his readers that they, like him—like nearly everyone—really hate war, that they are pacifist in spirit, that they would indeed stand up for its termination, if only a certain effort could be galvanized around the horror of war and a sense of how the conflict might yield a just peace. Thus, in the emphasized "will" can be found an essential facet of Wells's whole career and certainly of the writing of civilian identity we have been elaborating in this chapter: a fervent, almost manic, attempt to force events to move in the direction Wells hoped—with a nudge from him—would become our human destiny. We might note, further, the presence here of the word "scattered," a keyword for Wells, the obverse to his desired collectivity. What "scattered" conveys can be differentiated, however, from a term like "isolated" or "alienated," in its more external, less psychological suggestiveness. What has been scattered can certainly be (re)united.

The essays collected together as *The War That Will End War*, all of which were published in the days and weeks immediately after war was declared, along with later pamphlets *The Peace of the World* (1915), *What Is Coming: A Forecast of Things After the War* (1916), *In the Fourth Year* (1918), and the coauthored *The Idea of a League of Nations* (1919), comprise a remarkable set of texts that on their own were meant to move an agenda of ultimate peace. And we might add to these dozens of other short pieces Wells wrote for newspapers and other venues over the same period. These occasional texts, bristling with affect and changing in tone and content as the war progressed, figured regularly in newspapers like the *Daily Chronicle*, the *Times*, and the *New York Times* during the war and catapulted Wells into the position of war authority we have noted (he was invited to visit the trenches in 1916, for instance, and always to write more and more about the conflict). As one of the initial assembly of writers invited to join C. F. G. Masterman's new propaganda unit in September 1914—all men!—a somewhat ambivalent signer of its declaration in support of the war that same month, and for a short time in 1918 an active member of its later iteration, Wells would seem to have a straightforward relation of support for the British government cause, but in fact, such is far from the case. Wells's short tenure with Masterman's group suggests as much (and Masterman was an old friend), and similarly short lived was the later effort to recruit him. Wells was much too critical of Britain's management of the war and much too devoted to world government to make him a reliable campaigner, and, as we have seen, his major fiction about the war featured a narrative of indiscriminate violence and widespread psychic damage, in which the war's leaders were decisively critiqued. Wells's pamphlets are wildly idiosyncratic, in both their content and tone and in the widespread misreading they have occasioned. Most have responded to Wells's patriotic fervor in the first installment (of August 5, 1914) and, as one biographer puts it, hear a "prevailing note [of] jingoistic patriotism . . . which earned him considerable hostility in some quarters."[55] And indeed, in the first months of the war, Wells spewed much anti-German sentiment in newspaper articles and other formats, his argument against German "kultur" striking a patriotic chord in the initial weeks of war. The general verdict on the pamphlets today comes mostly from the title alone of the first collection, *The War That Will End War*. Slightly more elaborated views are that Wells was (a) so horribly wrong in predicting the outcome that the phrase can stand for a kind of blithe ignorance about how world events would actually move and (b) utterly conservative in sentiment, seeing the war as Germany's fault, England's to win, all expressed with a repellent righteousness. Yet what the pamphlets actually say is quite different. For all their seeming triumphalism, in fact, they lay out an agenda for those who are disempowered in times of war (and perhaps at any time), the civilians who, as we have seen, concerned Wells over the decades that led up to and followed the war. Thus, despite troubling elements in the pamphlets (blaming Germany for the war, condemning German imperialism while mostly ignoring Britain's, evincing a fighting fervor that upset his pacifist peers), they represent a robust textual experiment in thinking about the nature of war and peace, completing the long task of propelling the civilian into a position of world consequence that has, as its coin's other side, Bert Smallways's clutching and cowering in the teeth of mass destruction.

The central precept underlying Wells's approach to war in *The War That Will End War* is one that can be found throughout his writing: the incentive to transform the worst forms of carnage into the grist for a renovation of the world, a first step in the direction of peace. "Every sword that is drawn against Germany now" he wrote, "is a sword drawn for peace" (*WEW*, 16). In this trajectory, the anticipatory lurches into action; we must, in a sense, leap over the grisly necessities of the present, all the while planning assiduously for what will come, in order to make the (near) future into what we want to eventuate after the catastrophe of the war. Taken from a point of view just in advance of now, the horror of what will then be the past can be made to generate change. Yet this does not translate to the principle of enchanted violence. Violence is unredeemable, but out of the wastage one can force an outcome that will retrospectively confer a kind of necessary value on what came before. If such a conclusion was missing from *The War in the Air*, it most certainly characterizes *The World Set Free, Things to Come* (and *The Shape of Things to Come*), and many other works. Even *Mr. Britling* struggles in this direction, insofar as the novel's ending pairs the desperation and deconstruction embodied in Mr. Britling's final letter to Hugh (discussed in chapter 1) with his strange discovery of God—figured as a kind of principle of goodness in the world—and with his epiphany that all this suffering does have a purpose, in renovated political and national structures across Europe. Such may be in keeping with Wells's views, but he writes the principle as a necessary jolt, from the exceedingly personal and painful fact of loss to willed recovery in the revelation, as Mr. Britling puts it, of "the only possible government in Albania" (*MB*, 403). We have noted that *Mr. Britling* is organized all along by a division between personal, intimate, and local versus public, universal, and worldwide and that these principles never keep to their spheres. Here, as in the case of the violence against civilian bodies, the lurch of category slippage unsettles both the interior life of the story and the reader's response. Is it really possible to answer the intense grief of losing one's son or husband in the trenches with the balm of a reformed world government, exemplified by a small Balkan region? The novel wants, at least with one side of its energy, to insist that such transmutations of affect and purpose are not only possible but necessary. Only if we can make the dead son with a raw, red hole in his head into the carrier of a new world map will there be any way to make sense of—much less redeem—the horrors at hand. Or, to put it in reverse, Wells *will* turn extreme loss of one kind into lasting gain.

Thus the seemingly perverse innovation in *The War That Will End War* of finding in the war's very first shots the seeds of the last forms part of Wells's career-long identity; significantly, this hit a nerve with his contemporaries. As a phrase, "the war that will end war" (usually stated as "the war to end war," including by Wells in later years) caught the public's ear—as the MacKenzies claim, it "became the national slogan"—and its vibrancy in the war and postwar years has not waned: the phrase maintains a kind of tortured longevity.[56] Wells would continue for years to work out the meaning and promise embedded in his own phrase and to try to figure such leaps as an essential fact of history. From the moment when he first named the war that will end war, and still today, the questions it raises have confounded Western culture: can we separate one war from other wars? How do we reconcile the experience of the intense presentness of war's violence with a historical understanding that wars always have followed and generated one another? In the case of the First World War, when, exactly, does the culture recognize itself as living between two wars, and what, then, does the new condition of between-wars mean for our (and their) understanding of the First World War? In other words, we keep asking how each war enters into the larger history and general condition of war and, at least in Wells's terms, how it could ever be possible to terminate that seemingly endless sequence, bringing one and all to an end. One of the most interesting facets of the idea of a war that will end war is that it precisely conjoins the exceptional (this war is different, it will be the turning point and the one to change history) and the continual (this war is one in a long and, from some points of view, never-ending series of wars; it is really peace that is exceptional). Favret, as we have noted, pushes back against the principle of exceptionality, especially the idea that the total wars of the twentieth century were unique—in their scale of violence, their disregarding of the civilian/combatant distinction, their ferocity, and their global consequence. Instead, her idea of "wartime" traverses the categories of present and past. As she writes, "wartime . . . has trouble measuring its distance from other times of war: it produces a history of the present always permeable to other presents, other wartimes," and further, "Under the ever-present possibility of unlimited war, wartime itself seems increasingly difficult to restrict or seal off, always vulnerable to invasion from other wars."[57] More, as I will discuss more fully in the next chapter, Paul Saint-Amour has developed the important idea of "perpetual inter-war," such that the condition of recognizing oneself liable to mass violence, mostly in the form of aerial bombardment, becomes a shared facet of cultural psychology over many years, even decades. In a sense, then, Wells's formulation was only inaccurate factually; in its essential questions, it continues to press urgently on our understanding of these massive events.[58] We might thus hear Wells sounding through a formulation like this one, from President Obama, speaking in June 2015 at Hiroshima, at the seventieth anniversary of the bomb dropping: "The world was forever changed here, but today the children of this city will go through their day in peace. What a precious thing that is. It is worth protecting, and then extending to every child. That is the future we can choose, a future in which Hiroshima and Nagasaki are known not as the dawn of atomic warfare but as the start of our own moral awakening."

How, then, is it supposed to happen? How is the war, which Wells recognized from the start would be uniquely bloody and cataclysmic, going to interrupt the modern world's seemingly inexorable vector into conflict, given what works like *The War in the Air* or the later *Things to Come* have to say about wars' causes—not in any real way the progeny of a single nation or leader but the inevitable endpoint of many forces of modernity, such as international competition, armament manufacture, world interconnectedness, and the failure of political institutions and social traditions to confront these forces and stand for peace?[59] There are three primary answers: through a world organization dedicated to preventing future wars and securing international cooperation for its mandates; by a rigorous policy of disarmament and permanent control of arms manufacture across all nations; and by enlisting the large-scale efforts of those noncombatants who have, in Wells's view, the necessary freshness of mind, latent pacifist orientation, and outrage about the war and its leaders to demand change.

Not surprisingly, given his ongoing dream of a world state, Wells came very early—in the war's first weeks—to the idea of a world organization devoted to ensuring peace. In the essay "Opportunity of Liberalism," he exhorts liberalism to step up to its moment, eagerly predicting that if liberals "will insist upon a World conference at the end of the conflict, if they refuse all partial settlements and merely European solutions, they may re-draw every frontier they choose, they may reduce a thousand chafing conflicts of race and language and government to a minimum, and set up a Peace League that will control the globe" (*WEW*, 67–68). In essays like this one from *The War That Will End War*, the peace league is a fairly fleeting reference, but by early in 1915, it had become a primary concern. *The Peace of the World* lays out the rationale for a "World Council" that would follow upon a peace treaty and be charged above all with "the maintenance of the peace of the world."[60] Even beyond this mandate, the World Council could further "discharge a hundred useful functions in relation to world hygiene, international trade and travel, the control of the ocean, the exploration and conservation of the world's food supplies," and hence contribute to the welfare of humanity into the long future (*PW*, 31). From the World Council, Wells had moved by 1917 to the "League of Free Nations," naming himself a follower of President Wilson in maintaining that all-important "Free" in the League's conception and title. The League would embody "the idea of united human effort to put an end to wars," a permanent organization that would begin with the international armistice convention and live on from there, with powers Wells often likened to those of the United States federal government vis-à-vis the individual states.[61] By the end of the war, of course, the entity that Wells had been striving to imagine and promote consolidated as the League of Nations. We often remember the League today above all for its failure, and Wells, too, ceased to support the League as founded and wrote frequently in the 1920s and '30s about its tragic outcome, even as he envisioned new roads toward international unity, but during the years of war and just after, the League promised an innovative, even radical, solution for reorganizing the nations of the world in a new and better direction, and Wells advocated tirelessly for it.[62]

Most notable in its advocacy is the postwar *The Idea of a League of Nations*, which, though impressively coauthored, everywhere betrays Wells's hand; for instance, the opening pages establish the context of large historical trends swinging from unification to disintegration (and back) and proclaim the ongoing intensification of warfare as an ineluctable mark of the modern era, all with a notably Wellsian cadence. Setting up the stark choices of a world collectively governed in the interest of peace versus one of ever more destructive warfare and social/economic disintegration, the pamphlet makes its case for the League. "Only through counter-organization of the peace-will in mankind," it claims, "can the world be saved from a great cycle of disasters, disorder, and retrogression."[63] It was always Wells's conviction—or what we might read as his aspiration-as-conviction—that the populace was latently peace loving, that the "peace-will in mankind" stands ready for its institutions, here the League of Nations. "It is believed," he and his coauthors claim, "that the clear, deliberate, and methodical working out of the broad problems and riddles of the world-league idea will be a sufficient compelling force to bring it within the realm of practical possibility" (14–15).

Closely allied with his aspiration for a new world body to ensure peace was Wells's fervent demand for disarmament. Here he is in *The Peace of the World*, making the key points:

No one who has watched the politics of the last forty years can doubt the very great share the business and finance of armament manufacture has played in bringing about the present horrible killing, and no one who has read accounts of the fighting can doubt how much this industry has enhanced the torment, cruelty and monstrosity of war.... Modern war is entirely dependent upon equipment of the most costly and elaborate sort. A general agreement to reduce that equipment would not only greatly minimize the evil of any war that did break out, but it would go a long way towards the abolition of war.... It is necessary that the manufacture of war material should cease to be a private industry and a source of profit to private individuals, that all the invention and enterprise that blossoms about business should be directed no longer to the steady improvement of man-killing.

(*PW*, 47, 50, 52)

The combination of practical with aspirational sets the tone, as Wells toggles back and forth between the loftiest of his goals, where his rhetoric is invited to soar, and the more realistic concessions of what is possible. These, then, are the core political aspirations of Wells's writings on these subjects, though it should be added that the texts, with their breathless, hasty energy, are bursting with interest beyond the essential, reiterated ideas about how to control arms and ensure peace.

Amid this welter of ideas about war, politics, the logic of historical development, and the culture of home is Wells's empowering of the ordinary civilian as envisioner, promoter, and keeper of the peace. Let us return to two formulations we have already adduced and add several more to our inventory. In the section's epigraph ("we liberal English should draw our new map of Europe") as well as in the passage that closes *The War That Will End War* where, we recall, Wells calls upon everyone who has ever written, thought, discussed, or influenced another person to take this moment, *now*, as the opportunity to change things once and for all, Wells urges his readers to find themselves in the historical present, to accept a "now or never" challenge that, crucially, involves them in the war as it does their sons, brothers, friends, lovers, and husbands in the trenches. Two more such statements:

> By means of . . . books, newspaper articles, leaflets, tracts in English, French, German, Dutch, Swedish, Norwegian, Italian, Chinese, and Japanese we have to spread this idea, repeat this idea, and *impose upon this war* the idea that this war must end war.
>
> (*WEW*, 102, italics in the original)

> I admit a certain sense of presumptuous absurdity as I sit here before the map of Europe like a carver before a duck and take off a slice here and decide on a cut there. None the less it is what everyone of us has to do. I intend to go on redrawing the map of Europe with every intelligent person I meet. . . . No one, I hope, will suggest after this war that we should still leave things to the diplomatists. . . . The only alternative to diplomacy is outspoken intelligence, yours and mine and every articulate person's. . . . If we common intelligent people at large do not secure that, nobody will.
>
> (*WEW*, 56–57)

There is, of course, something a little uncomfortable in thinking about English civilians sitting at home carving up the map of Europe. But then, they are not taking such power away from their counterparts in, say, the Balkans, or even in

Germany—on the contrary, for all the Englishness either implicit or explicit in many of Wells's phrases, the larger idea is for citizens of all nations to be doing just what Wells is asking of himself and those immediately around him. Certainly this is Mr. Britling's view, who takes up the map and its potentialities as his very particular concern in the last segment of the novel, illustrating Wells's position as an urgent psychological necessity (to create meaning and value out of otherwise meaningless loss).

The real enemies are those world leaders who, in Wells's view, have brought Europe and the world to the awful place where it stands in 1914–1918, and these are to be superseded by ordinary civilians. Over and over in these pamphlets, Wells lays heavy blame on diplomats, embassies, "Welt Politik," and the Great Power machinations that he believes for two centuries have destroyed so much potential for progress and well-being around the world. If it is presumptuous for English citizens to consider their maps as a site for political action, it is more so, in Wells's assessment, in the hands of those power brokers whose adherence to an aggressively imperial, competitive approach around the globe has been so devastatingly destructive. We might note, too, the close proximity of this new alignment—ordinary, thoughtful citizens all across Europe versus leaders and diplomats who are, in essence, cynical, small-minded, and incapable—with the principle that the real enemies of soldiers on both sides are not one another but rather their own governments and military leaders who sent them off to be slaughtered.

To jump from the war years for a moment, Wells's contribution to the discussions surrounding disarmament at the Washington peace conference in 1921–1922, which he attended in the capacity of reporter, can be read as a continuation of his wartime pamphlets. Like the pamphlets, the essays from Washington are framed in terms of emergency and shape themselves around the largest issues—the survival of civilization, a last chance, it may be, to reorganize the world on sane, peaceful lines, lest total catastrophe engulf us all. As Wells writes in the opening essay, "The catastrophe of 1914 is still going on. It does not end; it increases and spreads. . . . If this downward drift toward disorder and war is not arrested, in a few years' time it will certainly catch my sons and probably mutilate or kill them" (*WHP*, 2, 7). Tonally, the articles epitomize the essential Wellsian trait of interleaving the darkest visions of chaos and catastrophe with crisp articulations of hope for triumph nonetheless, generously laced with Wells's own recommendations for bringing about such outcomes (quite apart, it should be stressed, from whatever might be developing at the conference). Thus from vivid visions of collapse, Wells can happily write that the Washington conference, as a beginning point for a new kind of international spirit, "may become the symbol and rallying point of all that vast amount of sane, humanitarian feeling and all that devotion to mankind as a whole, and to peace and justice, that has hitherto been formless and ineffectual in the world, for the need of such a banner" (*WHP*, 104). Meanwhile, as an artifact of the convention and, more broadly, of this moment of vastly insufficient world efforts at peace, Wells's book also models itself on his friend John Maynard Keynes's great work *The Economic Consequences of the Peace*, which famously detailed the events of the Versailles convention as a prelude to Keynes's dire forecast for what would follow from the treaty's vindictive mandates. For us, what is most compelling about the essays is the way these articles carry forward the pamphlets' aim to develop the role of civilian, to make her a crucial actor in pushing forward the peace effort. During the war years, the noncombatant without political authority occupied a starker position, yet even in this postwar climate, Wells constructs, once again, a live persona whose authority with respect to war is minimal but whose potential vulnerability to state violence makes her an actor in the drama of peace.

As quoted earlier, Wells reached out in these essays to "teachers and writers, parents and talkers and all who instruct and make and change opinion"; it was these who were tasked with "building up a new spirit in the hearts of men and a new dream in their minds, the spirit of fellowship to all men, the dream of a great world released for ever from the obsession of warfare and international struggle" (*WHP*, 154). The agents of war were many at the convention (political leaders, diplomats, legislators, and, in the background, the multiple capitalist interests ranged around the profitability of armed conflict), and Wells portrays himself—and by extension his reader—as decidedly exempted from such war connections. Wells as outsider and layperson can offer a specific perspectival openness, the essays suggest, to see past, present, and future in and around the issues at hand, to pan back and consider how the local questions being debated might fit into a larger picture. At the same time, he can indulge in hyperbole and gesture, in a fashion denied delegates or political leaders. Hence the essays veer disturbingly into dystopic forecasting of Europe's imminent decline and imagine a variety of horrific conflicts and depredations to come, in a spirit of violent extrapolation reminiscent of *The War in the Air*. Always, the idea is to jolt readers into demanding a solution that will bring ultimate—not illusory—peace.

This pamphlet language, from the Washington conference and especially from the 1914–1918 interventions, makes a remarkable gesture; it is a bold assertion of a creative approach to the politics of wartime modernity. As with his forging of an audience that defies ordinary categories, Wells brashly sets out to construct a new cohort of "common intelligent people at large" across England, Europe, America, and ultimately the world.[64] There are class implications to

such a group, naturally, something akin perhaps to Woolf's "daughters of educated men" in *Three Guineas* and harking to the vision of socialist international
antimilitarism that many believed, at least in 1914, could be a viable force for
combating world war. Then again, the class story is not at all clear. It may rather
be that the pamphlet form itself implies the kind of reader-activist whom Wells
is attempting to will into existence, in a form that brushes aside the infinite
complexity of class distinction. His plan in these writings is to swap out class for
audience, known social rubrics for those he, and the historical moment, are generating to answer the needs of the present. Wells's principle of "intelligence"
works to snub the ordinary dividing structures around inheritance and cultural
capital and instead to constellate an emerging cohort of men and women who,
for example, had benefited from the expansion in secondary education across
England since the 1870s (as had Wells himself). But it is not, finally, a preexist-
ing group to which Wells reaches any more than Woolf's daughters can be said
to have a meaningful community beyond the covers of her polemic. There is,
rather, a dialectic of reality (an expanding class of readers that can be charted in
different ways) and imagination (the speech act that authorizes this writer to
make demands for world change). Indeed, this dialectic might be placed alongside other Wellsian strategies that showcase his virtuosity in tapping into the
popular vein but also his ultimate isolation. There are so many cases over the
course of his career when he will say, "To this end [the goal of world unification]
a small but increasing body of people in the world set their faces and seek to
direct their lives," or "Never before [in 1919] can there have been so great and so
universal an awakening from assumed and accepted things. Never before have
men stood so barely face to face with the community of their interests and their
common destiny"—yet one wonders: isn't this really just Wells?[65]

There is no such ambiguity, however, admitted into the tone of the war pamphlets. If the alliance of "common intelligent people at large" is understood to
traverse class and other boundaries, it nevertheless coheres in one important
sense: it is generated in the first place by the same purpose it avows, the need for
civilians to take on all war's issues. Like so many strategic alliances that have
defined later twentieth- and now twenty-first-century political protest, Wells's
imagined—or, better, conjured—civilians are constructed and united as a group
by the force of the historical emergency. Here again, the idea that the most dire,
hellish, catastrophic episodes of violence and loss *will* beget a future that dramatically repudiates that violence stands behind Wells's immediate ideas. It is in
the moment itself—here, now, with all its shock, grief, outrage, fear, confusion,
and physical precariousness—that the opportunity arises. Such a call to turn the
violent crisis of the moment into a way of activating the community, rejecting

its violent norms, and thinking creatively forward has continued appeal, right up to our own times. As Anna Tsing notes, "The diversity that allows us to enter collaborations emerges from histories of extermination, imperialism, and all the rest"; for Wells, that would be war. Judith Butler makes a similar move, reflecting after the September 11 attacks, "These events posed the question, implicitly at least, as to what form political reflection and deliberation ought to take if we take injurability and aggression as two points of departure for political life."[66]

The idea of seizing on a moment of unique world violence becomes, for Wells as for later feminist theorists, an ethical imperative as well as a horizon-spreading gesture of self-empowerment. And it was one that Wells continued to foster over the decades. Writing in the *Times* in 1940, in the midst of the next war, Wells posted several letters in which he called for the crisis of the moment to yield, once again, a progressive future, now in the form of a Declaration of the Rights of Man, a human rights manifesto that served as a model for the United Nations' universal declaration in both form and content. "At various crises in the history of our communities," he wrote in the *Times*, soon published as a book, *The Rights of Man; or, What Are We Fighting For?*,

> beginning with Magna Carta and going through various Bills of Rights, Declarations of the Rights of Man and so forth, it has been our custom to produce a specific declaration of the broad principles on which our public and social life is based, and to abide by that as our fundamental law. The present time seems peculiarly suitable for such a restatement of the spirit in which we face life in general and the present combat in particular.[67]

It is not only wartime that generates these conditions of possibility but also the voices articulating it: Wells and others like him, citizens with no authority behind their defiant speech acts beyond their conviction that they speak for the conscience of the broader human population. To find a voice, a community, and a belief in the efficacy of challenging enormous, seemingly crushing world forces, from a position just outside the whirlwind, is something we can continue to admire and embrace. These are not the gestures of the naïve. They are the demands of the civilian.

# 3

# Time

nticipate, foresee, predict, prophesy, envision, plan, design, spec-
ulate, invent, imagine: these are Wells's verbs. No writer of his
era—no writer, perhaps, of any era—has been more virtuosic or
more diverse in these modes of thought. "The man who invented tomorrow"
became an epithet, and, in fact, no aspect of future life was outside the ambit of
Wells's vision. From the minute (the shape of doorways) to the global (the shape
of world government) and across the topical spectrum, Wells never stopped
looking ahead, creating spectacular settings and vistas to give rich life to his
many ideas about what the future might, will, and, above all, should entail.
Wells embraced the future as the absolutely critical temporality; it was his gift,
and also his burden, to take constant flight into the particular unknown of what
lies before us and to insist, at the same time, that the unwillingness to anticipate
has been one of the great failures of political and imaginative life, an unforgive-
able lapse in collective thought. Importantly, he took two different paths into
the future, and those verbs might be seen to divide accordingly. Some radiate
agency, the work of planners, Wells's dream makers of new and better worlds;
others suggest the hopeless task of the seer, whose primary fate is—and always
has been—to go unheeded. In the early works of fantasy, the world has taken its
often disastrous course outside of any agency, in scenarios that register the deepest anxieties of late-Victorian culture. These worlds act as a prism or—one of his
preferred metaphors—magic lantern to display the nightmares that haunted
the culture of the late nineteenth century in England, consumed by the twin
processes of evolution and decay, putting its faith only reluctantly in the science it nevertheless acknowledged as law, and experiencing with intense

self-consciousness the raw realities of industrialized modernity. They seem to bring together in uneasy balance the timeless with the specifically contemporary. Wells's science fiction is often recognized for the estrangement and other-dimensionality it imagines and produces, extracted from its culture and projected as distorted phantoms of the known world.

But there were also, of equal importance and as part of the same imaginative tendency, a whole host of forays into a future that we might—Wells would say, we must—plan. These two Wellsian iterations of the future belong together—those disturbing, uncanny visions of later/other life that are just recognizable as mirror, exaggeration, or allegory of the contemporary world, which provided the germ for so much modern science fiction, and the planned societies (utopias, mostly) whose actuality in the future, for Wells, furnishes proof that the violence, injustice, and general chaos of modernity—what he often calls our "age of confusion"—will have had an end goal, a meaning in the longer story of humanity. *Will have had*: Wells was a great writer in the mode of the future history, where a narrator or text from many years ahead scans back into the past (that is, the present or near future of the writing) to derive the conditions of that later time, a speculative temporal scheme that has come into its own in our era of ecological crisis and nuclear threat. *The Shape of Things to Come* (1933) is the most elaborate of his future histories, but it was always a congenial mode for Wells, in part because it fostered what we have seen to be one of his signature stylistic commitments, simultaneously to show, within the text's narrative world, and tell, providing commentary, often didactic in character, as explanation and analysis of how that present came to be and what it entails. Above all, Wells made it an article of faith that the willingness to take the future seriously as *something that can be known*, as a site for science-based extrapolation and reasoned political incitement, had real ethical ramifications. We have already noted, in considering the way his war pamphlets tackled the realm of the immediate future, that this orientation was closely tied to the empowering of civilian voices in the world history being made. It was Wells's particular genius to turn his imaginative powers toward the one temporality that was almost inevitably left out of literary world making in his era, the future.

Even before his breakaway into the future in *The Time Machine*, Wells had been experimenting with temporal imaginings in his scientific journalism, and he continued thinking about the essentially kinetic nature of all life until his last days. The very phrase "things to come" became associated with Wells, and under its rubric we can divine a variety of textual types. There were, most clearly, pioneering works whose primary conceit is to envision the near and middle future—whether in the form of fiction or direct prediction—and these share the thematic habit of blending an analysis of how current trends will naturally develop over time, in predictable, scientific fashion, with more ambiguous pictures of what Wells either hopes will transpire or dreads will terrorize our descendants—or both. These works envision complete worlds, in the manner of the classic utopia, though it should be emphasized that Wells's utopias are inevitably marked by internal self-critique, as we have seen in the seemingly forthright case of *A Modern Utopia*. In fact, most of his future-set works, beginning with *The Time Machine*, fall more into dystopic than utopic territory. Among other works that display a full future panorama are "A Story of the Days to Come" (1899), *Anticipations* (1901), *In the Days of the Comet* (1906), *The Sleeper Awakes* (1910) (formerly, *When the Sleeper Wakes* [1899]), *What Is Coming* (1916), *The Shape of Things to Come* (1933), and *Things to Come* (film, 1936).[1] Punctuating these works and scattered across many other writings are more local predictions about the future. These include, notably, the marketing and financial fraudulence of *Tono-Bungay*, which looks strangely like a forecast of our own economic conditions, and his many premonitions of future warfare.

But Wells's time travel has a tendency to run further and further into the future, and his forays into the extremely far future are particularly engrossing. Those last, spellbinding sequences of *The Time Machine*, thirty million years ahead, almost seem to throw down a gauntlet to the reader, challenging us to strain our mind's eyes as far as we can into the almost infinite distance yet demanding all the same that one employ scientific logic. What, those haunting passages of the earth's death seem to ask, would *you* see? And his immediate followers, notably Olaf Stapledon, did follow suit, creating stories set millions or even billions of years in the future. Closely related to these temporal journeys are works that are technically set apart in spatial terms yet easily transpose into fiction of the future. It was all, finally, about movement. The kinetic nature of all life, or what Wells often calls the "secularism" that characterizes organic processes, is more than a source of plots; it is a life principle that Wells endlessly plumbed. His experiments with time belong to a scene of flux and temporal instability. The movement along time's spectrum allows for no full stops, only glimpses of one object in motion as seen by another (the principle, after all, of relativity).

It also moves backward. "Wells and the future" is an iconic suggestion, especially in the context of science fiction, but, in fact, Wells was also one of the period's most influential envisioners of the past. Above all, he had a special attraction, like his modernist peers, to the farthest, oldest reaches of human and even antehuman history. All manner of prehistoric beings stalk his work. *The Outline of History* became the classic source for the period's engagement with prehistory, incorporating geology, paleontology, and the anthropology of early mankind. Wells's writing teems with reflections on time, evolution, and the longest reaches of life on the planet. In his early science journalism of the 1880s and early '90s, for example, the forays go backward as well as forward. In one instance, a narrator takes a dream visit to an unnamed prehistoric period, dominated by great reptiles, who, in a classic irony, complacently see themselves as the very pinnacle and endpoint of evolution.[2] Two tales published over a twenty-year span, "A Story of the Stone Age" (1897) and "The Grisly Folk" (1921), are particularly striking for the way they hone in on key moments of invisible yet violent transition in the evolution of mankind, concerning bands of early people as they unconsciously forge forward in the direction of recognizable humanity.

Bones have a way of firing the imagination, triggering new models of conceptualizing the past, and Wells gave vivid visual specificity to the more general rise in the period of an archeological imagination. As with the future, Wells looked backward in different temporalities; the longue durée is especially important in his works—but then *The Outline* quite spectacularly collated hundreds and thousands of years into a coherent and readable scheme of history, corralling the past into order and taking the narrative right up to the present or, rather, as we would expect, into the future. What makes Wells's writing of time so startling is its rich internal variety, the way time schemes collide and crash within a tale, or scene, or mind; the way scientific principles of temporal change (evolution, relativity, thermodynamics) coinhabit with dream spaces, folkloric motifs, and extraordinary fantasy; the way the staunch and unbreakable belief that we can plan and control our future is infiltrated by temporalities of long pasts and distant futures that disable such organizing energies. The aim of this chapter is to uncover Wells's great imaginative grasp of time in its multifariousness and to indicate what these figurations meant to twentieth-century thought and writing and, specifically, to modernism. In the end, Wells becomes a kind of philosopher of time. His articulations of both historical experience and of temporality veer away from the melancholic affect of many of his contemporaries because, for Wells, the future is not an inert space. It palpitates with its own life, an existence already destined, incipient and oncoming.

Modernism, of course, is famous for its own engagement with time. "The structure of history, the uninterrupted forward movement of clocks, the procession of days, seasons, and years, and simple common sense tell us that time is irreversible and moves forward at a steady rate," Stephen Kern noted in his landmark *The Culture of Time and Space, 1880–1914*, "Yet [in modernism] these features of traditional time were also challenged as artists and intellectuals envisioned times that reversed themselves, moved at irregular rhythms, and even came to a dead stop. In the *fin de siècle*, time's arrow did not always fly straight and true."[3] Kern and many other cultural historians point to the technologies of wireless transmission, telephone, sound recording, factory automation, film, motorized vehicles, and airplane flight, along with scientific developments stemming from Darwin in the nineteenth century and Einstein in the twentieth, as the sparks that helped ignite modernism's temporal experiments.[4] So many major writers of this period engaged time at thematic, formal, and philosophical levels as to make it almost the master figure of the period, such that Wyndham Lewis in *Time and Western Man* came to bemoan modernism, in its very heyday, as a literature swallowed by time, "all that welter of thought and sensation which has recently culminated in Relativity Theory," as he put it.[5] Lewis's critique was influential, but more centrally it shows how fully the immersion in temporality was recognized by modernism itself, its central object of study and also a constant reminder of literature's inevitable enmeshment in the principles it contemplates. Here, for instance, is Thomas Mann, perhaps speaking for all of modernism: "The cause [of a certain apathy and enervation] is our very sense of time itself—which, if it flows with uninterrupted regularity, threatens to elude us and which is so closely related to and bound up with our sense of life that the one sense cannot be weakened without the second's experiencing pain and injury."[6]

Such instances of reflexivity are part of the modernist temporal immersion, which takes a stunning variety of forms. These include the vast expansion of the present moment, a formal, thematic and theoretical predilection; the primacy and force of the past in determining the flow of thought, feeling, and action in the moment-by-moment experience of the present, as well as in establishing the fundamentals of psychic life; the indissolubility of temporal units from one another, where one time scheme mixes and confuses with others, as Bergson taught was its primary characteristic, time defined by fluidity and flux rather than by order or measurability; the suspicion that the management of knowable, official time is deeply rooted in Western regimes of power and thus the exploration of personal modes of experiencing time as they jar against (and perhaps resist) the chronos of clocks, timetables, schedules, and the whole welter of synchronic urban experience (Eliot: "The tolling bell / measures time not our time, rung by the unhurried / Ground swell, a time / Older than the time of chronometers"), what Kern calls, in a nice understatement, "the heterogeneity of private time and its conflict with public time."[7] Anchoring these large and canonical topics in the 1884 Prime Meridian Conference that sought to establish Greenwich Mean Time as the worldwide time standard, Adam Barrows writes,

> As political and scientific representatives of "civilized" nations argued over the value of synchronized civil time, literary artists were experimenting with the representation of human temporality in ways that would radically alter prevailing aesthetic forms.... The modernists negotiated, without ever necessarily resolving, a complex array of temporal models, alternately centered in the body, the mind, the state, the empire, and the globe.[8]

It would seem, then, that a rich harmony with modernism might appear as we consider Wells's temporal experiments, and, indeed, some of the most intense and productive entanglements between Wells and his modernist peers emerge in these interactions around time. However, the divergences in emphasis are ultimately even more stark than the mutualities. The success of *The Outline*, for instance, was particularly galling to some notable modernists, such as Eliot, representing an approach to the past that seemed to fly in the face of modernism's primary creeds, such as individual, private vision; expertise; refinement of audience; and the rejection of generalization and prizing of uniqueness. The utopias and other visions of planned worlds, too, triggered immediate responses. Wells's utopias and related works engaged his contemporaries and a century of later writers, many of whom sought very directly to critique the Wellsian ideal of hopeful futurity. "Overwhelmingly," Mark R. Hillegas writes, "the most important influences... in creating the modern anti-utopias were the scientific romances, utopias, and future histories of H. G. Wells."[9] But these critiques are only a small part of the story. The real difference is that when it comes to the future, modernism's theater goes dark. Ernst Bloch writes, in *The Principle of Hope*, that philosophy has entirely neglected the future—"essentially only 'backward dawning' has previously been described and investigated"—and this silence is especially remarkable when we consider modernism.[10] Perhaps the future is simply not amenable to a project tightly affiliated with the enlarged private world, the movements of interior life, the depths of memory, and the bubbling, Freudian cauldrons of early development.[11] There are clashes, too, in sensibility, since the belief in human progress, often entailed in Wells's futuristic thought, tended to incite deep skepticism among modernists, as it does among critics today. In Heather Love's influential account of queer modern writers, these "turn their backs on the future: they choose isolation, turn toward the past, or choose to live in a present disconnected from any larger historical continuum."[12] Critics have embraced the queer temporalities that Love and others have theorized, and for good reason. Nevertheless, the future need not be understood as inevitably embodying a suspect progressivism. When we read Wells, the living, vital quality of futurity becomes as sensory and determining as the present, and its contradictions present dynamic and often surprising structures of thought and feeling. In Wells's lifetime of writings, to make the strongest claim, new temporalities are envisioned that cannot be squared with the prevailing models we have inherited from the nineteenth and twentieth centuries.

Of course, modernism did see itself as having stakes in the future, though its futural forms and modes typically register uncertainty and hesitation, the future viewed from and into a place of semidarkness. Many of Yeats's most powerful poems end with questions—"The Second Coming," "Leda and the Swan," "Among School Children," to name a few—and these, in leaving the reader suspended, indicate a distinctive forward-leaning temporality, hovering on the edge of the future. "And what rough beast, its hour come round at last, slouches toward Bethlehem to be born?" would seem to press its reflections on two thousand years of Christian history into an unknown, frightening next stage and to do so in the form of vision, a prized mode for futurists of all kinds and for Yeats quite markedly. Yet even so, in another sense the future registers as a blank; the rough beast, after all, is an exuberantly uncertain referent. It is a poem that stands on a brink, troubled and looking, and it takes that very threshold as its temporality.[13] Such thresholds embody what I have elsewhere described as a structure of imminence characterizing modernist thinking about violence and what Saint-Amour has posited as a "perpetual inter-war," a way of experiencing and writing time as continually invaded by a threat of future violence, a modality, he argues, expressed most fully in modernist encyclopedic form between the wars.[14] Saint-Amour's work is important, among other reasons, for the way it shows how modernism—but not only modernism—embedded the future in its present. The idea of anticipation, of what Saint-Amour considers a shared *pre–traumatic stress disorder*, is revealed as an agonized center of modernism's psychic investments and as a primary driver of its formal achievements.[15] If we follow Saint-Amour, Wells suddenly and strangely appears right at the flashing hub of modernism, given Wells's prominence as the most famous and committed anticipator of the era. Still, we should be clear that Wells's reach into the future, strikingly varied and spread across his full writing life, breaks free of the dread of tense futurity. It is one of Wells's most moving attributes that he can always take a further step forward, always see into a yet more distant or different future. There are, of course, other currents in the literary life of the period to consider, most notably Futurism, yet even there the future can seem static and unreal. It is clear, reading the Futurist manifestos, that the movement generated its primary energies from its gleeful attack on everything "passéist" rather than on any sustained concentration on what might come next. If we return to our list of Wellsian verbs, the only one that really connects him with his peers in the period is "imagine." That is the joining, but also the parting, of the ways.

# PART 1: THINKING THROUGH TIME

## I. CLASHING TEMPORALITIES

"One cannot choose but wonder . . ." So muses the frame narrator of *The Time Machine*, in his final thoughts, closing out the Time Traveller's tale with his own observations:

> Will he ever return? It may be that he swept back into the past, and fell among the blood-drinking, hairy savages of the Age of Unpolished Stone. . . . Or did he go forward, into one of the nearer ages, in which men are still men, but with the riddles of our own time answered and its wearisome problems solved? Into the manhood of the race: for I, for my own part, cannot think that these latter days of weak experiment, fragmentary theory and mutual discord are indeed man's culminating time! I say, for my own part. He, I know—for the question had been discussed among us long before the Time Machine was made— thought but cheerlessly of the Advancement of Mankind, and saw in the grow- ing pile of civilization only a foolish heaping that must inevitably fall back upon and destroy its makers in the end. If that is so, it remains for us to live as though it were not so. But to me the future is still black and blank—is a vast ignorance, lit at a few casual places by the memory of his story. And I have by me, for my comfort, two strange white flowers—shrivelled now, and brown and flat and brittle—to witness that even when mind and strength had gone, grati- tude and a mutual tenderness still lived on in the heart of man.[16]

It is a great misreading. After all, if the narrator believes the Traveller's story at the level of factual truth—as his hypotheses on the Traveller's possible where- abouts in one or another ancient age confirm—then his further reflections are manifestly inappropriate. "But to me the future is still black and blank," even though he has just heard, in riveting detail and in all its lurid particulars, what that future will bring, in the long future of AD 802,701 as well as many millions of years further along, when the earth has waned, life nearly extinguished. The narrator's ideal of "the manhood of the race," his hopeful assumption that there will be a time when all the world's wearisome problems have been solved, jars badly against the spectacle of Morlocks and Eloi and indeed brings to mind the Traveller's own learning curve over the course of his eight days in the future, his initial hypotheses about the Golden Age as a time of perfect harmony between mankind and its environment turning out, of course, to be a grisly irony. In part, the narrator's flat misreading of the story is a matter of temperament. He and the Traveller, it seems, have always differed, his warm optimism sharply distinguished from the Traveller's brooding predictions that all our progress and modernity will only "fall back upon and destroy its makers in the end."

Notably, the narrator's attachment to the withered flowers stands as sign of a persistent Romanticism that the story has done nothing to foster. The flower is as overdetermined a symbol for Romanticism as one could find, but the sentiment attached to these blossoms—as distinct from what we might adduce, say, to Wordsworth's daffodils or Tennyson's flower in the crannied wall—seems entirely willed, even perverse. For one thing, the flowers in question, given to the Traveller by Weena (and of apparently minor interest to him except as a genetic token of the veracity of his travels) may be a reminder of "gratitude and a mutual tenderness . . . in the heart of man," but more certainly they recall the highly equivocal nature of the Traveller's treatment of Weena throughout his time in the future, especially in the ultimate negligence that leaves her to the wildfire and/or Morlocks. For their part, the flowers signify the one and only accomplishment of the Eloi. Interestingly, Wells's utopians and future dwellers always take special pride and care of their flowers, which invariably are figured as entirely different from—and hence an improvement upon—our own. But then, Wells could not select a more unimpressive token for the world's progress than flowers. What makes one flower an improvement over another, anyway? Plants played a key role in the initial science of genetics, but a million years in the future, their refinement signals the waning not only of progress but even of change. The sense of the world as a cultivated garden, where humans have the leisure to tinker with their blooms, functions less a sign of our return to Eden than as a nod to decadence and decay, always the nagging *doppelgängers* of Wells's previews of forward progress. As Vincent Sherry writes of *The Time Machine*, "This fiction of the future thus spells out an intractable paradox: a progressive history, which is sped ahead by the engine of progress that is its narrative vehicle and so advanced to its imagined conclusion, reveals the face of contemporary decadence."[17] If the far future marks the deeply disturbing endpoint of decadence in degeneration, heaving also a final gasp of Romanticism, then the frame narrator's attachment to the flowers signals how fully he has missed (or willfully ignored) the story's ramifications. In these senses, the epilogue fulfills the role of frame narration, in one of its recognizable iterations, to create counterforces and tensions against the main thrust of the internal narrative, a move in keeping with Wells's more general tendency to incorporate opposing voices into all of his texts.

But this is not quite satisfactory as an account of the epilogue's disturbance of the main narrative: what the epilogue showcases above all is the disruptive copresence of incompatible temporal scales. This clashing of timeframes resurfaces continually in *The Time Machine* and, more, can be named the essential principle of Wells's temporal journeys in many genres. The problem for the frame narrator is that he cannot reconcile what the Traveller has displayed of the far future with his own aspirations for the nearer future, forged from contemporary progressive theories (such as those germinating among the Fabians), cultivated in the club-like atmosphere that pervades the novella's frame, revealing a vaguely socialist idealism and, notably, overlapping with Wells's goals. In this nearer future, well in advance of the Eloi's soft, passive androgyny, "the manhood of the race" might be apprehended; a traveler to that manageable distance might well be catapulted into the world of Wells's utopias and anticipations—not yet written in 1895 but incubating. The frame narrator's stubborn refusal to think backward from the facts of the tale's later age is not simply willful, in other words; it is impossible to reconcile these differing futural schemes. Even when Wells's forays into the nearer future have nothing utopic about them, they remain qualitatively different from the far-future visions. To be sure, all require an analysis and extrapolation of current phenomena in the social and biological structure. Yet those set within a few hundred years still feature our own world, its trends exaggerated, its propensities realized, for better or for worse—so cities and transportation look higher, faster, more advanced and mechanized, either more congested and chaotic or more efficient and rational; class relations are either harmonized or on the brink of all-out revolution; the problems of food, homes, work, geography, and war have either been solved or run dangerously out of control.

But in the much later times, such questions have either disappeared or become elemental, the class warfare of the nineteenth century, say, made biological and endemic—the condition of existence—800,000 years later. The dramas of human desire and failure are reduced to acquiescence, and, even further along, all of humanity is swept away. " 'I cannot convey the sense of abominable desolation that hung over the world,'" the Traveller says of his brief venture into the late days of the earth, when humans have long since disappeared, the world has ceased to rotate, the only plants are mosses that live "'in a perpetual twilight,'" and for animal life there is only a screeching enormous butterfly and gigantic crabs whose tentacles, in tickling the neck of the Traveller, invite a primal terror (*TM*, 83, 82). In these sequences, Wells strikes the note of desolation, silence, stillness, an incoming darkness that washes in on the tide of an eclipse; ultimately, what is presented is the oncoming extinction of all life. For the Traveller to witness the end has something of awe about it, something magnetic and alluring: "'So I travelled, stopping ever and again, in great strides of a thousand years or more, drawn on by the mystery of the earth's fate, watching with a strange fascination the sun grow larger and duller in the westward sky, and the life of the old earth ebb away'" (*TM*, 84). As in the beginning, so in the end, life registers according to geology, astronomy, orbits, and cycles.

The nature of the objects of our imagination and the systems in which we understand them shift according to the temporal scale in which they are viewed. Such temporal extension is thus incompatible with the dreams of a few hundred years forward in time, demanding and providing a different imaginative and intellectual sensibility, logic, and language. It is a difference, too, in forms of science: if social science is asked to rule the nearer future, the far reaches succumb to the forces of evolution, thermodynamics, entropy. These temporal incompatibilities might be said to have generic analogues as well, with the novel's normative ranges and scales of attention hesitating in view of the longer schemes being deduced in the sciences; out of such disjunctions the scientific romance finds its space. As Aaron Rosenberg writes, in a brilliant assessment of *The Time Machine* as a key text in rescaling literary form to match the time-and-space dimensions of evolution and the Anthropocene, "*The Time Machine* . . . raises questions about whether attempting to write fiction on the scales at which the biological, social, and political become visible as planetary forces necessitates breaking with realism, and, if so, which genres are better suited to the task."[18]

Wells's science journalism strikes at moments late in the earth's life, moments similar to the farthest voyages of the Traveller, and it, too, suggests an order of thinking that jars against anything offered in more habitable ranges. Taking human evolution down a different path from the story of Eloi and Morlocks, his essay "The Man of the Year Million," published in 1893 in *Pall Mall Gazette*, prefigures our descendants looking like this: a huge brain; the body mostly atrophied (with the exception of the hand); a face no longer needing ears, nose, or brow ridges (hence mostly forehead and eyes); and the inner organs evolved so as to have eliminated that cumbersome requirement, the eating of food. Here we are:

"In the centre of [a] transparent chameleon-tinted dome is a circular white marble basin filled with some clear, mobile, amber liquid and in this plunge and float strange beings. Are they birds?

"They are the descendants of man—at dinner. Watch them as they hop on their hands . . . about the pure white marble floor. Great hands they have, enormous brains, soft, liquid, soulful eyes. Their whole muscular system, their legs, their abdomens, are shrivelled to nothing, a dangling, degraded pendant to their minds."[19]

Wells is having fun, I think, with the disgust these beings must offer to his readers, and the fact that the men of the year million are close in form both to the Martians in *The War of the Worlds* and the Grand Lunar in *The First Men in the Moon* indicates that this creepy nonhumanity might have moral as well as physical and aesthetic ramifications.[20] Still, for all the humor and revulsion of these jellyfish-like humans, and despite some distancing moves, pathos reenters at the essay's close, when the existential threat even to these highly specialized beings breaks into the narrative.[21] In the decades around the turn of the century, the received principle, dating primarily to the physicist Lord Kelvin's work in the mid–nineteenth century, was that the sun was slowly expending its energy, which in turn would lead to the earth's ultimate cooling. The question was simply one of time, how many millennia this would take, and with all estimates millions of years in the future, it carried no sense of emergency—thus the cooling of the earth as threat differed substantially from the nineteenth century's Malthusian predictions of worldwide famine, which had a significant impact on Wells, or our own climate-change crisis.[22] This ultimate cooldown loomed over the scientific imagination, especially for those thinking about the earth in these larger units of time, and Wells sends his latter-day humans in this little essay into all-out, hopeless survival mode, as they burrow underground, straining hopelessly to adapt their way out of the oncoming endgame.

We must imagine these creatures . . . in galleries and laboratories deep down in the bowels of the earth. The whole world will be snow-covered and piled with ice; all animals, all vegetation vanished, except this last branch of the tree of life. The last men have gone ever deeper, following the diminishing heat of the planet, and vast metallic shafts and ventilators make way for the air they need.

(*JP*, 9)

Extinction: this is the big threat, the overarching condition of the future, that which shadows all such reflections. Wells wrote several pieces on extinction, and it enters regularly into his longer works as well, always with the ultimate question abiding: will humans, too, become extinct? What are the right frames even to begin to think about that prospect? In one essay, he merges biology with the terms of literature. Thinking of Sophocles and Shakespeare as chroniclers of the tragic, he presses the issue onto a different scale: "The life that has schemed and struggled and committed itself, the life that has played and lost, comes at last to the pitiless judgment of time, and is slowly and remorselessly annihilated. This is the saddest chapter of biological science—the tragedy of Extinction" (*EWS*, 169). Tragedy is perhaps an inapt choice, however, since, for all its featuring of the individual reckoning with his minute place and utter insignificance in the universe, as a premise, the conflict matters, and the human story will always be the one that tragedy elevates. By contrast, the primary principle of Wells's extinction narratives is that there is no reason why mankind should fare any better than predecessors like the dodo or, more pointedly, those earlier creatures who had dominated the earth in their own day. "In the long galleries of the geological museum," a place Wells spends much imaginative time,

> are the records of judgments that have been passed graven upon the rocks. Here, for instance, are the huge bones of the "Atlantosaurus," one of the mightiest land animals that this planet has ever seen. . . . And yet this giant has passed away, and left no children to inherit the earth. No living thing can be traced to these monsters; they are at an end among the branchings of the tree of life.
>
> (*EWS*, 169)

Without fail, such reasoning points toward humankind, the planet's current rulers, and, with little fanfare, to a scenario like this: "the earth desert through a pestilence, and two men, and then one man, looking extinction in the face" (*EWS*, 172). To see the story of life from the point of view of those being eliminated radically darkens the mood, the emphasis on dead ends ramifying in both biological and epistemological terms:

> The long roll of paleontology is half filled with the records of extermination; whole orders, families, groups, and classes have passed away and left no mark and no tradition upon the living fauna of the world. Many fossils of the older rocks are labelled in our museums, "of doubtful affinity." Nothing living has any part like them. . . . Index fingers they are, pointing into unfathomable darkness, and saying only one thing clearly, the word "Extinction."
>
> (*EWS*, 170)

Here and throughout his writings on species and their fates, Wells fore-grounds questions of knowledge—or, better, of ignorance, what we can know and also where the great lapses and ineffable blanks emerge in what *The Outline* calls "the record of the rocks." In amplifying this idea of "the record of the rocks," Wells is in contemporary company; geologists had used the metaphor since at least the 1850s, and high-stakes debates about the age of the earth fueled Wells's writings from the outset.[23] (Interestingly, the one course Wells failed as a science student in London was geology.) Like Freud and the unconscious mind, Wells takes the tour of geology and paleontology in the spirit of the historian of knowledge, thinking about our ability to decipher, follow leads, and build scien-tific case studies and also stressing those places where the records end. These scenarios are meant to check our hubris and remind us of the nearly infinite stock of life that is already lost, and they create a strange sense of invisible forces of enormous, possible antagonism exerting themselves around us. It could be a cosmic catastrophe, it could be the advent of a more powerful competitor, it could be climate change, it could (most likely for Wells) be a pestilence: "for all we know even now we may be quite unwittingly evolving some new and more terrible plague—a plague that will not take ten or twenty or thirty per cent., as plagues have done in the past, but the entire hundred."[24]

In these scenarios, past and future, one animal has particular resonance: the American bison. Wells comes back to it on several occasions; in his accounts, as in many contexts today where the bison serves as object lesson in ecological and indigenous catastrophe, what most arrests the imagination is the spectacle of numbers. We are invited to turn our minds back to the mid–nineteenth cen-tury, not so many years before Wells's writing, to visualize those millions of bison crowding the plains (today it is estimated that up to thirty million bison roamed the Great Plains region), a field of shaggy brown in all directions, the very figure for multitude—and then, as if in a moment, gone. As an emblem of extinction, too, the bison casts a shadow over humanity that is stronger and more ominous than examples from the prehistoric age, not only because it is more recent but because it stands as analogy to the people with whom it is asso-ciated, Native Americans. The possible elimination of Native Americans as a people (or as many peoples) carries a different kind of affective weight from the specter of the last man, in the vastly distant future, staring extinction in the face. Both offer stark suggestions of the gravest and greatest threats to human life. But again, it is the scales that are different; events from the recent past and the foreseeable future invite affective and intellectual responses that, as with the frame narrator of *The Time Machine*, may not correlate with the spectacle of disappearance when the lever is set all the way forward. It is a matter, in part, of what is fathomable: the lost bison, the genocide of Native Americans, yes (incredible, but true); the evolution out of all recognition and eventual extinction of humankind, not quite. Wells does his best to keep the extinction of humanity always present and pressing: "No; man's complacent assumption of the future is too confident," he writes in "The Extinction of Man" (1898). "Even now, for all we can tell, the coming terror may be crouching for its spring and the fall of humanity be at hand. In the case of every other predominant animal the world has ever seen, I repeat, the hour of its complete ascendency has been the eve of its entire overthrow" (*CPM*, 179).

One thing, I hope, should have begun to emerge from these reflections on extinction and the end of earthly life: every journey into the future entails an equal and opposite journey into the past. There is a parallelism in Wells's approach to future and past, almost a harmony (if it weren't that the content of what is recognized is almost invariably so grim). If irreconcilable time schemes can clash and create a sense of discordant affect and understanding—the Time Traveller versus the frame narrator, that which makes for horror and resignation versus that which inspires one to work for social change in the present—here the view is of destiny, an aesthetically satisfying sense of time patterns falling into place. Thinking of the past and future balancing together in the mind makes for a larger sense of order in the scheme of the world. In that sense, it is only partially in accord with evolution, since evolution, like relativity, is largely affiliated with randomness; in both systems, a *sense* of order is produced by the sheer force of accumulated small occurrences transpiring over huge spans (of time, of space). As Wells writes in *The Science of Life*, "mutation seems in general to be a perfectly random process. There is no evidence of adaptive striving or set purpose in the way new varieties turn up.... Out of these random, purposeless gropings ... Evolution builds."[25] As we will see more fully in the next chapter, the idea that evolution represents progress, or even that it occurs according to a pattern, is a serious error, albeit one with real trenchancy. But in thinking about the past and future together, Wells wants nevertheless to stress the ways those patterns can be known. He was adamant about how the past and future can cohabitate in one intellectual setting, with a single set of mental operations covering analysis of both temporal realms. (Woolf: "behind the cotton wool is hidden a pattern ... the whole world is a work of art"; Eliot: "history is a pattern / Of timeless moments.")[26]

In essence, Wells proselytized for a new cast of mind, a temperament formed in scientific principles, driven by a curiosity and moral investment in the future, where the past and future are honed together as comparable schemes of understanding. He made this case most directly in a 1902 speech before the Royal

Institution, reprinted later that year as *The Discovery of the Future*.[27] In the initial audience were many from Wells's circle(s), scientists, writers, and political leaders, his friends Richard Gregory (a major figure in science culture and the editor of *Nature*) and Joseph Conrad among them, and at the time of publication, this little book, like countless others now forgotten, made a splash among such diverse and influential readers. As is often the case with Wells's nonfiction, *The Discovery of the Future* has the ring of mantra, Wells staking his claims boldly, making the type of ground-clearing move characteristic of modernism in its manifesto mood. There are, declares Wells, two types of mind:

> The first of these two types of mind, and it is, I think the predominant type, the type of the majority of living people, is that which seems scarcely to think of the future at all, which regards it as a sort of blank non-existence upon which the advancing present will presently write events. The second type, which is, I think, a more modern and much less abundant type of mind, thinks constantly and by preference of things to come, and of present things mainly in relation to the results that must arise from them. The former type of mind, when one gets it in its purity, is retrospective in habit, and it interprets the things of the present, and gives value to this and denies it to that, entirely with relation to the past. The latter type of mind is constructive in habit, it interprets the things of the present and gives value to this or that, entirely in relation to things designed or foreseen.[28]

One thinks, in this new schema, of how often modernism was "retrospective in habit," of how its claim to "make it new" was qualified by the long, deep inflows from many entwined pasts.

Seven years later, Futurism would establish itself as the movement that despised the past; eyes ahead, spurning the old Italian culture that Filippo Marinetti found so stifling, Futurism was to embody "the mind of youth," in Wells's phrase above. Marinetti and Wells share the sensibility of being weighed down (rather than inspired) by their respective traditions.[29] Marinetti will say, "You ought to fear everything from the moss-grown past. All your hope should be in the Future. Put your trust in Progress, which is always right even when it is wrong, because it is movement, life, struggle, hope," and the overlapping in spirit with Wells is audible, at least in a general sense. But Marinetti and his peers framed their agenda with a destructive glee. They famously denigrated women and lauded war in the most flamboyant terms. They sought a wild and reckless persona for their young movement, which would, for instance, "renounce the old Venice. . . . Your Grand Canal, widened and dredged, must become a great commercial port. Trains and trams, launched on wide roads built over canals that have finally been filled in, will bring you mountains of goods and a shrewd, wealthy, busy crowd of industrialists and businessmen!"[30] Wells may share Marinetti's resistance to sentiment about all things traditional, but he is after something quite different; to turn Venice into Liverpool is not his plan. Nor is there a cult of speed in Wells's futures. Speed is a fact, a premise and beginning point from which to construct larger anticipations or expand specific designs. Worldwide interconnection and rapid movement of people, things, and ideas stand as the foundations of the future—it will be shaped by these—but they do not warrant veneration. In fact, I think we can say that while Marinetti chooses the future as his motto, he does so more as a signpost of rejecting the past and as the temporality best suited to the new technology he embraces, while Wells is interested in the future itself, wanting to understand what it will entail in every detail and to shape it in concrete terms.

Certainly, for Wells the future requires no capital *F*. It can be known, just as we can know the long past; it is a kind of home for Wells, so much of his imaginative life being oriented there. "I am venturing to suggest to you," he wrote in *The Discovery of the Future*, "that along certain lines and with certain qualifications and limitations a working knowledge of things in the future is a possible and practicable thing" (*DF*, 69). Two points are bundled together in this key concept: the first is that the past, once scrutinized, seems far less certainly known than instinct or ordinary assumption allow. Memory is a form of produced knowledge and an unstable archive, rather than a fixed and absolute fund of truth from the past, as historiography since the 1960s has recognized and today's memory studies has elaborated. And modernism was at the forefront in pressuring memory's factuality. For Wells, if the past is much less securely known than it initially seems, the future is much more knowable; this is the second and more unsettling point. "About the past I would suggest we are inclined to overestimate our certainty, just as I think we are inclined to underestimate the certainties of the future" (*DF*, 69). Such a mindset belongs to the scientist, Wells wants to say, someone comfortable with principles of causation and evolution and possessing a quality of mind that, like the relativity principles that were already beginning to emerge, is ready to work according to hypotheses that might yield confirmation only many years, even centuries, later.

For Wells, what matters is a habit of thought, and his best analogy for how we might read the future is, not surprisingly, drawn from the lessons in how we have learned to decode the past:

And what I would insist upon is that this further knowledge is a new kind of knowledge, obtained in a new kind of way. We know today . . . the form and the habits of creatures that no living being has ever met, that no human eye has ever regarded, and the character of scenery that no man has ever seen or can ever possibly see; we picture to ourselves the labyrinthodon raising its clumsy head above the water of the carboniferous swamps in which he lived and we figure the pterodactyls, these great bird lizards, flapping their way athwart the forests of the Mesozoic age. . . . A vast amount of detail in that farther picture is now fixed and finite for all time. . . . We have become possessed of a new and once unsuspected history of the world . . .

I want particularly to insist upon this, that all this outer past—this non-historical past—is the product of a new and keener habit of inquiry, and no sort of revelation.

(*DF*, 71)

It is a unique portrayal of how we navigate our way through time and one that in a sense caps off Victorian controversies about the age of the earth, which had been fierce (and still were in 1902), given the essential challenge the earth's extreme antiquity posed to the biblical account of creation. Wells's rendering of his—and by extension his readers'—absolute confidence in the validity of the scientific reconstruction of the past suggests a new zeitgeist, where one's modernity is bound up with one's complete immersion in this way of assessing reality. In the passage, too, Wells not only declares his allegiances but demonstrates in his own prose how vitally the long past lives in the imagination; we can see its presence as we read.

The essay's key strategy, then, is to apply the logic of how we have come to know and believe in a past well before human existence to how we might know and come to believe in the future, including even a posthuman one. I am reminded, in considering Wells's reasoning here, of the landmark Armory show in 1913 in New York City, in which works of French postimpressionists and cubists were shown for the first time in the United States. In the exhibit, the organizers used the example of impressionism as a kind of lesson. Showing several once-groundbreaking works of impressionism, which had shocked initial viewers in the 1880s, the organizers made their case: now those works seem ordinary, for we have learned how to view them. Similarly will the works here, radical at the first encounter, become normalized once the viewing public finds the aesthetic idiom to receive them, and in so doing, whole new vistas of perception and thought will open. Modernism certainly wanted to shock, and at the same time, it knew that every generation has its senses and understanding jolted by arresting, unfamiliar forms, eventually to be normalized. Even T. S. Eliot could say, in "The Use of Poetry and the Use of Criticism," that all writers want to be widely read—want even to be popular—though of course for those in the vanguard, readers will only emerge over time, as the confusion of the first encounter becomes softened, the reading strategies learned.[31] Yet with *The Discovery of the Future* there remains something radical, even a hundred years later, about this proposal: "I believe that the time is drawing near when it will become possible to suggest a systematic exploration of the future," a "possibility of an inductive future to correspond with that great inductive past of geology and archeology" (*DF*, 73).

Wells reminds the reader that, strange as his assertion may at first seem, in fact all branches of science rely on a structure of prediction (hypotheses); all are essentially extrapolative. Here he follows Huxley, who had coined the term "retrospective prophecy" to describe the scientific method, in an 1880 lecture/essay that establishes a close parallel between how astronomers can predict planetary events hundreds of years in advance and how we can determine the nature of the far past.[32] And thus Wells:

> If I am right in saying that science aims at prophecy, and if the specialist in each science is in fact doing his best now to prophecy within the limits of his field, what is there to stand in the way of our building up this growing body of forecast into an ordered picture of the future that will be just as certain, just as strictly science, and perhaps just as detailed as the picture that has been built up within the last hundred years of the geological past?
>
> (*DF*, 74)

Even with such confident assertions, Wells recognizes that there remains, in his scheme, a necessary leap of faith, that there will always be some imbalance between past and future as realms of knowledge. In the second half of the essay, he shifts away from defining a process of temporal thinking that unlocks the future in the same way it has revealed the past and into a statement of optimism about what will be found when we do turn our attention to the next stages. This hypothesizing about what the future will bring culminates in a heady rendition of one of his core beliefs, that "All the world is heavy with the promise of greater things, and a day will come, one day in the unending succession of days, when beings, beings who are now latent in our thoughts and hidden in our loins, shall stand upon this earth as one stands upon a footstool, and shall laugh and reach out their hands amid the stars," thus welding his thesis of the future's knowability into a muscular, benevolent vision of what that future might hold (*DF*, 85). Of course, such a giddy endpoint is not at all entailed. On the contrary, Wells concedes that, like the frame narrator of *The Time Machine*, he chooses, against the best scientific surmises, to believe "in the coherency and purpose in the world and in the greatness of human destiny. Worlds may freeze and suns may perish, but there stirs something within us now that can never die again" (*DF*, 82–83). Wells's surging optimism threatens (or perhaps endeavors) to over-power even his own argument—and we should note that he reused the precise language of this ending, with future humans reaching out from the earth-footstool into the heavens, in at least two other works, *The Food of the Gods* and *The Outline of History*, two texts marked just as strongly by extremely dark and terrifying narratives of the violent, destructive quality of life welded to an unquenchable hopefulness. It expressed, with exactitude, the form of his highly willed, futural optimism.

There are other ways, too, in which Wells muddies his picture exactly when he is calling for a new form of clarity about the nature and scope of knowledge. If we return to that first passage from *The Discovery of the Future*, which established two frames of mind, one with a forward inclination, the other mired in the past, we find Wells concluding via a conventional East-West analogy, where the West is associated with all that is modern, active, and future oriented, the East with what is backward, passive, and past: "It is in the active mood of thought," he says of his futurist, "while the former is in the passive; it is the mind of youth, it is the mind more manifest about the western nations, while the former is the mind of age, the mind of the oriental" (*DF*, 62). Similar to Conrad in *Heart of Darkness*, Wells deploys the most familiar of East/West binaries in part as a way to deconstruct Western self-satisfaction (you think you are the Western, but really you are the Oriental). But such a move, as Conrad's critics have amply shown, drops him back instantly into the initial premises of a simple and unequal binarism; to tar one's nemeses with the slur of being Oriental is hardly a progressive tactic. Instead, what is striking is how these racial and imperial categories continue to undergird thinking that, in other ways, is so dramatically dismissive of their framing assumptions. Wells's recourse to the passive Oriental calls to mind, moreover, a surprising moment in the dying-earth sequence of *The Time Machine*, when the Traveller, having rested his machine, observes the sky those millions years in the future: "'Overhead it was a deep Indian red and starless, and south-eastward it grew brighter to a glowing scarlet where, cut by the horizon, lay the huge hull of the sun, red and motionless'" (*TM*, 82). The sun as a ship's hull, the sky Indian—here on this far fringe of the world's future history, the Victorian imaginary remains active, still helping organize the thought structures needed to consider the rela-tion of one Western man to the wider world into which he has voyaged. Such momentary reappearances of the ready-to-hand ideological forms of Victorian culture remind us of their hold on the imagination, a kind of rebuke to the modernizing aspirations motivating Wells's presentation of temporality.

So there are limits and internal checks that seem to pull Wells back to the present, yet his ideas about the way the future and the past together engender a new field of thought, with extensive ramifications for politics, literature, and consciousness, are a striking and unremarked aspect of modern(ist) thinking. The very idea that there is such a thing as a prophetic cast of mind specifically carved from science and enlarged in its name might make us pause. No era has ever really become comfortable with its prophets and fortune tellers, and modernism seems especially Eliotic in this respect; Prufrock's "for I am no prophet, and this is no great matter" yields to Gerontion's "concitation / Of the backward devils," reprising the twisted fortune tellers of the *Inferno*, not to mention the most canonical of false prophets, *The Waste Land*'s Madame Sosostris. We might think of Leopold Bloom's unsealed forecast, stashed in a drawer in *Ulysses*; more generally, as Saint-Amour notes, *Ulysses* "teems with allusions to prophets and prophetic texts, with diegetic instances of prognostication, with skeptical anatomies of prophecy's social function. It is as if Joyce's book were an encyclopedia of prophecy."[33] To be sure, foretelling, like all modes of speech, has its place in *Ulysses*, yet even in Saint-Amour's generous account of the vibrancy of such motifs, it is foreclosure that dominates. In *Ulysses*, and more fully in modernism, the future is restricted to tight spaces, and its traditional harbingers fare accordingly, highly present only to recount their obsolescence, inadequacy, muteness. The most overtly prophetic in tone of the British modernists is Lawrence, and we certainly hear the influence and affiliation of Wells in Lawrence's tirades against the present and in his calls for new worlds to be born from the ashes of the old. All of Lawrence's alter-egos, from Birkin to Somers to Cipriano to Mellors, not to mention his raging narratorial voice in the nonfictional works of social critique, carry overtones of prophetic utterance. Then again, Lawrence's speculative impulses almost always come down to rants against the present, Nietzschean in spirit; if there is a vision of the future, it is either a reconstruction of the imagined past (as in *The Plumed Serpent*) or a vague premonitional insistence, inevitably bound to his favored image, the Phoenix. As Forster declares in *Aspects of the Novel*, "Prophecy—in our sense [and here he is thinking in part of Lawrence]—is a tone of voice."[34] In Forster's iteration of the prophetic novel, there is no fortune telling.

Wells stood in many ways alone in his eagerness to test the dark waters of the unknown ahead, and he identified strongly with the many prophets who have appeared in every phase of Western history (to whom he gives special attention in *The Outline of History*), some revered, for example the biblical prophets, others despised. Anticipation as a project has always been dangerous, as Wells knew and, in a sense, embraced. One is reminded of the precarious lives of those

Scythian soothsayers in Herodotus's *The Histories* who are called in when the king is ailing and asked to divine what evil person may be responsible; after a complicated procedure, either the convict is brutally executed, or, if not, it is the fortune tellers who will be killed.[35] Risk aside, prognosticating was a calling for Wells, or perhaps a profession. As the decades passed, Wells was increasingly recognized as a kind of prophet and was regularly asked for prediction, to be given in the form of speech, article, or radio broadcast. When Wells suggested on the BBC that England might consider a Professoriate of Prediction, he certainly could cite the worldwide interest in his own predictive habits. There is a true stubbornness in this mode of thought for Wells, which had its first extended treatment in *Anticipations* (1901) and which bubbled up regularly over the years, in his rage that, as he worried, *no one has listened*. We might recall those prefaces to *The War in the Air* of 1921 and 1941, where Wells seethes with a sort of outraged pride in having predicted global aerial war, and now here was the real thing, more violent and unstoppable than ever. Like so many other writers, Wells scripted his own epitaph, which he hoped would read "I told you so."

## II. TIME TRAVELING

For Wells, this project has a name: *anticipation*. Of Wells's books, *Anticipations* is one that dates badly, in part because it comes laced with spasms of racism and callous complacency about such matters as the probable mass extermination of the unfit, also because his predictions range from uncannily accurate to entirely off course. Yet it is an important document of this period, for its bravado construction of a new temporal mode of thought and writing. For all we might wish to forget some parts of it, *Anticipations* is a significant work of the era, as was recognized at the time; it was very widely read and became the turning point in Wells's career, in his rise to fame and influence. It stands at a crux for the very particular and extensive manner of forward orientation it wills into existence. Right in the here and now, conscious of the immediate turning of the century, Wells announces that we can and should look ahead and that we will need to mold new genres accordingly:

> It is proposed in this book to present, in as orderly an arrangement as the necessarily diffused nature of the subject admits, certain speculations about the trend of present forces.... Hitherto such forecasts have been presented almost invariably in the form of fiction, and commonly the provocation of the satirical

opportunity has been too much for the writer. The narrative form becomes more and more of a nuisance as the speculative inductions become sincerer, and here it will be abandoned altogether in favor of a texture of frank inquiries and arranged considerations. Our utmost aim is a rough sketch of the coming time, a prospectus, as it were, of the joint undertaking of mankind in facing these impending years. The reader is a prospective shareholder—he and his heirs— though whether he will find this anticipatory balance-sheet to his belief or liking is another matter.[36]

In these opening lines, Wells forcefully makes the case for a new and unsettling textuality, suggesting a form of imaginative writing overlapping with the speculative fiction that inaugurated his career yet departing just as radically. Listen to how he recruits the reader, with tongue-in-cheek economic metaphors, but seriously enlisting her as *interested*. We all have a stake in the future, "the joint undertaking of mankind," so that the effort to discern its lineaments, from as many angles as possible, becomes a universal necessity. We hear in these lines, and even in his slightly self-mocking, eighteenth-century-sounding title— *Anticipations of the Reaction of Mechanical and Scientific Progress Upon Human Life and Thought*—that he is marking out a new space in the consciousness of his contemporary age, where speculating is unleashed from the dubiousness that typically surrounds it (as in real estate, as in fortune telling) and instead takes its rightful place in the area of respectable discourse in the large realm of scientific imagining. There is a sense in this and other works that the future is contained in the present (Eliot's version, "Time present and time past / Are both perhaps present in time future"). As should be clear, the specific predictions Wells makes in *Anticipations* are of less importance here than the cast of mind, the relation to temporality it begins to build, and the literary or generic ramifications it promises. Wells's model of anticipating not only conjures individual forecasts but, more richly, represents a sensibility, a way of thinking and feeling about time. Forster begins "The Machine Stops," a Wellsian exercise in antiutopian thought, with the injunction, "Imagine, if you can . . ."[37]

Imagine, if you can: it would be hard to overstate Wells's reach into the future. Anticipation means many things in his textual world. It means, clearly, prediction about all manner of life, from transportation to cities to gender to warfare to the structures of government, and beyond, to the way both world and inhabitants might eventuate over short, medium, and the longest of spans. Wells loved predicting, as his mind traveled into the minute details of, say, what people might be wearing in the year 2060 or 2106 or 802,701 or into how children would be birthed and reared. Prediction about economic and commercial life were staples (as in *When the Sleeper Wakes* or *Tono-Bungay*), along with vivid imagining of the weapons and destructive capacities in store (*The War in the Air, The World Set Free, The Shape of Things to Come*), and all manner of technological futurities fill his texts. Anticipating also conjures the prospect of dread or terror, and much of the energy of Wells's more dystopic futures is generated around a sense of inevitability, the way the future is nestled in and haunted by the present, as in Saint-Amour's account of perpetual interwar, where the future carries along the threat of destruction. On the other hand, the fun of many of Wells's works comes from such speculative fervor, as readers are invited to envision all manner of future machines, devices, scenarios, configurations of people and things. Mostly, though, anticipating carries with it an ethical charge. It is, quite simply, what we must do; if we are going to evade the obliteration of ourselves he so vividly conjured, we must leap into the temporal next stage(s).

For Wells, this is more than an exercise. It is as if he lives half in and half out of the present. If Marcel in *Remembrance of Things Past* is drawn out of the present into a living past, Wells is always falling forward, and like time traveling itself, the experience is disquieting, and the psychological and intellectual effects uncertain. Here he is at the opening of *The Future in America* (1906):

> This [anticipatory] habit of mind confronts and perplexes my sense of things that simply *are*, with my brooding preoccupation with how they will shape presently, what they will lead to, what seed they will sow and how they will wear. At times, I can assure the reader, this quality approaches otherworldliness, in its constant reference to an all-important hereafter. There are times indeed when it makes life seem so transparent and flimsy, seem so dissolving, so passing on to an equally transitory series of consequences, that the enhanced sense of instability becomes restlessness and distress.
>
> (*FA*, 4)

The beauty and wonder we might adduce in a forward-moving imaginary are checked by the repeated reminder of "distress," a kind of nausea. This profound orientation toward what might be, as Wells ruminates here, carries dramatic consequences for his full writerly project, his angle of vision, his primary motivations. "I am curiously not interested in things," he writes, "and curiously interested in the consequences of things," a distinction also at the back of what he declares, in *The Future in America*, to be his motto, discovered independently and soon affiliated with one of his favorite Greek philosophers, Heraclitus, that " 'There is no Being but Becoming' " (*FA*, 3). Branka Arsić discovers in Thoreau a theory of such endless transformation: "Beings and minds are found to fuse and switch, substances mix, and everything is on the move, in becoming, as if substances were itinerant and everything existed in a zone of process."[38] With Wells, one hears also the biological resonance of Huxley, whose teaching always came back to the fact of biological processes, of development. As Wells put it simply in *The Science of Life*, "one fact remains, that all the life we know is one continuing sort of life, that all the life which exists at this moment derives, so far as human knowledge goes, in unbroken succession from life in past time" (*SL*, 1:6). But how, one wonders, can any mind focalize a present as always and only giving way to the future? There is something uncanny in this prospect of the world around Wells as ever-becoming, suggestive of a time-lapse photographic cycle of, say, a flower blossoming; for Wells, to see the bud is immediately to watch its next stages, eradicating any fixity or stability in the present. One thinks of Bergson's temporal flux or even of the nonstop mutations and transformations that characterize the "Proteus" chapter of *Ulysses*, where the possible enters into the stream of history along with its more muscular partner, the actual. Wells is, by his own admission, simply more interested in tomorrow than he is in today: " 'Think of the men who have walked here!' said a tourist in the Roman Coliseum. It was a Futurist mind that answered: 'Think of the men who will.' "[39]

The sensory aspects of this forward orientation generate Wells's version of impressionism. The story of modernism and impressionism has been well told, and I have touched on it, too, in considering some of the Conradian aspects of Wells's style, but here is something that disorients the mode. The essential instability in the world of objects, or in any kind of fixed reality, comes not from the undermining of stable epistemological principles, or from the vagaries of psychological flux, or from an essential subjectivism, but from an extreme cognitive involvement with the future. This is, he argues in many works, the nature of living in the modern world: its principle is change. In *The World of William Clissold*, such change is expressed in one after another iteration. The novel's creed is that "in truth there is no underlying permanent stratum to the changes of our world. It all changes, root as well as flower. Less rapidly, indeed, but as surely, the peasant changes with the rest of mankind" (*WWC*, 115). The principle that modernity is defined by its accelerated temporalities, driven by its attendant technologies, and hitched especially to the rhythms of urban existence and the pace of voracious capitalism is so widespread at this point as to seem intuitive (think of Edna Duffy's *The Speed Handbook* or Kern's *Culture of Time and Space*). For Wells, though, the spirit of kineticism as a consequence of technological modernity, with its always accelerated pacing, is only part of the story—and perhaps not the most interesting part. As we will see more fully in the next chapter, "Biology," Wells circled in his writings around the general principle of growth, the essential feature of organic life. There are, in Wells's works, a few basic premises, and insights about the nature and meaning of organicism fill his writing at the level of image, meaning, narrative, prediction, and sentiment. Sometimes the biological proclivity to increase is figured in literal terms, as in *The Food of the Gods*, a brilliant and troubling (and often extremely funny) fantasia of possibility about the fate of the world after an experimental formula that leads to unchecked growth is let loose, initially on a decrepit farm in Kent, later spreading over the globe. What begins as a threat to the human world that we assume will be overcome by plucky humanity slowly transforms into an allegory of bigger as better, and we humans are to be elbowed aside by our giant successors. *The Food of the Gods* features passages like this: "We fight not for ourselves but for growth—growth that goes on and on. Tomorrow, whether we live or die, growth will conquer through us. That is the law of the spirit for ever more. . . . To grow, and again—to grow. To grow at last into the fellowship and understanding of God."[40] Notwithstanding the particular tenor of the allegory here (and the counterintuitive demand that we readers root against ourselves in the cosmic reckoning), what is striking is how Wells shuttles the idea of change from a local diagnosis of modern conditions to a universal one of the progress and movement of humankind—even if, in *The Food of the Gods*, the meaning of such progress and change is the ultimate eclipse of us all.

Yet despite the positing of pure, biologic growth driving the earth's story, and for all the claims of a kind of inevitable, scientific process at work in taking us mentally into the future, Wells's writings return again and again to the disorienting quality of time travel into the future—otherworldly, dissolving, unstable, and alienating to the inhabitant of the present. To see the universe in perpetual motion is both a testament to reality, as Wells conceived it, and a check on our mental conditioning. "The practical reality . . . is that nothing is permanent," he considers. "A is always becoming B more or less or ceasing to be B more or less. But it would seem the human mind cannot manage with that. It has to hold a thing still for moment before it can think it. . . . It cannot contemplate things continuously and so it has to resort as it were to a series of static snapshots. It has to kill motion in order to study it as a naturalist kills and pins out a butterfly in order to study life."[41] Darko Suvin writes that "Wells's science fiction makes an aesthetic form out of hesitations, intimations, and glimpses of an ambiguously disquieting strangeness," and there is, alongside this general quality of aesthetic estrangement, a specific temporal dimension to Wells's portrayal of the ineluctable and strange.[42] Thus Mr. Barnstable, the protagonist of one of his later utopias, *Men Like Gods* (1923), is launched into Utopia by an accident of a space warp, a kind of cosmic crossing of worlds (of which, incidentally, the novel posits an infinite number). Unlike his fellow humans, Mr. Barnstable is full of yearning to belong to this beautiful and impressive world. The catch is that for those like him (and Wells) who have spent so much effort devising a future to supersede and redeem the hideous injustice, waste, and cruelty of the past and present, the better future is out of bounds. Mr. Barnstable only slowly recognizes his necessary banishment from Utopia, and when he does, his epiphany tells a story with wide aptness in Wells's writing:

> It was with something like awe that Mr. Barnstable realized how clean a sweep had been made of the common life in a mere score of centuries, how boldly and dreadfully the mind of man had taken hold, soul and body and destiny, of the life and destiny of the race. He knew himself now for the creature of transition he was, so deep in the habits of the old, so sympathetic with the idea of the new that has still but scarcely dawned on earth.[43]

Such then, are the consequences of inhabiting the position of inventor of tomorrow: a sensibility of confused insufficiency, a quality of being squeezed out of history (including future history), an atemporality that emerges just at the moment when the future comes into full, embodied reality.

Wells's short stories are often built around such temporal disjunctions, as they are around unusual warps in space. We might consider, in this context, "The New Accelerator," first published in 1901 (the same year as *Anticipations*), which features the testing of an experimental drug that accelerates the body's movement up to around one thousand times its usual speed. While its inventor, Gibberne, muses about its salutary mental effects—allowing hyperintense thinking and intellectual stamina, along the lines of the 2011 film *Limitless*—what the story actually dramatizes is the experience of bodily suspension between timeframes, as the narrator and inventor sample the potion and undergo its effects. As with so many of Wells's texts about wonderful inventions (*The Invisible Man*, "The Man Who Could Work Miracles"), this one cannot refrain from a certain amount of small-time, small-town, trick playing (here Gibberne takes revenge on a neighbor's dog), but mostly it figures the experience of living briefly out of time. With one's own body moving at unimaginable speed, the effect is to make the rest of the world appear to be still, as if, that is, one's visible surroundings were moving at one one-thousandth their usual pace. A sample:

> The band was playing in the upper stand, though all the sound it made for us was a low-pitched, wheezy rattle, a sort of prolonged last sigh that passed at times into a sound like the slow, muffled ticking of some monstrous clock. Frozen people stood erect; strange, silent, self-conscious-looking dummies hung unstably in mid-stride, promenading upon the grass. . . ."Lord, look here!" cried Gibberne, and we halted for a moment before a magnificent person in white faint-striped flannels, white shoes, and a Panama hat, who turned back to wink at two gaily dressed ladies he had passed. A wink, studied with such leisurely deliberation as we could afford, is an unattractive thing. It loses any quality of alert gaiety, and one remarks that the winking eye does not completely close, that under its drooping lid appears the lower edge of an eyeball and a line of white.[44]

Even more disorienting than extraordinary speed is the stasis that constitutes very slow movement to the human eye. One thinks, here, of the frozen world Woolf displays in *Orlando*, when the young Orlando and her elusive Russian princess observe, as a kind of delightful theater, various groupings of immobilized people during the great London freeze. There as here, the effort of literary description to approach the still life—photography, or painting, or perhaps a wax museum—conjures an arrested world, one whose unnaturalness is emphasized not as beauty but as a kind of mild horror, as with the too-bodily look of the winking eye, whose charm, we now realize, depends entirely on its speed. We might compare the moment, too, to the famous photographic sequences of Eadweard Muybridge, the mid-nineteenth-century photographer whose breaking down of the horse's running motion into a series of stills inaugurated a tradition that leads all the way to the child's flipbook of my own 1970s childhood. As Louise Hornby notes of Muybridge's sequences, "His photographs reveal stages of motion that are otherwise invisible, glossed over by the moving body that does not stop."[45] "The New Accelerator" offers a quite precise literary equivalent. More generally, its playful maneuvering of time runs in parallel with its scientist/experimenter, himself manipulating bodily motions. There is something a little smug, perhaps, in these fantasies ("the whole world had stopped for our convenient inspection," the narrator muses, and this, in fact, is what also happens in "The Man Who Could Work Miracles," only just sparing the earth's destruction [*CSS*, 940]). Meanwhile, we are told that he is also working on a "Retarder," the reverse of the "Accelerator," which will slow down the body, enabling "the patient to spread a few seconds over many hours of ordinary time, and so to maintain an apathetic inaction, a glacierlike absence of alacrity, amidst the most animated or irritating surroundings" (*CSS*, 941). As is typical of Wells's fiction, "The New Accelerator" literalizes its key ideas, here both the Bergsonian individuation and relativity of time and the Muybridge principle that time can be viewed as a series of infinitesimally distinguishable instants, what Garrett Stewart calls the "photogram."[46] The story's traffic is in the momentary, as it thematizes and itself turns on the nature of temporal experience, felt as such, and disrupting any fiction of a simple, naturalist portrayal of lived time.

*The Time Machine*, above all, is built on such moments. A quality of disjunctive temporalities is there from the start, as when the guests initially gather at the Traveller's Victorian home in the comfortable, middle-class suburb of Richmond and are invited to sit on his patented chairs. The Traveller, clearly, is thinking along different lines from his peers; the fact that he has a laboratory in his home at all suggests as much. At this gathering (and the follow-up a week later, when the tale of his voyage is recounted) is a small group of professionals, given epithets rather than names (though there is Philby and the oddly titled Blank). The professions represented at the Traveller's home might be said to embody the latest in knowledge production in the England of 1895: a Medical Man, an Editor, a Journalist (of the modern school), a Psychologist. The Traveller is a member of this community, to be sure, but he is also, in another sense, the appropriate *object* of these new fields of study. After all, he may be eccentric and extremely accomplished in an entrepreneurial way, but he also seems vaguely neurasthenic, as indicated by his recurring dizziness, faintness, and nausea. There is, too, a strange passivity that emerges at various times in his story, often while the Morlocks paw him or slowly begin to drag him off, and his attraction to the androgynous child-woman Weena seems to cast a questionable light on his masculinity. One might then read the Traveller's final escape into time as a form of resistance to the modern forms of knowledge, interpretation, and disciplinarity so well represented by the men at his salon.

Whatever kinds of subtle temporal distinctions the present may suggest in its plural modernities, the primary narrative in the future is made up, dramatically, of dislocating criss-crossings of temporal scales and motifs. From the moment when the Traveller first arrives in the Golden Age, he is presented with an astonishing range of shadings and mixings among scales of time. Here, for instance, is the Traveller's first apprehension of the sphinx. He has righted himself after the fall from his machine, and in finding his initial bearings, sees the statue:

"My sensations would be hard to describe. As the columns of hail grew thinner, I saw the white figure more distinctly. It was very large, for a silver birch-tree touched its shoulder. It was of white marble, in shape something like a winged sphinx, but the wings, instead of being carried vertically at the sides, were spread so that it seemed to hover. The pedestal, it appeared to me, was of bronze, and was thick with verdigris. . . . It was greatly weather-worn, and that imparted an unpleasant suggestion of disease. I stood looking at it for a little space—half a minute, perhaps, or half an hour. It seemed to advance and to recede as the hail drove before it denser or thinner . . .

"I looked up again at the crouching white shape, and the full temerity of my voyage came suddenly upon me. What might appear when that hazy curtain was altogether withdrawn? What might not have happened to men? What if cruelty had grown into a common passion? What if in this interval the race had lost its manliness, and had developed into something inhuman, unsympathetic, and overwhelmingly powerful? I might seem some old-world savage animal, only the more dreadful and disgusting for our common likeness—a foul creature to be incontinently slain."

(TM, 21–22)

The passage packs in one after another instance of temporal overlapping: far out into the future, the first object the Traveller meets is a statue resembling the iconic figure from ancient Greek and Egyptian civilizations, one associated with the passage and principles of time, via its famous riddle; the figure is on a pedestal, whose material instantiates the ancient world (from a slightly later time, the Bronze Age), a pedestal that, moreover, shows signs of its own existence through time, via its verdigris; the experience of time, in the present, has become murky and imprecise, with a half-second indistinguishable from a half-hour; the Traveller suddenly remembers that the passage of all this time has not been empty, that there have been stages and development all along the way, so that any given stop on the spectrum of time has many histories that might have shaped it; in relation to the future, the Traveller takes on the possible role of "some old-world savage animal," a figure that interestingly could refer either to the shared old-world savagery of the present and the future (the prehistory common to all humans) or to the seeming savagery of a late Victorian in the face of people living hundreds of thousands of years later. To find oneself standing in the far future, then, is an immensely complex experience, where the range of time exerts itself *as range*. It is not that time spans collapse, though the appearance of the sphinx, of all figures, does suggest such a comingling, but more that they jump in and out of order, like atoms in the episteme of relativity, rather than in the measurable Newtonian universe. The spans of time are never invisible, nor are they ever exactly visible, since any given instant—like this present of first perceiving the sphinx—gives way to the many other temporalities that penetrate it from all sides. If for writers like Eliot and Pound the palimpsest of pasts upon pasts dominates a poem's texture and meaning, in a sense filling each line (or even word) with its presence, here the text is filled by temporalities with not even such stability; it is crowded, instead, by futures' pasts, past's futures, different stages along the temporal trajectory. The result of such temporal miscegenation is a feeling of discomfort. To inhabit this strange location is, perhaps, to experience a kind of nausea, as in the Traveller's sense of the sphinx as somehow diseased, replicating the unpleasant and disorienting sensations of time travel itself.

This early moment in the future, with its multiple tenses jostling together, inaugurates a narrative made up of many such interludes, and more generally, *The Time Machine* presents a folding over of the long past onto the far future. The evolution of Eloi and Morlocks out of the working and upper classes of the nineteenth century provides the most sensational discovery in the novel and, as any reader will observe, seems to suggest reversion more than progression. As we have noted, Wells often remarked that adaptation is in no way synonymous with improvement (in this he follows Darwin), as in an early essay debunking "Bio-Optimism" (1895). Evolution, for all its association with the idea of progress, in fact features as many dead ends as fruitful continuations of species, as in those passages cited earlier where Wells points, with a sigh and a warning finger, to evolutionary finales, those many "branches of the tree of life" that have no further outgrowths. And the progressive premise is even less secure in a moral or civilizational sense, as epitomized by Wells's Martians, with their huge brains and negligent ethics, or the even more questionable men of the year million.

Clearly, the overwhelming feeling of *The Time Machine* is of a species decayed in nearly all respects. On the Eloi branch, most damning is the species' lack of curiosity or imagination. With literacy at an end (books are only to be found in the ruined palace of green porcelain, where they are no more than heaps of dust), a spare language that is "'excessively simple—almost exclusively composed of concrete substantives and verbs . . . [with] few, if any, abstract terms . . . little use of figurative language,'" and having developed no technology whatsoever, the Eloi have passed the Utopian dream of a life free of toil ("'the whole earth had become a garden,'" *TM*, 30) to settle instead in the realm of degeneration, as it was obsessively figured in the late nineteenth and early twentieth centuries (*TM*, 39).[47] Their semisexlessness, resulting from a lesser need for sexual differentiation, in Wells's terms, and vegetarian diet may follow some of the newer trends of the 1890s, but one cannot blame the Traveller for being overcome with disappointment when he becomes acquainted with their childlike ways and intellectual nullity. The Eloi have moved backward and forward simultaneously; the phylogenic principle in which species rearticulates the development of the fetus, a concept urged by Huxley among others, here operates to highlight their regressive character, while their soft passivity also suggests adaptation to the nature of work and life in the year 802,701. Even the number of the year, as critics have noted, suggests regression (from 8 to 7, 2 to 1; it should also be noted that the year configuration is quintessential Wells, in that he builds in a reader-friendly device for remembering it). More, once the Eloi's status as "fatted cattle" has been deduced, this overlapping of evolution and devolution is fully revealed in all its sensational gruesomeness. And the Traveller responds in kind, at once recognizing his affinity with them (in relation to the Morlocks, toward whom he feels a visceral abhorrence) yet in other ways mirroring the Morlocks' own attitude toward the Eloi, as when he feels an irrational desire to throttle the soft little folk or when he describes them in passing as "'these delicious people'" (*TM*, 33, 37). For their part, the Morlocks provide a textbook case of adaptation, their bleached features and intolerance of light a result of many centuries underground ("'Living, as they did, in what appeared to me impenetrable darkness, their eyes were abnormally large and sensitive, just as are the pupils of the abysmal fishes, and they reflected light in the same way'" [*TM*, 53]), while their eating habits call to mind early humanity, with its taste for raw meat and cannibalism. In both directions, moreover, the Traveller reacts with powerful disidentification: "'You can scarce imagine how nauseatingly inhuman they looked—those pale, chinless faces and great, lidless, pinkish-grey eyes!'" as if to say, humanity falls somewhere in the interim of these huge spans of time; it cannot see itself at all in this infolded time of past/future (*TM*, 55).

In global and local terms, in other words, *The Time Machine* fully interpenetrates the scales of time, with significant effects, at the level of narrative—including suspense, horror, intrigue—and at the level of content—with the forecast of a future decidedly loathsome and frightening, in part for its replaying of prehistoric motifs, yet also recognizable, telling the present something essential about itself. To take just one more sequence from the novella, in the palace of green porcelain, a "latter-day South Kensington," the Traveller again stands at the vortex of different vectors of time. In this case, the setting is contemporary to Wells (rather than ancient in relation to him, as with the sphinx) and indeed bespeaks a deep Victorianism; after all, one could not select a more perfect artifact of the period's scientific, imperial, and domestic-cultural personality than a natural history museum (*TM*, 65).[48] This sequence, moreover, resonates beyond the tale, in the sense that it inaugurates many such moments in Wells's fiction, when a character stands in a museum face to face with some kind of long-extinct figure. Such is not quite possible in the palace of green porcelain, since the bones themselves have decayed, though in its day, as the Traveller remarks, the museum seems to have prized its "'Palaeontological Section, and a very splendid array of fossils it must have been'" (*TM*, 65).[49] The entry hall of the green palace is inhabited by "'some extinct creature after the fashion of the Megatherium,'" and "'Further in the gallery... the huge skeleton barrel of a Brontosaurus'"; these compelling giants thus provide a literal entry into the enormous museum that branches off, like the tree of life, into various sectors (*TM*, 64, 65). Standing amid the dust all these millennia in the future, the representative of Wells's age is not particularly moved by these bones ("'this spectacle of old-time geology in decay'"), perhaps because he is in the midst of an early/late evolutionary fold in real time; instead, the novel suggests that what the Megatherium offered to the nineteenth century (that is, to the novella's readers) as a way to experience the great gaps in temporalities has been superseded by the striking visibility of temporal change in the present. The Traveller may have little use for fossils, but he regrets the ruination of a hall of taxidermy, which might have helped account for the present, "'because I should have been glad to trace the patient readjustments by which the conquest of animated nature had been attained'" (*TM*, 66). It stands to reason, as we have seen in the temporal schemes surrounding the sphinx, that no such clear march through time *could* be on view. In the evolutionary scheme as Wells presents it, there are always and only gaps, jumps, leaps, spaces. In this sense, Wells calls to mind the theory of "punctuated equilibrium," formulated in the 1970s by Niles Eldredge and Steven Jay Gould, which sees evolution not as a smooth and gradual process but as formed of uneven spans of quick change and stasis. In truth, none of these exhibits can be seen; instead, it is the museum itself, as an index of culture, that has become the relic. A vast ruin, built centuries in the past, it is always already old, like all the architecture of the Golden Age. It is a place of dust—metonymical with its books— and in fact is sloping downhill, in a sense becoming buried once and for all, or perhaps going the way of the subterranean Morlocks, whose hand the Traveller detects in some raiding of the cases, as he too will soon do.

But the Traveller, true to his status as a Victorian lay scientist, nevertheless feels at home in the museum, as usual ignoring Weena's rightful anxieties about their danger, musing among the aisles. The museum presents, once again, a temporal meeting ground. After all, the project of the natural history museum was always bound up with the cycles of time, its central illusion being a certain kind of static time, where both temporality and geography are collected and controlled. When the Traveller wanders the museum, he seems to revert not so much to the age from which the museum comes but rather to something simultaneously earlier (prehistory) and later (the present of 802,701). We might then take his final gesture in the museum, signing his name on an idol, not only as a suggestion of a certain residual adolescence but also as a sign of reversion to something primal, that early human whom Wells is always finding just behind our exteriors—"The cave man, the ancestral ape, the ancestral brute."[50] Scribbling on the idol reminds us of other impulses woven into the Victorian museum in the first place, what Wells in *The Outline* names as the flag-planting form of discovery, travel, and imperial encounter, which he sees as one of humanity's worst tendencies (and which he contrasts with the genuine globalism epitomized by the world's great religions). Such flag planting is epitomized in *The Outline* by the villain of that story, Napoleon, whom Wells presents as a kind of sulky adolescent bully. Mostly, though, the Traveller exits the museum better armed. He now has a handy mace, a weapon he longs to use on some Morlocks, and a box of matches. It is back to the beginnings: a club, fire.

*The Time Machine*, it turns out, really is a story about time. It makes its own kind of theoretical foray into the meaning of temporal existence, pressing the idea that different scientific epistemes—that of space-time, of evolution, of the Victorian pseudosciences—when overlapped yield a disorienting experience of being, in a sense, "nowhen" (a word Wells quite likes, along with "somewhen"). In the Traveller's opening lecture to his guests, Wells rehearses some of the principles of fourth-dimensionality as he had derived them from his formal studies, recent reading, and scientific society attendance. In one sense, his lecture functions as a guarantor, or reality effect, for the tale that follows, giving an up-to-date scientific framework for the work of fantasy, in what would become classic science-fiction style. The opening primer in the physics of time-space is important in a different sense, too, as it establishes a theoretical premise for the idea of time as essentially disruptive of expectations, mutable, thick with its own unanticipated realities. It might be instructive to recall that "The Chronic Argonauts" (1888), the precursor to *The Time Machine*, seems to have shared little with the final version of *The Time Machine* when it comes to the journey itself (which, if it was narrated, is now lost). It does, however, present the theory of time travel and the fourth dimension as expostulated also in the published novel. This was true of all initial drafts. What was essential for Wells in this retold story, it seems—its origin and central idea—was the play in and through time, not the particular eventualities a time traveler might encounter (such as Eloi and Morlocks, which intuitively read as the germ of the story). We can go further: time travel for Wells is a capacious signifier for the imaginative release into clashing worlds, multiplicity of experience, thinking and feeling experimentation in the very flesh. What this means, in practice, is not so much that

Wells follows Pater in embracing the fragile, sensorially rich nature of each moment as it is lived but, almost the reverse, that each moment becomes so layered and infiltrated with other spots on the spectrum of time that, in some sense, it cannot be experienced at all.

## III. THE PAST IN THE PRESENT

*The Time Machine* inaugurated Wells's career; later works return in their own idioms to the spectacle inaugurated by museum and sphinx, generating a trope of temporal juxtaposition that extends through his full oeuvre, fluctuating and modulating in each setting, and offering readers a continual provocation about the meaning of existing in time. Consider these three examples, spanning nearly three decades, from *Ann Veronica* (1909), *The World of William Clissold* (1926), and *The Croquet Player* (1936):

> She stood for a time looking at the dry limbs and still human face of that desiccated unwrapped mummy from the very beginnings of social life. . . . It was wonderful to think this thing had lived, had felt and suffered. Perhaps once it had desired some other human being intolerably. Perhaps someone had kissed the brow that was now so cadaverous, rubbed that sunken cheek with living hands. . . . But all of that was forgotten.[51]

> Men have lived among these hills [in Provence] for scores of thousands of years, and one could think that here if anywhere in the world was peace and permanent adaptation. A short automobile journey to the east would take us to the caves of Grimaldi, where some of the earliest of human skulls were found, and Moustiers, which has traces of men even more ancient, is as close to the west. Cro-Magnon, in Dordogne, is five or six hours of motoring beyond. The soil everywhere is rich with human traces, from chipped flint fragments to Phoenician beads, Roman brickwork, and medieval crockery. . . .
>
> But, indeed, this fair and spacious scene is a mere mask of calm beauty upon the face of change. . . . All these peasants seem to be giving up their olives for jasmin, and they are growing that for the perfume factories in Grasse which serve the transitory, unstable world of luxury in Paris and London and New York.[52]

> "More and more did the threat of that primordial Adamite [an ancient skull seen in a museum] dominate me. I could not banish that eyeless stare and that

triumphant grin from my mind, sleeping or waking. . . . It became as vast as a cliff, a mountainous skull in which the orbits and hollows of the jaw were huge caves. . . . In the foreground I saw his innumerable descendants, swarming like ants, swarms of human beings hurrying to and fro, making helpless gestures of submission or deference, resisting an overpowering impulse to throw themselves under his all-devouring shadow. Presently these swarms began to fall into lines and columns, were clad in uniforms, formed up and began marching and trotting towards the black shadows under those worn and rust-stained teeth. From which darkness there presently oozed something—something winding and trickling, and something that manifestly tasted very agreeable to him. Blood."

And then [the internal narrator] said a queer thing. "Little children killed by air-raids in the street."

(CP, 69–70)

What leaps out of these three passages is the primacy and richness of prehistory as signifier. In each case, a particular conjunction of factors animates the moment of contemplation of the prehistoric past: the presence of a relic (skull or mummy or the many discoveries that have made a region famous for its archeological finds); the startling placing of those relics in the present; the simultaneous recognition that we learn something important about ourselves when we confront these objects and life-worlds of the prehistoric past—and that, in fact, we may only be learning about ourselves and not actually delving into the past at all; and above all, the fact that in crashing together, these temporalities generate a distinct sensibility, or feeling, or philosophy. In other words, these are cruxes because there is something sensual, affective, stirring, *living* about the confrontation of one era with another.

Yet all scales are not equal. Wells is at pains, in text after text, to stress the immensity of time spans that preceded our human entrance into the world, and in this he follows Victorian predecessors such as Charles Lyell, in his *Principles of Geology*, which had attempted to generate a sense of enormousness in the scales being hypothesized. Here, for instance, is a characteristic early passage in *The Outline*:

Speculations about geological time vary enormously. Estimates of the age of the oldest rocks by geologists and astronomers starting from different standpoints have varied between 1,600,000,000, and 25,000,000. The lowest estimate was made by Lord Kelvin in 1867. Professor Huxley guessed at 400,000,000 years. . . . That the period of time has been vast, that it is to be counted by scores and possibly by hundreds of millions of years, is the utmost that can be said with certainty in the matter. . . . And be it noted that whatever the total sum may be, most geologists are in agreement that *half or more than half of the whole of geological time had passed before life had developed to the Later Palaeozoic level*. . . . For ages that stagger the imagination this earth spun hot and lifeless, and again for ages of equal vastness it held no life above the level of the animalculae in a drop of ditch-water.

Not only is Space from the point of view of life and humanity empty, but Time is empty also. Life is like a little glow, scarcely kindled yet, in these void immensities.

(OH, 1:13–15, italics in the original)

It is the point he makes with more force than any other in *The Outline*: the accelerating temporality of human history needs to be placed in vastly longer perspective. "Time is empty also." Then again, if such a perspective were in any way organic to Western (or any human) thought, Wells would not need to keep reminding his readers at every turn of these disproportionate time spans.

Returning to the three passages, it is clear, seeing them together, how powerfully the mixed scales of history come to express whatever preoccupations a text or character may be harboring. Ann Veronica, in seeing sexual love (perhaps even illicit love) in the mummy is quite transparently filtering her own dawning sexual self-awareness, the central subject of the novel. Yet the mummy is not simply a screen for such projections; it exerts its own pressures. If the novel's primary metaphor for the experience of young women stifled by middle-class respectability is "wrappered," the mummy provides an eerie new articulation, a startling literalness. As we have noted, when the metaphor becomes literal—the animal/human continuum actually constructed in *The Island of Dr. Moreau*, the figure of upper and lower classes extended to its logical endpoint in *The Time Machine*—the social idea at its root is exposed, and the world's categories seem ready to collapse. More, for Ann Veronica, her coming of age as a sexually emancipated woman involves a variety of passages, importantly including a recognition of her own primal femininity, as she and the novel conceive it. "Modern, indeed!", she thinks of her radical sexual choices. "She was going to be as primordial as chipped flint" (*AV*, 258).

For *The World of William Clissold*, the ramifying quality of these reflections on the prehistoric past as it juts into the present, itself understood in terms of accelerated change, chimes in with the larger themes in this meditative novel. The sensual reality of the long past is especially important; one of the novel's primary structural features, in a generally very unstructured novel, indeed almost a pure deconstruction of novelistic order, is the swing back and forth between the very specifically contemporary and other, longer spans of time. At times Clissold is seized by despondency, that he is wasting away "these nights of beauty in mental toil, in plotting, planning, writing and re-writing" for no likely result, since in this moving modern world no one is listening, yet he can also switch on to a different scalar frequency, where value can be reconceived: "But here in this secluded peaceful place," he writes of his villa in Provence, "and especially at night when everything is still, one can take a larger view, see things upon the scale of history, see the wide-sweeping radius of destiny tracing its onward path across the skies" (*WWC*, 743–44). As with other works considered above, to shift the temporal (and here also spatial) dimension is to enable a particular cast of mind, one with impressionist affinities, where optimism can thrive and one's work for the future be redoubled. As noted, this novel makes explicit and extensive its Heraclitan affinities; it has as epigraph the philosopher's "flux universal," about which Clissold further dilates: "It is only because I may sit at this window for so brief a time that I do not see this scene dissolve visibly and pass and give place to other unprecedented and equally transitory appearances. Of one thing only can I be sure, that all this goes, peasants and pleasure cities, ships and empires, weapons, armies, races, religions, all the present fashions of man's life" (*WWC*, 116).

The three-volume, eight-hundred-page *World of William Clissold*, itself generous with time, opens with a melancholy reflection on aging and temporality, as the narrator of exactly Wells's age wonders, rues, and regrets the bodily facts of entering his sixth decade. These early pages are especially wonderful, Montaignian in spirit, with something haunting in them, dwelling first on the physical side of temporal change, eventually widening out to consider many angles on the question of time and flux. Like *The Magic Mountain*, a kindred work in spirit and interest, the novel takes the exploration of living in time—and in the times—as its primary object. That it ends with the narrator's death (violently, as is typical of death in Wells's novels) must, in retrospect, seem a given. William Clissold seems to live, like the Time Traveller, too completely on the margins of stable time, and seems to reflect too precisely on the meaning of its passage, to expect a future in the indefinite space of the end of a novel.

Of the three examples cited above, *The Croquet Player* is most fully engaged in conjuring great folds in time and in reckoning the present by comparison and juxtaposition with the old past. Written in 1936, at a time when the culture of English intelligentsia was wracked with painful self-scrutiny about what they saw as the essential barbarism at the root of Western culture, *The Croquet Player* comes down firmly on the side of an old, inherited propensity toward savagery and violence.[53] It takes the form of a gothic tale, with allegorical overtones—until, that is, the allegory is shattered by some surprising formal moves toward the novella's end. In departing from both realism and didacticism, entering instead a realm somewhere between dark fantasy and absurd theater, the novella represents a return to aspects of Wells's early scientific tales, though here the contemporaneity of the story is directly manifest. In the passage above, that is, the prehistoric skull registers not only the human bestiality of all eras but more particularly the political extremities of the 1930s. *The Croquet Player* relays the story of a strange set of occurrences in the fictional village of Cainsmarsh, where the internal narrator, Dr. Finchatton, had taken refuge from an unpromising medical career in London, only to find a strange illness of spirit infecting the region, which seems to be emanating from the marsh and taking forms that range from sleeplessness to anxiety to the beating of animals to murder. Explanations differ among the townspeople Dr. Finchatton consults in his search for answers: it is the hand of god, punishing those who have left the true church, corrupted by a new minister! It is the handiwork of archeologists who have tampered with the order of things by digging up old bones that should have been left buried! It is—here is the psychologist (Dr. Norbert) who enters toward the end of the story, draining its metaphysical and gothic elements, to focus instead on subjective experience—that " 'we have been probing and piercing into the past and future. We have been multiplying memories, histories, traditions; we have filled ourselves with forebodings and plannings and apprehensions. And so our worlds have become overwhelmingly vast for us, terrific, appalling. Things that had seemed forgotten for ever have suddenly come back into the very present of our consciousness' " (*CP*, 88–89). We have, says the psychologist, "broken the frame of time," his term for the destruction of mental ease at the root of Dr. Finchatton's experience of unchecked evil in the marsh. Norbert sounds, in a funny way, as if he is diagnosing Wells's work as the cause of our trouble; who more than Wells has furthered such forebodings, plannings, apprehensions? Who else has disturbed time by interleaving past with future? Wells, as we know, was fond of placing himself in his texts, often as the object of some satire, but here the suggestion is less a playful self-referentiality than an exemplification of the principle that to live in the imaginative realm of mixed temporalities is to inhabit a disorienting, almost diseased space, where time is both moving and stopping, the past engulfing and the future taunting. Here is the outcome, in Dr. Norbert's words:

"Man is still what he was. Invincibly bestial, envious, malicious, greedy. Man . . . unmasked and disillusioned, is the same fearing, snarling, fighting beast he was a hundred thousand years ago. These are no metaphors. . . . What I tell you is the monstrous reality. The brute has been marking time and dreaming of a progress it has failed to make. Any archaeologist will tell you as much; modern man has no better skull, no better brain. Just a cave man, more or less trained. There has been no real change, no real escape. Civilization, progress, all *that*, we are discovering, was a delusion."

(*CP*, 89)

We know that Wells's works operate according to the dialectic of darkness and light, deep skepticism canceled by a resurgent optimism, and back again. In the 1936 vision of the cave man whom we are—and whom we must own—*The Croquet Player* gives the most unmediated version of the grimmer half of this prospect, where civilization has all been a terrible waste. It also reminds us that among the infinite points on the spectrum of time, one span became especially alluring for understanding our world and for recognizing the profound limitations that beset the utopian promise: the long, unrecorded years of prehistory.

## PART 2: HISTORY AND BEFORE

### IV. PREHISTORY

It is time to check back in with modernism. If Wells's endorsement of the future set him and modernism on separate paths, his equally powerful engagement with the distant past offers one of the most salient points of overlap and exchange. Modernism was absolutely taken with prehistory. Like so many others in the first half of the twentieth century, writers reacted with creative expression to the archeological discoveries that had begun in the mid–nineteenth century and to the sense of the earth's age as theorized by midcentury geologists. Prehistory presented a temporal edge toward which the modernist text loved to creep and peer. In some cases, prehistory is nearly interchangeable with the primitive, and critics have long noted the deep and problematic reliance on primitivism that quietly (or more loudly in some cases) sustains modernism, including in the visual arts.[54] But with Wells as our prism, we can see especially clearly that prehistory did not always, or even most interestingly, correspond with primitivism. It made its own distinctive call, invoking temporal schemes where the unity, or at least universality, of the human story stands as premise and where questions of unstable temporalities—also of historicity, evolution, and the meaning of humanity when understood in these varying scales—become pivotal for both formal and thematic concerns.

Avoiding generalization from across a dazzling array of prehistoric formulations in works by Hardy, Conrad, Lawrence, Woolf, Eliot, Joyce, and more, we can nevertheless make a few observations. One is that, implicitly or explicitly, juxtapositions among temporalities, such as we have been discovering in Wells's works, give these passages their jolt. Lawrence in *The Rainbow* has Tom Brangwen muse: "Having occasion to go to London, he marvelled, as he returned, thinking of naked, lurking savages on an island, how these had built up and created the great mass of Oxford Street or Piccadilly. How had helpless savages, running with their spears on the riverside, after fish, how had they come to rear up this great London, the ponderous, massive, ugly superstructure of a world of man upon a world of nature! It frightened and awed him."[55] If Lawrence puzzles over the prehistoric people who somehow yielded modernity, Woolf's Bernard in *The Waves* instead sees only the blink of an eye. The cave man, Bernard thinks, "he squats in me."[56] More widely, the perception in the present of an extremely ancient past gives a sense of something extraordinary—in sensibility, psyche, thought, aesthetics, or in the drama of the present situation. These recognitions seem to occasion, that is, a certain kind of perceptual or affective heightening, of the sort we often associate with modernism's signature temporality of the sudden insight, the moment of rapture, disillusionment, or exceptional clarity. In slightly different terms, prehistory enters the modernist text at moments when the apparatus of meaning making is in especially high gear. Of course, the reasoning could be circular: trained by modernism to read the interruption of the long past as crux, one then recognizes in the prehistoric that very significance. But there is, I think, more than hermeneutical good training here. It would be difficult to elaborate any reading of *A Passage to India*, say, that did not take the extremity of the caves, figured according to varying indices, including their enormous age, as essential. And similar observations prevail across the modernist scene.

Two insights, in particular, help account for the particular power and the pressure prehistory exerts on circumstance, text, and narrative in so many modernist works. One is the sense of continuity in the long past. Such persistence exerts itself as potency in the "Proteus" scene on the beach in *Ulysses*, as Stephen imagines the ages of time that eventuate in the "damp crackling mast, razorshells, squeaking pebbles, that on the unnumbered pebbles beats, wood sieved by the shipworm, lost Armada," or, more simply, "dead breaths I living breathe."[57] Eliot evokes such figures in "East Coker," echoing James Frazer (and hence *The Waste Land*, so Eliot's own literary history), as "ashes to the earth / Which is already flesh, fur upon faeces, / Bone of man and beast, cornstalk and leaf."[58] We stand face to face with the long past—it was here all along, indeed contained within us, ingrained in what we would now call our DNA—and there are no breaks in the temporal line. Gillian Beer argues, in relation to Woolf's ruminations on prehistory, that the "missing link" has evaporated, that key invisible bridge Victorians understood to connect—but especially to separate—themselves to/from earlier forms of mankind.[59] So much of the past washes up on the beach, or mixes in with a handful of dust, as if, Tennyson-like, to contain the global past in the single flower.

Yet the aesthetics are not of the flower, not gemlike, not beautiful. That savage is grotesque, the dirt's richness comes from feces, Stephen's walk on Sandymount is marked by corpses, not to mention urination and other reminders of our very biological dogsbodies. Next to these accounts of persistence—and even in the same passages—comes another insight: the recognition of the old past is one of shock, perhaps dismay, certainly dislocation. Here, again, one runs fully into modernism's most recognized affective and aesthetic motifs, what Eliot canonically described as the poet "amalgamating disparate experience," "forming new wholes" out of what is "chaotic, irregular, fragmentary."[60] In the case of prehistory, such juxtapositions have destructive force, yet they are also alluring, potent, that which the text will continue to approach or circle. For *A Passage to India*, what transpires in those ancient caves unravels all that has been accomplished via the very human, cultural achievements housed in the mosque. For Conrad in *Heart of Darkness*, the trip along the Congo comes freighted with heavy fictions of the world before and beyond civilization, as in reflections such as these: "Going up that river was like traveling back to the earliest beginnings of the world, when vegetation rioted on the earth and the big trees were kings," or "We were wanderers on a prehistoric earth, on an earth that wore the aspect of an unknown planet."[61] In all of these works, the forces of modernization—or, perhaps more generally, the experience of modernity—in relation to very old pasts are largely at stake. It is so overt and pressing, as in *Tess of the d'Urbervilles*, a novel that continually stages the overlapping or sundering of stages in the passage through time, and so at Stonehenge, where Tess's narrative closes, these dynamics reach culmination. She is found by the rising sun sleeping on a plinth. If she is at one with the prehistoric monument, her pursuers starkly contrast it, emerging from dots on the landscape into military-style police, who "walk as if trained."[62] Eliot goes straight there too, in his ambiguous claim in "Tradition and the Individual Talent" that "the mind of Europe" is embodied in three artist-figures, Shakespeare, Homer, and, bizarrely, the "Magdalenian draughtsmen," Eliot having visited the Dordogne caves with the Pounds in 1919.[63] In all, the instant when prehistory becomes perceptible—either when it breaks into view, or when it is felt as hint and suggestion, as a lurking reminder about all kinds of unwelcome facts in the nature of inheritance, or when it is claimed as the origin of our expressive potential—charges the present with a sense of affiliation, if often unwanted. "Make men and women only sufficiently jealous or fearful or drunken or angry," writes Wells, as he contemplates the miniscule amount of time, evolution-wise, that has passed between modern humanity and the days when humans ate raw meat, "and the hot red eyes of the cavemen will glare out at us to-day" (*OH*, 1:377).

Detached from concerns of the primitive per se, what all these sequences underscore is the prevalence and richness of modernism's archeological imagination. In her wonderful book *Shadow Sites*, the art historian Kitty Hauser defines a phenomenon she calls "topophilia"[64] as "an interest, sometimes amounting to an obsession, with local landscapes marked by time." In such a construct, "the landscape is seen not so much as vista, picture, or space, but as *site*, the place where things have occurred. . . . For those who see the landscape and its elements in this way, appearances are simply the end products of more-or-less hidden stories, an agglomeration of traces of past actions, processes, and occurrences."[65] If this habit of perception and thought seems especially pertinent to contemporary writers like W. D. Sebald or Graham Swift (or to the photographers and preservationists who are Hauser's main subjects), it is also an apt evocation of, say, Eliot—of how he considers place in *Four Quartets*, especially, and how location, like the interior life of the mind, seems endlessly to display depth beneath depth, story under story, a kind of resonating effect in the very principle of the buried becoming revealed or, equally, not quite revealed.

Prehistory ignites (also demonstrates) that aspect of twentieth-century literature which draws one to the mummy or, perhaps better, turns even a living body into a site of archeology. Karin Sanders, in a cultural history of the "bog bodies" found preserved in peat in northern Europe in the 1950s, traces how these intact corpses have fueled ongoing imagining in the last half-century, finding in them a case study for the seemingly inevitable attraction to long-dead human remains and, indeed, for an archeological sensibility more generally. What makes archeological thought so pervasive, Sanders writes, is "the way in which the stubborn *thereness* of archaeological objects as material testimony seems to leave an element of something both unavoidable and mysterious, something that begs for imaginary fill-ins and fill-outs . . . in archaeology the very materiality of the artifact appears to simultaneously offer itself up for interpretation and refuse to be *known*."[66] In literary modernism, a close parallel is an archival attitude to the basic unit of the writer's craft, as the word or even phoneme becomes a vessel for so many records and traces, filtering through time. But the archeological habit is primarily extralinguistic, and prehistory is intriguing precisely because it predates the written word. For modernism, there is something essential in the moment of reckoning in the cave, the moment, perhaps, when humans first experienced an urge for expressive signification and made their extraordinary marks on the walls of the caves. "And by the way, speaking of cave-men," writes Lawrence, "how did these prognathous semi-apes of Altamira come to depict so delicately, so beautifully, a female bison charging, with swinging udder, or deer stooping feeding, or an antediluvian mammoth deep in contemplation. It is art on a pure, high level. . . . Hadn't someone better write Mr. Wells' History backwards, to prove how we've degenerated, in our stupid visionlessness, since the cave-men?"[67] Lawrence's romantic claim for the purity of the bison (figured in a large color plate in *The Outline of History*) and other wall images as artistic figuration is in many ways less eccentric than typical.

Wells's writings form a crucial missing piece in our understanding of how modernism came to prehistory, nurtured its archeological imagination, and conceived the relation of the long past to the present. All of the writers just named learned from Wells's writings on prehistory, reacted against them, and treated them to their modernist praxis. Lawrence's quip is only the most overt and instructive; everyone knows what "Mr. Wells' History" is and can be assumed, moreover, to have a sense of what it would mean to write it backward (that is, to work against Wells's progressive hypothesis). The relation could be symbiotic (as, for instance with Wells and Conrad; *Heart of Darkness* rewrote *The Time Machine*, transposing its literal time travel onto a more figurative form). That modernists at times openly disdained Wells or despaired of his authority should not blind us to his importance in their creative directions. It is also, less tendentiously, a story of shared intellectual and cultural milieu. All of these writers, including Wells, exemplify Gillian Beer's argument that it was at this moment, when Freud met Darwin, that the history of mankind was discovered (often figured *as discovery*) inside the psyche, or in childhood, or hiding within our cultural artifacts. It is a zeitgeist, constellating cultural interest in terms that range from biological (Darwin, Huxley), to psychological (Freud), to collective or holistic (Jung, Western accounts of Buddhism), to anthropological and archeological (Frazer, Freud, Weston, Harrison, Malinowski). With the exception of Freudian psychology, Wells wrote about and within each of these disciplines, and his own imagination was powerfully formed in relation to their narratives of the origin and progress of humankind. Whereas modernism approached prehistory with caution, however, dipping in a toe here, considering its lingering effects there, Wells immersed himself in the long ages before writing with the same gusto and knack for catching readerly interest he also brought to the future. Its style was visual, expressive, descriptive—as needed to recreate these long-lost scenes—one especially attuned to the breaks, clashes, and disjunctions that, for Wells, characterize all of our movements through time.

Three additional works, beyond the passages in *The Time Machine, Ann Veronica, The World of William Clissold*, and *The Croquet Player* we have considered, contribute to the rich panorama of prehistory in Wells's corpus: the first hundred pages or so of *The Outline of History* and two stories from earlier and later in Wells's career, "A Story of the Stone Age" (1897) and "The Grisly Folk" (1921). Together they model an immersive relation to prehistory, where a full range of textual temporalities is considered. Along with those moments of rupture when the past invades the present via its relics and traces, and complementing the awareness of continuity in the long historical scheme, what these texts offer is the direct encounter with early humans. Their visions are often harsh, violent, and off-putting yet also compelling and uncanny. And, for all the shared cultural surround, the depictions here differ from modernism and from some of the other Wellsian texts we have considered, stepping forward to fill in the gaps and unknowns, rather than dwell on features of fragmentariness and mystery. In their direct, unabashed entry into prehistorical time, they invaded the scene of early-twentieth-century imagining.

"Can these bones live?" This is how Wells begins one of his prehistoric musings, with a nod to the prophet Ezekiel, filtering modernism's and the more general public's archeological interests:

> Could anything be more dead, more mute and inexpressive to the inexpert eye than the ochreous fragments of bone and the fractured lumps of flint that constitute the first traces of something human in the world? We see them in the museum cases, sorted out in accordance with principles we do not understand, labelled with strange names. Chellean, Mousterian, Solutrian and the like, taken mostly from the places Chelles, La Moustier, Solutre, and so forth where the first specimens were found. Most of us stare through the glass at them, wonder vaguely for a moment at that half-savage, half-animal past of our race, and pass on. "Primitive man," we say. "Flint implements. The mammoth used to chase him." Few of us realise yet how much the subtle, indefatigable cross-examination of the scientific worker has been extracting from the evidence of these rusty and obstinate witnesses during the last few years.

> (*CSS*, 607)

The emphasis, in these last lines, is on science—on its branch of archeology, and especially on its practitioners, with their patience and open-minded attitude to the past. Scientists here are indispensable, yet they also have their traditions (the use of place names to label early beings, say), which may stymie rather than generate broader interest, much less awe. Likened to lawyers, they work with the recalcitrant, silent material that represents the genesis, Wells always wants to proclaim, for the great story of all of us, even if they are not, ultimately, the tellers. It is these specialists who first unlock a huge lost world, opening the way for writers and artists to follow. Perhaps Wells is their medium. Perhaps it was his role to move the idiom from such passing phrases as "Primitive Man . . . Flint implements" to a full envisioning of prehistoric worlds. In so doing, Wells spoke very forcefully to his contemporaries.

Let us recall Woolf's gestures, in *Between the Acts*, toward far-off temporalities. It is her last novel, a writing suffused with end-of-life affect, attuned to the pressing question of survival and harking back more than any other to the prehistoric past. In the novel's penultimate lines, she takes us back most directly, in a vivid tableau: "The house had lost its shelter. It was night before roads were made, or houses. It was the night that dwellers in caves had watched from some high place among rocks" (*BA*, 219). As in the beginning, so now, the basic units of human existence, shelter from storm or predator, become the pressing questions. Characters become silhouettes, the drama plays in starker and more elemental terms. Like her author, Miss La Trobe also has an attraction to the idea of human origins, her next play rising out of the mud in a kind of primal utterance, as she sits in the pub and feels the germination of a new work stirring, herself perhaps channeling the same primordial beginnings as her envisioned characters. And then there is Lucy Swithin, who is reading *The Outline of History* at the beginning and the end of the novel. Or is she?

> She had stretched for her favorite reading—an Outline of History—and had spent the hours between three and five thinking of rhododendron forests in Piccadilly; when the entire continent, not then, she understood, divided by a channel, was all one; populated, she understood, by elephant-bodied, seal-necked, heaving, surging, slowly writhing, and, she supposed, barking monsters; the iguanodon, the mammoth, and the mastodon; from whom presumably, she thought, jerking the window open, we descend.
>
> (*BA*, 8–9)

Lucy turned the page, quickly, guiltily, like a child who will be told to go to bed before the end of the chapter.

"Prehistoric man," she read, "half-human, half-ape, roused himself from his semi-crouching position and raised great stones."

(*BA*, 218)

As we know, *The Outline* was a bestseller, and Lucy Swithin seems an excellent encapsulation of one of its readers (today we might chart her within Wells's reading demographic), that generous swath of the public that cannot easily be categorized according to high-, middle-, or lowbrow.

To set the passages together, therefore, shows how the two works and authors illuminate each other, in an intricate and complex partnership. Woolf's renditions are generalized and impressionistic; prehistory ferments in Lucy's mind and in *Between the Acts* as a category and space for dreaming. It plays on fears and visions, allowing the mind to imagine difference. These passages have traveled far from Wells's prehistory segments, which are scientific and detailed, marked by divisions, subdivisions, and charts. The closest passage to this portion of *The Outline* would have to be this one:[68]

But at Trinil, in Java, in strata which are said to correspond either to the later Pliocene or to the American and European First Ice Age, there have been found some scattered bones of a creature, such as the makers of these early implements may have been. . . . The creature was not a man, nor was it an arboreal ape like the chimpanzee. It was a walking ape. It has been named by naturalists *Pithecanthropus erectus* (the walking ape-man). We cannot say that it is a direct human ancestor, but we may guess that the creatures who scattered these first stone tools over the world must have been closely similar and kindred, and that our ancestor was a beast of like kind. This little trayful of bony fragments from Trinil is, at present, apart from stone implements, the oldest relic of early humanity, or of the close blood relations of early humanity, that is known.

While these early men or "sub-men" were running about Europe four or five hundred thousand years ago, there were mammoths, rhinoceroses, a huge hippopotamus, a giant beaver, and a bison and wild cattle in their world . . .

After this first glimpse of something at least sub-human in the record of geology, there is not another fragment of human or man-like bone yet known from that record for an interval of hundreds of thousands of years.

(*OH*, 1:68–69)

What a difference! Lucy is, like Woolf, engaged in imaginative rather than literal reading. She is a dreamer more than an exact reader, and she certainly must have been drifting during the relevant biology lesson, since Wells overtly refutes any claim of direct human descent from the great reptiles or from most of the early humanlike creatures. Yet one apprehends Wells here, and throughout *Between the Acts*, excavating and building up the rich, descriptive world behind and absorbed in Woolf's spare artistry.

At the same time, others of Wells's prehistory texts attend to these same questions of the first appearances of humans on the European scene in a spirit more akin to storytelling than to the *Outline*'s scientific narration. Let us listen to the opening of "A Story of the Stone Age," originally published in 1897 (collected 1899) and included in the 1927 *Complete Short Stories of H. G. Wells*:

> This story is of a time beyond the memory of man, before the beginning of history, a time when one might have walked dryshod from France (as we call it now) to England, and when a broad and sluggish Thames flowed through its marshes to meet its father Rhine, flowing through a wide and level country that is under water in these latter days, and which we know by the name of the North Sea. In that remote age the valley which runs along the foot of the Downs did not exist, and the south of Surrey was a range of hills, fir-clad on the middle slopes, and snow-capped for the better part of the year. The cores of its summits still remain as Leith Hill, and Pitch Hill, and Hindhead. . . . Fifty thousand years ago it was, fifty thousand years—if the reckoning of geologists is correct.
>
> And in those days the spring-time was as joyful as it is now, and sent the blood coursing in just the same fashion.
>
> (*CSS*, 656)

Or again, in the later story "The Grisly Folk" (also in the *Complete Short Stories*): "They were still savages, very prone to violence and convulsive in their lusts and desires . . . the true men drifted northward from the lost lands of the Mediterranean valley into the high Spanish valleys and the south and centre of France, and so on to what is now England—for there was no Channel then between England and France" (*CSS*, 611). We find in these lines, and throughout the stories, ample signals of a different Wells, a storyteller willing to plunge into the erased days of early humanity just as he dwelled in the speculative future, hundreds and thousands of years forward, a voice closer to modernism, perhaps, than to the historian of *The Outline*.[69] Wells stands out through this long period as a creative force generating the idea of the early life of the earth and its inhabitants.[70]

"A Story of the Stone Age" and "The Grisly Folk" are violent tales—we should not be fooled by the pleasant springtime of that opening—both of which transpire in and around moments of transition in the early epochs of human life. "The Grisly Folk" is not really a story but rather a musing, a Montaignian *essai* on the subject of early human and prehuman types, those named in the museum cases, which Wells sets out to awaken into visual life. In tone and content, he vacillates between scientific explication (this is what archeologists have found and hypothesized) and a more individual conjuring, as the storyteller takes over from—or perhaps encroaches on—the specialist. From an idiom of this sort— "Scientific authorities already distinguish four species of these pseudo-men"— the story shifts into a tentative stage where sentences or paragraphs might begin "We can understand" or "We can imagine," until such caveats are abandoned and the narrator simply tells his story of these lost days. We thus watch as Wells brings the silent bones in the museum case into vibrant narrative, complete with his habitual self-commentary on the process and meaning of his narrative mode. The story's conclusion, in good Wellsian form, makes this premise explicit: "A day may come," he forecasts, "when these recovered memories may grow as vivid as if we in our own persons had been there and shared the thrill and the fear of those primordial days; a day may come when the great beasts of the past will leap to life again in our imaginations, when we shall walk again in vanished scenes, stretch pained limbs we thought were dust, and feel again the sunshine of a million years ago" (*CSS*, 608, 611, 612, 621). That day has come in the reading moment, and it is equally accurate to find that day slowly emerging, if more tentatively, in the literary inquiries of modernism.

The concluding paragraphs of "The Grisly Folk" capture with special clarity, and with Wells's familiar style of intuition, one way of expressing the relation of stone age to present age, a formulation that conjoins all the elements we have been finding across the range of prehistorical thought:

> What leapings of the heart were there not throughout that long warfare [between Neanderthals and early humans]! What moments of terror and triumph! What acts of devotion and desperate wonders of courage! And the strain of the victors was our strain; we are lineally identical with those sun-brown painted beings who ran and fought and helped one another, the blood in our veins glowed in those fights and chilled in those fears of the forgotten past. For it was forgotten. Except perhaps for some vague terrors in our dreaming life and for some lurking element of tradition in the legends and warnings of the nursery, it has gone altogether out of the memory of our race. But nothing is ever completely lost. Seventy or eighty years ago a few curious *savants* began to suspect that there were hidden memories in certain big chipped flints and scraps of bone they found in ancient gravels. Much more recently others have

begun to find hints of remote strange experiences in the dreams and odd kinks in modern minds. By degrees these dry bones began to live again.

This restoration of the past is one of the most astonishing adventures of the human mind.

(*CSS*, 620)

Whatever is triumphalist in these sentiments, they remain largely a salutation for all humanity. They are fictional counterparts to *The Outline*, which was explicit in its goal of recruiting the common history of all people into a political drive for a single world community. Equally, what stands out is the picture of emerging humanity as formed by violence and terror, leaving its traces in nightmare and in the unconscious mind—this we might have expected—but also as cooperative and progressive, bound for better things.

For Wells, then, the discovery of a universal prehistoric past is hitched to the prospect of an improved futurity, and in this, once again, he and modernism push in their divergent directions. In all the modernist works discussed here, and more widely throughout the period, to recognize what is truly ancient persisting here in the present is to come face to face with a grave threat; at the minimum, it means taking stock of one's own potential barbarity. Typically such reckoning is the epitome of danger and force: Forster's caves work that way, as do the final lines of *Between the Acts*, the canonical imperial violence named in *Heart of Darkness* ("exterminate all the brutes"), and Wells's own *The Croquet Player*, with its vivid recognition of the caveman as fascist dictator. At the same time, as critics have long noted, the primitivism thesis is, in essence, a narrative of liberation: to find the primitive is to free the modern, industrialized person from his shackles, discovering in the naturalized self the unbounded possibilities (erotic, artistic, psychic) associated with earlier cultures and people. These familiar tropes are, in terms of prehistory, perhaps channeled into the Eliotic claim of the cave artists as ancestors of "the mind of Europe." Wells's stories, like *The Outline*, share with modernism the fertile ground of imagining prehistory but differ in having, we might say, an agenda, a view of prehistory as grounding a cooperative world community.

If the conclusion of "The Grisly Folk" catapults the story back to where it began, in the present, where one might think of conjoining the long past with the desired future, the primary narrative of the tale, like "A Story of the Stone Age," concerns a time in history when the first stirrings of self-consciousness are, Wells intimates, germinating. Above all, it treats an intriguingly speculative feature of the landscape of fifty thousand or so years ago, the confrontation of two

groups or subspecies, early *Homo sapiens* (us), as we arrived on the scene, in ultimate conflict with our predecessors, the Neanderthals (or grisly folk). "Almost
certainly they met," Wells writes of this great exchange across the European
expanses, "these grisly men and the true men. The true man must have come into
the habitat of the Neandertaler, and the two must have met and fought. Some
day we may come upon the evidences of this warfare" (*CSS*, 610). In advance of
possible discoveries, it is the storyteller who steps in to provide the lineaments
of such engagement. There is a kind of tension, in fact, between the way the past
stands out vividly, its fantastic story demanding to be told, and the murkiness
and unreliability of what we actually know, so that it is above all the fiction writer
whose craft is generated. Listen, for instance, to this construction: "The tribe
travelled light. They were mainly naked, but all of them were painted with white
and black and red and yellow ochre. At this distance of time it is difficult to see
whether they were tattooed. Probably they were not" (*CSS*, 612). *At this distance
of time*, one might wonder how we can see the red, white, black, and yellow so
precisely; it is the work of Wells's texts simultaneously to show us in brilliant
detail these exceedingly unfamiliar worlds yet remind us of the speculative and
scientific work underlying all such imaginative projects.

Even within the story's action, Wells emphasizes moments when the visual
becomes at once acutely important and uncertain, such as when the two groups
encounter each other for the first time:

> The eyes of the whole tribe swung round to the pointing finger.
>
> The group became one rigid stare. . . .
>
> Far away down the slope with his body in profile and his head turned
> towards them, frozen by an equal amazement, stood a hunched grey figure, big-
> ger but shorter than a man . . .
>
> For a little while this animal scrutiny held discoverers and discovered
> motionless. . . . Then he [the Neanderthal] halted again for a moment to look at
> the newcomers, waved an arm strangely, and then dashed into cover.
>
> The shadows of the thicket swallowed him up, and by hiding him seemed to
> make him enormous. It identified itself with him, and watched them with his
> eyes. Its tree stems became long silvery-limbs, and a fallen trunk crouched and
> stared.
>
> (*CSS*, 613–14)

The drama is one of mutual spectatorship, an uncanny mirror stage in the
development of the group, generating in the watchers some kind of primary

consciousness; one knows the self by seeing the other. Wells is free with suggestions about how the humans take stock of this new development in their world, though he always demurs on the Neanderthals, whose thoughts, he concludes, are just too far from ours to allow for the imaginative articulations of fiction. If he can enter the *mind* of an early human, he is thwarted by the *brain* of those beings who evolved along a different branch. Such impenetrability is figured, here, in the shadows that absorb the Neanderthal and "make him enormous," as Wells plays with his own brand of psychoanalytic theory. He comments in these works on the way these early forms of conflict and terror might carry over into our world, perhaps in the dreams of childhood or in folkloric motifs, and he hypothesizes the Neanderthal as the original for the ogre. It might be that self-consciousness itself is born here, in these confrontations and clashes. We might also note—it is irresistible—that the Neanderthals, as they streak by in the shadows, grayish, eerie, us and not us, figure as doubles of the Morlocks, especially as the Traveller first encounters them in the twilight. Perhaps, eight hundred thousand years from now, the whole world narrative has come full circle, and the grisly folk, eventually eliminated and superseded by humanity in the far past, are getting the last laugh.

From the stress on such moments of arrested looking, "The Grisly Folk" shifts easily into a tale of violent exchanges between the groups. Violence in "The Grisly Folk" is the telos more than the object of representation, as the story makes its way from the museum, through hedging speculation, into the vivid colors of painted bodies and the first encounters, and then quickly into children vanishing, new forms of war and conflict, "a nightmare age" of kidnapping and fear, an epoch of enmity. "Many and obstinate were the duels and battles these two sorts of men fought for this world in that bleak age of the windy steppes, thirty or forty thousand years ago. The two races were intolerable to each other" (*CSS*, 619). The logic of such fighting is absolute, a kind of destiny, claimed as the trajectory of prehistory, reinforced at the level of narrative.

Violence, loss, trauma, occluded memories, extinction, victory, continuity . . . these mark the Wellsian prehistorical world. In "A Story of the Stone Age," much more than in "The Grisly Folk," these arrive in gruesome excess. This time, the early humans are caught in a struggle against themselves. It details an early human community that constitutes itself by violence; the group ejects its own (in this case a young couple), to reinstate them only when subdued by force. The young people, outside the circle of the group before violently reestablishing themselves, also fight an elemental struggle against the great cave bears, who function, along with the Old Man of the tribe, as the primary adversary for the couple at the center of the story. "A Story of the Stone Age" is, in a funny way, conventional: the tale of a Eudena (the young woman) and Ugh-lomi (her lover) who choose each other over the security and stasis of the group and its leader. Their romantic choice precipitates a crisis in the community, a period of exile in the wilderness where their strength is tested, and a final return to the tribe, now readjusted to their (victorious) position as leaders. One could neatly map the tale onto, say, the shape of the European bildungsroman. Yet the trials, suffering, and victories are excessively bloody—one of the innovations the story tells is of the first time a man thought to attach a stone to a branch, making a club, and I think we know what follows—with both of the young protagonists put through intensely horrific bodily torment. Return to the group comes not with any metaphorical Oedipal overturning but with the actual killing of the leader and his allies. The message is blunt: the movement through time represented by evolution should not be sanitized or smoothed. It is fought tooth and nail ("red in tooth in claw," as Tennyson has it). The story of humanity as it emerged by the time of recorded history may be, in Wells's telling, one of destined victory, but in these stories he stresses the blood and injury that accompanies any change in the biological and sociological order. Literary patterns are like that too, Wells's story suggests; they metaphorize and make spectral the intense violence standing beneath and before. In entering prehistory directly, Wells will make little accommodation to such attenuations.

## V. PREHISTORY IN *THE OUTLINE OF HISTORY*

These stories, then, make their mark in figuring the prehistory of humanity in terms of conflict and bodily trial, slow innovation (again violent), and the dramatic moments when change suddenly becomes visible. They also call attention to *how* one manages these extremely strange and disorienting subjects—subjects, after all, whose defining quality is that they cannot be known in any concrete way. In *The Outline of History*, Wells recalibrates the balance to some degree, as the history attempts a full consideration of how and what we know of these early days, complete with a full roster of charts, maps, and renderings of flints, skulls, cave drawings, and the like. In the first edition, serialized over twenty-four installments, there were also several standout color plates from this part of the history, including a depiction of one of the most beautiful and oft-discussed of the Altamira cave drawings (the bison so admired by Lawrence—no doubt he saw the reproduction here) and an especially sensational, fanciful rendering of a pair of Neanderthal-related prehumans standing in a cave entrance. In a certain way, *The Outline* provides, in the form of its illustrations, some of what Wells's fiction rendered as red, blue, yellow, or ochred bodies. The pictorial qualities of *The Outline* are essential to its overall function and appeal; in the case of the prehistory sections, they do a special work, since the injunction to visualize is unusually pressing and overt when the archive is so partial, fragmentary, and speculative. As with the project of anticipation, moreover, there is some risk in making all these explicit forays into unknown temporalities, and Wells received some of his harshest and most contemptuous criticism in relation to his treatment of the Neanderthals and other early people. His tendency to follow the essay "Primal Law" (1903), by the archeologist James Jackson Atkinson, which lays out a social organization based on an Old Man at the center of tribal life, was particularly ripe for derision.[71]

Yet there is good reason why the public, not heeding the wagging fingers of historians, was engrossed by these early segments, from the fiery origination of the earth as it broke off from the sun (the prevailing theory in 1919 when Wells was writing) through to the segments on early historical cultures. Prehistory in *The Outline* has three key characteristics: it is accessible, it is also uncanny, and its temporal phases are unfathomably long. As we have noted (in the passage that began, "Speculations about geological time vary enormously"), the misapprehension of recorded and recent history in relation to the scale captured in the longue durée is one of Wells's reiterated motifs throughout *The Outline*. These prehistory sequences require that we constantly check and recalibrate our temporal apparatus, and this mental exercise adds to the overall interest, a kind of magnetism, in these pages. One could name any number of passages where the stretches of prehistoric time are elaborated with especially rich, engrossing results. To take one such: Wells's spellbinding description of the Mediterranean basin filling up is characteristic—an event that would seem never to have entered most readers minds *as event*—of how he takes us down the reaches of time, elaborating the tremendous ramifications of these nearly unfathomable experiences. The passage captures the flavor and style of the early stages of *The Outline*, particularly its treatment of time and scale:

> But if this reasoning is sound, then where to-day roll the blue waters of the Mediterranean there must once have been great areas of land, and land with a very agreeable climate. This was probably the case during the last Glacial Age.... Certainly there must have been Grimaldi people, and perhaps even

Azilian and Neolithic people going about in the valleys and forests of these regions that are now submerged ...

This refilling of the Mediterranean, which by the rough chronology we are employing in this book may have happened somewhen between 30,000 and 10,000 B.C., must have been one of the greatest single events in the pre-history of our [human] race.... Suddenly the ocean waters began to break through over the westward hills and to pour in upon these primitive peoples—the lake that had been their home and friend became their enemy; its waters rose and never abated; their settlements were submerged; the waters pursued them in their flight. Day by day and year by year the waters spread up the valleys and drove mankind before them. Many must have been surrounded and caught by the continually rising salt flood. It knew no check; it came faster and faster; it rose over the tree-tops, over the hills, until it had filled the whole basin of the present Mediterranean and until it lapped the mountain cliffs of Arabia and Africa. Far away, long before the dawn of history, this catastrophe occurred.

(OH, 1:120–21).

Infusing the vast events of the past with a sense of present urgency and reality, Wells sets the tone; what rivets is the mixture of event and slow passage that characterizes historical time. Sequences like this one move in a constant back and forth between notations of scale (the huge distance in time or the massiveness of the geological event) and a feeling for how such situations would have been experienced in their present. *The Outline*, in fact, proffers the same masterful blending of detachment with deep sympathy that characterizes modernism; both see history with a cool eye, both drop into it as into a funnel, expressing its granular reality as if from within. But for Wells, that rendering of the distant past is complete, systematic, and accessible; its meaning is more textured than in the fragmentary treatments that have become canonical from the period, at once more personal and more worldwide.

The other two qualities that exemplify prehistory in *The Outline* are closely allied with the way scale is handled—it is the combination of accessibility and strangeness that gives these pages their distinctive flavor, and established the ground, I think, for the book's worldwide success. Wells is at his pedagogical best in the early sequences, as in the first short chapter, "The Earth in Space and Time," which offers a mini astronomy lesson, making use especially of analogies to orient the reader to the immensity of scale, giving familiar frameworks that allow one to ponder these immensities. Of greatest import in these few pages is to establish a sense of the planet's apartness, silence, singularity. As Wells notes, having run through the parameters of the major celestial forms, *"All the rest of space about us and around us and for unfathomable distances beyond is cold, life-less, and void"* (*OH*, 1:4, italics in the original). Wells's technique in these first pages is reiterated and refined over the next few hundred, as he creates an easy congress between seemingly straightforward presentation of historical/scientific narra-tive and these pauses over what remains stupendous, astonishing, disorienting, and transfixing in the long passages of time and the wide traverses of space. As in the depiction of the Mediterranean filling up, Wells's invocations of the great events in the earth's past invite the reader to pause on stimulating facts and ideas, and these are often about scale itself, about our systems for knowing the past and the tricks time plays on our understanding. It is perhaps easy to overlook the accom-plishment, but we should not. All the early chapters have this quality of balance, combining lesson with wonder, with the provocation to stop and think. In these ways, *The Outline* teaches, shows, and reveals, developing a unique reading expe-rience, especially well tuned in the prehistory sections.

Here, for instance, the first traces of life on the planet are deduced, through painstaking attention to the "Record of the Rocks":

> First comes the evidence of a diversity of shell-fish, crabs, and such-like crawling things, worms, seaweeds, and the like; then of a multitude of fishes and of the beginnings of land plants and land creatures. These rocks are called the Palaeo-zoic (ancient life) rocks. They mark a vast era, during which life was slowly spreading, increasing, and developing in the seas of our world. Through long ages, through the earliest Palaeozoic time, it was no more than a proliferation of such swimming and creeping things in the water. There were creatures called trilobites; they were crawling things like big sea wood-lice that were probably related to the American king-crab of today. There were also sea-scorpions, the prefects of that early world . . .
>
> It was not a display of life to excite our imaginations. There was nothing that ran or flew or even swam swiftly or skillfully. Except for the size of some of the creatures, it was not very different from, and rather less various than, the kind of life a student would gather from any summer-time ditch nowadays for micro-scopic examination. Such was the life of the shallow seas through a hundred million years or more in the early Palaeozoic period. The land during that time was apparently absolutely barren. We find no trace nor hint of land life.
>
> (*OH*, 1:10)

Perhaps these crustaceans, giant wood-lice, sea-scorpions, and waving weeds are not such as to fire our imaginations, but, then again, the comparison used to demonstrate their commonality works, contrary to Wells's suggestion, to stimulate wonder and trigger thought, as it transforms a bucket of swamp water in a child's science class into the original seas of the world. And then, one cannot fail to notice that Wells had ended the world in *The Time Machine*, thirty million years from now (or twenty-five years ago in actual time), with very similar, enormous crablike creatures, their long tentacles tickling the Traveller's neck. In the beginning, so in the end, the Wellsian temporal fold encompasses these passages, creating the kind of metatextual conversation across his works we saw in chapter 1 to be one of his signatures. Within the passage and throughout these chapters, Wells enlists his figures to make distant spectacles present and recognizable ("the prefects of that early world"), while stretching our thinking to the edges of what's comprehensible (those long millions of years, a teeming ocean next to entirely lifeless land).

All throughout the prehistory segments, *The Outline* creates a form of suspense as it unfolds the story of our world. Each stage has its surprising revelations, showing us the earth's history in ways that ring true and new—and how much greater this newness must have seemed to the book's first readers, who would not have had the kind of regular, generalized familiarity with earth sciences, anthropology, and world history common today. Thus, after the dominance of the seas, life slowly spreads up out of the water. A particularly exciting development here is the evolution of the internal lung; the humble amphibian turns into a major actor in the outcomes of all life on land. Next come the great ages of the dinosaurs (or "reptiles") and mammals, and *The Outline* is rich in illustration and description of these creatures, often unusual versions of an animal we can almost recognize, visually arresting testaments to the nature and particularity of evolutionary diversity.

Wells's approach to early humankind, like his treatment of the evolution of life in the text's previous sections, is to place it concretely within its history and context, teasing out the available scientific hypotheses and attempting judgment as needed, always setting the sensational and strange alongside the recognizable. Such thoroughness furnishes a strong contrast with the solitary prehistoric event or singular cave encounter that most often transfixes modernism, a key outcome of his generic experimentation. And it is not solely the past and surrounding context that grounds his speculations about early humanity. These sections also lead forward into discussion of early thought, languages, the world's races, the first civilizations, the relationship of sea to land. Prehistory, in other words, is not an isolated time in the reaches of the past and lurking somewhere in our unconscious minds—or rather is not only that—but a placeholder that names the slow, always ongoing movements in the inevitable, forward slide of time. Recall the encounters that structured "The Grisly Folk" and "A Story of the Stone Age"; those dynamic, violent periods when (pre)historical change comes into view. There is no singular moment when we arrive at history. Instead *The Outline* figures these two great epochs as a continuity. In some ways, in fact, the invisible shift from prehistory into history is even more startling than the strangeness of the early seas or the parsing out of the confusing traces of different stone-age men. Homer's famous warriors, to take one instance, are proffered in *The Outline* as instances of a particular human moment, one common at various times and places across history, products of systemic change. These classic characters, so deeply engrained in Western notions of cultural and literary beginnings, look entirely unfamiliar when we come to them from the thousands of years leading into their world, rather than from our habitual stance of looking back at them through the tunnel of millennia and the haze of mythology:

> The *Iliad* . . . gives us that [neolithic] life already well on the move towards a new state of affairs. . . . Now, as the climate of great portions of the earth was swinging toward drier and more open conditions again, the primitive neolithic life was developing along two divergent directions. One was leading to a more wandering life, towards at last a constantly migratory life between summer and winter pasture, which is called NOMADISM; the other, in certain sunlit river valleys, was towards a water-treasuring life of irrigation, in which men gathered into the first towns and made the first CIVILIZATION. . . . The Greeks, as the *Iliad* presents them . . . are primitive nomads in an excited state, because they have just come upon civilization, and regard it as an opportunity for war and loot.
>
> (*OH*, 1:176–77)

Wells is always happy to debunk whatever is cherished in high culture, and the Iliadic heroes here certainly look shoddy next to the honor-loving, beautifully spoken warriors created by Homer. But the primary point is not to debunk; it is to rehistoricize. The epic itself becomes a reading tool, like the record of the rocks, and one, above all, that tells of the infinite modality of history's moments, how each period in history exists in constant, moving relation to what came before and what will supersede it. There is nothing static, fixed, finished about any moment in the past, any more than the Time Traveller can find in the natural history museum of the far future the lineation from his world to the age of the Eloi and Morlocks. A is always becoming B, more or less. *The Outline*, like so much of Wells's work, is a testament to unending change and movement. It begins "The earth on which we live is a spinning globe" and ends with an invocation of "Life, for ever dying to be born afresh, for ever young and eager," stretching itself into outer space (*OH*, 1:3, 2:595). The principle of growth, it turns out, is also the principle of history. There are no origins, no beginnings, only what came before and what follows.

## VI. HISTORY

The prehistory sections represent, in so many ways, the quintessence of *The Outline of History*, that felicitous mixture of education, evocation, wonder, and analysis that enabled its phenomenal reach. They exemplify its readerly pleasure and must have performed especially admirably in the initial serial format, where the suspense—the construction of an engrossing story whose next stages beckon—takes formal shape in the short biweekly block. Here, moreover, the principle of choice is less visible or controversial than it becomes when the history moves toward the modern era, the likelihood of snubbing any group minimal, Neanderthal enthusiasts notwithstanding. Thus the eminent American historian Carl Becker recognizes in these early segments the genius of the history; in the prehistory discussion, he intuits, Wells is "on good terms with his subject."[72] But *The Outline* functions at two scales: there are the smaller passages, engrossing, suspenseful, friendly to excerpting, and these recount, in the later stages, all manner of human foible and failing, and there are the large themes and agendas, where Wells establishes historical patterns, making his case for the slow but inevitable development of the world community. That each of these two registers does not always support the other should not surprise us. Thus *The Outline* will make this point as one of its creeds:

> Our history has traced a steady growth of the social and political units into which men have combined. In the brief period of ten thousand years these units have grown from the small family tribe of the early neolithic culture to the vast united realms—vast yet still too small and partial—of the preset time.... If our *Outline* has been faithfully drawn, and if these brief conclusions are sound, it follows that we are engaged upon an immense task of adjustment to these great lines upon which our affairs are moving. Our wars, our social conflict, our enormous economic stresses, are all aspects of that adjustment. The loyalties and allegiances to-day are at best provisional loyalties and allegiances. Our true

State, this state that is already beginning, this state to which every man owes his utmost political effort, must be now this nascent Federal World State to which human necessities point. Our true God is now the God of all men. Nationalism as a God must follow the tribal gods to limbo. Our true nationality is mankind.

(*OH*, 2:579–80)

At this point in our study, these statements ring familiar, the faith in united humanity driving Wells's effort, *The Outline* concluding where it began, with the promise that universal history might yield universal peace.

Yet anyone who has read the full history might ask herself, does this actually characterize what I have read? It is not only that Wells is reading *history* through a prism (looking back in order to find the genesis of what he dreams will be our happier future), but he is also reading *his history* through the same prism. The primacy of internal contradiction and critique is one of Wells's writing codes, and *The Outline* exemplifies this practice to a very high degree, since its two scalar reading levels contradict each other in stark ways. The narrative of history he relates is varied, marvelous, textured, sometimes questionable, and almost never amenable to the moral just stated, that the history of humanity is one of increased unification pointing to ultimate harmony. Wells tells of the great aspirations and inspiring potentiality of his many subjects and then equally of the failure, disappointment, and crushing loss that, in one context after another, finally ensue. One such example finds Wells commenting on the extraordinary failure, as he views it, of Alexander the Great: "Here was the great world of men between India and the Adriatic ready for union, ready as it had never been before for a unifying control. Here was the wide order of the Persian empire with its roads, its posts, its general peace and prosperity, ripe for the fertilizing influence of the Greek mind. . . . Here was Alexander in many ways gifted above any man of his time, and he was vain, suspicious, and passionate" (*OH*, 1:377). Over and over, *The Outline* charts a pattern of tremendous promise, followed by awful waste and disaster (in history), followed at some point by an unexpected, perhaps unjustified upsurge in enthusiasm for humanity's accomplishments and hope for our future (in this history).

This practice is most fully exemplified in the last two chapters of *The Outline*, which swing from the First World War, presented in all its garish slaughter and futility, the spotlight on its political idiocy, into the imagined future of a unified globe, where humanity has conquered its hitherto insoluble problems and is moving forward into a promising future. Wells concludes *The Outline* on a note of defiant enthusiasm, retrofitting the crescendo he had parlayed in *The*

*Discovery of the Future* and *The Food of the Gods*, a favored image of humanity on its quest for happiness and progress: "Gathered together at last under the leadership of man, the student-teacher of the universe, unified, disciplined, armed with the secret powers of the atom and with knowledge as yet beyond dreaming, Life, for ever dying to be born afresh, for ever young and eager, will presently stand upon this earth as upon a footstool, and stretch out its realm amidst the stars" (*OH*, 2:595). Yet this last chapter rolling forth the bright future follows jarringly from what immediately precedes it, which details, first, the war, and, perhaps even more ominous for the future, the catastrophically vindictive peace treaty of Versailles. It should be manifest that this utter betrayal of the possibility of a just, lasting peace, one that would retroactively confer redemption on the war, is deeply resonant for Wells and *The Outline*. After all, Wells's creed that the war must become the one to make future wars impossible was, by all rights, crushed by the terms of Versailles. Yet *The Outline* continues to will such outcomes. It thus maintains—though it is hard not to scent a spirit of creeping desperation—that this *has to have been* the war that will still end war. The tense is shifting into a time of the impossible, a temporality where what the war will do becomes what the war will have done or what we still must do to make it have done: "The catastrophe of the war was not an unnecessary disaster; it was a necessary fulfillment of such an age of drift [as just described]. Only through a catastrophe, it may be, could a new phase of human thought and will have become possible" (*OH*, 2:573).

The only way, indeed, for one to retrofit the details of what actually happens to the larger pattern and goal of *The Outline* is by a leap of faith—or rather of history. "It is absurd to despair of mankind because of these treaties," Wells declares, "Creation was not there [at Versailles]. But a great process of thought spreads throughout the world; many thousands of men and women, in every country . . . are awakening to their responsibility . . . and upon them it is that we must rest our hope" (*OH*, 2:566–67). As Forster noted in his perceptive review of *The Outline*, the problem with Wellsian optimism is that it can always be retemporalized: if the present has turned bleak, we can look to the future; if the immediate future will not deliver, we can jump another few hundred years. "There is no collaring these optimists," writes Forster, "They asked for science in 1914, they got it, and in 1920 they still ask for science."[73] And he is right. Wells can thus write briskly that

> Sooner or later [world] unity must come or else plainly men must perish by their own inventions. We, because we believe in the power of reason and in the increasing good-will in men, find ourselves compelled to reject the latter

possibility. But the way to the former may be very long and tedious, very tragic and wearisome, a martyrdom of many generations, or it may be travelled over almost swiftly in the course of a generation or so.

(OH, 2;580)

As Forster intimated and as we have noted in the persistent dialectic of hope and despair that governs Wells's works, such a proclivity crops up in many other places. In *The Shape of Things to Come*, written fifteen years later, at a time when Wells's plan for world unity looked more and more like a mockery, the temporality for our future triumphs is spelled out according to a series of these leaps and bursts, with an especially long period of vast destruction and worldwide want before the new world begins to build itself up. It is Wells's most elaborate future history, and takes full advantage of its affordances. In the swoop from the failure of Versailles to the success of worldwide peace efforts articulated in *The Outline*, however, the incompatibility cannot be reconciled by genre: Wells the historian is shunted aside by the visionary. It is an elision almost identical, if on different temporal planes, to his move in *Discovery of the Future*, which shifted from arguing that prediction is a legitimate scientific enterprise to making some large predictions—enormously hopeful ones that even Wells admits derive more from his faith in a brilliant human destiny than from scientific evidence. The principle enumerated in *The Outline*, moreover, is familiar to us from Wells's wartime pamphlets; here, as in 1914, he can be seen willing into existence these "many thousands of men and women, in every country" who share his convictions and are imagined as instigating the revolution in their quiet way, the same "common intelligent people at large" envisioned and invoked during the war. Thus the pattern, once established, does not depend entirely on the history being narrated. The historical generalization may, at one level, be the story, but it also operates independently of the story's own contours.

This internal disruption of the spirit of outlining by the details of what is outlined might be seen as the history's most visible structural feature (or rather anomaly), and it is one that reaches across Wells's work. Wells, as we know, believed in the feasibility and value of planning: he proselytized endlessly for a scientific, systematic, comprehensive understanding of the world around us— around, before, and after us—even as his fictions are saturated by all the dark, creepy, anachronistic realities that might undermine those systems. The green ghosts of "The Plattner Story" (1896), which hover in a space adjacent to our own, watching and shadowing us in our oblivious activities, might stand as emblems of this writerly habit. As the next chapter will show more fully, Wells's great nemesis is waste, that which is always ready to mock Wells's efforts, a reminder, at the base level, of the mere organicism that humblingly defines us as living animals and, at the more singular level, the sign of inevitable failure that stalks Wells himself, no matter how furiously he writes or how widely he disseminates his ideas. We might think of the Martians who helped launch Wells's imaginative career, those seemingly impervious, omnipotent, highly evolved beings whose bodies, in the end, are shockingly vulnerable, easily and immediately destroyed by the tiniest and most abject of sources, invisible bacteria. The grand plan, for Wells, is always threatened by the infusoria. That the very same threat almost wipes out the Utopians in *Men Like Gods*, or that the possibility of pandemic always lingers as a potential cause of humanity's swift future extermination, suggests the trenchancy for Wells of this little worm in the vast woodwork. But the insecurity of systematicity is more ingrown; logic, reason, analytic thought, scientific reasoning and learning—these are great fonts of belief for Wells, but they are also dialectically composed of their many others, all their antagonists and complements.

Another version of this story is of the ongoing fluctuation, within so many of Wells's writings, between the principle (and/or the representation) of immense variety, the interest in peculiar detail, on one hand, and pattern, order, scheme, outline, on the other. Here is George in *Tono-Bungay*, modeling the process his author both will and will not follow and providing a miniature for Wells's very expansive project in *The Outline* and elsewhere. Having relayed his impressions of London, he will enter the Wellsian stream toward comprehensiveness, as an analytic frame emerges: "At first, no doubt, it was a chaos of streets and people and buildings and reasonless going to and fro. . . . Yet in time there has grown up in me a kind of theory of London; I do think I see lines of an ordered structure out of which it has grown, detected a process that is something more than a confusion of casual accidents, though indeed it may be no more than a process of disease."[74] Two operations, then, tussle in a mutual and ongoing operation, the specificity giving way to the pattern, the pattern belied by the specificity. "Reasonless going to and fro . . . a confusion of casual accidents": how perfect an encapsulation of what *The Outline* must systematize—and also a signpost for what makes it so exuberant and plural. Read in such terms, *The Outline* has an uncanny resemblance to another big book of its decade, which followed it a scant two years later and shares its passion for making and undoing its frameworks, building and toppling its scaffolds: *Ulysses*.

Wells unfurls several large patterns to organize and make sense of the thousands of years of history he encompasses, in addition to the primary motif of gradual world unification; if the latter has a tendency to deconstruct, others are notable for the way they encode the principle of regular, continual change. We have already seen Wells pushing back against shibboleths that would fix and isolate the heroic ages as they have come down to us. He is even more resistant to the idea that there is any reality behind national identity. Racial unity and purity are thoroughly dismissed, and Wells will corrode the basis even for something as seemingly straightforward as the continuous habitation of a people in a place. All of these principles used to naturalize nationalism are discredited from the roots. The mantra throughout is mixture, migration, adaptation, and mutability. Of the world's races, which he attempts to address with care and detail, the primary point is that "for thousands of years there have been two sets of forces at work, one tending to separate men into a multitude of local varieties, and another to remix and blend these varieties together before a separate species has been established" and that "in the present age, man is probably no longer undergoing differentiation at all. Readmixture is now a far stronger force than differentiation. Men mingle more and more" (*OH*, 1:136, 140).

It should be said that Wells's handling of race, though progressive for his time, reads equivocally in the present. Wells aims to tell the complete story of mankind, but his focus tends to drift back to Europe. *The Outline* engendered protests in India for the treatment of its modern history, to take just one example; also, the Aryans do have a way of grabbing more than their fair share of discussion. In the first books, covering prehistory and early civilizations, this emphasis on Europe and the Middle East stems from the fact that much more archeology had been undertaken in those areas. Too, we should not overlook the radical nature of such statements as "We must, for the sake of precision, repeat here two warnings we have already given the reader: first, that we use the word Aryan in its widest sense, to express all the early peoples who spoke languages of the 'Indo-Germanic' or 'Indo-European' group; and, secondly, that when we use the word Aryan we do not imply any racial purity" (*OH*, 1:298). Still, in weighing the effects of *The Outline*, the critic William T. Ross stresses what he sees as an inordinate emphasis on Aryan culture, arguing, for instance, that the drawings and photographs included in "The Races of Mankind" are troublingly hewed to stereotype.[75] The ideal of racial unity is easier for *The Outline* to embody in the long past and in the imagined future: in the here and now, Wells fails to express radical unity across races and geographies and hints instead at familiar connotations of racial difference.

"Men mingle more and more": in Wells's concept of *how* people have tended to generate the mixtures he names as universal are the lineaments of a theory of broad fluctuation, where history is envisioned according to great swings among states of being. There will be slow evolution, followed by a moment of crisis (what we might call "event"), then a shift back to gradualness, succeeded again by an event. Here, for instance, is an account of the relation between nomadism and civilization in the early historical periods:

> Down pour the united nomads on the unwarlike, unarmed plains, and there ensues a war of conquest. Instead of carrying off the booty, the conquerors settle down on the conquered land, which becomes all booty for them; the villagers and townsmen are reduced to servitude and tribute-paying, they become hewers of wood and drawers of water, and the leaders of the nomads become kings and princes, masters and aristocrats. They too settle down, they learn many of the arts and refinements of the conquered, they cease to be lean and hungry, but for many generations they retain traces of their old nomadic habits, they hunt and indulge in open-air sports, they drive and race chariots, they regard work, especially agricultural work, as the lot of an inferior race and class.
>
> This in a thousand variations has been one of the main stories in history for the last seventy centuries or more.
>
> (*OH*, 1:187–88)

Whatever the accuracy of Wells's claim, arguments like these sustain *The Outline* at the level of structure and pattern. Wells detects similar forces at work in other aspects of early human cultures, such as the two organizing sites that he argues were the polar—and ultimately competing—centers of the first civilizations, the palace (king) versus the temple (priest). Or again, another structuring motif Wells names is the emergence at different times and places of the capacity for free thought and writing. Not timeless human ambitions, these abilities thrive under certain conditions ("They appear [first] side by side with the development of social security and private property" [*OH*, 1:259]) and are among several traits especially extolled in *The Outline*.

Wells typically (though not always) places developments in human ideas above those of technology or social organization, and these, in turn, cannot be severed from the individual historical actors who are, at least temporarily, lifted out of the panorama for closer scrutiny and appraisal.[76] Of Pericles, for instance, Wells has this to say: "The reader must bear in mind that illuminating remark of Winckler's, which says that this renascent Athens bore for a time the face of Pericles. . . . Athens wore his face for a time as one wears a mask, and then became restless and desired to put him aside" (*OH*, 1:346). In the balance enacted here, Pericles neither dominates and dictates the course of events nor functions merely to exemplify them. Wells wants to extol Pericles and others like him throughout this long story; he also finds himself exasperated by them and by the constant retarding of possible greatness in the name of all that is small, incompetent, petty, and violent.

Wells stays attuned to how social forces, technology, and other factors limit or encourage intellectual expansion. For instance, he argues that China would in all likelihood have become the dominant world power long ago if its writing techniques had been on the Roman model. Thus:

> Now it is manifest that here in the Chinese writing is a very peculiar and complex system of sign-writing. A very great number of characters have to be learnt and the mind habituated to their use. The power it possesses to carry ideas and discussion is still ungauged by western standards, but we may doubt whether with this instrument it will ever be possible to establish such a wide, common mentality as the simpler and swifter alphabets of the western civilizations permit. . . . Probably it is the complexity of her speech and writing, more than any other imaginable cause, that has made China to-day politically, socially, and individually a vast pool of backward people rather than the foremost power in the whole world.
>
> *(OH, 1:226–27).*

What is striking is Wells's relativism with respect to the nature of power. At the same time, the language of backwardness and the extolling of Western models of writing and thought indicate his adherence to racist stereotypes, captured in the phrase "vast pool of backward people." In *The Sleeper Awakes*, to take another case, the novel is constituted by a series of mob struggles, often fought in the dark, and the final horror, to which the protagonist Graham cannot assent and which drives him to take up the mantle of leadership, is that his opponent has called up black colonial troops to quell the rebellion in London. Wells continued to harp on the outrage of training black African soldiers for duty in Europe in his collection from the Washington disarmament conference of 1921. This is a recurrent horror, begun allegorically in *The War of the Worlds*: the colonized (Martians) arriving in the metropole to swarm, crush, and eliminate the colonizers (English). Here in *The Outline*'s casual reference to contemporary Chinese as a "vast pool" the metaphor is more circumscribed, but Wells's embrace of some nasty figuration—of the sort, moreover, that he seemingly is working to oppose—cuts against the history's progressive tone and ideals. Still, Wells's claims about why China is not the world's dominant power are radical, and in ways that are characteristic of *The Outline*'s convictions, that the development of world power represents no great embodiment of a people (much less a race) but rather the outcome of technological processes and the accidents of development.

For all the stress on historical forces that obscure the individual actor, *The Outline* has its protagonists at each stage, and Wells can be a brilliant storyteller. Not surprisingly, he also singles out many storytellers along the way, beginning with the Neolithic bards.[77] Prophets and forecasters do extremely well, as one would have intuited. Wells gives particular emphasis to biblical prophets, whom he casts as great critics of religion, speaking from outside the precincts of religious power and recasting its large ideas. Another who is isolated out of the general scheme is Herodotus, the first historian, whom Wells extols for exerting an independence and individuality that breaks free of the ordering principles of Greek culture. Others among the most celebrated in *The Outline*, too, are Jesus, Mohammed, and Siddhartha Gautama, all of whom are praised for their magisterial visions of universality and commonalty, for envisioning a world united in sacrifice and conviction. Wells reads these in stark contrast to their followers, including the very consequential early disciples. From the very moment when the great religious teachers come into history, those followers, in Wells's accounting, lard their bright, simple, global messages with the dross of religious practice, priesthood, cult, caste, and the excessive embellishment that, for Wells and *The Outline*, distort, efface, and finally absorb the sublimity of the teacher's message. At a smaller scale, *The Outline* will take up other figures to serve as hero, like Roger Bacon, the thirteenth-century Franciscan whom Wells casts as a prophet, genius, and entrepreneur "two centuries ahead of his world," a restless thinker never content to accept what was given, always looking at the world as if from first principles (*OH*, 2:172). In the modern era, we have Darwin. In all cases, reflecting in and across these diverse figures is Wells, another eclectic futurist and world unifier who aligns with no group, movement, or creed. As we know, Wells was among the most autobiographical of the era's writers and the most likely to write himself into his protagonists. There is certainly a healthy dose of narcissism on view in this mimesis, but his identification with *The Outline*'s cast of iconoclasts, seers, and scientists is less interesting as a matter of self-aggrandizement than as a writing praxis. The author and the world mirror, interpenetrate, and mutually express each other.[78]

The ambivalence about historical figures, those whom he lauds and those whom he loathes (and there are many more of the latter), points to another pattern that emerges in *The Outline*, the duel between two traditional, competing forms of understanding history: as a matter of great world forces versus as a story of great men. On such a canonical division, one would expect Wells to have a position, and indeed he does. In *The Discovery of the Future*, addressing a probable objection to his claim that using scientific methods, we can predict the future—what about the unpredictable rise of someone like Napoleon who comes along and changes everything?—he writes that "these great men of ours are not more than images and symbols and instruments taken, as it were, haphazard by the incessant and consistent forces behind them; they are the pen-nibs Fate has used for her writing" (*DF*, 77). That we may disagree is less germane than to register the claim. Anyone interested in history was (and perhaps still is) required to weigh in on the matter of Great Men (the subject of Jacob Flanders's essay at Cambridge, "Does History Consist of the Biographies of Great Men?").[79] In 1920, as in 1902, Wells declares himself a reader of structures—he who deciphers the record of the rocks—a maker of outlines, rather than a scribe to personalities. Again, his assessment of Pericles expresses the conundrum, as he teases out the causalities and interactions among one person (Pericles), a small group of Athenians and others who were attracted there by its culture (slightly larger group formation), and the historical trajectories and conditions that together made for a "remarkable outbreak of creative power, which for three and twenty centuries has been to men of intelligence a guiding and inspiring beacon out of the past" (*OH*, 1:345). We should add that by the 1930s, with the rise of Hitler and the other dictators, this problem of individual historical actors had become urgent. Wells's greatest and most elaborate consideration of it forms the core of *The Holy Terror*, his 1939 anatomy of the rise of a homegrown English dictator, in which he toggles among different views of whether and how much Rud Whitlow, the would-be English Hitler, matters in the revolution that he, almost unwittingly, helps bring about. In the end, Wells settles on the individual as a transitional actor, helping galvanize and articulate world forces and directions, eventually to be superseded (in this case, assassinated) once the revolution has fully succeeded.

This question of people versus forces has come back repeatedly in our reading of Wells, and it forms a crux in how modernism distinguished itself from him. We recall Woolf's critique of *Joan and Peter*, that the novel abandons its protagonists, drowning them (like the novel's initial protagonist) in a deluge of commentary. *The Outline* brought these differences to the fore, showcasing Wells's greatest imaginative capacities but also, for some modernists, his unforgivable clumsiness on human individuality. In his two-part review in *The Athenaeum*, to take a revealing instance, Forster admires Wells's capacity to evoke the great movements of the past, his way of making these vast, old events stand before us. "His history 'lives,' . . . in a peculiar way: by its fundamental soundness, expressed through brilliant parallels and metaphors."[80] Yet of course, the catch comes in the form of Wells's failure, in Forster's estimation, to bring equivalent life to the past's personae. *Bring to life*: always, this is modernism's standard and its self-assignation. As Woolf so canonically has it in "Modern Fiction" and

"Mr. Bennett and Mrs. Brown," it is her Georgian club, which of course includes Forster, that will bring Mrs. Brown *to life*, while Wells's characters, like the others in her invented circle of "materialists"—alas, "if life should refuse to live there?"[81] In this vein, Forster writes of *The Outline*, "Wells' lucidity, so satisfying when it comes to peoples and periods, is somehow inadequate when individuals are thrown on to the screen. The outlines are as clear as ever, but they are not the outlines of living men ... the eminent humans appear as diagrams ...; the lecturer [Wells] points to the lettering and then passes on."[82] The values that have become ingrained as common literary standards, crisply invoked by Forster here, become stark when placed so squarely against Wells. Nobody wants matchstick figures, diagrams, characters who fail to live. But *The Outline*, with its massive readership, scratches back at modernism's developing self-recognition; the history has its own claims to a progressive view of the kinetic world, where past and present and future become part of an inexorable unit, a global view that shadows the big personalities of history behind the *life itself* of each of us, of humanity, of the spreading sense of community. In a strange way, Forster's critique offers a kind of endorsement of Wells's own stated aims, to magnify the steady, ineluctable movements and to minimize the individual's imprint on the world over the long term.

Well beyond modernist critics, *The Outline* became a lighting rod for debates across the spectrum, with skirmishes between Wells and some of his most conservative critics, notoriously, in an exchange with the Catholic polymath Hilaire Belloc, as well as with his sometime friend G. K. Chesterton.[83] Wells's contempt for religion as it has been organized throughout history (and for many of history's religious leaders), stood at the basis of these arguments, as well as his vociferous embrace of evolution and his denigration of nationalism and other traditionalist ideologies. The controversy had a certain moment of celebrity, with Wells and Belloc each publishing pamphlet rejoinders to the other.

It should also be noted that Wells was sued for plagiarism by a Canadian woman, Florence Deeks, who claimed that Wells had read her own manuscript of world history at Macmillan, where she had sent it. Deeks argued that there were striking similarities between the two works not otherwise explicable, and her feminist vision of the past is one that merits interest from us today. Her lawsuits went nowhere, but recently, in an award-winning book, A. B. McKillop has returned to Deeks and finds in her story an account of a suppressed feminist voice whose ideas, he argues, formed an essential part of Wells's book and were never acknowledged. Like all of Wells's biographers, I am unconvinced by this argument, though even so, it is worth remembering that, amid the welter of sources and ideas on which *The Outline* depended, some may never come to light. Its collective quality was something Wells wished to elaborate, but there may also be unrecognized dimensions to this fact, and in particular one wonders if other women's contributions could and should have been acknowledged by Wells, not least that of his wife, Jane, whose tireless work on the manuscript is a moving testament to her own great abilities.[84]

Wells was, in some sense, ready for the backlash from historians and eager to frame his work in collective terms. In writing *The Outline*, he convened a roster of eminent historians, classicists, and scientists to be his guides and internal correctors: Ernest Barker, H. H. Johnson, Ray Lankester, and Gilbert Murray, all among the most distinguished scholars of the period. And in a characteristically Wellsian innovation, he included dissent from these advisors within *The Outline*, as footnotes or at times in the main body of text. It is an extraordinary experience even today to be reading along in *The Outline* and to come, at the bottom of the page, upon rejoinders by the advisory experts, signed with their initials. In one case, Wells added an entire chapter to give Murray the space to expostulate on what he felt were inadequacies in Wells's presentation of Athens: "The preceding section raised an interesting discussion between Professor Gilbert Murray and the writer . . . what he had to say was so interesting and informing . . . that it seemed better, instead of modifying what had been written . . . to leave that as it stood and to supplement it by quoting Professor Murray" (*OH*, 1:352). Wells strove in all of his genres to enfold dialogue, contradiction, and multiplicity of approach. In *The Outline*, such principles are exerted in several ways—at the level of the competing scalar effects, for one, and in the footnotes, which also include critique beyond the advisory staff, in cases where Wells consulted experts in some of the many subfields covered in the history.

Such progressive tactics might align with our contemporary understanding of the dialogic and relative nature of historical truth, but at the time and in the years after its initial publication, as *The Outline* went through multiple editions—even its abridged version, *A Short History of the World* (1922), became a bestseller—the profession was aggravated by Wells's book. *The Outline* got under professional historians' skin. They critiqued Wells on various grounds: his questionable claims, his many inaccuracies (some corrected over time in subsequent editions), and his more idiosyncratic conclusions, including his utter disdain for such historical actors as Julius Caesar and Napoleon, his manifest impatience with the Roman Empire, and his dismissal of the whole project of European, national statesmanship from the end of the eighteenth century to the Versailles treaty. Above all, what worried historians was Wells's violation of the profession-defining ideal of objectivity. As Peter Novick writes in *The Noble*

*Dream*, "At the very center of the professional historical venture is the idea and ideal of 'objectivity.' . . . It has been the quality which the profession has prized and praised above all others."[85] Wells's history made no secret of its goals and agenda, and historians responded with the skepticism their profession demanded (and still demands). To give just one example, a "Symposium of Opinions Upon the *Outline of History*: Views of Historians" was published in 1922, in response to what the convener feared was the "menace" of *The Outline*, namely that it would be introduced into American schools and universities as a textbook and thereby infect American youth with its radical socialist propaganda.[86] All of this Wells courted with his brash and ambitious attempt to rewrite global history in twenty-four installments—with color pictures. As Wells put it in his introduction, "The writer will offer no apology for making this experiment. His disqualifications are manifest. But such work needs to be done," and, he implies, if professional historians are too specialized to take on the task, here is a volunteer without such compunction (*OH*, 1:viii).

Behind these stated grievances stand three major facts: the project's staggering ambition; Wells's dilettantism, as many saw it; and then, of course, the book's sales. Wells, who was not a professional historian, who made proud use of the *Encyclopedia Britannica* as a source, was read by vastly more people around the world than any living historian could expect for his own work.[87] It was this discrepancy between readership and professional accreditation that irked the profession. Several critics have noted this feature of *The Outline*'s place in its own moment, how its nonprofessionalism troubled the professional community of historians. As Cliona Murphy puts it, with a dose of understatement, the "concern about Wells, a non-historian, writing a history of mankind may have been behind much of the hostility he received from the profession. While his unorthodox approach, ambitious subject matter, and admitted agenda drew criticism with some justification, it was more than likely compounded because he had not jumped through the hoops of becoming a professional historian."[88] It was not only historians who bristled at Wells's untrained status. Lisa Fluet, in an elegant analysis, connects the question of disciplinary privilege to modernism, arguing that "Wells's version of modern intellectual professionalism refuses to see specialization as a compensation for what has already been irretrievably lost, because he lacks the requisite sense of loss in the first place," instead yoking his efforts to rewrite history to his larger goals for universal education. Fluet is thinking in part about Eliot, whose comments in a review of the Wells-Belloc debate in his journal *Criterion* reveal a great deal about his own class biases and about his fetish for expertise. His fear is that "the brilliant and voluble amateur" is on the ascendancy in the writing of history, elbowing aside the master.[89] The master and the dilettante return as foils, echoing the rivalry and split between Henry James and Wells.

However, and perhaps of greater interest, the response was not all territorial, or narrow, or in fact always disciplinary. Even the modernists I have cited on *The Outline*—Eliot, Forster—saw the grandeur, ambition, bravura, and indeed a kind of sui generis forcefulness and wonder in Wells's vision that they could not help but admire. Writing in the *Criterion*, Eliot was willing to grant Wells "a prodigious gift of historical imagination, which is comparable to Carlyle's,"[90] and Forster saw in *The Outline* a "great book" more impressive than the sum of its faults, one that, as he concludes in his review, should be bought—not borrowed. *The Outline* was in the world, acting on it, *creating*, and modernists were among the multitude who responded to its vital, sweeping energy. I have noted the eminent American historian Carl Becker, whose 1921 review of *The Outline* in the *American Historical Review*, "Mr. Wells and the New History," represents this more generous stance, a way of seeing in Wells's effort something that professional historians might disdain, no doubt, but also emulate. Becker recognizes that Wells's reorganization of the past according to his own categories might help even the "well-drilled" historian to see things anew—modernism's imperative, after all—including, in this case, in the realignment of Western versus universal models of historical organization and valuation. Too, Becker hones in on the way Wells's approach to history ramifies through his vision of the future. Becker, that is, recognizes a version of Wellsian temporality as I have been developing it, in this case manifesting in the writing of history. He is very funny, for instance, on the whole question of how Wells scolds the past for failing to live up to his standards. As Becker puts it, Wells "has his idea of 'the next stage of history,' of the 'world as it might be like, were men united in a common peace and justice.' This idea is what inspired him to write the *Outline*; and it is this idea which gives him a standard of *values*, which enables him to say what history ought to have done and miserably failed to do."[91]

In some sense, Becker articulates what any reader of *The Outline* would see; after all, Wells makes no secret of his forward-looking objectives, and those utopian hopes for the united future of mankind, as we too have noted, most certainly do not follow in any logical way the thousands of years Wells has documented in his history. Becker's recognition that there is, in this configuration, a philosophy of history and a way of organizing it by values accurately characterizes *The Outline*. It is quite clear that Becker is friendly to some of what Wells is doing with his blatantly nonobjective, progressive approach. Wells may be an iconoclast, but he is also, in important ways, an exemplar of "The New History," the movement Becker and others championed in the first decades of the century, as they sought a history that would recognize its situatedness (as we might call it today) in a present context that can never be purified into strict objectivity. Becker, in other words, can find in Wells's flagrant flouting of the objective premise a version of what new historians were producing. But of course, in the end, Wells is not in the club, nor would he want to be, and perhaps, by the end of Becker's review, one wonders if the club is a place Becker himself much enjoys: "'Ah, but this is not *History!*' I hear someone exclaim. Very well, call it what you like. If you like not the term history for Mr. Wells's book, call it something else—for example, the adventures of a generous soul among catastrophes!"[92]

I have cited Becker at length because his little piece so beautifully encapsulates the way *The Outline* jostled and jutted within the matrix of contemporaneous historical thought. To see how and by whom Wells was attacked is finally less illuminating than to see how and by whom he was called upon to invigorate ambitious projects, to stimulate broad visions.[93] As his biographer David Smith puts it, "*The Outline* and similar books created a small revolution in the teaching of history."[94] Wells's was progressive history, in both senses—because it tells a narrative of progress (with the caveats we have stressed, of its internal deconstructedness) and because, as history, it sits with other progressive historical efforts in the twentieth and now twenty-first centuries. The French Annales school, which became an important counterpoint in midcentury France to the more traditional, nation-based approach that dominated academic history, took as its guiding principle that traditional categories constrained a richer understanding of the past. It bridged the study of social, ecological, and national histories, paying attention to the life practices of ordinary people along with leaders, seeing historical understanding in intricate webs of experience, events, and the gradual movements that often characterize change. It slowed down the clock, taking the long time of ecology and geology into account. Fernand Braudel's great work, *The Mediterranean* (written over several decades, completed in 1949), is the monument of this school, a massive effort to rethink a region by reframing categories of knowledge to yield more productive insights and to draw light upon a whole range of people and dynamic processes often left out of historical study. Braudel is willing to think about social, environmental, and temporal totalities, a Wellsian temperament spurned by modernists and many historians of their era. "The question of boundaries is the first to be encountered," writes Braudel,

> from it all others flow. To draw a boundary around anything is to define, analyse, and reconstruct it, in this case select, indeed adopt, a philosophy of history.

To assist me I did indeed have at my disposal a prodigious body of articles, papers, books, publications, surveys, some purely historical, others no less interesting, written by specialists in neighboring disciplines.... But, dare I say it, at the risk of seeming ungrateful to my predecessors, that this mass of publication buries the researcher as it were under a rain of ash. So many of these studies speak a language of the past, outdated in more ways than one. Their concern is not the sea in all its complexity, but some minute piece of the mosaic, not the grand movement of Mediterranean life, but the actions of a few princes and rich men, the trivia of the past, bearing little relation to the slow and powerful march of history which is our subject.[95]

And here is Wells:

This book ... has been written primarily to show that *history as one whole* is amenable to a more broad and comprehensive handling than is the history of special nations and periods.... This outline deals with ages and races and nations, where the ordinary history deals with reigns and pedigrees and campaigns.... And many topics of quite primary interest to mankind, the first appearance and the growth of scientific knowledge for example, and its effects upon human life, the elaboration of the ideas of money and credit, or the story of the origins and spread and influence of Christianity, which must be treated fragmentarily or by elaborate digressions in any partial history, arise and flow completely and naturally in one general record of the world in which we live.

(*OH*, 1:v–vi, italics the in original)

Separated at birth, these twinned historical approaches each stood against the dominant grain, bucking both disciplinary tenets and the more buried class, national, and regional biases underpinning the academic traditions they sought to dethrone.

The connections between Wells and Braudel make for an illuminating crosscurrent; equally notable is the resonance with a new model of history that bypasses the profession's emphasis on specialization altogether, today's Big History. Big History is "the approach to history in which the human past is placed within the framework of cosmic history, from the beginning of the universe up until life on Earth today." As its name suggests, Big History changes the scale, both geographically and temporally, taking the planet as its primary unit, with the earth's lifespan as its salient temporal range. It is big not only in this scalar sense, moreover; with such a wide focus, it must encompass a variety of scientific disciplines, offering, in a sense, an ecology of historical approaches. "A historical theory of everything," is how Fred Spier, one of the field's exponents, characterizes the effort.[96] Unity, integration, narratability: these are the attributes that motivate Big History and stand out in its conclusions. As articulated by one of the field's pioneers, David Christian, describing how he became persuaded to abandon the academic premise of specialization and see the world according to a single story, "beneath the awesome diversity and complexity of modern knowledge, there is an underlying unity and coherence."[97] Several operations and features jump to the fore in this model of historical study, in keeping with its overall conception: an emphasis on process, where the kinetic qualities of the past dominate the view (slow change as it interacts with cataclysmic events, say); foregrounding the dialectic between complexity and simplicity; comfort with the notion that the historian can never achieve the ideal of objectivity, since in any field of inquiry one is always in *some* relation to one's object; and an admission that the force and significance of the work does not lie in discovery (this kind of work is not centered on original research findings) but rather in synthesis and analysis, a formula for explaining the past that will have tangible, positive ramifications for the future. I hope that it is becoming evident, as we scan its self-presentation, that Big History shares just about all its defining aspects with *The Outline*, including its origin in a sense of present urgency.

In a similar vein, Wai Chee Dimock's influential discussion of "deep time" in her book *Through Other Continents* takes "the abiding traces of the planet's multitudinous life" as a more productive archive than that of more familiar iterations of American literary study, those traces that "arise and flow completely and naturally in one general record of the world in which we live"—to borrow Wells's phrase again. Aiming to break American literary study out of its temporal, linguistic, and national limitations by infusing it on all sides with a broader, older archive of sources, connections, and histories, Dimock hopes to bind "continents and millennia into many loops of relations, a densely interactive fabric."[98] Dimock fails to name Wells as a precursor (not surprisingly), though she does note the importance of Braudel. Perhaps owing to its more independent personality—defining itself significantly in opposition to so much in academic history—Big History, by contrast, claims *The Outline* as one of its own, naming Wells as the only big historian over a more-than-hundred-year period, between the early nineteenth century and the 1970s.

From the point of view of modernism and of our inquiry into twentieth-century forms of thought and writing that have been overlooked, dismissed, or generally left without subsequence, this gap becomes symptomatic of something larger to grasp about the period. It is a deep suspicion of totalizing discourses or forms of knowledge. Modernism has its big books with omnivorous appetites, and these have often been named as "epic" and recognized as registering a desire for coherence and order within the "immense panorama of futility and anarchy that is contemporary history" (T. S. Eliot), but when we think about what *Ulysses*, say, values in its huge encompassing of the social world, it is impossible not to hone in on its perspectivalism, multiplicity, detail, smallness, even modesty, to a degree that outweighs (or deconstructs, cancels, and overrides) its totalizing energies.[99] It is the creed of *Ulysses* that there can and must always be at least two opinions on all matters—this is one reading of its parallax—and Joyce's attack on unitary thinking, orthodoxy, and fanaticism is essential to the novel's workings. *Ulysses* in this sense is well representative of modernism, which staked its authority on the private idiosyncrasy of vision, the panoply and heterogeneity of experience, the infinite sensation made available in modern culture. Paul Saint-Amour has made a concerted and convincing case to this effect, arguing that the interwar modernism of *Ulysses* and other works may be encyclopedic but never epic. These terms, often conflated, come in Saint-Amour's *Tense Future* to stand for opposed valences with regard to the grasping of social or national breadth. Where epic imagines the potential for a totalizing, coherent vision—aligned in Saint-Amour's account with the totalizing, coherent vision of *total war*—the encyclopedia recognizes its own cataloguing mission as partial, subjective, infinitely correctable, and existing always in relation to the threat of massive destruction. In Saint-Amour's account, then, those sites of modernism that might seem glibly to comprise the largest swaths of culture instead register a deep anxiety about any such holistic effort. Modernism in these works does achieve scope, span, even epic dimension, but it gets there through the modest and partial.

*The Outline* differs from modernism, as it does from professional history, in having no qualms about the value of thinking big, no doubt that totality is and must be for the betterment of humanity, and no ambiguity about its own goals when it comes to scale. Wells's aims were clear, forceful, urgent. We have quoted these lines before:

> There can be no peace now, we realize, but a common peace in all the world; no prosperity but a general prosperity. *But there can be no common peace and prosperity without common historical ideas.* Without such ideas to hold them together in harmonious co-operation, with nothing but narrow, selfish, and conflicting nationalist traditions, races and peoples are bound to drift toward conflict and destruction. This truth, which was apparent to that great philosopher Kant a century or more ago—it is the gist of his tract upon universal peace—is now plain to the man on the street.... A sense of history as the

common adventure of all mankind is as necessary for peace within as it is for peace between the nations.

(OH, 1:vi, italics in the original)

Wells is at his most clear-sighted here, with no self-division, no reservations, no tugging violent reality mocking his ambitions. The first and necessary step in setting forth toward worldwide peace is education, and specifically historical education framed in world terms. Wells places his book at a crossroads, a moment when it might be possible, given the recent mass violence and disillusionment of the war, to reconceive relations among peoples, but to do this, it seems so clear to him, we must have an idea of a shared past. That line is so quintessentially Wells—"A sense of history as the common adventure of all mankind is as necessary for peace within as it is for peace between the nations"—and his history is written to give this adventure its first guidebook. Views of history are *realized*, as he further declares; they must be given life in new genres, new forms. Following the book's success, Wells sought to build two more legs into his tripod of popular education, one on biology, one on economics, thinking thereby to complete the preliminary education of mankind. Together, as he wrote in *The Open Conspiracy*, these writings "present altogether, first a complete modern world outlook, politically speaking, then the moral data of the new time, and then the forecast of a collective economic policy, in a form accessible to a person of ordinary education . . . the three will help in a great number of cases to pull people's minds together into a shape that will dispose them to full participation in the movement" he calls "open conspiracy," the early formations of his world state.[100] We have left modesty far behind.[101]

Immodest and inspired, Wells's goals shape *The Outline* in a variety of aspects, all the way to its conclusion. By the last pages of *The Outline*, Wells is ready to elaborate in euphoric detail how our united future might look; he is also quick to remind his readers of how precarious the line is between achieving such a heady outcome and once again missing the opportunity. Most famous today in pithily capturing this dynamic is one line, to be found toward the close of the book: "Human history becomes more and more a race between education and catastrophe" (*OH*, 2:594). These divergent outcomes, education versus catastrophe, might be attached to the two dominant streams that flow continuously through *The Outline*. Education carries with it the optimistic, progressivist ideals that drive the history, this statement itself following from the soaring last sequence in which Wells opens his text to utopia, where we glean a harmonized world no longer the prey of war, greed, chaos, and tumult, one where resources—of the earth, of its inhabitants—are fulfilled rather than exploited.

For Wells, *The Outline* enters on the side of education; indeed, it *is* education. Catastrophe we know.

It seems fitting, for a text whose essential fabric is woven of opposing forces and tendencies, to close our discussion with two of its key personages, whom we might nominate as hero and antihero: Herodotus and Napoleon. They are not parallel figures—one of the monarchs whom Wells lauds for attempting to unify the world under right auspices, such as the great Indian ruler Asoka in the third century BCE, might be a more apt antagonist for Napoleon, and a more exact foil for Herodotus would be a paranoid tyrant who stifles dissent, of which this history furnishes some choice examples—but I choose these two because each epitomizes the goals and obstacles of *The Outline* so exactly, and each takes us, finally, outside of *The Outline*, ramifying for the larger Wellsian project of world writing that, perhaps more than any other aspect of the history, breaks out of the norms and constraints of its interwar, modernist setting to address us today. Napoleon haunts Wells's writing, as he does so much of Western thought since 1815. He is there, memorably, in *Tono-Bungay*, Edward Ponderevo's not always unconscious foil ("the Napoleon of Notting Hill," as the press calls him), and similarly for Rud in *The Holy Terror*. Napoleon is there, too, among the boys and young men of Wells's social fictions, where he could be found throughout the young male Western imaginary for a century or more. Clearly, Napoleon presents the blunt counterexample to Wells's theory of historical change, as we have noted, the major actor who seems to belie any attempt to account for the past without acceding the centrality of individual personality. Wells's readers noticed Napoleon's presence: when Orwell critiqued Wells in 1941 for, in his estimation, having failed to understand the dangers of fascism and the nature of fanaticism, he notes that the "principal villain of his *Outline of History* is the military adventurer Napoleon," a key symptom for Orwell in diagnosing the outmoded nature of Wells's historical sensibility.[102] The historians who reviewed *The Outline* went straight there as well; Becker quotes the passage (to be discussed shortly) in which Napoleon is derided for his utter failure to realize the possibilities at his behest, who looks, in the end, no better than a "cockerel on a dunghill."

And Napoleon does spark *The Outline's* obsessions—with waste, disappointment, and catastrophically missed opportunity. Wells devotes a chapter to Napoleon, one of the liveliest and most passionate in the history, and one senses a personal dimension to his investment in Napoleon's failure. It is in this last third of *The Outline* that Wells drifts away from writing a true world history to concentrate almost exclusively on Europe, and here, too, the reader is confronted with some of *The Outline's* worst lapses in historical judgment, such as Wells's utter failure to say anything of value about black slavery in America.[103] In this context of the history's uneven progress, the Napoleon passages, with their intensity of viewpoint and driving theoretical energy, are particularly engrossing.

Napoleon matters because he embodies everything Wells continually wishes—and promises—we need not forever be. A quintessential passage:

> Now surely here was opportunity such as never came to man before. . . . The old order of things was dead or dying; strange new forces drove through the world seeking form and direction; the promise of a world republic and an enduring world peace whispered in a multitude of startled minds. Had this man any profundity of vision, any power of creative imagination, had he been accessible to any disinterested ambition, he might have done work for mankind that would have made him the very sun of history. All Europe and America, stirred by the first promise of a new age, was waiting for him . . .

Of course, what follows is the great "but, alas" that inevitably characterizes this scenario for Wells. Alas, then:

> Napoleon could do no more than strut upon the crest of this great mountain of opportunity like a cockerel on a dunghill. The figure he makes in history is one of almost incredible self-conceit, of vanity, greed, and cunning, of callous contempt and disregard of all who trusted him, and of a grandiose aping of Caesar, Alexander, and Charlemagne which would be purely comic if it were not caked over with human blood. Until, as Victor Hugo said in his tremendous way, "God was bored by him," and he was kicked aside into a corner to end his days.
>
> (*OH*, 2:354–55)

Wells is at his best here in part because there is so much of him in his antagonist, the creeping sense of wasted opportunity, the abyss that separates what might have been from what was. If Wells need not fear leaving a legacy "caked over with human blood," he nevertheless continues to refract himself through all these figures on the historical stage, and the image of the failed little man atop a pathetic hill, its mere simulation of a mountain emblematic of a larger inefficacy, seems a primal one for Wells—the inverse of his regular invocation of mankind standing on the earth as on a footstool, arms stretching to the sky. Mostly, though, in the configuration of tremendous letdown, and in the contemptibility of the person relative to what he might have accomplished, Wells gives body to the essential historical pattern *The Outline* traces. Napoleon's story, as Wells tells it, cries out for what we, as Wells's readers, have learned to expect—the upswing that never has come but is forever imagined. The structure is not so much of hope deferred as of deferral being the genesis of potential.

If Napoleon is *The Outline*'s nemesis, Herodotus is its guiding spirit. How could it be otherwise? The first historian, with his limitless capaciousness, willing to see other cultures evenly and without judgment, one who encompassed as much of the world as was known at the time, a storyteller and a synthesizer: he is Wells's model. As a figure, he is more like a shadow or *anima* than a character. He swims in and out of the first volume, often referenced for historical data, quoted directly at length, treated by Wells on many occasions (as by many historians of the ancient world) as a source. Wells keeps the biography of Herodotus to a minimum and makes no detailed scan of *The Histories*, which he treats as its own natural magnet. "It is a book," he writes, "to which all intelligent readers come sooner or later, abounding as it does in illuminating errors and Boswellian charm," and indeed he finds himself distracted by Herodotus's storytelling, an all "too alluring . . . companion" who writes what "may not be exact history, but it is great poetry" (*OH*, 1:262, 326, 335). At the narrative level, Wells has a specific and important role for Herodotus, who limns "a new factor . . . becoming evident in human affairs. . . . A new sort of people . . . were asking questions, exchanging knowledge and views, and developing ideas. So beneath the march of armies and the policies of monarchs, and above the common lives of illiterate and incurious men, we note the beginnings of what is becoming at last nowadays a dominant power in human affairs the *free intelligence of mankind*" (*OH*, 1:262, italics in the original). Herodotus becomes, in essence, a figure for writing and for intellectual life taken out beyond the precinct of what is comfortable, of home. That Herodotus was not born in Greece, moreover, makes his Greek identity all the more appealing as an exemplification of the cosmopolitan ideal to which he is yoked. Later Aristotle is joined to Herodotus as another instance of this empirical brand of free thought, which Wells presents as an essentially scientific cast of mind.

But what positions Herodotus, finally, as Wells's twin is not solely the overt role he plays in *The Outline* of world writer, free thinker, traveler, and exponent of scientific method in the realm of the human past, but also the way his story is guided by two unique, and never exactly reconcilable, impulses: the desire to tell many stories, all stories, and the imperative to tell one story, in a gradually cohering narrative. For Herodotus, the unifying narrative that eventually shapes his *Histories* is the conflict between Greeks and Persians, a binary episteme that dominated political and racial thought for many centuries. It would be hard to overstate the resonance of Herodotus's gradual shift, in his massive book, from multiplicity to duality, from absolute manyness to a story with a single plot. Yet the structure never quite inheres, and what makes his writing so utterly pleasurable is its immense variety, its plurality and love of detail, a tolerance and indeed attraction to all manner of human whimsy, caprice, desire, failing, triumph, confusion, and even, now and then, dignity. And so with Wells. *The Outline*, too, forms a double helix, as it builds up a world shape, making out of the immense welter of the sprawling past some kind of knowable pattern; as he writes in the introduction, "History is no exception amongst the sciences; as the gaps fill in, the outline simplifies; as the outlook broadens, the clustering multitude of details dissolves into general laws" (*OH*, I:vi). And yet, as with Herodotus, the material is never quite reducible to that shape, and its marvelous readability stems precisely from the bottomless nature of its inquiry, its sheer energy. Similar to Herodotus's work, one can dip into *The Outline* almost anywhere and be immediately pulled inside the tale's dynamic. This flexibility with historical time ought not to surprise us, since Wells never believed in straightforward temporality. He lived in the future at the same time as the past; his worlds may be distant in time, but they fold, overlap, and express one another. *The Outline of History* is Wells's greatest work because it captures *the* world but also multiple worlds. It is his most quintessential work because it expresses the grasp of totality but also the infinite ways such totality can and must be split, undone, dissolved, resisted. It is far from perfect, but then, as Wallace Stevens reminds us, "the imperfect is our paradise."

# 4
# Biology

A lunar morning begins. The sky has been the deepest pitch black, the surface of the moon is frigid, lifeless, covered in plumes of snow and frozen air. No person could survive in such inhospitable cold, bereft of sustaining atmosphere, the very picture of a human desolation. The sun appears in the morning sky, but violently, "and hurl[s] a shaft of heat . . . as though it were a spear"; quite quickly a thaw commences, the snow hissing as it turns to vapor, and without warning the brightness of the sun scalds the eye.[1] Night and day are opposed in light and heat, equally inhospitable. But then, something happens:

> How can I describe the thing I saw? It is so petty a thing to state, and yet it seemed wonderful, so pregnant with emotion. I have said that amidst the stick-like litter were these round bodies, these little oval bodies that might have passed as very small pebbles. And now first one and then another had stirred, had rolled over and cracked, and down the crack of each of them showed a minute line of yellowish green, thrusting outward to meet the hot encouragement of the newly risen sun. For a moment that was all, and then there stirred and burst a third!
>
> "It is a seed," said Cavor. And then I heard him whisper, very softly: "*Life*!"
>
> (*FMM*, 55, italics in the original)

Life: it is Wells's great subject. We have heard his triumphant conclusion to *The Outline of History*, that "Life begins perpetually. . . . Life, for ever dying to be born afresh, for ever young and eager, will presently stand upon this earth as upon a footstool, and stretch out its realm amidst the stars."[2] It turns out life was the subject of that history, the test and consequence of Wells's analysis of the past and his aspirations for the future. Inseparable from the idea of birth, as the language of the lunar morning testifies, life as subject means that the focus returns emphatically to the body, its essentially productive and reproductive facticity. Life begins perpetually: Wells's language, accordingly, is of movement, cycle, beginnings, striving, combustion, and expression. That the dimension of life is both immense and diverse (the universal generativity of evolution over the eons meeting the minuteness of the individual seed case) makes it particularly congenial to Wells, with his attraction to mutable scales. As with his rendering of time, Wells is undaunted by the multiplicity of registers at which the life processes must be analyzed, his training under Huxley having attuned him to the phylogenic principle underlying biological thought in the nineteenth century, that different scales of development recapitulate and express one another. Nothing less than life tout court will do for Wells as subject, the rich entangling of divergent forms and branches of knowledge a source of attraction to the writer who sought totality amid welter.

If biology is the study of living forms and the processes that enable them, such indeed might be seen not only as Wells's subject but as his own undertaking. His is a form of literary biology or biological textuality in which life is figured as form, function, process. More, Wells understood that biology in fact comprises a variety of subfields and entwines with other branches of science, such as chemistry (the study of matter) or physics (force and movement), and thus it requires an inquiry that seeks outward alliance along with its inner complexity. The study of life is expansive in other ways as well—it can be seen in a different sense as the primary subject of philosophy, anthropology, and indeed literature, and it also becomes a primary motivator for human aspirations when the religious orthodoxies wane, the ultimate arbiter of value for a secular age. This excess of meaning and daunting demand for methodological agility are no obstacles; they conform exactly to Wells's imaginative style.

Wells is calm in the face of massive data and enthusiastic for the encompassing quality that biological systems can provide, yet he was always—"perpetually"—stunned by the sheer force of life in its many guises. Wells's writings never quite lose the sense of awe, expressed by Cavor and Bedford on the moon, of this simple fact that the seed does crack open, that the plant grows. We have considered this quality of the mystical penetrating and at times undoing the scientific in various guises: as an impulse toward community and sacrifice despite the most acute visions of human failure and catastrophe, as a repeated dialectic of light and dark surging across the Wellsian canon, and as a willingness to leap into hopefulness in defiance of his own scientific analysis. In the case of the material world as such, Wells's work is especially marked by these double attributes of wonder and skeptical interpretation. One strain in his writing pulsates with scientific wonder; the other is guided by scientific method. Indeed, the riveting of awe with scientific principle—what Michael Page describes as a mysticism that accompanies Wells's scientific attitude—is a touchstone across Wells's works. As Page writes, "Wells maintained the visionary capacity of the Romantic poet mixed with the systematic reasoning of the research scientist. And like the great Romantic synthesizers, Wells could hardly be constrained by the limitations of a purely scientific perspective."[3] We might borrow one of Wells's favorite metaphors, appropriately biological, to register the systole of imaginative expansion around the sheer power of life in constant play with the diastole of careful, reasoned analysis.

But if Wells can buttress these principles in mutual support, he has no such sanguinity about his fictional scientists, who almost uniformly demonstrate a blinding incapacity to see and share the profundity of their work.[4] They are limited, almost maimed, by a smallness in outlook that stunts the grandeur of their discoveries—unless, that is, they are dangerous egomaniacs, as in the case of Doctor Moreau or Griffin of *The Invisible Man*. Even such innocuous figures as Redmond and Bensington of *The Food of the Gods* are unable, as scientists, to recognize the sublimity of their material. In the case of these two, they unleash a world revolution through a combination of vanity, indiscretion, and sheer sloppiness. The novel's comedy is set in motion initially by Redmond's obsession with graphs, a way of figuring growth in two-dimensional designs that suggests their authors' own flat imaginations. Or, as Wells has his narrator opine:

> There is no doubt about what is not great [in scientists], no race of men have such obvious littlenesses. They live in a narrow world so far as their human intercourse goes; their researches involve infinite attention and an almost monastic seclusion; and what is left over is not very much. To witness some queer, shy, misshapen, grey-headed, self-important little discoverer of great discoveries, ridiculously adorned with the wide ribbon of some order of chivalry and holding a reception of his fellow-men. . . .
>
> And withal the reef of science that these little "scientists" built and are yet building is so wonderful, so portentous, so full of mysterious half-shapen promises for the mighty future of man! They do not seem to realise the things they are doing![5]

Wells, hoping neither to play god nor to miss the significance of what science embodies and can teach, aims to differ from such caricatures. The reach and power of biological meaning instigates for him an exuberantly diverse literary output. I will elaborate, in this book's conclusion, on how Wells's lifelong effort to foster scientific education represents one of his most prolific and important forms of worldwide advocacy, and it is worth keeping in mind that Wells's writings on science are often conceived as part of a global, cross-class educational project.

In all his forms of writing, Wells wants to scrutinize life root to flower, from the smallest units we can know through the microscope—those infusoria that are such regular protagonists in his writing—to the great expanse of the earth's ecosystems and into the planetary cosmos. At the same time, the largest views of scientific systems motivate Wells's imagination in other directions, to consider how the world might ultimately be one. All that is organic, grows, and reproduces—"whatever is begotten, born and dies," as Yeats might have it—these are the constituents of life, and they occupy Wells in such terms. He emphasizes, too, that the units of life are entirely interdependent, that they form an ecology, from the minute interactions of cells within the body to the many "life communities," as he calls them, that make up diverse habitats and ecosystems.[6] Today's theorists might call these "assemblages." Ecology is a basic precept in Wells's writings and one that connects him to modernists like Woolf or Joyce, who may not have had particularly strong affinities to the biological questions surrounding natural habitats or scientific systems but whose writings foster rich, far-reaching ecologies within their textual worlds. Wells's ecological orientation also bespeaks an attunement to environmental crisis and precarity, questions of great relevance for us today. His interest in the astonishing fact of life's urge to flourish is suggestive of environmental critics who, for instance, are exploring how life finds its forms amid "capitalist ruins" or within particularly devastated urban regions.[7] More, in *The Outline of History*, as we recall, Wells demands an ecological approach to the past, rebuffing the arbitrary cordons of national history just as he resists the atomistic approach to individuality.

Most generally, Wells is looking to make analogies, to take *representativeness* as his essential category, so that the individual narrative can become a telling of the human story—or the life story—and back again. As he writes in the late work *The Conquest of Time* (1942):

> If a species survives, then it survives only by and through its individuals. It is a great mass of individuals rolling toward that maw of time, and every one of these individuals is contributing to the movement. The species may or may not survive; it will struggle to survive as stoutly as its collective will—or, if you prefer it, the algebraic sum of its wills—to survive determines. So long as it holds

out, the life of every individual must contribute some consequence to the struggle. Every individual life without exception changes the species, and its contribution is permanent so long as the species endures.

A species lives and dies in its individuals, and obviously the extinction of a species and the death of its last individual is one and the same event.[8]

The species, the individual, the species, the individual: so it will always oscillate, or rather cohere. To understand the workings of life in such a dialectic is one of Wells's primary goals as a writer and scientific philosopher.

In the lunar day, the principle of life is condensed and made visible, providing in short form what would become Wells's lasting work of literary, scientific, and social-scientific exploration. After the first remarkable seeds burst, the action is quick, as the moon *bios* rushes into existence:

> Every moment more of these seed-coats ruptured, and even as they did so the swelling pioneers overflowed their rent-distended seed-cases and passed into the second stage of growth. . . . In a little while the whole slope was dotted with minute plantlets standing at attention in the blaze of the sun.
>
> They did not stand for long. . . . The movement was slower than any animal's, swifter than any plant's I have ever seen before. How can I suggest it to you—the way that growth went on? The leaf tips grew so that they moved onward even while we looked at them.
>
> (*FMM*, 56)

And so over the course of fourteen Earth days, the moon's single day acts out the birth, growth, and spread of its flora, followed of course by its decay and death. By the time Bedford leaves the moon, frantically entering his sphere and blasting off before absolute night consumes him, the whole process of life has been completed. At the dawn of the next lunar day, there will be nothing but desolation once again, to renew itself with the onset of the sun. Without atmosphere or tides, moreover, there is no variation. Every day on the moon is the story of life; every night, its eclipse.

It is a scenario of irresistible imaginative possibility. In *The War of the Worlds*, when the Martians come to colonize, they drag in their wake a voracious red plant that quickly dominates the English landscape. In carpeting the recognizable features of the local area, the red weed might be said to allegorize colonization, but more to the point here, it also epitomizes the same spirit of seemingly uncontrollable growth that each moon day replays. *The Food of the Gods* reboots such plant efflorescence as a primary scenario, a gigantism that takes visual potency in the form of enormous vegetal spread, creepers and branches and weeds that dwarf gardens, homes, countryside, and ultimately the human habitat. The gargantuan chickens, wasps, and rats make for good comic horror in the novella, but it is the lasting spread of those vast and always-extending plants that entirely transforms the landscape of human habitation. The visuality of growth is part of Wells's representational praxis, with its insistent pressuring on the medium of seeing and its adherence to the principle of movement. In the passage just noted, as Bedford struggles to fix the speed at which the eye can see change, Wells makes the scene of moon growth filmic, as if we are watching a film and watching it being made at the same time. Wells often plays back and forth across media, here with writing and film, a technology whose resonance in *The First Men in the Moon* is felt in sequences like this one that engage the scopic magnetism of such basic organic processes. Nevertheless, technology in this novel is a somewhat chastened presence, in the face of these raw encounters with the lifecycle, which seem to dwarf our own small interventions (as the primary technological object to leave Earth, the sphere, is easily buried by the emergent shrubs).

The awakening and quick death of the moon's surface bloom opens out onto very broad questions, which probe the indissoluble connections among the basic biological processes—birth, growth, development, reproduction, evolution, decay, death—and make them the elemental source for Wells's inquiry into personal and shared cultural life. "Each man and woman," he writes in *A Modern Utopia*, "to the extent that his or her individuality is marked, breaks the law of precedent, transgresses the general formula, and makes a new experiment for the direction of the life force."[9] Wells comes back over and over in his writings to the big questions: What constitutes life, species, humanity, the biological imperative? And how do we write such processes? His stories take shape around a dense array of biological topics, from the gruesome spectacle of Dr. Moreau's experiments, to the sexual self-discovery at the center of *Ann Veronica*, to *Tono-Bungay*'s expansive foray into the social and financial consequences of unbridled growth translated into capitalist form (a theme, too, of *The Sleeper Awakes*).

But whether the subject is organic processes or economic forces (read in biological terms), one physical prospect always accompanies Wells's thought: waste. We have met this relentless double before, the bitter and perpetual taunt that this whole enormous effort of his might represent no more than so much wasted time and paper. Like time, waste is a Wellsian subject that also held the imagination of his modernist peers. All find themselves agonized—and often also energized—by the prospect of these principles of life that seem to belie the logic of productivity. Given the cultural fetish of efficiency in the period (Wells belonged for a while to a group called the "Coefficients"), it is not surprising that waste, its natural other, might have outsize presence. Scholars have considered modernism on either side of the waste binary: obsessed by purity, anxiously seeking to banish all the excess and recrudescence of modernity, capitalist surplus, queerness, femininity, the body, essentially conservative and looking to harden, cleanse, and masculinize the arts; or, on the other side, as reveling precisely in the waste of the land, making its art out of refuse, the flotsam and jetsam of a world that accumulates, generates, and casts off in such enormous profusion, works that take joy in the sheer materiality of the modern world and its effects.[10] Waste, as Christopher Schmidt writes, "in its various literal and metaphorical manifestations—detritus, garbage, trash, shit—is a crucial influence on twentieth-and twenty-first-century aesthetics," a site of both incubation and contradiction.[11]

For modernists, as for Wells, waste is not only about actual material stuff—it is also about the idea of progress, as all of these writers took stock of the Enlightenment and its outcomes and wondered what proportion of its narrative of amelioration was myth, self-satisfaction, or a mere cover story for abuse, a huge waste of the West's energies. As the idea of "civilization" coalesced as the modern world's key product, one had to ask, no doubt without solution: Does such a thing exist? Is it valuable? What enormous fund of life has been lost in its name over the centuries? Was it worth it, and for whom? In its Conradian guise, the problem takes the form of futility, a deep irony that Conrad presents as the only available response to the insane doings of modernity, where the enterprise of civilization teeters on the verge of meaningless effort, the tremendous movement of the ages coming down to a senseless hole blasted into a hillside or a boy tripping over a tree root and blowing himself up. Or for Woolf, Western culture can be read, with numbing regularity, as an endless circling round the mulberry tree of war, violence, and more war and violence. For Wells, as we know, there is nothing more pressing than to ward off the nullity of a modernity in which war has simply been a useless squandering of life and resources, its bloodshed yielding no salvation, its destruction no improvement. Wells and modernism stand together in such consternation. But perhaps the strangest and most moving partnership when it comes to waste is with its other great visionary in the period, Eliot. Both Wells and Eliot took the measure of the dialectic of waste and germination, and both saw in the latticing of these mutual principles some basic patterns in the world's history. In his waste poem, Eliot gave modernism one of its most stunning self-iterations. I suggest that we now explore this other waste land.

## I. BIO = LIFE

We will begin our summary [of *The Science of Life*] by asking what is meant by life? What are its distinctive characteristics?...Firstly, a living thing moves about.... Life may move as swiftly as a flying bird, or as slowly as an expanding turnip, but it moves. It moves in response to an inner impulse.... And not only does it move of itself, but it feeds.... In addition, life seems always to be produced by pre-existing life. It presents itself as a multitude of individuals which have been produced by division or the detachment of parts from other individuals, and most of which will in their time give rise to another generation. The existence in the form of distinct individuals which directly or indirectly reproduce their kind by a sort of inherent necessity is a third distinction between living and non-living things.[12]

(*SL* 1:4–5)

By 1929, Wells, in collaboration with Julian Huxley (grandson of Thomas and brother of Aldous) and his son G. P. Wells, was ready to offer a mass reading public an elaborate consideration of life, in the form of a science book for the ordinary reader. This was not a new enterprise for Wells, whose first published book was a biology textbook (1893) and whose writing had taken up the problem and the wonder of life for decades. Moreover, *The Science of Life* (1929) was envisioned as a sequel to *The Outline of History*, the second of the three disciplinary introductions that would together pave the way for the global thought at the basis of his world community. Even in that early textbook Wells was thinking broadly, writing in his preface that his book is addressed to "a vast number of solitary workers [in biology]...scattered through the country, to whom sustained help [in the form of classroom teaching] is impossible, or possible only in days stolen from a needed vacation."[13] In the earlier lines from *The Science of Life*, in accord with his principles of popular science writing, we have a crisp definition of life. It has three attributes: movement, ingestion, reproduction. Crisp but never dry, and never straightforward, Wells's language is marked, through these long volumes, by the telling example, the extended metaphor, and by the very definite stress, and as such, it follows predecessors like his hero Thomas Huxley, whose science writing for the layman was peppered with idiosyncratic conceits and figures and who was ready to guide his readers to his own positions, some quite controversial. It also mirrors *The Outline*, in that both texts want the reader, amid the flood of data and fact, to find herself constantly stopping to pause and to stretch her mind.

What stands out here in this opening definition of life is the emphasis on inherency, the "inner impulse" that distinguishes a living being's change of form from what could be stimulated, say, in a chemical compound. Wells is always attracted to the moment when the inner stir is activated, that instant just before the seed cracks open, when the very thing that constitutes life—nameable and at the same time ineffable—may be apprehended. Wells is drawn to life at its points of ontological saturation, and these often turn out to be thresholds, edges, or sites of incipience. Eggs often feature in his writing, and there are many instances when science seems to yield up something fundamental about our biological nature. *Ann Veronica* begins at such a juncture—"She had trembled on the verge of such a resolution before, but this time quite definitely had made it"—and the novel, cast in biological terms from beginning to end, figures Ann Veronica's coming of age as a story of *life*.[14] At the same time, these scenarios of discovering life, figured in terms of urgency and inner necessity, inevitably create extreme disturbance in Wells's fiction, overwhelming the clarity they seem to provide, and become entangled quickly with violence and power.

That phrase "trembled on the verge of" at the opening of *Ann Veronica* is familiar to modernists from Woolf, who prophesied a decade later in "Mr. Bennett and Mrs. Brown" (1924) that "we are trembling on the verge of one of the great ages of English literature," and Woolf, too, concentrates on the key figure of "Life" in this essay and in "Modern Fiction" (1919/1925), her two statements of artistic creed, which have become some of British modernism's most recognizable self-presentations. In "Modern Fiction," she uses that word (or its verb cognates) thirteen times. Life, which might also be named "truth, or spirit, or reality," is cast as the intangible engine of fiction, its essence, that which testifies to the text's value and import for the modern reader, as against a whole series of conventions that have grown stale, leaving fiction bereft of its germinating substance. Henry James, too, in rebutting Wells's harsh parody of him in *Boon* (1915) turned to the figure of "life" as his descriptor for what his fictional effort was seeking. "Of course for myself I live, live intensely and am fed by life, and my value, whatever it be, is in my own kind of expression of that," he wrote, countering Wells's suggestion that in his pronounced attention to minutiae James missed what is essential and important, a commitment to style that *Boon* concluded to be desiccating and deathly.[15] These modernist statements are too familiar to need elaboration, but their uses of "life" become suddenly rife with unspoken interests, newly revealing as the staging ground for literary modernism, when Wells's own massive engagement with the same vital force stands in the foreground and when, in the case of James, the confrontation is so direct.

It is not only fiction, in other words, that James and Woolf are trying to repossess in these key statements of modernist ethos but also "life," which has its own Wellsian purchase, a powerful one. Wells's writing was motivated by a dynamic conception of material life, an understanding of people caught within a cycle of vitality that gives meaning to the individual but also snatches it back from her. Mrs. Brown in her railway carriage is part of that story, too. If she finds herself swamped out in the Wellsian universe, it is not because he is too interested in the details of her railway carriage but because her place in that universe, her flickering existence in the evolution of life, is so precarious. Let us return to a passage from *The Future in America* (1906): "This [interrogative] habit of mind confronts and perplexes my sense of things that simply *are*, with my brooding preoccupation with how they will shape presently, what they will lead to, what seeds they will sow and how they will wear. . . . I am curiously not interested in things, and curiously interested in the consequences of things."[16] For Wells, what it means to seek life is not to plumb "the dark places of psychology" (Woolf) or to assert that "it is art that *makes* life" (James, his italics) but rather to dramatize the foundational qualities of living beings—that they move, interact with the biological world around them, and belong in a generational trajectory.[17] From these will follow innumerable scenarios, some of them frightening, others sobering, still others exhilarating; the human animal finds its quintessential qualities when it is closest to its past, its future, or its near kin. And vice versa: "It may seem a strange contradiction in me," says Prendick in *The Island of Doctor Moreau* (1896) at a late moment in the narrative of the beast people. "I cannot explain the fact—but now, seeing the creature in a perfectly animal attitude, with the light gleaming in its eyes, and its imperfectly human face distorted with terror, I realized again the fact of its humanity."[18]

Wells begins his definition of life with movement, and all of his engagements with life muster around one particular form of slow movement and transformation, evolution. If there ever was a master narrative, one that gives shape and significance to the place of the human in the scheme of the world, it is evolution. And if ever there was a theory that stood ready to provide a thick account of origins right where religion falls short, this is it too. "Evolution is," Wells puts it simply in *The Science of Life*, "*the* life-process" (*SL*, 1:317, italics in the original). Numerous critics have described Wells as an apostle to evolution, its literary avatar as Huxley was its scientific proselytizer. Huxley's place in Wells's imagination, and Darwin's before him, was indeed profound, including in his writerly techniques. Huxley's science writings in particular provided the model for Wells's own efforts, straddling as they do the line between addressing specialists and lay readers. These writings covered many topics; one important category includes works like *Man's Place in Nature* (1863), in which Huxley patiently, carefully, slowly makes his case for seeing humans in proper relation to other apes and primates. Man is an ape, that's the sensational point for which he argues, but Huxley gets there by working calmly and evenly through the details of comparative anatomy—of, say, the enormous importance of the structure of a hip joint, or the bones in the hand, and of course the all-important jaw bone. Such temperate persistence is the hallmark of biology in general, and Huxley's gift in writing for a wider audience was to build edifices, slowly and without melodrama, that nevertheless ultimately undo expectations and confront conventional thinking about the biological world and the scientific structure of the universe.

And Huxley knows how to use an extended conceit, to create the kind of analogy essential to all scientific writing for nonspecialists, a legacy that reaches far into the twentieth century, and that, of course characterizes Wells's science writings. In a wonderful essay, "On the Method of Zadig" (1880), first published in *The Nineteenth Century*, as an example, Huxley begins his analysis of what we might today call "scientific method" with the case of the (fictional) Babylonian philosopher Zadig, whose seemingly miraculous predictive talents were, according to him, merely the consequence of exemplary attention to detail. In essence, Huxley wants to say that there is nothing in scientific research that differs in kind from our ordinary habits of perception and documentation. Or, in "Evolution and Ethics" (1893), an essay Wells took to heart, among other things, for its rendering of life as perpetual movement, Huxley argues that evolution, far from being a new discovery, presents the essential principle of chaotic violence against which all religions, Eastern and Western, have launched their ethical visions. This essay, with its pitting of evolution against human ethical community, stands at the heart of Wells's endeavor in so many writings, where the imperative to work toward human betterment seems taunted by the longer time schemes and other evolutionary realities that render such efforts laughable. Most generally, in seeing science, especially biology, entirely intertwined with intellectual change, Huxley stands as the predecessor that Wells sought, a father figure par excellence (in real life Huxley remained the great man and Wells the distant student and admirer).[19] Too, Huxley is credited with coining the term "agnostic," cementing the ties between secularism and evolution, a pairing Wells went far to encourage. Wells was known by some as an enemy of religion—even if he often characterized his world state as a new "religion" and regularly enlists God on his side—and this avowed antagonism to the inherited religions certainly finds affinity with Darwinian discoveries and Huxley's elaborations.

It is hard to overstate the centrality of evolution, and of Huxley, in Wells's vision.[20] Roslynn Haynes notes that "the chief formative influence on Wells's thought was that of Huxley," and more fully, "evolutionary theory . . . seemed to Wells . . . the nearest approach to a unifying factor in contemporary thought. . . . No other concept ever made an equivalent impact on Wells—rather the criteria of biology became his yardstick to measure the claims of all other disciplines— astronomy, physics, sociology, politics, even theology and art."[21] Michael Page agrees, writing that "in the anonymity of Huxley's lecture hall and through Huxley's writings, Wells found the evolutionary vision that was to dominate his career as writer and public figure."[22] These and other critics have stressed a neat line from Darwin, to Huxley, to Wells, each later writer a disseminator and cre- ative reimaginer of the earlier. Such a line might, of course, be too straight; thus Leon Stover asks, "But does it follow that just because he worshiped Huxley as man and teacher, Wells stuck to the man's teachings?" Stover's answer is no: "far from adhering to [Huxley's 'Evolution and Ethics'], Wells contradicts it."[23] Sto- ver is right to challenge the assumption that Wells slavishly followed Huxley. Huxley's ideas fueled Wells's intellectual projects, but Wells runs along his own lines, and his lifelong interest in evolution, which produced ongoing imagina- tive ferment, intersects with Huxley's even as it veers off in new, often unset- tling, directions.[24]

But what is impossible to miss is the presence, urgency, and longevity of evo- lution in Wells's writing. Evolution is an underlying principle from his first novel *The Time Machine* (1895), an evolutionary parable at the level of class and species, to his last work *The Mind at the End of Its Tether* (1945), an evolutionary riff on how the running down of the world registers in one whirling conscious- ness. Sometimes evolution is the active subject, at others a principle of growth and change, at still others a way to give narrative to some of the anxieties about biological life that haunted his generation and Wells himself. Evolution takes many forms in Wells's writing; it can be a solid truth, what he calls in *The Science of Life* "The Incontrovertible Fact of Evolution," or a check to human hubris on the model of his early science journalism (recall those giant reptiles who think themselves the pinnacle and endpoint of life on earth). It is an endlessly fertile source of imagination and forecast, and a reminder, finally, that these vast processes governing the history and future of the planet are not so much irrespective of individual life as arrows shooting through it. Wells described his scientific edu- cation, and especially biology, in terms of imaginative reorganization and stimu- lation, "an extraordinary mental enlargement as my mind passed from the printed sciences within book covers to these intimate real things and then radi- ated outward to a realization that the synthesis of the sciences composed a vital interpretation of the world" (*EA*, 160). Vitality, growth, and synthesis are the tenets of both evolution and life, and thus in framing his own learning in their terms, he enfolds his developing mind within their broad capacities.

However dominant it was as an idea in Wells's corpus, evolution is no subject for veneration. He was particularly contemptuous of Social Darwinism, which he felt was based on a skewed understanding of evolution, an excessive adherence to the non-Darwinian idea of "survival of the fittest," a conservative and self-serving ideology that gave the entire enterprise of evolutionary theory a bad name. Among the other problems with such models is that they mistake the time scale of evolution. As discussed in the last chapter, Wells stressed in his works the disproportionate temporal scale of human, and especially historical, existence versus the vastness of time in more evolutionary, geological, or cosmological schemes. He reminds his readers regularly, even obsessively, of the caveman's red eyes staring through ours—all of ours, not specified by any narrow inheritance. In an early essay, very much influenced by Huxley, he tries to be as plain as he can, in declaring "that man (allowing for racial blendings) is still mentally, morally, and physically what he was during the later Palaeolithic period, that we are, and that the race is likely to remain, for (humanly speaking) a vast period of time, at the level of the Stone Age. The only considerable evolution that has occurred since then, so far as man is concerned, has been, it is here asserted, a different sort of evolution altogether, an evolution of suggestions and ideas."[25]

In *The Undying Fire* (1919), which, we recall, stages a modern reenactment of the biblical story of Job set during the final year of the war, Wells gives to one of Job's four interlocutors an adherence to evolution as mantra, in a configuration that is instructive for evolution's ambiguous presence in Wells's thinking more generally. Of the four antagonists, Doctor Barack has the clearest affinity with his author (he is an exponent of science, after all), and it might seem that his affiliation with evolution stands as some kind of endorsement, yet *The Undying Fire* has an unambiguous *pro*tagonist and four *ant*agonists. Barack is always and only one of Job's tempters, not righteous but misguided. Barack calls evolution "the Process" and has this to say about it:

> The Process is complex. . . . It isn't . . . playing the part of a Providence just for our comfort and happiness. Some of us are hammer and some of us are anvil, some of us are sparks and some of us are the beaten stuff which survives. The Process doesn't confide in us; why should it? We learn what we can about it, and make what is called a practical use of it, for that is what the Will in the Process requires. . . .

[Unlike Job] *I* think we struggle against one another by nature and necessity; that we polish one another in the struggle and sharpen our edges. I think that out of this struggle for existence comes better things and better.... But [Job] Huss does not believe in the struggle. He wants to take men's minds and teach them so that they will not struggle against each other but live and work all together.[26]

Wells makes Barack's case simultaneously persuasive and odious. It represents aspects of Wells's own thought, particularly in the notion that as individuals we cannot expect evolution to offer personal affirmation. Nor need it be kind; as we will discuss later in this chapter, Wells's partial attraction to biopolitical planning with eugenic affinities belongs to the larger category of applied evolution, and Barack's idea that "some of us are anvil," though not a replica of Wells's own experiments in eugenic logic, belongs in the same family. So there are ways in which Barack's commentary channels Wells, along with others in the cultural history of the period who saw in evolution a system and theory that rationalized inequality and championed the idea of winners and losers in the epochal schemes of history. As in the biblical model, however, Job's "friends" are no friends, and their discussion bears only spurious likeness to the truth both the biblical and this mimic scripture espouse. The use of the word "struggle" five times in this passage alone testifies to the misleading couching of evolution as anthropomorphic and progressive. More, in Barack's attack on Job, it is clear that Wells himself is the target; after all, no one more than Wells was working to "take men's minds and teach them so that they will ... live and work together."

*The Undying Fire* was composed simultaneously with *The Outline*, and Job as headmaster elaborates an educational formula based on universal history as the spur to universal betterment that concurs with what Wells provided in *The Outline*. Evolution, with its immensely coherent logic, falters for Wells when it diminishes human aspiration. We might recall the frame narrator of *The Time Machine*, who could not reconcile the terrifying story of evolution in the long run with the nearer goals for social harmony; his choice (like that of Wells in *Discovery of the Future*) was to ignore the longer duration of evolutionary time altogether. But evolution is not really checked by the inconvenience it creates for our plans. It is, rather, one of the great laws of the universe, acting according to its own inner demands yet operating in the field where our essential narratives are construed and reimagined.

We might think of evolution in Wells's works as akin, say, to social and racial difference in Forster's writing or sexuality in Lawrence's, one of the large, organizing facts of human experience. Even if we cannot see evolution (or, rather, because we cannot), its power and presence course through Wells's universe. It is the source of plots and action but also, more revealingly, a pervasive force in the world, that which is always acting on and through us, a reality that can never be superseded. But then, need it be one's destiny? At the end of *A Passage to India* (1924), Forster wonders if two men of different races can be friends, which is to ask if the power of difference and intolerance can be overcome. As we know, he does not supply a definitive answer ("no not here, no not yet"). And so with Wells, he will never quite reach a conclusion about how, if at all, we go about overcoming the aspects of biology that seem tied to destiny versus controlling our collective future. It is an especially thorny knot because the idea of destiny is so central to Wells's optimism in general. Evolution, made up of untold millions of random changes over millions of years, despite the misleading rhetoric that has always surrounded it, is neither predictable nor friendly. As early as 1895, Wells cautioned against "Bio-Optimism," declaring, "The names of the sculptor who carves out the new forms of life are, and so far as human science goes at present they must ever be, Pain and Death. And the phenomena of degeneration rob one of any confidence that the new forms will be in any case or in a majority of cases 'higher' (by any standard except present adaptation to circumstance) than the old" (*EWS*, 209).[27] He wrote several pieces on this subject, arguing forcefully that "there is almost always associated with the suggestion of advance in biological phenomena an opposite idea, which is its essential complement . . . degradation" (*EWS*, 158). Just think of the Eloi and Morlocks. The idea of evolutionary fate is no panacea, and Wells toggles between seeing evolution as a world system like Barack's Process, with its own logic and unstoppable directionality, and his many schemes to plan and imagine our way into a harmonious future that has little in common with evolution's demands. In still another formulation, seeming to refute his caution that devolution is just as common in the world scheme as progress, Wells's surging optimism links to evolutionary history, as, for instance, "If that self-same stream of life that flows through our human generations and that we call man was once fish . . . without the aid of conscious purpose in any of the pre-human forbears, who shall prophesy what our race may not achieve and into what it may not transform itself before another such period in the history of life on earth has passed?" (*SL*, 1:423–24). Mostly, though, evolution stands in Wells's writing as crux, that place of imaginative generativity to which the reader of the story of life will inevitably be pulled. Wells writes with some amusement in *The Science of Life* about how "our grandparents" were always searching for "missing links" in the evolutionary chain, but the idea that there is some mystery at the heart of the evolutionary story, that the condition of humanity brought into view by evolution remains in some fundamental way inexplicable, is something Wells too takes as a starting point.

The essential mystery accumulates around the outlines of the human, how we delineate, know, and ultimately construct that figure—ourselves. Let us return, for a moment, to the morning on the moon's surface when life bursts into view. Here the biological imperative manifests overtly; these processes simply happen, in accordance with their own internal drives, an emphasis seen also in Wells's definition of life at the opening of *The Science of Life*. Yet when it comes to people, Wells is less willing to succumb to the sense of organic inevitability; in the case of humanity, there is equal part expression and making. We know that Wells believed in planning to an almost manic degree. That the all-important category of human beings would be left to develop on its own seemed, to the biologist and planner, wildly irresponsible. We must, he felt as conviction, do better; we must not only see ourselves as made but actively make our species and our future. But what does it mean to make a person? Frances Galton, the founder of eugenics and a massive figure in thought for over a quarter-century, laid out one system for creating a population, based on identifying strengths and weaknesses in families and promoting selective breeding. Wells proclaimed himself opposed to Galton's views and methods, on practical as well as theoretical grounds. Still, for all his overt disidentification with Galton, the generational timescale and the potential for a human engineering of the biological world Galton envisioned also permeate Wells's thinking. More normatively, "making men" and building "character" had been Victorian fetishes, and Wells hoped to stride away from these ideals, loaded as they were with middle-class British, often imperial, values. The base idea of making was released in Wells's imagination into the fertile terrain of evolutionary thinking, with the goal of improving the health and well-being of the polity along new lines.[28] His texts turn not on the good form associated with character production but on the literalization of the metaphor of man making. Following in the path of Mary Shelley, twisting away from Galton and back again, snubbing the respectability of Victorian character formation, Wells considered the very overt ways in which humans can be forged, constructed, bred—in a word, made.

The enthusiastic fashioning of people is the agenda of *Mankind in the Making* (1903), a sequel of sorts (by Wells's account) to *The Discovery of the Future* and to a lesser degree *Anticipations* (1901), two works where Wells lays forceful claim to the future as a site of knowledge and a proving ground for the imagination. In the later text, Wells provides a full-throated analysis for how we might construct humanity in the interest of these better futures. *Mankind in the Making* wants to rewrite the human and social plan according to the logic of the reproductive calendar—taking birth as the keystone event in people's lives and in the well-being of the community—and to see in the idea of generationality the crucial link between evolutionary process and the amelioration of the social body. The life cycle, understood in evolutionary terms, thus becomes the orienting idea in considering what "the New Republic," as Wells names his future society, will have as its core principles and goals.[29] He writes of this society:

> *Any collective human enterprise, institution, movement, party or state, is to be judged as a whole and completely, as it conduces more or less to wholesome and hopeful births, and according to the qualitative and quantitative advance due to its influence made by each generation of citizens born under its influence towards a higher and ampler standard of life.*
>
> Or, putting the thing in a slightly different phrasing, the New Republican idea amounts to this: the serious aspect of our private lives, the general aspect of all our social and co-operative undertakings, is to prepare as well as we possibly can a succeeding generation, which shall prepare still more capably for still better generations to follow.[30]

These lines sound a certain refrain with Wells's declaration that he can only see becoming, never being. Here too, though on a different scale, the suggestion is of each moment (or generation) slipping into the next, with human movement in and through time the object of state action. Wells's conception of generation is multiple and far-reaching. As a figure for cohorts among people, the usage of "generation" was recent (though soon to become widespread by the end of the First World War, as in "lost generation"), with other meanings also abounding. For Wells, evolution and generation are partners, both naming forces of living change through time.

In Wells's view, evolution makes this kind of rich generativity possible because it erases the primacy—or even the possibility—of stasis over time, one of his basic creeds. Life is movement, and the trajectory must always be to find ideas and language that accord with the Heraclitan mobility and mutability that is the universe. As for evolution, then:

> Directly the discovery is made clear . . . that one generation does not follow another in *fac simile*, directly we come within sight of the reasonable persuasion that each generation is a step, a definite measurable step, and each birth an unprecedented experiment, directly it grows clear that instead of being in an

eddy merely, we are for all our eddying moving forward upon a wide voluminous current.

(MM, 17)

Birth itself becomes a form of progressivism, and the idea that there might be a
better destiny for humanity in the future infuses these lines and the whole of
*Mankind in the Making* with its motivation. Because we know that birth can
mean change, we must make it a change for the better; because life begins perpetually, we must constantly be urging it toward more ideal conditions. The
principle is simple, really. Yet *Mankind in the Making* is a strange book, beginning with these invocations to life as revealed by evolution yet mostly made up
of all manner of nitty-gritty detail, a Home Depot in written exhortation. A
reader today is likely to be taken aback by the specificity and detail with which
Wells attempts to answer a hundred questions about birth, child rearing, education, and the polity. The Wellsian voice in *Mankind in the Making* projects an
unusually expert character on topic after topic, weaving these local discussions
into the larger plan for humanity's improvement. As he puts it toward the end of
the book, "Throughout these papers a disposition to become concrete has played
unchecked. Always definite proposals have been preferred to vague generalizations" (*MM*, 357). One senses that Wells is enjoying himself, down in the muck
and mud of so many "definite proposals," airing his interests around seemingly
limitless features of individual and social welfare.

*Mankind in the Making* thus stakes its claim firmly in the nurture field, taking on the problem of "making" with relish. Wells severely rejects the viability of
isolating natural hierarchies and abilities in groups or families—even in
individuals—and instead takes up the mantle of a reformer working with the
material at hand, those human bodies and beings that he sees as the signal
responsibility of the state to make, mold, nourish, and set loose to do their part
in improving the next generation. What he shares with eugenic forerunners like
Galton (whose 1883 *Inquiries Into Human Faculty and Development* he names in
the text) is, in fact, that motivating sense of generationality, the same principle
of movement that characterizes his overall understanding of the constituency of
life and his approach to time. Yet *Mankind in the Making* operates not in the
flux of time but in the absolute presence of each stage of the growing person. It
knows what it wants to make—healthy, productive, educated citizens with a sac-
rificial attitude toward the collective and a belief in world community over
national loyalty—and is ready to get down to business in realizing the vision.

Like *A Modern Utopia*, published two years later, *Mankind in the Making* is
in full social-engineering mode, and as such it releases Wells's human-planning

energies to an excessive degree. As biopolitical theory has demonstrated, such efforts ally the control of both animal and human bodies with the forces of governmentality, and Wells enters into this fray with gusto, though along his own lines. For Martin Danahay, considering Wells and Galton together as major figures in the nineteenth century's efforts to manipulate the body politic, with largely conflicting approaches (Galton treating humans as animals to be "bred," Wells seeing human rationality as his operating assumption), it is finally the commonalties uniting Wells with Galton that stand out: "both . . . ultimately had faith in evolution being used as a technology to solve social problems on a large scale and both thus supported the instantiation of biopower and the redefinition of 'mankind' as a 'human species' or 'human animal' that was subject to management by a technoscientific elite."[31] Whereas Danahay finds it difficult to pinpoint Wells's politics in relation to his schemes to manage and improve the populace, John Carey has made an extreme case against Wells as a kind of genocidal fascist (all the literary figures of the modernist era, other than Arnold Bennett, fall into this category for Carey), arguing that Wells's fantasies of extermination represent a real animus against working people, the middle class, women, and more. Seeing "anxiety about overpopulation, rooted in his childhood vision of woods and fields destroyed at Bromley . . . [as] the key to Wells's reading of modern history," Carey declares that "reducing the world's population became an obsession. In fantasy he took—again and again, and with mounting savagery—a terrible revenge on the suburban sprawl that had blighted Bromley."[32] At the same time, Carey somewhat grudgingly recognizes that Wells fell, in other ways, on the side of humanity, and in his chapter "H. G. Wells Against H. G. Wells," he qualifies his claims of Wells as largely a writer of hate. In general, contemporary criticism has difficulty with Wells as social engineer, and most readers today would strenuously reject the ideal of perfecting the polity under any rubric. Given the West's ghastly history of racial cleansing and eugenics, this is fair enough, but, as often with Wells, when we open and close the case here, we lose most of what is interesting and illuminating, such as, in the example of *Mankind in the Making*, the relish in getting into the weeds of person making. And we miss, too, the internal checks and contradictions Wells scripts into his works, including his penchant for writing his dreams as, also, nightmares.

Such nightmares take shape across his writing, most powerfully in two books that precede *Mankind in the Making* by ten and five years, *The Island of Doctor Moreau* (1896) and *The First Men in the Moon* (1901). It is almost as if *Mankind in the Making* is needed to alleviate what these two earlier novels have exposed in the extremely vivid prospect of making people. We began this chapter with

*The First Men in the Moon*, whose sequence on the lunar surface so beautifully encapsulates the lasting wonder that life's processes can stir. But underground, deep within the moon's hollow interior, a wholly different life story is told: a Selenite civilization that seems to have drunk equally from Moreau's and Galton's cups. In the bizarre world fantasized here are elements common to Wells's other dystopias, including the Grand Lunar, who refigures the Martians (and the men of the year million) as a giant brain with no body, a kind of floating intelligence with no further need of other organs. Where the Martians failed in their attempts at sovereignty, the Grand Lunar is successful, ruling like a sultan over a society constructed according to a most extreme and intricate hierarchy. Each Selenite is formed, by minute specification, to its task, from the job of cattle herding at one end of the social spectrum to that of remembering at the other. Once again, it is a civilization without books, all knowledge being retained by those bred as the culture's brain depositories. There is, naturally, a robust center of activity around reproduction, this being the one and only function of Selenite females. Women readers today will naturally be both offended and disgusted (and perhaps a trifle amused) by our situation in this moon culture.

But the most memorable and haunting spectacles in Wells's dystopic parody of a eugenic paradise are those involving this actual making of beings in the most hideous of ways. Cavor, now our only access point to the moon, Bedford having escaped in the sphere, has glimpses like this one:

> "I am still much in the dark about it, but quite recently I came up on a number of young Selenites, confined in jars from which only the forelimbs protruded, who were being compressed to become machine-minders of a special sort. The extended 'hand' in this highly developed system of technical education is stimulated by irritants and nourished by injection while the rest of the body is starved. . . . It is quite unreasonable, I know, but these glimpses of the educational methods of these beings have affected me disagreeably. I hope, however, that may pass off and I may be able to see more of this aspect of this wonderful social order. That wretched-looking hand sticking out of its jar seemed to have a sort of limp appeal for lost possibilities, it haunts me still, although, of course, it is really in the end a far more humane proceeding than our earthly method of leaving children to grow into human beings, and then making machines of them."
>
> (*FMM*, 184)

A similarly upsetting sight is one Cavor stumbles across one evening, when he sees the comatose bodies of working-class moon-folk lying in a field in a drugged stupor; for them, it seems, such breaks from work are inherent to their original construction, much as the elongated hand is for the machinist Selenites. Cavor works hard to banish such sights from his mental vision, straining to admire the rationality of the Selenite world—which, after all, has a great deal in common with Wells's forthcoming utopias, right down to the Selenites' shock at learning from Cavor about that distinctly human activity, war. But for all the irony leveled back toward the blue planet ("our earthly method of leaving children to grow into human beings, and then making machines of them"), Cavor's and, even more, the reader's disgust at how these beings are formed and the utter determinism of this world cannot be erased. More, there remains something deeply injurious to literary method in the literalization made manifest in the Selenite system, as the realities of inequity on Earth, and specifically of the class structure of industrialized England, are made actual, in a scenario that is becoming familiar (the Eloi and Morlocks, the country of the blind). Even if these literalizations come tinged with an ironic retort to the contemporary world, they blast, once again, through the conventions of language and thought. The text, like Cavor, cannot tolerate the biological impingement on humanity; it is too direct, too actual. The Selenites in jars or lying drunk in the fields give a kind of back-alley view of *life* as it is forged and expressed in this culture of creature creation. And of course, that helpless hand: is it reaching out to us, and does it suggest the work of the writer or artist no less than the soon-to-be machinist?

There are, then, two fundamentally opposed life principles at work in the novella, the organic wonder purveyed on the surface of the moon and the murky, violent world below, in which the extreme, indeed boundless, fabrication of men has reached staggering levels, fit for its own genre of visual display. The famous early bar sequence in *Star Wars* (1977), filled with a miscellany of wonderfully mutant beings (subsequently copied by innumerable later films and present throughout the *Star Wars* franchise), might have been set squarely in the Selenite community. More, the novel's own structure is jarringly divided, consisting of two very different parts: its first two thirds (largely the original text, serialized in *The Strand*) with the initial setting in Kent, the buildup to the moon voyage, the moon adventure, Bedford's departure and his return to Earth; and the second segment, after Bedford has returned home, consisting largely of Cavor's broken transmissions from the moon in which he relays what he has learned of the Selenite world, before his transmissions are ominously cut off, his communications slashed with the very disconcerting partial word "uless" (*FMM*, 203).[33] For all the metatextuality of the last portion, in which, for instance, Bedford takes up the pen name "H. G. Wells" and discusses the serialization of his book, and the continuing humor throughout the novel (which is really very funny), the two-part break cannot easily be reconciled, and the first half, which is clever and delightful but also haunting and metaphysical, holds more appeal, I think, than the strange second part, which seems to indulge a kind of extreme, overheated social imagination, grating against the novella's earlier trajectory from mild social comedy to sparseness and essentiality. If they are to form a whole, at the level of interior logic, their dual experiment with envisioning life as principle is the most potent linking motif. In the upper air, the vibrant innate necessities of biology assert their full energies; within the eerie depths of the moon's lower rungs, it is craft, ingenuity, and reason that retake such forces for themselves. Those horrifically cramped beings, limbs hanging from their jars, might stand as the uncanny endpoint of the effort to envision evolution as a process we might control, or mirror, or reproduce.

It is in *The Island of Doctor Moreau*, above all, that Wells offers a stinging and unforgettable dramatization of what it might mean to forge humanity. Preceding *Mankind in the Making* by nearly a decade, it registers what no amount of activist biopower is ready to recognize, that taken to its logical extreme, such making is no better than unmaking, to use the word in Elaine Scarry's sense from *The Body in Pain: The Making and Unmaking of the World* (1985), where unmaking stands against and undoes creation, language, and the alleviation of bodily pain. If we believe Foucault and his followers, such is the inevitable insight about biopolitics, that it delivers state power (governmentality) enacted through bodies, hence representing the most chilling outcomes of modernity and its controls, always in the interest of power itself. But *The Island of Doctor Moreau* registers the terrors of man making, rather, in the quintessentially Wellsian form of literalization. Doctor Moreau's experiments, of creating human beings out of animals imported for the purpose, sears through the metaphor, and that is just the beginning of the trespasses in this short, explosive tale of revelation, culminating in the death of Moreau and the return of the beast people to their previous states.

It is a book that defies categories and expectations. Published in 1896, one year after the success of *The Time Machine*, *The Island of Doctor Moreau* dismayed readers right from the start. Compared to its predecessor, *The Island of Doctor Moreau* drained away the charm of protagonist and setting, the wonder of scientific imagining, and the safety of a story set nearly a million years in the future to force an even harsher and more violent view of the status of humanity. The island, with its sealed nature and its overt unreality, may be a classic literary setting for testing out the limits and possibilities of the social, but Wells took his anti-Eden a few steps further than readers cared to go. Some samples of early reviews include:

> The distinction between legitimate and illegitimate use of horror seems to lie not in the form of the horror, but in the purpose for which it is used . . . the disgusting descriptions arouse loathing without any equivalent personal interest. The sufferings inflicted in the course of the story have absolutely no adequate artistic reason.
>
> (*Athenaeum*)

> We should have thought it impossible for any work of fiction to surpass in gruesome horror some of the problem-novels relating to the great sexual question which have been recently published, if we had not read the *Island of Doctor Moreau*, by H. G. Wells. Having read it, we are bound to admit that there are still lower depths of nastiness, and still cruder manifestations of fantastic imbecility.
>
> (*Speaker*)

> Those who have delighted in the singular talent of Mr. Wells will read *The Island of Doctor Moreau* with dismay. . . . For Mr. Wells has put his talent to the most flagitious usury.[34]
>
> (*Saturday Review*)

The overwhelming sense is of horror, a word that comes up repeatedly in these responses to the novel, as reviewers lashed out at Wells for pushing too far in the direction of blood and disgust, "nastiness," as well as for the story's scientific extravagance (reviewers questioned the verisimilitude of the outcome of Moreau's experiments). Perhaps a deeper uneasiness about what such transgressions are expressing stands at the base of these critiques. But there is, in truth, a great deal of blood in *Moreau*, much of it dripping, splashing, forming pools and puddles, and of course awash through the enclosed yard Moreau has converted to a vivisection chamber. An alarming amount of it is also consumed—even by Prendick, or so it might be, his first drink after being rescued by the *Ipecacuanha* being "some scarlet stuff, iced. It tasted like blood, and made me feel stronger" (*IDM*, 10). As Peter Kemp has noted in delectable detail, the drinking of blood is a replete Wellsian trope; in Kemp's phrase, the Wellsian human is "The Edible Predator."[35]

But the difficulty of *Moreau* is not only its ferocious attack on the niceties of Victorian fictional decorum ("decency") or the relentlessness of its focus on physically revolting details, including the regular feature of blood-drenched faces. There is a larger question in all of this, of what this short novel is trying to *do*. If we are asked to experience these grotesqueries, there must be a reason, a larger message, as the anonymous *Athenaeum* reviewer stressed. And the story does seem to demand an allegorical reading; everything seems to point toward allegory, from the setting in a magical yet sinister island to its creation myth and religious ritual, its robust literary associations, and its tapping into basic questions of what constitutes human nature. Yet it is not entirely clear whether allegorical technique is even appropriate, let alone what the referent might be. Given the literalization at the story's center, that is, allegorical reading seems pitted against a different kind of hermeneutical force, as if the concretizing of one central metaphor—making men—wreaks havoc on the more general metaphor-using habits to which readers of fiction are accustomed. The violence of vivisection, made not so much visible as audible, wafts through the story, continually calling us back to the primal scene of the female puma being torn apart and reconstructed, similar to the way the beast people are kept in line by being constantly drawn back in memory to the House of Pain. Wells makes the initial experience of the puma's torture nearly unbearable, for Prendick, who is driven out into the island by her howls, and also for the reader, who may not share Prendick's opinion that "surely, and especially to another scientific man, there was nothing so horrible in vivisection" (*IDM*, 35). Wells, in the introduction to the Atlantic Edition (1924), wrote this about the question of allegory:

> There was a scandalous trial about that time [of Oscar Wilde], the graceless and pitiful downfall of a man of genius, and this story was the response of an imaginative mind to the reminder that humanity is but animal rough-hewn to a reasonable shape and in perpetual internal conflict between instinct and injunction. This story embodies this ideal, but apart from this embodiment it has no allegorical quality. It is written just to give the utmost possible vividness to that conception of men as hewn and confused and tormented beasts.[36]

Of course, we need not follow Wells's exhortation to avoid allegory (much less his takeaway from the Wilde trials), and, as Jorge Luis Borges and many other readers have noticed, *Moreau* distills a sense of human truth that seems to promise widening circles of meaning: "Not only do [Wells's scientific fantasies like *Moreau*] tell an ingenious story; but they tell a story symbolic of processes that are somehow inherent in all human destinies."[37] Wells and Borges are in agreement, perhaps, that the way meaning works in *Moreau* is less by allegory than by holding before us, in a contained space and a time seemingly out of time, a series of provocations about what it means to be human, and also animal, what evolution shows us about ourselves.

Such questions are at the heart of the story and of Wells's more general investigation into the principle of life, but we might, before shifting to the knot at the tale's center, linger further on the question of allegory and other symbolic reading habits, to ask: what—if we want to pursue these for a moment—would it be allegorizing? Most directly, it reads as a conservative fable about the folly of colonial attempts to "civilize the savage." Neatly put by Paul A. Cantor and Peter Hufnagel, "The Beast People Moreau creates correspond to natives in the British colonial imagination; imperialist romances often pictured non-Europeans as animals (think of Kipling's *Jungle Books*). Indeed Moreau's fear that his creations will be unable to abide by the laws he has laid down for them reflects the central concern of British colonial rule."[38] In such a scenario, that project is hopeless, since the beast people can never be more than parodies of men and will revert, in any case, back to their animal ways. These are mimic men par excellence. Such an allegory of colonization has a number of supporting themes, the white-haired Moreau playing the part of the White Man, even Europe (as with Kurtz after him, it could be said that all of Europe went into the making of Moreau), the savages who can never be real men, the parodic European community set up on the island, even the expected catastrophe for whites who go native: Montgomery's fate, he who "half likes some of these beasts" is fittingly to be killed in a drunken confab with his bestial pals (*IDM*, 78). Wells also pushes against this reading, in the sense that Moreau's version of empire is bereft of all that Wells, for one, felt the empire was supposed to be doing: there is no project here other than experiment and egotism.

More urgent, perhaps, than the complex substitution demanded by allegory, *Moreau* offers the simpler reading formula of fable: about the dangers of science, playing God, the human aspiration to tinker with the universe. As we have noted, Wells's dialectical thinking is never greater than when science is the topic—science, our savior, that which will allow us to tackle our own biological infelicities, conquer matter, perfect our lives and our institutions, and build our utopia, but also science, our downfall, that which acutely shows how much humans are capable of achieving and how inescapably inadequate they are to such discoveries. It is a decidedly sinister moment when Moreau notes, learning that Prendick has some scientific training, " 'That alters the case a little . . . As it happens, we are biologists here. This is a biological station—of a sort' " (*IDM*, 29). A biological station: perhaps the yoking of the laboratory to the outpost, of an undertaking that thrives only through publication and collaboration to the rule-free universe of the colonial enclave, necessitates the corruption. Here on the outer edge beyond the populated world, science can carry on without the social restraints epitomized in the novel by Moreau's earlier exposures back in the Western metropolis, the press reports that drove him out of London. The result of unfettered scientific investigation is this, the island of Doctor Moreau. Science left alone, without its culture, becomes a matter of egomania triumphing over the common good. Restraint, as we see in other stories too (*The Food of the Gods, The Invisible Man*), becomes an essential accessory to ethical science.

In plumbing the question of scientific ethics in a sensational and unforgettable riff on creation, Wells's Dr. Moreau keeps company with various literary antecedents and especially with Shelley's Dr. Frankenstein. The parallels between the tales are clear, from the excitement of scientific discovery, to the blurring of the line between art and science under the rich sign of "creation," to the violence that eventually overtakes the narrative, to the ultimate showdown between creator and creation. And it is not only *Frankenstein* that Wells's tale calls up; of all his scientific fantasies, *The Island of Doctor Moreau* is the most saturated in literary history. *Frankenstein, Robinson Crusoe, Faust*, the Bible, *The Origin of Species, The Tempest, Comus*, "The Rime of the Ancient Mariner," Aesop's *Fables, The Odyssey, Treasure Island* . . . and the list continues.[39] Yet there is a strange way in which none of these literary references adds perceptibly to the experience of reading or helps in decoding the tale's meaning. Almost the reverse—these affinities show how ruthless and intransigent Wells's story is and underscore the essentiality of its central idea. *Moreau* is after something primal, raw, almost impervious to literary technique. Even under the rubric of the fable or parable, the moral import remains murky, a fact that very palpably worried all of the early reviewers quoted earlier. Returning to the question of the island's activity being offered as an allegory for the "civilizing" mission of the British Empire, what the story does, rather, is to degrade the foundations of that ideology by diluting the meaning of its stabilizing principles: civilization, higher and lower forms of mankind, progress, the value of Christian law and practice. Wells's own later assessment, that the tale was an attempt to get right down to the hewn human animal, rightly steers the reader toward something other than the substitutive logic of allegory. Yet in other ways, Wells's judgment does not entirely help matters, since the novella never heeds the call of clarity.

Rather, *The Island of Doctor Moreau* confounds categories as its primary mechanism, beginning with the central axis of human and animal. Take the excessive blood drinking that touches nearly every aspect of the story. The Law stipulates several key proscriptions against regression for the beast people: chasing other creatures, scratching on trees, lapping water from on all fours, and, above all, meat eating. Reciting the law (or rather chanting it, in a combination of self-hypnosis and crowd intoxication) as a prophylactic to prevent backsliding, the beast people go about their human ways—though, right from start, as early as Prendick's first exploration of the island, signs abound of their transgressions. As Moreau rues it, "First one animal trait, then another, creeps to the surface and stares at me . . . As soon as my hand is taken from them, the beast begins to creep back, begins to assert itself again" (*IDM*, 78). One transgression naturally stands above the rest as a threat to the system and a sign of resurgent instinct, the eating of prey, figured in the text largely as a matter of drinking blood (and as we know, once tasted . . .). But what is odd and symptomatic in all of this is that many of the animals figured as reverting to their blood-drinking ways are not natural predators. Certainly a leopard, puma, or hyena would be a frightening killer once returned to that identity, but why an ape? Or the swine men and women, not an appealing lot, are seen "bloodstained . . . about the mouth," and this follows immediately from the most domesticated of all the beast people, M'ling, displaying "ominous brown stains" around his jaws, though with some bear and dog in his pedigree, we can forgive him (*IDM*, 101, 100). Meanwhile, to state the obvious, humans on their side belong to the omnivore designation, and in Wells's fiction they are a heartily meat-eating species, beginning with the Time Traveller's craving for mutton, which so disconcertingly marks his return from the future, where he only just escaped the flesh-loving Morlocks (who of course favor their meat uncooked). Prendick too seems undaunted by an "ill-cooked rabbit" for breakfast on the morning after his conversation with Moreau, despite his encounter with a mutilated rabbit as the first sign of violence on the island (*IDM*, 80). Indeed, as Kemp points out, the Wellsian world divides with suspicious regularity into a game of predator and prey; on Moreau's island the question of who's who is part of the suspense, but what's missing in the menagerie is the possibility of any creature who does not harbor the predatory tendency. Even the rabbit-like creatures on the island, purpose-built by Moreau for food, end up eating their young. Wells the biologist is after something other than species fidelity, clearly. At the level of plot, such miscegenation makes sense, since what the island dramatizes is the mixture, confusion, and criss-crossing of different kinds of being.

Once the animal/human divide has been so entirely breached, it seems that all categories break down; "a kind of generalized animalism" emerges, in lieu of the distinct categorizations beloved of biologists, and also of the nineteenth century's cataloguing and displaying zeitgeist (*IDM*, 124). As noted in the previous chapter, "Time," Wells recognized the natural history museum as one of the quintessential institutions of his century. It is a place where his fiction often tends and lingers, but could there be an aisle for the beast people, who stand against the ordering compulsion that defines Victorian ethnography, natural history, biology? Some of the island's creatures, after all, are composed of several different animals—the hyena-swine and so on—and Prendick regularly uses the term "monster" and its cognates to describe all of the beast people (or beast monsters, as he also dubs them). In his first conversation with Moreau, he uses the term "abomination," picking up a religious intonation, another stride away from biology. From the natural history museum to the freak show might indeed be less of a distance than these distinctive attractions would proclaim.[40] The monstrous is a loaded term, one with powerful cultural implications in the late nineteenth century (as today), but on the island, it stands above all for the erasure of distinctiveness, a quality of indeterminacy that hovers over the beast people, with their species impurity, and seems to turn one and all into blood-drinking threats.

There is, of course, no monstrosity (or abomination) in biology. To the extent that the novel's speakers take recourse to its figuration, they enter a different terrain, where issues of essence and being come to the fore, raw forces in the world that cannot be fitted into proper scientific categories. Moreau, who presents himself as the pure investigator unbothered by ethics or consequences, waves away Prendick's concerns about the beast people being "abominations," yet he too recognizes that there is something in the animal that he cannot control, fix, or eliminate. " 'But I will conquer yet,' " he insists, " 'Each time I dip a living creature into the bath of burning pain, I say: this time I will burn out all the animal' " (IDM, 78). Moreau knows that the "animal" cannot be burned out, since the human is no less animal than any other, and so, in a sense, he has created a nonscientific goal for himself, an end in the realm of fantasy rather than material reality. And Prendick, for his part, is no scientist at all. Moreau may welcome him (warily and unenthusiastically, it is true) into the biological circle, but Prendick has few qualifications for the task. By his own account his "eye has no training in details—and unhappily I cannot sketch" (in his biology textbook of 1893, Wells reminds his would-be science students that anatomical drawing is a crucial skill for them), and of course observation of detail is a given for biology, as Huxley had so deftly argued in "On the Method of Zadig" (IDM, 82). More generally, as readers inevitably notice, Prendick is an unimpressive figure for the task at hand, given to fatigue and terror, utterly unresourceful. Rescued from the Lady Vain, our Prendick does not progress far from the laxity such a name promises, more the plaything of fate than its maker; this is no bildungsroman. Prendick is unreliable as a scientific guide, then, and his attachment to the idea of monstrosity is also shared around the text, as it takes us from the realm of biological classification to that of fantasy, folklore, and, more generally, literature.

Once again we feel the force of *Frankenstein*'s presence; after all, Mary Shelley made little effort to convince readers of the biological likelihood of her protagonist's creation. Wells takes pivotal biological questions and, releasing them into the hothouse atmosphere of the possible, infuses the narrative with a combination of biological and fantasmatic urgency. *The Island of Doctor Moreau* seems to grip the Victorian imagination by the throat, insisting that it watch its own most potent fears reach culmination. Like so many monstrous figures in literary history, the beast people play out the drama of admixture, kinds and differences that won't keep to their places, in a form that upends key principles in the culture of late-century, high-imperial Britain. Gillian Beer places the novella in the context of the Victorian obsession with "the missing link," that half-century-long reckoning with evolution's troubling provocation: what actually separates us from the apes? Wells, as we have seen, generally follows Huxley in reframing the question, considering the hermeneutical puzzles of man's genealogy, looking for common ancestry, asking where and when the split happened, deducing hypotheses from the careful study of animal and human anatomy.

Yet here in the novel, no such comparative biological conversation is underway. It is a place, rather, where the uses of science, and its overarching aura, create a surround for the novel's richer ore, the challenges to human self-understanding that abound in the face of what Moreau has constructed. In an article published the same year, Wells considered the "limits of plasticity," suggesting in his journalistic voice that such work as his novella imagines could one day be actualized in reality.[41] And so we ask again, what makes a human? "Stripped of its melodramatic trappings," Kimberly Benston writes, "*The Island of Dr. Moreau* makes visible thresholds of being and understanding that shape the metaphysical crux of humanity's relation to its own and other creatures' animality."[42] Prendick's response to the confusions is clear. Once he has experienced the beast people, neither category can ever return to its simpler status. The animal staring defensively on all fours from the bushes suddenly displays its residual humanity (in a passage quoted early in this chapter, "seeing the creature in a perfectly animal attitude, with the light gleaming in its eyes, and its imperfectly human face distorted with terror, I realized again the fact of its humanity"). And back at home, the tarnishing to human dignity evinced by the island's experiments with hybridity becomes permanent. The beast people of the island hover over the ordinary people of London, a kind of photographic transparency pressed over the picture to alter the view. "Then I look about me at my fellow men," says Prendick, "And I go in fear. I see faces keen and bright, others dull or dangerous, others unsteady, insincere; none that have the calm authority of a reasonable soul. I feel as though the animal was surging up through them; that presently the degradation of the Islanders will be played over again on a larger scale" (*IDM*, 130). Prendick may filter the experience as his own anxiety ("I go in fear . . . will be played out on a larger scale"), but Wells wants us to feel it too, to worry that we cannot specify the line that demarcates our humanity, that the hairy ears or coarse snout or ravening jaws of the beast people are, after all, not so very unlike our own features. We are mammalian at the core—and with the exception of the early failed snake-man, Moreau sticks to mammals for his creations.

But what makes *The Island of Doctor Moreau* such an unforgettable reading experience is not solely the hybridity it literalizes or its narrative arc of sensational discovery, but the way we watch species return to their norms. "They were reverting," is how Prendick describes the situation on the island after Moreau's death and the disintegration of the Law—"and reverting very rapidly" (*IDM*, 123). As Moreau had rued, the time of species admixture has a half-life, and some of the most wonderful, haunting sequences in the novel transpire in the last few chapters, when the beast people slowly, almost imperceptibly, revert to their animal natures. They move back to the trees and the forest, lose their ability to walk upright, and their use of language gradually slides into grunts and howls—"Can you imagine language," Prendick asks the reader, "once clear-cut and exact, softening and guttering, losing shape and import, becoming mere lumps of sound again?" (*IDM*, 122). One thinks of Elaine Scarry's magisterial account of the creation of language out of pain, here inverted; as often with Wells, it reads like a film effect, now in reverse, the acquisition of language from "mere lumps of sound" reeling backward. Thus Prendick's loyal companion becomes, once again, an actual dog. In some ways, these returns have the feel of cosmic order, each back to its place. Yet not quite. For all that Moreau's experiments are unjustified and loathsome on ethical grounds, once here in the world, the beast people exert a certain calling. The challenge they have offered to the natural order, with all the ideological weight that carries, has been almost exhilarating, and the creatures made by human hubris, whether by Frankenstein or Moreau, have about them a true pathos, not least when they begin to fall out of the human pantheon. "The change was slow and inevitable," Prendick says of these forces, somewhat contradicting his comment of rapid reversion made on the same page, as he tries to hash out what these forms of change mean, in time among other dimensions (*IDM*, 123). The reversion can seem simultaneously fast and slow in part because we only notice change when confronted by some jolting symptom. Wells was often thinking about the many ways time refuses to be measured or experienced singly, and his reflections on regression can be especially Bergsonian in this novel. Thus Prendick "scarcely noticed the transition from the companion on my right hand to the lurching dog at my side," but then, "the dwindling shreds of their humanity still startled me every now and then, a momentary recrudescence of speech perhaps, an unexpected dexterity of the fore feet, a pitiful attempt to walk erect" (*IDM*, 123, 124).

These mixed qualities of recognition come, too, because Wells is playing throughout the novel with the temporality of evolution and indeed more generally with the principles underlying evolution as an idea and a force in the natural arena. As noted, Wells consistently probed the question of what kind of force, exactly, evolution is, what the nature of its presence might be in the lived, contemporary world, and whether its powers should be understood as a matter solely for biological learning or, like alchemy in the past, as a potency that might be captured by the skilled practitioner (Victor Frankenstein, we recall, began his own career with alchemy). We know what eugenics says: yes, through selective breeding and even exterminations, the gene pool can be manipulated, improved, ultimately perfected. Moreau's island is the site for a different kind of genetic experimentation, a laboratory where the premise that humans have evolved from earlier forms of animal life can be tested in the present as a matter of will. Moreau may not so much be playing god, then, as channeling Darwin, and the setting of this unnamed island in the vague Pacific vicinity of the Galapagos points to the analogy between these sites of species scrutiny. Of course, nothing in Moreau's work actually corresponds to the principles of evolution: his species cannot reproduce (their offspring almost always die), their adaptability to habitat is decreased rather than increased by virtue of his interventions, and, above all, the longue durée needed to account for evolution is missing here in this eleven-month stay, itself the last portion of a mere ten-year experiment. Moreau is not replicating evolution, then, but is conjuring its inner dynamics, the way species ultimately generate surprising variation, adding new traits to old, each animal a composite of what has come before in its line. There is, in evolution, always that fact of ghostly remainder, inherited traits and qualities from the long past, and these are grist for Wells's mill. What stares through us with its red eyes is not so much some foreign, earlier being but the substance that constitutes ourselves. "We have the same family secrets in our embryonic cupboards as the rest of our mammalian relatives," Wells writes in *The Science of Life*, and every one of us "began his existence as a single cell, passed from the stage of protozoan resemblance through the stage of the cell-colony ... recalled the furry, four-footed stage of his genealogy by his tail, all ready to be wagged, and his coat of flaxen down; and even, after birth, was unable to help recalling what he later regarded as a blot on his escutcheon—his simian past.... We are thus no exception to life's rule" (*SL*, 1:416–18). And at the same time, the experiment fails; there is no engineering of new beings, no common animality either to be made or to be burned out of us, no acceleration of evolution, which must always function according to its own slow logic. One can manipulate, plan, extend, transform, mutate in a certain circumscribed sphere, but life, in the end, cannot really be made. It has its own mysterious power.

## II. LIFE'S ENERGIES

So much of what defines any living being is to be found inside, invisible. Wells and modernism agree on this, and their separate efforts to plunge into the mysterious interior of the human mind or body constitute an exceptionally provocative, shared enterprise. One has only to think of Joyce's assignation of an organ to every chapter of *Ulysses* (1922) to recognize how tightly interlaced these interior spaces are for modernism, material with immaterial. Organs certainly have pride of place in *Ulysses*, from their initiating gesture in Calypso ("Mr. Leopold Bloom ate with relish the inner organs of beasts and fowls"), making sure to remind us, as we immerse ourselves in the endless fluctuations of the mind, that the brain, too, is one organ among many. If the distinction—or unity—of mind with brain has occupied thinkers since the eighteenth century, modernists seem less anxious than overjoyed to explore such interstices. In *Ulysses*, we move at ease into and out of mind and body, each of which can be, at times, utterly opaque or beautifully legible, their mutuality and overlaying a key aspect of the richness Joyce accords to human experience. Or we might consider the wonder and horror of the X-ray in *The Magic Mountain* (1924), when Hans Castorp sees his cousin's and then his own body through the fluoroscope. In the dark space of the sanitarium's laboratory, he "gazed tirelessly at Joachim's sepulchral form . . . he saw the process of corruption anticipated, saw the flesh in which he moved decomposed, expunged, dissolved into airy nothingness—and inside was the delicately turned skeleton of his right hand."[43] Wells, too, anatomizes himself; in his autobiography, he makes much of the idea that it is the "brain" (and an "ordinary" one at that) that constitutes his subject, no lofty mind or soul or self: "And now," he writes in concluding his short introductory chapter,

> having conveyed to you some idea of the quality and defects of the grey matter of that organized mass of phosphorized fat and connective tissue which is, so to speak, the hero of the piece . . . I will try to tell you how in this particular

receiving apparatus the picture of its universe was built up, what it did and failed to do with the body it controlled and what the thronging impressions and reactions that constituted its life amount to.

(*EA*, 20)

For Wells, as for Joyce and Mann, the interior body in its fully organic, biological aspect is an unstinting trove of imaginative possibility, the pulsating home of what, in this chapter, I am calling *life*.

In Wells's work, to consider the body's tiniest units and hidden locales is to see its function in the long evolutionary scheme. Invisible microbes save humanity in *The War of the Worlds* (and nearly doom the Utopians in *Men Like Gods*), bacteria themselves the products of millions of years of evolution. Here is how the narrator of *The War of the Worlds* articulates it:

> For so it had come about [the Martians' death]. . . . These germs of disease have taken toll of humanity since the beginning of things—taken toll of our prehuman ancestors since life began here. But by virtue of this natural selection of our kind we have developed resisting-power; to no germs do we succumb without a struggle, and to many . . . our living frames are altogether immune. But there are no bacteria on Mars, and directly these invaders arrived, directly they drank and fed, our microscopic allies began to work their overthrow. Already when I watched them they were irrevocably doomed, dying and rotting even as they went to and fro. It was inevitable. By the toll of a billion deaths man has bought his birthright of the earth, and it is his against all comers; it would still be his were the Martians ten times as mighty as they are. For neither do men live nor die in vain.[44]

Wells's narrator may partake of a conventional Providential tone here and there—"neither do men live nor die in vain," and, just before this, he had noted that the Martians were doomed by "the humblest things that God, in his wisdom, has put upon this earth" (*WW*, 168)—but there is no disguising the evolutionary timescale or logic or the essential satisfaction evinced in such pure, random, organic trajectories. Biology's incredibly slow action through gigantic time spans produces the visible world in all its brilliant diversity and expansiveness, and it also has quieter effects, equally consequential. Evolution has generated every aspect of our bodily worlds, the great majority of which are entirely invisible and unknown to us. Microscopes, laboratories, operating rooms: these return and recur as key settings in Wells's fiction, sites of interaction where the enterprise of science meets its subject, the body's core; yet, as Hans Castorp also found, what is there seems both the very essence of what science teaches and, at the same time, somehow entirely resistant to its technologies of knowledge.

There is a quality of swarm, multiplicity, and infinite diversity in these newly discovered inner biological worlds, and Wells pays homage to such fester, even as he brings his trademark systematizing fervor to bear. He was writing, we should recall, during a period of explosive technological and theoretical development when it came to the sciences. The massive improvement and dissemination of both microscopes and telescopes in the nineteenth century, potentially making visible to nonspecialists what the unaided eye cannot see—that which is too small, or too far—had powerful imaginative consequences. Seeing the surge of interest in astronomy, in particular, as a spur for modernists to reconsider our own planetary status and meaning, critics have honed in on how these technologies fed into a form of planetary thinking with a distinctive scientific focus. Holly Henry writes that "advances in astronomy . . . had a shaping effect on work by Woolf and other British writers . . . [as] large astronomical telescopes . . . brought into the purview of popular audiences spectacular vistas of spiral nebulae whirling millions of light-years from earth."[45] In a similar vein Cóilín Parsons has shown the very deep engagement of *Ulysses*, and modernism more broadly, with developments in astronomy: "The astronomical telescope is a key structure of feeling for global modernity. In the early twentieth century, with the proliferation of telescopes and observatories throughout the world, the telescope brought some of the most breathless scientific headlines, as the size of the universe became apparent, and the scale of the planet came into sharp focus."[46] Wells, ever on the inside track of scientific imagining, wrote several stories that prominently displayed such devices and the forms of knowledge they hearken ("The Stolen Bacillus" [1895], "A Slip Under the Microscope" [1893], "In the Avu Observatory" [1894], and the opening of *The War of the Worlds* [1898], which conjoins the telescopic and microscopic); at the same time, he pushed these developments into dizzying new directions, probing key questions about, for instance, the essence of matter. *The World Set Free* (1914), as we recall, was the first book to envision atomic explosion.

Inside many of Wells's laboratories, scientists are at work on the interior essences of the body, like the doctors in "Under the Knife" (1896), whose dissection of the narrator's body is shockingly viewed by him, or Dr. Moreau, who rips, cuts, sutures, and reconnects the tissues of his animal subjects. In fiction and nonfiction, Wells thought about what it means for a body to be made up of smaller and smaller units, working amid the increasingly counterintuitive discoveries about these concepts as physics unveiled them. As he argued in *First and Last Things* (1908), it seems instinctive that the atom is like any other object, one that could be cut through with a knife, only much smaller—except that it isn't: "If you think of the universe, thinking at the level of atoms, there is neither knife to cut, scale to weigh, nor eye to see. The universe *at that plane to which the mind of the molecular physicist descends* has none of the shapes or forms of our common life whatever."[47]

One key principle that helps shape and order these many forces is energy. Energy, in the decades around 1900, as now, could mean many things, ranging from a quality of personality or character ("energetic"), to a source of industrial generation ("power plant" or "power source"), to the earth's fuel, to a simple unit of heat. Today, energy can be measured as joule, watt, therm, calorie, and electronvolt, and such multiplicity took quantitative shape during Wells's writing life. Modernist critics are becoming increasingly interested in energy, tracing today's climate crisis to key patterns of industry, economics, geopolitics, and thought of the early twentieth century. How might the question of fuel open up new ways of reading modernism, linking it with earth sciences and with philosophical and literary traditions that have profound consequences for the relations between people and the planet; conversely, can modernism offer compelling paradigms for reengaging the present, with its energy and climate crises? Or, in a slightly different direction, Enda Duffy has made the dazzling claim that "Modernism . . . is the literature of the era between the patenting of adrenaline in 1901 and the theorizing of stress in 1936. High modernist writing . . . enacts a movement in modernity to . . . focus on human energy, valorized for its intensity, and considered as the concern of science."[48] Duffy is especially interested in the path of energy in and through the body, to see a somatic force burning through modernist language. These are powerful new directions in critical study, helping us recognize how fully the body's materiality intertwines with large questions of ecology, politics, and economics. Duffy writes,

> If modernist literature made human energy its central concern, it was merely one component of a vast new interest in energy, including but by no means limited to human energy, that grew up in the late nineteenth and early twentieth century. In part, this was the result of a plethora of new technologies invented and popularized in these years, from the internal combustion engine to electric light, with which human energy had to compete.[49]

For Wells, the mutability of energy's scales and meanings, its crossing over from biology to physics to chemistry and from the sphere of industry to the mechanism of the cell, made it particularly forceful as an idea, and he reflected on what it was and how it might be harnessed across his genres. We might recall the central plot of *The World Set Free* as well as the final lines of *The Outline of History*, both of which take the unleashing of atomic energy as a crucial threshold for humanity. Atomic energy was inescapable as a Wellsian idea even before it had scientific credence in the world, and he continually found his way to the potential, whether for good or apocalypse, of the isolated unit of energy. *The World Set Free* tells the story of humanity as a narrative specifically of energy, carried forward by those entrepreneurial dreamers throughout history Wells calls the "sun snarers." Beginning with prehistory, according to *The World Set Free*, humanity is marked by its ability to harness energy: "hidden from him by the thinnest of veils, were the untouched sources of Power, whose magnitude we scarcely do more than suspect even to-day." The story goes on through steam, industrialization, and electricity, up to the early twentieth century, when, as one of the novel's scientists puts it in a lecture:

> "And we know now that the atom, that once we thought hard and impenetrable, and indivisible and final and—lifeless—lifeless, is really a reservoir of immense energy. . . . This little bottle contains about a pint of uranium oxide; that is to say about fourteen ounces of the element uranium. It is worth about a pound. And in this bottle, ladies and gentlemen, in the atoms in this bottle there slumbers at least as much energy as we could get by burning a hundred and sixty tons of coal. If at a word in one instant I could release that energy here and now, it would blow us and everything about us to fragments; if I could turn it into the machinery that lights this city, it could keep Edinburgh brightly lit for a week. . . . We stand to-day towards this radio-activity exactly as our ancestor stood toward fire before he had learnt to make it. . . . This—this is the dawn of a new day in human living."[50]

*The World Set Free*, characteristically, envisions both apocalyptic and utopian consequences of the energy revolution (in succession, the world nearly wiped out by nuclear bombs and the world saved by disarmament and unification), suggesting, as ever, that the question is what humankind will do with the great forces that are out there, in the process of being understood, giving substance and potential to the material world.

Wells was eerily prophetic about the atomic age, but he is on stable modernist ground with the more general attraction to radiation and the theory of atoms as a significant, reorienting construction. The discovery of radioactivity is a story closely intertwined with both the timeframe and deep concerns of modernism, from the first use of X-rays by Wilhelm Röntgen in 1895 (the year of *The Time Machine*) and on from there in quick and overlapping succession: Henri Becquerel's discoveries around uranium in 1896; the work of Pierre and Marie Curie throughout the period; Frederick Soddy and Earnest Rutherford's work, together and singly, on radium from the turn of the century until World War I, to name a few key stages. Wells was tuned closely into these developments and had been reading Soddy when he wrote *The World Set Free* (he modeled his scientist lecturer on him). These new ideas, in their aggregate, were important in shifting the idea of matter and being from a general picture of stability to one of interior corrosiveness and ultimately mutability, in creating new ideas for how the world is constructed, and for instigating startling ways of thinking about the quality of energy and its effects.[51]

Interested in what drives the basic life processes, Wells took energy to be one such factor, and as such he understood it to stand at the absolute center of world affairs. Many of his short stories pivot on some aspect of the theme of energy, on the play of atoms in random form, or on the strange ways these systems might disrupt or enhance perception. As I have noted, "The New Accelerator" (1901) imagines a potion that propels the swallower to metabolize thousands of times faster than the normal cellular pace. As the narrator discovers, such speed, as one's body races inconceivably fast, heats the accelerated person up to dangerous levels. It also offers up a world that looks, by comparison, nearly frozen in its sluggishness. In "The Remarkable Case of Davidson's Eyes" (1895), it is the presence of several large electrometers that seems the most likely candidate for the vision at the center of the story. Or, in "The Plattner Story" (1896), a strange accident involving a chemical explosion opens up a world populating the seemingly empty space around us; it is full of beings that have crossed the life threshold, who watch, and reach, and come close to us, as if sharing our energy. These scenarios and others like them allow Wells's imagination to wander around the idea of a continuous field of energy, whose effects and meanings are up for speculation and manipulation, with arresting visual and cognitive effects. Over Wells's writing life, the scientific community moved away from a consensus that there is an invisible substance filling the universe, which was called ether. (Our modern conception is dark matter.) Ether comes and goes within Wells's thinking, but the idea of energy as a force in the physical, chemical universe, linking the world in unexpected ways, was suggestive of intriguing ordering principles in the world in and well beyond his writing. One might pause here, too, on Woolf's or Joyce's visions of interconnected urban spaces, those mists and threads and filaments that connect the residents of London or Dublin.

But it is not all metaphysical; in his world schemes, Wells gave energy pride of place in practical terms. It was, in one formulation, to be the new unit of global trade, an idea he first floated in *A Modern Utopia* (1905). "It is possible to use as a standard of monetary value no substance whatever, but instead, force, and . . . value might be measured in units of energy. . . . In my Utopia . . . this has been done; the production and distribution of common commodities have been expressed as a problem of the conversion of energy" (*MU*, 56, 58). Wells goes to some length, here and again thirty years later in *The Shape of Things to Come* (1933), to explain why such a scheme represents a major improvement either over unregulated currency exchange or the gold standard, why it would correlate more exactly to the bedrock notion of work and productivity without being hinged specifically to human labor, and how—in some specifics—it would be carried out. In these musings, he taps into (while also diverging from) a variety of schemes and ideas that ran through socialism and anarchism in the nineteenth and twentieth centuries, where the underlying precept was to imagine labor as the meaningful unit of value. In *The Shape of Things to Come*, moreover, Wells takes energy as the key force for assessing a question that always cultivated real anxiety in his utopias: once social and economic problems have been solved, how to prevent humanity from lapsing into the decadence he had so memorably envisioned at the outset of his career, with the Eloi.

*The Shape of Things to Come* calls the problem not decadence but "surplus energy," and it has this to say about how, in the utopian world of 2106, it will have been utilized:

> This release of human energy from primary needs is a process that seems likely to continue indefinitely. And all the forces that have made our world-wide social life and keep it going direct that released energy towards the achievement of fresh knowledge and the accumulation and rendering of fresh experience. There is a continual sublimation of interest. . . . This planet, which seemed so stern a mother to mankind, is discovered to be inexhaustible in its bounty. And the greatest discovery man has made has been the discovery of himself.
>
> (*STC*, 440–41)

Wells's invocation of humanity released into its creative potential recalls the end of *The Outline of History*, both works focusing their most ardent visions of a fulfilled humanity around this principle that, once liberated from the millennia-long ordeal of deprivation, warfare, competition, and struggle, human beings will not sink into lethargy but instead will discover new outlets for the wasted energy of our shared past. Such tracing and balancing of lines of energy is a running theme throughout *The Shape of Things to Come*, as it is in others of Wells's social-diagnostic and forecasting texts. He argues, for instance, that the dominance of the militarized state is bound up entirely with economic forces, themselves understood in terms of the problem of overproduction, the wastefulness of capitalism, the rendering redundant of human labor: "And so the ever-increasing productivity of the [human] race found its vent in its ancient traditions of warfare, which admitted the withdrawal of a large proportion of the male population from employment for a year or so and secreted that vast accumulation of forts, battleships, guns, submarines, explosives, barracks and the like which still amazes us" (*STC*, 55). In other words, in addition to a socialist analysis of the way capitalism inevitably fuels the armaments industry, imperial competition, and ultimately war, Wells welds this to a theory of productivity in which energy is the central principle—a principle, moreover, that courses through and shapes history. Here, too, one glimpses the planetary vision that makes Wells into such a strange mirror (radically similar and dissimilar) for us.

Energy may be read in Wells's works, then, in terms of the macro forces that contour our world, sources of productivity that, he ardently predicts, will be repossessed in our future toward the fruitful development of the species; it is also, like the invisible bacteria encoding evolution into our bodies, a source of internal vitality. This latter has especially strong ramifications in his works that center on sex and its manifestations. For Wells and his contemporaries, the energy, drive, and physical concentration that were conceptualized as thriving sources of mental and psychic life function as descriptors, too, for sexual vitality. Wells's idea of energy and internal life, so pivotal for his analysis of the human being in its worlds, also overlaps, interlaces, and in some ways expresses a more biographical fact, Wells's well-known sexual activity.

We know that Wells was widely recognized from the first decade of the twentieth century onward as a prolific lover, and he was also a campaigner for sexual liberation. In his *Experiment in Autobiography*, he claims himself to have been a person of normal libido, much as he presented himself as a "very ordinary brain." The plausibility of such claims is not at issue here; rather, we recognize how sexual energy as a major topic entered the Wellsian fray, both in his public reputation and activism, and in his many works. Wells was marked by sexual scandal for most of his adult life, thanks first to his divorce in 1893 and remarriage, and soon in relation to affairs with many women, including several extended domestic relationships; his two children born out of wedlock were also no secrets. This public sexual context was interwoven into the reception of his works and indeed into their conception (and vice versa, with Wells appearing in the texts of his lovers). Over the course of his life, mores changed enough that by the postwar period his affairs were less vital to his persona, even if his long affair with Maura Budberg, a possible Soviet spy, brings back some glamour to the occasion. In the years around the turn of the century, however, these were significant and explosive stories. Within the Fabian Society, at the height of these scandals, there was general knowledge of his sexual liaisons, including with Rosamond Bland (daughter of Hubert Bland, one of the senior members) and then the more notorious, full-blown relationship with Amber Reeves that began in 1908. Reeves's birth of their child in 1909 was partially diverted in the public by her marriage to Rivers Blanco White, arranged to cover for the child, though none of this was fully suppressed—nor, in some respects, did Wells or Reeves want it so—and certainly not within the Fabian circles where Wells's writings had a natural circulation. The personal sexual scandal is of a piece with Wells's overt themes about marriage, sexual emancipation, and the battle against Victorian respectability in so many writings of these years (*A Modern Utopia* [1905], *In the Days of the Comet* [1906], *Ann Veronica* [1909], *The New Machiavelli* [1911], *Tono-Bungay* [1909], *Marriage* [1912], *The Passionate Friends* [1913], *The Wife of Sir Isaac Harman* [1914], and others). Wells's attitude toward sex and gender, expressed in his writings as much as in his life, was one of the dominant features in his appeal to younger writers. Such sexual self-revelation is one aspect of his more general autobiographical methodology, but also, in works that focus on the life principle, there is a specific bond uniting these different challenges to normative ideology around sex, birth, the family, and the body. Wells's biological formulations touched close to the collective nerve, especially in those texts that place the reproductive engine of life at the forefront.

Nevertheless, though it is never possible entirely to disentangle Wells's own sexual self-interest from his political positions, his contemporaries generally saw his advocacy for such radical causes as birth control and the state subsidization of motherhood (for which he began to argue as early as 1900) as more than mere cover for his personal peccadilloes. Wells was in the forefront in pushing for women's reproductive and sexual autonomy and for reconceiving the status and meaning of motherhood, advocating over many years for monetary remuneration for mothers and for changes in the structure of the family. These arguments could take what today seem like a conservative turn, orienting their radical suggestions about motherhood around the ideal of bettering the national stock. Thus in "The Endowment of Motherhood" (1914), Wells framed the principle in terms of the improvement of the "race" (an unusual usage of "race" for him, with a nationalist connotation), arguing—or rather taking it as a given—that the state had a major interest in supporting "good-class" parentage and preventing inferior births. Wells toggles in these texts (*A Modern Utopia, Mankind in the*

*Making*, and *Anticipations* all take up these questions) between pressing for progressive policies that empower women and reinstating noxious views about inheritance that characterize the literature of eugenics. Still, the liberation of middle-class women from their husbands was a constant and very public theme in his writing and advocacy and one that puts him into conversation, once again, with Woolf.[52]

All of his utopias feature major revisions in the family, and nowhere is his anti-Victorianism more overt than in his gleeful repudiation of the saintly mother and Holy Trinity as bedrock forces of social stability. "In Utopia," he asserts, having detailed the precise differentiations and policies around marriage and parenting that the government will institute, "love-making is no concern of the State's beyond the province that the protection of children covers" (*MU*, 141). Such positions help account for his long friendship with Margaret Sanger, the radical American women's reproductive rights campaigner (they also had a sexual affair). He was a member of the Neo-Malthusian League, a conservative organization whose sponsorship of birth control made it a plausible site to help launch what Wells believed should be a form of sexual revolution, without the banner. The hysteria that tended to greet his texts in which sexual freedom is envisioned reminds us that such positions were far outside the norm, preceding Bloomsbury's version by two decades. In the Fabian years, Wells saw himself as the leader of the group's progressive wing when it came to the women's program and attributed his ostracization from the group to his being too forward thinking on gender issues. In his resignation letter from the group in 1908, he wrote:

> My chief objection to the Basis is its disregard of the claim of every child upon the State which is primary and fundamental to my conception of Socialism. A scheme which proposes to leave mother and child economically dependent upon the father is to me not Socialism at all but a miserable perversion of Socialism. It forbids the practical freedom of women and leaves the essential evils of the Individualist system untouched.[53]

Around all of these issues of female sexual emancipation, feminism, and the question of a residual masculinist perspective, Wells and modernism intersect and overlap, though it bears repeating that Wells's positions had much greater exposure at the time than did followers like D. H. Lawrence. And of course, the attitudes differ. What Lawrence figures in his writings as a kind of inner sexual divinity—which throbs in us and must be nourished as the germ of individual fulfillment and a counter to the dulling, deadening nature of industrial modernity—Wells presents in less exalted terms as the reality of sexual energy, the organizing fact of life that demands recognition not so much for personal enrichment as for the ongoing nourishment of the species.

*Ann Veronica* (1909) is Wells's most notorious work to have taken up inner sexual life as an urgent demand at both the private and public levels, a novel in the realist tradition that stamped the generic signature of bildungsroman onto a story of biological imperative. Though dropped by Macmillan for fear of scandal, it was published by Fisher Unwin and immediately provoked the uproar Macmillan had anticipated. Conservative social voices rose in outrage, and there were calls for the book to be censored. Several sample comments in this vein: "We have headed this article 'A Poisonous Book,' and that is the epithet which we desire deliberately to apply to it. It is a book capable of poisoning the minds of those who read it" (John St. Loe Strachey, in the *Spectator*); "I wonder if [Wells] has reflected upon the influence exercised by his books upon enormous circles of readers" (R. A. Scott-James, in the *Daily News*); "Decidedly, then, *Ann Veronica* will be read and talked about this winter by the British daughter. All I can say is that I hope the British daughter will keep her head. That Mr. Wells's story may do considerable mischief is too clear" (John O'London, in *T. P.'s Weekly*).[54] D. H. Lawrence, never timid about public opinion, nevertheless worried in 1911 whether his own novel *The Trespasser* (1912) is "*so erotic*" that it might "be talked about in an *Anne* [*sic*] *Veronica* fashion."[55] Such responses were far from devastating for Wells, though there were social consequences following his often very transparently personal self-representations in this and other novels of the period, such as *The New Machiavelli* and *Tono-Bungay*, where his own affairs were represented with little effort at cover. With all of this swirling around, the novel blazed into the social conversation, becoming one of the most prominent texts to press on matters of women's sexual and personal freedom at this moment, when there was ferment on both sides of the Atlantic to advance not only suffrage but reproductive rights, sexual autonomy, compensation for motherhood, employment and educational reform for women, and the possibility that women might create their own narratives around all of these crucial issues. In literary history, we know the long pedigree of writings that press these questions, and Wells's novel sits among immediate predecessors and followers as diverse as George Eliot, George Gissing, Grant Allen, Thomas Hardy, Lawrence, Woolf, and Radclyffe Hall. While literary history recognizes works by these and other writers to have played a crucial role not only in fiction but in cultural history and gender politics, lost to our critical ears has been this novel's resonance in and through the period.[56]

Ann Veronica's narrative is given partly in the language of social comedy, partly of cultural exhortation, partly of the domestic novel. It is, in its essential outlines, a story in the tradition of nineteenth-century domestic fiction, where the young female protagonist struggles against her family/father and the social status quo to forge a meaningful, autonomous identity. Such self-direction manifests first in the decision to live independently in London and eventually in her (radical) choice of husband. The novel begins in richly satiric mode, with Ann Veronica taking the battle for women's rights to the question of whether she will be allowed to attend a fancy-dress ball and involving a consummate standoff between her and her father in the confines of the suburban home, and featuring the struggle over a doorknob. Interestingly, combat over a locked door comes back in a later and more serious sequence, when Ann Veronica wards off the sexual assault of one of her suitors. In this repeated focus, Wells highlights the essential fact of female domestic and sexual imprisonment—inside the locked room—so central to feminists of the period.

As Ann Veronica moves through the various challenges that follow her flight from home, many of which revolve around the bare facts of the limited options for middle-class women to earn a living, the novel moves in and out of social comedy. It comprises, for instance, several harrowing sequences that give the novel a distinctly serious tone (Ann Veronica being stalked in London by an unknown man, on her first day alone in the city; Ann Veronica in prison); an equal number of humorous send-ups of various radical gatherings, which allow Wells to make tremendous fun of his friends and colleagues (always a favorite pastime for him); and the sober consideration of how a young woman can fend off sexual predation. These are compelling plots, which showcase the novel-as-social commentary, yet this novel also wants to keep its protagonist in the forefront. Ann Veronica thus tilts the balance from, say, *The War in the Air* (1908), its near contemporary, which diminishes its protagonist at every turn in favor of the span of world affairs. As an early review noted of her as character: "The heroine from whom the book takes its name begins as an impetuous capricious girl, with a sense of humour, and ideals which she does not understand. She becomes a woman, experienced, self-reliant, reflective, capable of discipline, yet with a capacity of concentrated passion which she is willing to regard as the true channel of her destiny."[57] Though Ann Veronica may get sidelined by one or another social cause, and though her various battles with voracious men remind her (and us) of the stark forces—power and sexual domination—exerted against the will of a young, vulnerable woman, her story remains fully her own, a narrative of self-realization that turns, ultimately, on sexual fulfillment.

And so, as early as chapter 2, the basic tenet of this story is isolated: "her manner was one of quiet reserve, and behind this mask she was wildly discontented and eager for freedom and life. She wanted to live" (*AV*, 7). Early reviewers pounced on that line, "she wanted to live," which so disconcertingly inaugurated a novel that might, so they feared, influence young women to take action to realize their own similar urges. And for us, as well, "life . . . to live" captures one of Wells's essential objects, that driving, inexorable fact of the biological being, composed of so much living tissue and cell, pulsing with inner energy, expressing its interiority in this novel in the form of sexual self-empowerment. Ann Veronica is virtually defined by the urgency of desire, initially unspecified, eventually focused on her lover Capes, the external manifestation of the sexual energy that, so this novel wants to say, proves the essence of humanity and especially youth. Even Ann Veronica's pinched and desiccated aunt flashes a little life, at least in Ann Veronica's imagination, insofar as she can be the heir to a shared primitive past full of passionate possibility: "After all, she found herself reflecting, behind her aunt's complacent visage there was a past as lurid as anyone's—not, of course, her aunt's own personal past . . . but an ancestral past with all sorts of scandalous things in it: fire and slaughterings, exogamy, marriage by capture, corroborees, cannibalism! Ancestresses with perhaps dim anticipatory likenesses to her aunt" (*AV*, 38). No doubt we are listening in here to Ann Veronica's fantasy life rather than to any truths about what lurks in her aunt's DNA, but as this sensational conjuring of early human experience suggests, the novel also plays with the suggestion that all of the overwhelming social forces leveled against women might in fact be contrary to "nature," whipping up an old and unresolved Victorian debate about what constitutes womanhood in the first place. Whether her aunt might legitimately be seen as an ally (and she does support her wayward niece in London), the larger point is to see the ubiquity and ferocity of social force in keeping women from actualizing, or even knowing, their libidinal potential. And so the classic novelistic opposition between fulfillment and suppression takes shape as the sexual stifling of women by their fathers, sometimes the literal father, always also the figurative.

The primary metaphor for all of this in the novel, filtered through Ann Veronica's interior monologue, is of the "wrapped" life, a usage that begins early in the novel:

> All the world about her seemed to be—how can one put it?—in wrappers, like a house when people leave it in the summer. The blinds were all drawn, the sunlight kept out, one could not tell what colours these grey swathings hid. She wanted to know. And there was no intimation whatever that the blinds would ever go up or the windows or doors be opened, or the chandeliers, that seemed to promise such a blaze of fire, unveiled and furnished and lit. Dim souls flitted about her, not only speaking but it would seem even thinking in undertones . . .

> (*AV*, 7–8, ellipses in the original)

From here, Ann Veronica will have recourse to the "wrappered life" or "the most wrapped things in all [her] wrappered world" as a kind of private shorthand, shared with the reader as per novelistic convention and later with Capes, who declares near the end of the novel, " 'The wrappered life, as you call it—we've burned the confounded rags! Danced out of it! We're stark!' " (*AV*, 276). We might note here that Wells's method of using and also explaining or emphasizing his figurative language (as discussed in "Voice") is effective as usual, with reviewer after reviewer borrowing the term "wrappered" to parley this shorthand. The wrappering conceit has its particularities, of course, including its highlighting the novel's emphasis on textuality, with its plethora of letters, telegrams, poetry, even transposed real-estate signs. Ann Veronica's architectural metaphors also signal her middle-class background, and like the ferocity of struggles over keys and doorknobs, they reinforce the actual, material spaces in which women live alongside the less tangible layout of their psychic situations. Victoria Rosner has shown how fully modernism implicated the physical textures of women's domestic living into their writings (and back again); here as well, what is so striking is the way imagination and affect are fully shaped in and around the kinds of spaces that define (and limit) Ann Veronica's material experience up to now.[58] The wrappering is suggestive of other issues as well, including its sexual insinuations, as Capes's delighted declaration that "We're stark" makes clear. As Wells's contemporaries saw, Ann Veronica, with her yearning to be unwrapped, held the potential to become an icon—a dangerous one—and the unabashed sexual joy that gushes through the novel in its penultimate sequences, when the lovers are fully engrossed in each other, a physical euphoria matched by the very beautiful Alpine locale where they take their scandalous vacation, can hardly be excused by their later marriage.

For all the jouissance it purveys and despite the appeal of Ann Veronica herself, not to mention the novel's brilliant exposure of patriarchal rapacity and hypocrisy, *Ann Veronica* nevertheless disappoints a modern feminist readership, as it also disappointed some of its initial women readers. This is partly because Wells's satire is so devastatingly successful when it comes to the suffragists, but mostly because the nature of Ann Veronica's adventure only partly conforms to our understanding of women's emancipation or the range of their potentialities. The novel's first two thirds lean strongly feminist—its protagonist seeks to set her own terms and carve her own future amid a welter of competing visions of women's roles (as demanded by the conservative father and family, reimagined by an array of suffragist peers, and also part of the dialogue among the socialists gathered in London, who have their own views of the struggle), and she handily repels suitors who range from the adoring, Romantic oaf to the rapacious married predator. Ann Veronica is witty, at times ironic, at others serious, and most notably courageous. That she is also physically lovely makes her especially Hollywood-ready. Thus there is tremendous deflation when Wells falls back into a disappointing vision of sexual submissiveness, as Ann Veronica comes to cringe and crave in front of her lover, her tremendous fight for independence seeming to have meant, in the end, the right to choose her own lord, her professional career as a biologist forgotten:

> "I say," she reflected, "you *are* rather the master, you know." [his title in the biology lab.]
>
> The idea struck him as novel. "Of course, I'm manager for this expedition," he said, after an interval of self-examination.
>
> She slid her cheek down the tweed sleeve of his coat. "Nice sleeve," she said, and came to his hand and kissed it.
>
> "I say," he cried. "Look here! Aren't you going a little too far? This—this is degradation—making a fuss with sleeves. You mustn't do things like that."
>
> "Why not?"
>
> "Free woman—and equal."
>
> "I do it—of my own free will," said Ann Veronica, kissing his hand again. "It's nothing to what I *will* do."
>
> (*AV*, 274–75)

Wells's particular fantasy, of an equal partner who also chooses to dedicate herself to him, makes regular appearances throughout his writings, and it jars particularly badly here. Ann Veronica surely does not fit the mold! That her radicalism comes down, finally, to the choice of husband raises the question: how far have we actually come from the familiar contours of the domestic novel? Charlotte Perkins Gilman, whose own novel on these subjects has retained its influence in contemporary literary culture, was disappointed, noting in 1910 that Ann Veronica "wanted to be human, and tried to be. Her masculine interpreter, seeing no possible interests in the woman's life except those of sex, dismisses all that passionate outgoing as comparable to the mating impulse of insects."[59]

As Gilman indicates, a key factor needs to be isolated in the novel: its essential biological vision. Biology is the novel's world, its context, its motivating force. "She wanted to live," coming from this author, tips us off immediately that this bildungsroman will be concerned with inner life in its richly animate aspects, and the novel is steeped in biological thought. Ann Veronica is studying biology at London's Imperial College (similar to the Normal School of Science), and many of the novel's scenes take place in the laboratory, where Capes is demonstrator, the assistant to the novel's Huxley figure, here called Russell.[60] "The biological laboratory had a character that was all its own," and as such it anchors the novel, providing a foil for so many other fraught spaces (home as prison, actual prison, the private dining parlor where one of Ann Veronica's suitors attempts to assault her sexually) (*AV*, 130). And it is not only the lab. As Wells writes,

> But the influence of the science radiated far beyond its own special field—beyond those beautiful but highly technical problems with which we do not propose for a moment to trouble the naturally terrified reader. Biology is an extraordinarily *digestive* science. It throws out a number of broad experimental generalizations, and then sets out to bring into harmony or relation with these an infinitely multifarious collection of phenomena ... not only did these tentacular generalizations gather all the facts of natural history and comparative anatomy together, but they seemed always stretching out further and further into a world of interests that lay altogether outside their legitimate bounds....
> It was the same Bios whose nature and drift and ways and methods and aspects engaged them all. And she, in her own person too, was this eternal Bios, beginning again its recurrent journey to selection and multiplication and failure or survival.
>
> (*AV*, 134–35)

Among other things, these lines embody the familiar Wellsian style of teaching and performing their idea, showing us how to read this novel, with biology as its keystone, radiating out into the many areas named here, finally resting with Ann Veronica herself. Biology shapes the novel, as it shapes the thinking of its students, and nearly everyone in the novel has caught the idiom. Miss Miniver, Wells's send-up of a suffragist, makes many sorts of argument in favor of her cause, including vaguely biological statements such as, "We are the species. ... Men are only incidents. ... In all the species of animals the females are more important than the males; the males have to please them" (*AV*, 34). Sequences take place at the zoo, where Ann Veronica and Capes go to study "a point of morphological interest about the toucan's bill" and make observations about the animals on display ("'so much more human than human beings'" is their consensus about the chimpanzees) (*AV*, 221). The talk within the lab among the group of students and Capes often takes a biological turn, in particular on the subject of gender, on which the group is predictably split (as, for instance, on the question of the "case for the primitive matriarchate and the predominant

importance of the female throughout the animal kingdom" [*AV*, 141]). Even
Mr. Stanley, Ann Veronica's stodgy, stockbroker father and the text's early nemesis, has a place in the scientific mélange, since his primary hobby is "microscopic
petrography," which involves the careful inspection and polishing of geological
specimens. It is not too difficult to see the contrast between the geological realm,
steeped in inanimate substances, whose closest ties to life are the long-dead fos-
sil remains occasionally preserved in its layers, and the science of living forms,
biology. Ann Veronica and her father spar as youth against age, female against
male, organicism against rock, and, also importantly, practicing science against
the hobbyist. By the end of the novel neither Ann Veronica nor Capes is practicing any science, yet there remains something pure and laudable about the laboratory that Wells reveres, even as, in other works (*Moreau*), it is also the site of the
most egregious forms of human hubris.

What the laboratory and the study of biological science more generally signify in this novel is not so much the pursuit of truth as the principle that the raw
facts of biological existence can here be treated without social constraint. It is a
place where some kinds of things are isolated and studied and the rest sidelined.
It facilitates equal relations between men and women (at least potentially so)
and epitomizes a happy balance between work and social value. Biology, then, in
its various guises, is context, setting, and subject of the novel. When Ann Veronica confronts her father at the beginning of the novel, kicking off her rebellion,
she establishes the motif in distinctly Wellsian terms, declaring, "I want to be a
human being" (*AV*, 27).

What it means to desire one's own active humanness should be predictable
from all we have seen in this chapter and in the previous one, "Time": that Ann
Veronica's inner worlds are shot through with forces from the long past; that she
is working out, in her own narrative, consequences of biological imperative; that
sex and gender do not exactly overlap, formed diametrically out of the evolutionary history and the social present; and that literary expectations will never hold
up under these powerful directives, producing a text whose innovation comes
precisely in its construction of an imperfect, always troubling, female *life* story.
A key spot amid this flurry of biological contexts is the passage that charts Ann
Veronica at the British Museum. Here is a location saturated with physical
reminders of the longue durée and of the stages of history, read as stage:

> She got a bun and some cocoa in the refreshment room, and then wandered
> through the galleries upstairs, crowded with Polynesian idols and Polynesian
> dancing garments, and all the simple immodest accessories to life in Polynesia,
> to a seat among the mummies. She was trying to bring her problems to a head,

and her mind insisted upon being even more discursive and atmospheric than usual. It generalized everything she put to it.

"Why should women be dependent on men" she asked; and the question was at once converted into a system of variations upon the theme of "Why are things as they are?"—"why are human beings viviparous?"—"Why are people hungry thrice a day?"

"Why does one faint at danger?"

She stood for a time looking at the dry limbs and still human face of that desiccated unwrapped mummy from the very beginnings of social life.

(*AV*, 185–86)

In some sense, Ann Veronica channels her culture well, finding ideal space for reflection amid the signs of otherness collected in these exotic sections of the British Museum, a key metropolitan site of imperial largesse. In other ways, however, her meditations amid the idols and mummies are eccentric, Wellsian, carrying on the novel's restless inquiry into the clash between inherent bodily substance, with its potent, invisible connections to the past, and the sexual mores of the present. "Why are human beings viviparous?" is a perfectly formed question for this novel. As we know, Wells made it a habit to pepper his texts with specialized terms, and in *Ann Veronica* as in many other works, these emanate from the biological sciences. Ann Veronica, a science student, is taught to bundle together questions that her culture ordinarily cordons off into separate zones: about different aspects of physical adaptation, say (those involving sex and reproduction next to matters of digestion and fright), or about the relation between biology and culture (can the fainting reflex, once fully biologized, be segregated from its overweighted social meanings?). Not only does science give us a framework for asking new and powerful questions, but it supplies material for developing answers. Here in the museum, these mostly swirl around sexuality, desire, power, and freedom. Ann Veronica is drawn to test out her culture's essentialism in a locale meant, on the contrary, to foreground racial and temporal difference. What, she needs to know, can the far past, filtered through biology, teach us about our own potential for satisfaction in the present?

The mummy becomes a vehicle for Ann Veronica's own daydreams, but there is more to it than that, as we can now see more fully; it joins a rich aggregation of suggestion within the novel that it is our collective pasts, understood through the prism of evolution, premised on the invisible ferment within the body, and figured as a kind of energy, that determine physical fulfillment and, even more broadly, give shape to *life*. Ann Veronica circles back repeatedly to evocations not just of ancient cultures but of prehistory, as in the passage in which she muses about her aunt's potential for a spark of connection with her cavewoman ancestresses and their "fire and slaughterings, exogamy, marriage by capture, corroborees, cannibalism!" (*AV*, 38). Prehistory and early cultures provide Ann Veronica and the novel a space of fantasy where sexual desire can be imagined as unfettered. As we know, Wells's accounts of prehistory typically figure the far past not as a static space open to modern fantasy but as constituted by the same continual flux as the present. In *Ann Veronica*, however, the protagonist has a more conventional—or, we should say, "modernist"—approach; it is not knowable, nor would one wish, in fact, to know it. For Ann Veronica herself the long past is doing psychological work, giving a language for sexual freedom that stands against the ferocity of sexual control in the contemporary world. Thus in a late conversation with her most dangerous suitor, who proclaims the two of them modern, Ann Veronica, about to elope with her married lover to Switzerland, has this response: "Her heart leapt within her as she caught that phrase. That knot also would be cut. Modern, indeed! She was going to be as primordial as chipped flint" (*AV*, 258). It is a serious proposition, since the novel is torn between taking its cues for women's emancipation from modern causes and claims, such as those espoused by Miss Miniver and the other suffragists, or perhaps from the values associated with work in the science lab, where we as contemporary readers no doubt wish Ann Veronica to remain, and a wholly different premise, that it is culture that has always held women down. The earlier one travels back before cultural norms are established, the more likely to find a social order answering to biology in the least encumbered way. Yet, all that said, the novel seems to recognize that there is no simple liberatory prospect to be found in the distant past. The mummy, after all, epitomizes the "wrappered" condition in the most literal way, and Ann Veronica recognizes, when she gazes at it, that this ancient woman would have lived under harsh patriarchal constraints. The novel knows, really, that all of human history has been a story of women's subjection.

And biology is no panacea. The story of life that Wells tells almost never follows easy directives—as we have seen so emphatically in works like *The Island of Doctor Moreau* or *The First Men in the Moon*—and in *Ann Veronica* the hard facts of biology may offer a rationale for sexual fulfillment, but they also draw up the reins on her euphoric sense of sufficiency just as they do on the ease of the domestic novel's solution of marriage. The turn comes in the epilogue, four years later, when Ann Veronica and Capes have become an established and accepted married couple. What happens is simple: she becomes pregnant. Viviparous as she is, this should come as no surprise, but the deep biological realities encompassed in pregnancy break the bounds of expectations. Ann Veronica's whole persona, in this last scene, is of a woman whose body has now taken back control over her wider ego. She sinks on the floor "into a crouching attitude," moaning and weeping as she recognizes that "Oh, I've loved love, dear! I've loved love and you, and the glory of you; and the great time is over," and when Capes sympathizes, "Blood of my heart . . . I know. I understand," his figure is well chosen (*AV*, 291–92). In her crouching pose and his evocation of blood, the two intuit an ancient, bodily dimension to their impending retrenchments. Recognizing the end of her adventure in the physical condition of pregnancy, Ann Veronica sees the forces of sociality closing back in: "And the great time is over, and I have to go carefully and bear children, and—take care of my hair—and when I am done with that I shall be an old woman" (*AV*, 291). Age, the body, respectability, and back to the body, and age—the vicious cycle Ann Veronica intuits through her pregnancy, recognized in the social and economic success she and her husband have substituted for their former pariah status, cannot be halted. In thwarting his protagonist at what might have been a moment of triumph, Wells is bucking genre, having followed along the path of the domestic novel (scandalous version though it is) only to reject its usages in the final pages. Marriages are never really happy in his cosmos, in part because Wells does not believe in marriage in the traditional sense (as expressed in his utopias, which typically refigure marriage and the nuclear family quite dramatically) and also because the elevation of the couple over all other units flies in the face of his ethos of species writing. "It is not the individual that reproduces himself," he writes in *First and Last Things* (1908), published one year before *Ann Veronica*. "It is the species that reproduces through the individual and often in spite of his characteristics. The [human] race flows through us, the race is the drama and we are the incidents" (*FLT*, 102). But *Ann Veronica* has been a novel headed toward marriage and has figured women's sexual self-determination finally in terms of marital choice, so that the defeat of *life* by a combination of biology and social normativity—their precise meeting point being, in fact, pregnancy and reproduction—is especially stark. Wells, we know, is no bio-optimist. What has driven life onward for all these millennia is a subject for study, reflection, and representation, but it is not something to champion nor to assume one's ally. On the contrary, the critical fact about evolution and its signal operation, adaptation, is its utter indifference. As Doctor Barack insists in *The Undying Fire*, it acts through us, not for us. This is why Ann Veronica's bildungsroman cannot end with fulfillment: as genre, the novel is an individualist form (most of all in its *bildung* mode), but biology, Wells wants to insist, is a force pressing through and quickly beyond the individual. The human body, it turns out, is hitched to the same temporal wagon as experience more generally, in its Wellsian guise. Biology, even at the level of the human, is a force of forward momentum, moving inexorably always into futurity. It is, as Wells displayed in context after context, always in process, forging, pressing ahead, always—in a word—*generating.*

## III. WASTE

Where there is generation, there is waste. What could be more essential? From the individual cell to the power plant, to produce means to generate and hence leave something behind, even if only as mere heat. Here is Wells in *The Science of Life*, in the opening segment on the most basic facts and needs of the human body: "Three or four times a day he ['Mr. Everyman'] loads his stomach to keep his wheels going round—and several times, we must note, he has to deposit the residue of their working in appropriate places" (*SL*, 1:26). For someone whose willingness to broach subjects anathematic to normative culture rivaled Joyce's, that slight hesitation ("we must note") might seem a little surprising, and the comparison with *Ulysses* reminds us of that novel's thorough immersion in the aesthetics of defecation, as Leopold Bloom in his opening chapter memorably heads to the outhouse for a shit and a perusal of the paper. To know Bloom is to follow the body's movements—its humanness. Such humanness is the subject of the novel, in many senses, as in the Hades chapter, where the body's decay and dissolution stand as a challenge to the culture's many sanguinary rituals for demarcating the passage out of life. The body in Hades refuses to keep to its demarcated zones, despite the elaborate work by church and community to control its meanings. Rather, as Bloom muses, "I daresay the soil would be quite fat with corpsemanure, bones, flesh, nails. Charnelhouses. Dreadful. Turning green and pink decomposing. Rot quick in damp earth. The lean old ones tougher. Then a kind of tallowy kind of a cheesy. Then begin to get black, black treacle oozing out of them."[61] Wells may be less committed than Joyce to making human waste per se a central part of his textual worlds, but he was no less motivated—urgently—to think out the dialectic between what is made and what is left behind or, rather, how the very fact of making entails residue. Waste is produced by making something else, but for Wells the real danger is that it might also be the ultimate product, all that remains of work, strife, war, history, life. At the other end of generation stands the prospect of sterility, of failure.

Waste was Wells's nemesis, the sinister *doppelgänger* of his own enormous productivity. There is no more perfect epitome of his inner oppositionality—alternate and contradictory viewpoints cohabitating throughout his thought—than this constant, nagging prospect of waste. Perhaps, after all the books and articles and speeches and radio broadcasts, after mounting decades of forging a voice to be heard throughout the world, after the fame and influence, it will all have amounted to so much paper, so much noise. As George Ponderevo writes of his novel, his nation, and his life:

> It is, I see now that I have it all before me, a story of activity and urgency and sterility. I have called it *Tono-Bungay*, but I had far better have called it *Waste*. I have told of childless Marion, of my childless aunt, of Beatrice wasted and wasteful and futile. What hope is there for a people whose women become fruitless? I think of all the energy I have given to vain things. . . . It is all one spectacle of forces running to waste, of people who use and do not replace, the story of a country hectic with a wasting aimless fever of trade and money-making and pleasure-seeking.[62]

The word "waste" (and cognates) populates this short sequence five times, covering a gamut of forms, from the family line stubbed out, to the personal story rendered pointless, to the activity of a nation misguided and meaningless. These are the subjects of *Tono-Bungay* as novel, and they also represent an overarching, hostile force running throughout Wells's work. As another of his alter-egos, Mr. Britling, agonizes, "Beneath that hollow, enviable show there ached waste. Waste, waste, waste—his heart, his imagination, his wife, his son, his country . . ."[63] Even at moments of triumph, the prospect of futility was always staring at Wells, like the many ghostly figures in his short stories who reside just on the other side of the perceivable world, gazing and reaching across the almost unbreachable divide, or like the Eloi and Morlocks, who inaugurated his career by mocking our aspirations for humanity, or indeed like so many species dead-ends in his science journalism, branching out into nothingness and extinction. At the scale of the species, extinction is the ultimate evolutionary expression of waste, the nihilistic endpoint.

The prospect of waste, then, is both personal and global. It expresses together three large categories: the unavoidable reality of how life operates (expending and excreting); the question of humanity's progress and its future, which may, after all, be a giant, many-millennia-old exercise in pointlessness; and the volatile story of the reach or value of any one life. Here is Wilfred Owen's "Futility," kindred in spirit:

> Move him into the sun—
> Gently its touch awoke him once,
> At home, whispering of fields half-sown.

Always it woke him, even in France,
Until this morning and this snow.
If anything might rouse him now
The kind old sun will know.

Think how it wakes the seeds—
Woke once the clays of a cold star.
Are limbs, so dear achieved, are sides
Full-nerved, still warm, too hard to stir?
Was it for this the clay grew tall?
O what made fatuous sunbeams toil
To break earth's sleep at all?[64]

It is a poem of the war, of course—and the "waste of war" is as old a problem as war itself (Owen calls it "the pity of war"). Read in the context of Wells's reflections on life, the poem's organicism leaps to the fore, with its powerful reflections on growth as a process, expressed in the poem at divergent scales and in different kinds of bodies. That word "clay" triggers a powerful force of making and, given the war frame, unmaking. There is, indeed, no simple processing in the organic vision of the poem: all is toil, work; fields will not complete their own sowing. And the making of mankind, to use Wells's phrase, is no mere matter of easy godly touch. The Adamic creation is thoroughly mixed with its outcome, work. Owen's exquisite tableau figures so exactly the Wellsian insight, to recognize in the varied scales of existence a common set of life processes, and to ask, of each and all, "Was it for this?"

As with Owen's poem, the issue of waste is simultaneously expressed as a personal dilemma (in the poem as a matter of one life come and gone, and for what?) and as vastly exceeding the individual, figured instead as world-scale problem, the other side of *life*. Life does not oppose death, for Wells; it opposes meaningless death. The events of the historical past threaten constantly to tell a larger story of failure and the nullified value of existence, the entire collapse of human promise. Such is the urgency of a passage like this one from *The Salvaging of Civilization*, a 1921 work typical of Wells's 1920s attempts to squeeze from the war's receding horrors the substance of a better future, when war will—finally, still, after all—have ended itself (the subtitle of this book being *The Probable Future of Mankind*):

The urgent need for a great creative effort has become apparent in the affairs of mankind. It is manifest that unless some unity of purpose can be achieved in the world, unless the ever more violent and disastrous incidence of war can be averted, unless some common control can be imposed on the headlong waste of man's limited inheritance of coal, oil, and moral energy that is now going on, the history of humanity must presently culminate in some sort of disaster, repeating and exaggerating the disaster of the great war, producing chaotic social conditions, and going on thereafter in a degenerative process toward extinction.[65]

Waste within waste: the profligate usage of resources feeds into and expresses a larger and longer profligacy, that of our human and communal capacities. For Wells, the war and waste dynamic is an utterly motivating problem, and he asks again and again how to extract from the destructive vortex of war a force for ultimate betterment. That his phrase "the war that will end war" has come to stand as an extreme irony is actually entirely appropriate to the urgent concerns that engender its logic. In so many senses, the full Wellsian canon can be seen to bend and strain around war and waste as they entwine their way through history, repeatedly asking how the world might untether them. Of the First World War, he wrote, in agonized terms, "Intellectual energy, industrial energy, are used up without stint to make this horror [of poison gas] possible; multitudes of brave young men are spoilt or killed. . . . Along such lines can you imagine men or life or the universe getting anywhere at all?" (*UF*, 163).

If Wells continually stages this conflict between war and waste, he also widens the scale to the question of the species. Here is the Time Traveller, right at the outset of Wells's career: "Had I been a literary man," the Traveller notes at seeing the dust to which all books have been reduced, "I might, perhaps, have moralized upon the futility of all ambition. But as it was, the thing that struck me with the keenest force was the enormous waste of labour to which this somber wilderness of rotting paper testified" (*TM*, 67–68). Or again, forty years after *The Time Machine*, in the soaring, melodramatic exhortation that closes *Things to Come*, Cabal, looking out on the stars, amid which the "space gun" (a rocket) is now on its way around the moon, offers two possibilities for humankind's future, one in which he has "conquered space and time" and opened up its mysteries, the other in which, failing this, he has fallen back to a mere animal, whose own extinction is of no more consequence than that of some minor species lost along the evolutionary way. "It is that," he says, gesturing to the stars, "or this. All the universe—or nothingness . . . Which shall it be . . . WHICH SHALL IT BE?"[66] *The World Brain* essays (1938) ask the same question—which shall it be?—though they invite a note of irony, as for instance: "Never was a living species more perilously poised than ours at the present time [1937]. If it does not take thought to end its present mental indecisiveness catastrophe lies ahead. Our species may yet end its strange eventful history as just the last, the cleverest of the great apes. The great ape that was clever—but not clever enough."[67]

In all of these cases, we might see waste as motif, and so it is, but it is also, more robustly, a dynamic antagonizing force in the panoply of life, as ineluctable to the story of life as Wells's three defining facets—movement, growth, reproduction—and as such, it has its own pull, a corroding quality visible throughout Wells's thought and writing. It is not only Wells who might fail, his works crumbling away like the long-forgotten books of *The Time Machine* or the worldwide illiteracy that closes *The War in the Air*, but the rest of us, too, if we don't follow his program and reform our world. Like the individual and the species, which prosper or die out together, in Wells's universe there is always the suggestion that our future and Wells's success precisely dovetail. Think of the prefaces to *The War in the Air* of 1921 and 1941, which offer his frustrated epitaph, "I told you so, you *damn* fools." It's not only hubris or the self-appointed role of prophet that drives such thought (Peter Kemp describes this habit as playing God, and others of Wells's contemporaries shared this view), but the conviction of immediate peril, of a world on the brink of destruction. The race between education and catastrophe is also a race between productivity and waste, in other words, and one whose outcome seems closely allied with Wells's own fate as an accurate and effective world advocate. It is also, more uncomfortably, allied with the question of eugenics, which, in its fervor to perfect the polity, is constantly needing to rationalize or even eliminate those parts of the social order that fall away from the ideal—the impure, the nonprogressive.

The constant nagging problem of waste thus links Wells closely to some of the most sinister cultural movements of the nineteenth and twentieth centuries. We have been running into Wells's dark side from the beginning, his science fiction that so happily wipes out the human race making a strange companion for his salvational efforts and epic optimism. Wells's embrace of principles allied with eugenics is the most decisive case in point, collecting together his interest in evolution, his desire for the perfection of human life (though not, to be clear, of human beings, whom he believed too biologically akin to our cave ancestors to be perfectible), and his faith that social-scientific methods might enable society to come together. Wells's biopolitical enthusiasm is among the most overt among his peers, his linking of the management of reproduction with social amelioration a critical feature of his thought. Wells's views on social perfectibility were not racial; his world polity was meant to be drawn from around the globe, as were those who would fall out of this republic, those failures or lost causes for whom, as we have seen, he envisions little compassion among the world's future rulers. Frequently, Wells expresses frustration at the "nonsense," as he usually calls it, that passes for racial science. Racial categorizing as a way to determine ability, intelligence, or promise was, he strongly believed, false as well as dangerous. Here again is how he puts the question of racial singularity in *The Outline of History*: "In the present age, man is probably no longer undergoing differentiation at all. Readmixture is now a far stronger force than differentiation. Men mingle more and more" (*OH*, 1:140). Nevertheless, his politics of reproductive management were allied in important ways with eugenics, whose history in the twentieth century is one of egregious racial violence, and thus for all Wells's progressive caveats about race, his work is peppered with comments, recommendations, analysis, predictions, and anxieties that suggest a shared basis with the racial theories he criticizes. Angelique Richardson notes that questions around biology, breeding, reproduction, gender, class, and the racial politics of Britain, framed in specifically eugenic terms, powered the popular and intellectual culture of England in the last decades of the nineteenth century and into the twentieth.[68] For modernism as for Wells, these crosscurrents, sweeping together ideals of purification (often in aesthetic terms) and distaste for anything that falls outside the pale, have a strong presence throughout the period's aesthetic politics. As Maurizia Boscagli writes of art and trash, even beyond modernism, "To manage junk either through its disposal or its return as art is to affirm the anxious dream of a world without a residue."[69]

In this sense, Wells joins the club, or perhaps bears the standard, for eugenic modernism. His whole orientation toward sweeping out the mess can be chilling and inhuman, a biting irony for someone who in so many ways saw himself as humanity's tireless champion. The ferocity of this impulse is dramatized throughout his writing, beginning with *The Time Machine*, where he so perfectly figured what was dank and murderous in his own instincts. Rather than overlook what does not belong, Wells comes back, armed, at those undesirable beings who will not get with the program. Here he is in *A Modern Utopia*, from the chapter alarmingly entitled "Failure in a Modern Utopia," dilating on the fate of those who, after all the utopian blessings, still cannot desist from their dangerous ways and are thus to be sent to self-governing islands, there to live among their peers:

> Quietly the outcast will go from among his fellow men. There will be no drumming of him out of the ranks, no tearing off of epaulettes, no smiting in the face. The thing must be just public enough to obviate secret tyrannies, and that is all.

There will be no killing, no lethal chambers. No doubt Utopia will kill all monstrous and evilly diseased births, but for the rest, the State will hold itself accountable for their being. . . . Crime and bad lives are the measure of a State's failure, all crime in the end is the crime of the community. Even for murder Utopia will not, I think, kill. . . .

The State will, of course, secure itself against any children from these people, that is the primary object in their seclusion, and perhaps it may even be necessary to make these island prisons a system of island monasteries and island nunneries.

(MU, 100–1)

There is much to puzzle and dismay in these sequences. The sequence of "There will be no X's" shocks for the suggestion that one ever would, reading this novel, have imagined these eventualities. At such moments, Wells seems to be in conversation with a totalitarian, violent interlocutor/self, whose very presence is strange and troubling. The more affirmative, socialist voice that intervenes—"all crime in the end is the crime of the community"—reassures, but not by much, since it is surrounded by other startling, violent suggestions, such as the possibility of forced sterilization.

Nevertheless, true to form, Wells does not embrace anyone else's idea of eugenics, heredity, or how to create a healthier population. Even *A Modern Utopia*, happy to play with these ideas of cordoning off those who don't conform to utopian perfection, is at pains to remind its readers that these "failures" are not defined by race or any inherited characteristics. More generally, Wells wants to draw a hard line (where we, no doubt, see a very porous border) between his schemes and plans for biopolitical regeneration and the false trails he attributes to eugenics, with its deterministic and unscientific reliance on race, family, and other reductive categories.[70] Quite early (in an essay in 1895), he dismissed the basic principle underlying eugenics. "The generalizations of heredity may be pushed to extremes," he writes, "to an almost fanatical fatalism." And further:

It often seems to be tacitly assumed that a living thing is at the utmost nothing more than the complete realization of its birth possibilities, and so heredity becomes confused with theological predestination. But after all, the birth tendencies are only one set of factors in the making of the living creature. We overlook only too often the fact that a living being may also be regarded as raw material, as something plastic, something that may be shaped and altered.

(EWS, 36)

Wells held to this position, and by 1904, in a symposium organized to respond to Galton's "Eugenics: Its Definition, Scope, and Aims" and reprinted in the *American Journal of Sociology*, Wells rebutted Galton's essential assumptions, arguing, in essence, that we cannot attribute "success" in families to inherited characteristics and casting a critical eye on such views as, for instance, that criminals are hereditary failures (on the contrary, he rather likes criminals, in this piece noting that "I am inclined to believe that a large proportion of our present-day criminals are the brightest and boldest members of families living under impossible conditions. . . . Many eminent criminals appear to me to be persons superior in many respects—in intelligence, initiative, creativity—to the average judge").[71] Instead of breeding them, Wells wants his future polities to *create* their own citizens—along lines he is ready to specify. His writings gravitate regularly to so many efforts to make humanity in the body, rather than to selective breeding, the cornerstone of eugenics, as in *Mankind in the Making*.

But perhaps this is a distinction without a difference, since a key feature of both programs is to eradicate failure and to construct a society in which citizens are harmoniously matched to the state's needs. Again, the issue so often comes down to residue, that which cannot or will not be purified, those elements or beings that refuse to join the Wellsian project of standing on the footstool and reaching up to the sky, where so many of his fantasies end. One listens with real dismay to some of Wells's statements about how the weak will—or should or do—fare in the world. Here, for instance, in his late meditation *The Conquest of Time* (1942), having lamented the state of the world and the possibility of total dissolution or even extinction, he can write:

> Much of what is happening in the world now is hideous, dismaying, cruel, and shameful; it is a wild storm of elimination, yet nevertheless it is not a biological catastrophe. . . . It is easy to exaggerate the mortality due either to pestilence or warfare. We are told that twenty-three million people were killed by the influenza epidemic of 1918. But most of those twenty-three millions were old people, weak people, feeble children who had to die somehow. If there had been no influenza they would have died very shortly in some other fashion. War casualties in the past have been mostly the premature deaths of young men, but a considerable proportion of the present holocaust has meant the miscellaneous killing of defenseless people, already earmarked for an early death.
>
> (*CT*, 72)

There are stunning factual inaccuracies here: the 1918 flu epidemic, for instance, was unique in part because it tended to be fatal not for the elderly or immune compromised but for young and otherwise healthy people. And then, in what possible sense can the civilians killed during World War II be considered "earmarked for early death" other than the fact that they were killed? Even if there were truth in its claim, that these millions were on their way to death, it would not be possible to "exaggerate" the horror of their loss. And of course, there is no context in which it would be meaningful to frame these catastrophes as somehow beside the primary point, since no point could be of greater urgency than protecting the lives of millions of innocent people.

The problematic of waste, then, inspires some of Wells's most despicable ideas and reactions, yet it is appropriate, given the fundamentally dialectical nature of his thought, that it also stands as the basis of his greatest novel, *Tono-Bungay* (1909). I don't think this represents simply a neat irony. Wells was moved to produce his most astonishing works, and to bring out his most innovative and important ideas, in the context of what terrorizes him. In so many ways, the conflict between his best and worst impulses turns out to be the motivating center of his genius. *Tono-Bungay* stands especially close to the fire for several reasons. Like countless other works, it is autobiographical, but here George Ponderevo comes near to Herbert George Wells at a critical place, his family and background, and the class analysis the novel performs has deep roots in Wells's formative experiences. The correspondences established in the novel—George and Herbert George; George's mother and Wells's mother; Bladesover and Uppark, where Wells's mother was a lady's maid; Marion in the novel and Isabel, Wells's first wife—are always loose, but together they concentrate the affinity of novel and life. George joins many other Berts and Georges in Wells's works, but he also stands out as one of the self-portraits most suffused with identity, in part because he is particularly Wellsian (and particularly attractive) as a boy. His key quality is skepticism, an attitude Wells liked to think of himself—as a radical, freethinker, and scientist—as embodying, and he fights back against class privilege and religious orthodoxy with satisfying determination. George's observations of the world, colored by the perspective of his older, narrating self, have about them a quality of observed truth as he reacts to his world, a complete social system that presents itself as a given.

In fact, that givenness is in many ways the subject of George's analysis of his surroundings, which in turn represents such a vital thread in this novel, Wells's contribution to the Victorian "condition of England" tradition.[72] As George notes early in the story, "In that English countryside of my boyhood every human being had a 'place.' It belonged to you from your birth like the colour of your eyes, it was inextricably your destiny" (*TB*, 16). One can hear, even in this short statement, how fully the organicism that entwines class with biology will be scrutinized in this novel. From the start, the novel embraces as its task to apply the attitude of the skeptic to these very assumptions, taking account of what George names the "Bladesovery" of England, his shorthand for the gentry-estate system that, in his view, persists at the basis of all English social formations, even when disguised by more contemporary forms of social power. The novel, which tells the story of George Ponderevo, his uncle Edward, founder of the useless product Tono-Bungay and capitalist extraordinaire (until his fall), the wives and women who populate their emotional universe, and ultimately England itself, partakes of the rise-and-fall structure, interweaving these private stories with larger analysis of the social and economic system.

As this chapter has found, Wells approaches the large stories of our world with biology as guide, taking the idea of *life* to encompass what *The Science of Life* reminds us are intertwined and mutual principles: biology, ecology, and the economy of systems. Hence there is a specific cadence to be heard in George's declaration, "I suppose what I'm really trying to render is nothing more nor less than Life—as one man has found it" (*TB*, 12). The life this novel tracks is actually several simultaneous lives—of George, of Edward, of Tono-Bungay the business venture, whose story orients the novel, and most generally, of England. This layering of multiple stories telling and retelling one another conforms to Wells's multivalent approach throughout his *life* writing, where the subject is less any given person that the life principle as it works its way through person or context (or here, business empire). Like Ann Veronica, who wants *to live*, or the seeds cracking open on the moon that exemplify the biological imperative, or the beast people whose transformations remind us of the mutability and strangeness of all life, the narrative of George and his uncle is one that fluctuates according to the forces of generation: making, expanding, rising, falling, deteriorating, and ending. These operate at different registers, as the novel brings together overt thematics about science, such as the chemical corrosiveness of quap (the radioactive substance George journeys to Africa to steal, with disastrous effects), or the physics and engineering of aeronautics, or even the liver effects vaguely associated with Tono-Bungay, with a story whose inner dynamics are also fully conceptualized in biological terms, digging in to the bases of life.

The theme of expansion, for instance, has the force almost of necessity in *Tono-Bungay*. The Ponderevo empire grows according to the ineluctable logic of capitalism, which also applies to Edward's real-estate habits, with their ever-accumulating gigantism. It is this constant growing, or *out*growing (as with Edwards's houses), that helps create the novel's aura of propulsion and activity, its "hum." Some of the most appealing sequences in the novel, in this spirit, concern the life of Tono-Bungay, as, for instance, in the "How We Made

Tono-Bungay Hum" section, when Tono-Bungay first takes off, with Edward and George, each with his special skill set, together turning the snake oil into a thriving business.[73] Behind it all, the sheer drive of capitalism thrusts this meaningless commodity out into the world. As George regularly reminds the reader, all will end in failure and demise, and this incorporation of death and endings into the story of birth and wild growth ought to be read not only in cautionary or moral terms (the Herodotan lesson, that one cannot judge a life until one has seen its end) but as registering death as embedded in all activity, a story of life as cycle rather than as progress.

Growth, waste, growth, waste: these are the partners whose interchange the novel tracks and whose seemingly pointless significance in the playing out of life it rues. Tono-Bungay, needless to say, is a product with no value in terms of its physical contents; critics have mused about its ingredients, in the face of George's coy refusal to specify the solution ("No! I am afraid I cannot give it away"), with guesses ranging from wastewater to cocaine to, in Edward Mendelson's brilliant suggestion, the new product of Coca-Cola, but what is clear is that its value in the market is independent of its contents (*TB*, 131).[74] Edward understands the principle deeply: " 'The old merchant used to tote about commodities,' " is how he explains it to George's artist friend Ewart, " 'the new one creates values,' " and to George he extols the nasty stuff for " 'giving people confidence' " (*TB*, 159, 135). And he is right, to a fantastic degree; the life of the product manufactured entirely by advertising and fueled by desire, containing no physical substance of value, goes a long way in this novel, creating enormous wealth and generating in Edward, in his last phase before the fall, an insatiable urge to consume, accumulate, build, and even—always the endpoint of such stories in the English imagination—to ascend the class hierarchy. From unreality to unreality, it is entirely fitting that the last phase in this sequence would be a title and coat of arms, pure signs whose immense value in one sense is met by total fictionality in another. For his part, George remains suspicious of the Tono-Bungay phenomenon, consistently naming it as rubbish and its success as absurdity. Early in the proceedings he thinks, somewhat wistfully, " 'Some businesses are straight and quiet, anyhow; supply a sound article that is really needed, don't shout advertisements,' " and for all his complicity in his uncle's affairs, he remains contemptuous of Tono-Bungay, whose science is no science at all but rather the art of advertising, the play of language, and the imperially charged incentive to spread and morph (*TB*, 136). George is especially unnerved by this combination of exponential increase (in money, power, range of influence) and the continued nullity of substance to any of these events, beginning with the initial product, Tono-Bungay.

The novel offers several resonant metaphors for all of this, including whirl-pool and bubble, but one has primary explanatory value: cancer, a metaphor taken, as one would have predicted, from biology. Of London's sprawl, for instance, George writes, "All these aspects have suggested to my mind at times, do suggest to this day, the unorganized, abundant substance of some tumorous growth-process, a process which indeed bursts all the outlines of the affected carcass" (*TB*, 102). London and disease have a long history of signifying each other, and George's version hews to the theme of uncontrolled and damaging growth. Moreover, such biologized readings of the social sphere and built envi-ronment are attached to a more chemical understanding of matter, with its own destructive properties. It is quap that delivers the insight most forcefully, invit-ing George, in familiar Wellsian fashion, to press his literary figuration very far, to the point, as we have seen many times before, of literalization:

> But there is something—the only word that comes near it is *cancerous*—and that is not very near, about the whole of quap, something that creeps and lives as a disease lives by destroying; an elemental stirring and disarrangement, incal-culably maleficent and strange.
>
> This is no imaginative comparison of mine. To my mind radioactivity is a real disease of matter. Moreover it is a contagious disease. It spreads. You bring those debased and crumbling atoms near others and those too presently catch the trick of swinging themselves out of coherent existence. It is in matter exactly what the decay of our old culture is in society, a loss of traditions and distinc-tions and assured reactions. . . . I am haunted by a grotesque fancy of the ulti-mate eating away and dry-rotting and dispersal of all our world. So that while man still struggles and dreams his very substance will change and crumble from beneath him. . . . Suppose indeed that is to be the end of our planet; no splendid climax and finale, no towering accumulation of achievements, but just—atomic decay!
>
> (*TB*, 329, italics in the original)

For us, there is much here that has become familiar from Wells's writing—the use and explanation/dilation of his figures ("It is in matter exactly what the decay of our old culture is in society"), the engagement with contemporary science, the obsessive draw toward extinction, the play with time, literalization ("to my mind radioactivity is a real disease of matter"). In *Tono-Bungay*, these persistent motifs are yoked to an analysis of the class system ("the decay of our old culture . . . a loss of traditions and distinctions and assured reactions") and refracted through the prism of the life story, in its most pessimistic form

("something that creeps and lives as a disease lives by destroying," as he puts it
[*TB*, 329]). George, too, lives by destroying, even before he finds a career in
building destroyers. He kills at least one man, the unknown African whose gratuitous murder stands as an emblem of imperial violence and its outrageous
impunity, and possibly also a second, his uncle, who is perceptive when he com-
plains after their all-night glide, "'You know you're not saving—you're killing
me'" (*TB*, 361). Such contradictions are part of the larger scientific cosmos Wells
is summoning in his analysis of the social order, where biology, chemistry, and
physics are figured as critical explanatory discourses.

London, though, would seem to resist categorizing within George's class-
based conception. His first visit there is overwhelming, well summed up by his
simple response, "But this London was vast! it was endless!" and even as he
becomes a resident and settles in to life as a science student, its thronging potentialities easily distract him from his studies (*TB*, 87). London, moreover, does
not seem particularly amenable to George's theory of England as an extension of
the gentry system; then again, the onus of the novel is to bring the large, systemic thinking embodied by the sciences to bear on these swarming and swelling social and geographic units as well. And so, in a passage that epitomizes
Wells's intellectual habits over much of his career, George declares a kind of
cognitive victory:

> London!
> At first, no doubt, it was a chaos of streets and people and buildings and
> reasonless going to and fro. I do not remember that I ever struggled very steadily
> to understand it, or explored it with any but a personal and adventurous inten-
> tion. Yet in time there has grown up in me a kind of theory of London; I do
> think I see lines of an ordered structure out of which it has grown, detected a
> process that is something more than a confusion of casual accidents, though
> indeed it may be no more than a process of disease.
>
> (*TB*, 99–100)

It is a concise articulation of the novel's attempt to imagine counterforces of
continuity and order in a domain defined by both wasteful growth and decay.
Of course, "it may be no more than a process of disease," setting us right back
into the figurative landscape such ordering is supposed to oppose in the first
place. Or perhaps the point is that biology lines up on both sides; it is the hypertrophy that stands for disorder and also the system that makes it possible to
detect a countervening order. Chaos, too: if chaos is defined as that which has
no system or logic, the very epitome of what cannot be controlled or predicted,

chaos theory, initiated as early as the 1880s with Henri Poincaré's experiments, puts a different spin on the random and unpredictable. For Wells, who was always in his comfort zone in the realm of long time scales, the fact that chaos theory shows predictability and pattern only at a vast scale is no obstacle. Somehow this is cold comfort in *Tono-Bungay*, however, where disease determines health, corrosion shows us the meaning of matter, and chaos seems the predictor of pattern. The big, long structures of chaos may come in too late to offer solace to the cancer patient.

One group in particular comes to stand in for the most worrisome chemical properties: Jews. From the early description of how Bladesover is now let to "Reuben Lichtenstein," exemplifying a quap-like decay right at the heart of England, as George sees it, to his disgust and contempt for the "bright-eyed, eagle-nosed people talking some incomprehensible gibberish between the shops and the barrows" (that is, another language, no doubt Yiddish) encountered in his London perambulations, and back to the debasement of the estates, which persistently bothers George's narration, the novel is gripped by what seems an altogether gratuitous anti-Semitism (*TB*, 16, 103). By the logic of the novel, though, it is not so gratuitous. In George's relentless figuration, Jews belong to the region of strange growth, in this case chemical rather than tumorous: "To borrow an image from my mineralogical days, these Jews were not so much a new British gentry as 'pseudomorphous' after the gentry. They are very clever people, the Jews, but not clever enough to suppress their cleverness" (*TB*, 16). The pseudomorph is a crystal formation that has taken on the exact shape—in fact having replaced in entirety—the formation that preceded it, so a handy scientific image for the logic of substitution and seriality that organizes the novel's objects. There is in this metaphor a temporal elasticity, as the old and new inhabit separately but also together. The memory of what came before has a determining quality, as if of presence but in fact of absence, the originary form now superseded. Yet the ugly feelings at issue here overshadow the cleverness of the metaphor (clever, we might say, but not clever enough to suppress its cleverness). Wells's anti-Semitism takes different forms, as noted in the introduction; here he calls up a series of nasty associations involving aesthetics and ugliness, financial ruthlessness, and a threatening survivalism about the Jewish people. The problem for *Tono-Bungay* is how available Jews are to step into the old forms, to push out what came before; they function as ready signs for all the biological and chemical residues, accretions, adaptations, and mutations that in this novel stand as so many mocking antagonists. Jews have long been associated with ambulation in Western culture (wandering) and with all manner of invidious qualities of infiltration, infection, pollution, and parasitical replacement. To the extent that

*Tono-Bungay* taps into these suggestions, it reignites the most familiar and repulsive stereotypes. The novel's most totalizing and pessimistic view of the futility of human culture becomes entangled, then, with aspects of the Western imaginary that are as atavistic and rearguard as any the novel might be ready to ironize.

As the emphasis on disease suggests, *Tono-Bungay* takes up the story of life from the vantage of its ends, reading backward. Its formal experiments to a large degree map to such backward looking. As in other novels (*The War of the Worlds*, *The Time Machine*) but to an even greater degree, Wells frontloads the plot, often articulating the outcome at the opening, whether of novel, chapter, or segment. The novel's first paragraphs sum up the plot, signaling the narrative arc to come, and this self-predictive habit persists throughout the text. These frontloadings, which recur throughout the novel, act as little précis of what will follow in the chapter, in an undercutting of the narrative logic of storytelling. Such is also the dominant strategy of *The War of the Worlds*, as in its opening lines, which establish for the reader what those within the story cannot yet know, that they are being watched, that the Martians are coming. The layering of time in these plot previews can be discomfiting, as they call attention to the oddities of readerly temporality when the tale is being told in this distinctly reversed fashion. When George tells us as early as the second page that "once (though it is the most incidental thing in my life) I murdered a man . . . ," he both creates and undermines the principle of suspense, putting the reader in an ambiguous position of being told something that, at the same time, we have no power to judge (*TB*, 10, ellipses in the original).

Other devices share in the behindhand mood. George, for instance, repeatedly alludes to the chaos of his notes to signify the vision of a world post-events. This quality of being "post" is the condition of writing, which is then figured as a kind of reassembling; thus in an early passage "Tono-Bungay still figures on the hoardings . . . but its social glory, its financial illumination, have faded from the world for ever. And I, sole scorched survivor from the blaze, sit writing of it here" (*TB*, 11–12). Many of the novel's formal conceits take this temporally reversed approach, with the end writing the beginning. Here, for instance, is how George sets up the chapter to describe his marriage: "As I look back on those days in which we built up the great Tono-Bungay property out of human hope and a credit for bottles and rent and printing, I see my life . . ." (*TB*, 162). Of all the chapters, "Marion" is the most intensely retrospective, and it tends to interrupt its narration of the past with a sense of present afterthought, with many statements taking temporally conscious forms, such as "Now that I am forty-five, I can look back at her with all my old admiration and none of my old bitterness" or "Who can tell the story of the slow estrangement of two married people . . . ?. . . Even now, with an interval of fifteen years to clear it up for me, I still find a mass of impressions" (*TB*, 166, 183). Emphatically, the marriage story is told by way of its failure. Such an approach follows the novel's biological fixations, since it is death and waste that here determine life and productivity. To a remarkable degree, each episode in the life story of *Tono-Bungay* is marked by its negative capabilities.

In fact, the theme of waste and futility seems not so much to reach an apex as to overtake the novel, with multiple endpoints in the plot and narration. In addition to metaphoric usages, there are, too, the plot developments, Edward's bankruptcy, the running down of Edward by fever and delirium, the love among the wreckage that dictates no future for George and Beatrice together (and no children for any of the couples). George, who can never resist an opportunity to sum things up, has this to say about the overall spirit of the *post*-world of the novel's close:

> What a strange melancholy emptiness of intention that stricken enterprise seemed in the even evening sunlight, what vulgar magnificence and crudity and utter absurdity! It was as idiotic as the pyramids. I sat down on the stile, staring at it as though I had never seen that forest of scaffold poles, that waste of walls and bricks and plaster and shaped stones, that wilderness of broken soil and wheeling tracks and dumps before. It struck me suddenly as the compactest image and sample of all that passes for Progress, of all the advertisement-inflated spending, the aimless building up and pulling down, the enterprise and promise of my age. This was our fruit, this was what we had done, I and my uncle, in the fashion of our time. We were its leaders and exponents, we were the thing it most flourishingly produced. For this futility in its end, for an epoch of such futility, the solemn scroll of history had unfolded . . .
>
> "Great God!" I cried, "but is this Life?"
>
> For this the armies drilled, for this the Law was administered and the prisons did their duty, for this the millions toiled and perished in suffering, in order that a few of us should . . . make our lives one vast dismal spectacle of witless waste! So it struck me then . . . This was Life! It came to me like a revelation, a revelation at once incredible and indisputable of the abysmal folly of our being.
>
> (*TB*, 347–48, ellipses in the original)

One looks ahead to Owen: "Was it for this the clay grew tall?" And to Yeats: "Was it for this / The wild geese spread the wing / Upon every tide?" And back to Conrad, an integral presence in *Tono-Bungay*, via the quap interlude, which is both homage and extension to *Heart of Darkness* (1899/1902), another tale about the violent waste and folly of Western culture. Then again, at his most modernist, Wells reminds us of his particularities and divergences from the era's more familiar voices. We would not, surely, find Yeats equating the pyramids with the extravagance and vulgarity of contemporary capitalism's excesses. Wells is ready to cast a mordant eye on the achievements of the past; his scale is expansive, his timespans long, his categories (humanity) encompassing. More, as this chapter has attempted to show, it was Wells's intensely diverse, biologized purchase on "life" (here capitalized, Life) that gave him access to such heightened meanings and such profound expressions of defeat.

The novel's vision of totalized waste, with its formal correlative in his retrospective, written-from-past-the-end style, meets little resistance, but George does present himself as something of a lone holdout against the principles of substanceless wealth and wasteful growth, summed up in his phrase, "And now I build destroyers!" (*TB*, 381). Before these, it was gliders that provided a personal antidote to the expanding Tono-Bungay empire. Neither of these objects can be said to stand on solid ground (at the literal level), but their basis in engineering and practical usage—and, as Wells of all people knew, specifically military usage—sets them apart in George's mind from his uncle's realm of the romance of commerce, the heady and ultimately toxic mix of fiction and uncontrollable growth, and the governing trope of waste. "Sometimes I call this reality Science, sometimes I call it Truth," George states, yet it is difficult to credit these as plausible or sufficient counterweights to what the novel has been diagnosing as constitutive of its world. (*TB*, 388). As William Kupinse argues, the serial sequence of the gliders and destroyers, each modifying, superseding, and replacing the former, mimics the waste-producing form of commerce epitomized by the Tono-Bungay empire. Tono-Bungay not only produces waste; it is waste. But this does not set it apart from the novel's other forms of production. Rather it becomes the exemplification of production-as-waste that dominates all aspects of the novel. Kupinse writes, "Himself a young creator, George's apprehension at his first sight of the quap deposits arrives in the form of his realization that every act of creating value involves a process of discarding, and his suspicion that matter itself might ultimately participate in the same waste-driven value system informing Edwardian England."[75] Or perhaps the question is, once the life process has been so fully postulated by its ends, what kind of alternative vision can be offered, given that this is, above all else, a *life* story, writ at multiple levels and indicating a series of back-and-forth mimeses among the different figures (George, Edward, Tono-Bungay, England)?

A literary answer would be that storytelling itself offers what all the other realms of analysis can only handle as so much waste. This is Kupinse's argument, that the serial literary styles of *Tono-Bungay*, like those of Joyce, formally instantiate the principle of sequentiality that the novel embodies through its successive houses, gliders, and destroyers, all of this in turn representing an economic structure of capitalist overproduction: "just as a serially-defined, waste-driven value schema underlies the social, economic, and scientific commentary of Wells's novel . . . so too does this notion of a series of discarded and soon-to-be discarded items undergird the serial presentation of *Tono-Bungay*'s stylistic pastiches."[76] Unlike those other entities, the way language evolves opens up expansive prospects for meaning, insofar as modes such as imitation, parody, and appropriation are not so much replacements that imply discarding their source texts/styles as references back and forth across time, so that the earlier modality partially inhabits the new one and is partially superseded by it. James Longenbach, in a study of Eliot and Pound, writes that "for these poets the present is nothing more than the sum of the entire past—a palimpsest, a complex tissue of historical remnants," and in playing with literary style as a moving and accumulating system of accruing meaning, Wells is bumping shoulders with these two articulators of the "historical sense."[77]

Language is always, for Wells, about change. It is a view that comes up repeatedly in his works, as, for instance, in the language of *A Modern Utopia*, which, as the narrator stresses, differs from other composite languages like Esperanto in their stasis, its mutability. From the moment of its appearance, Wellsian utopian language remains in continual motion, like any living language. And so here, if Wells is playing with different literary prototypes to embody over the course of his text, the most pronounced being his Conradian interlude, this mutability is less about the half-life of style than it is about its constant need to keep up with the swarming "impressions" that George attempts to pin down in (and as) his narration. With evolution, in turn, flood in the many questions of generation, extinction, progress, and endpoints that hover around this most important of Wellsian life principles.

Is language, then, also subject to the cancer (or the corrosiveness) that the novel diagnoses as the disease of modernity? Certainly there are some worries, first and foremost involving Tono-Bungay, a product and indeed empire made of language, via advertising, in its most deconstructive guise—all signifiers and no signifieds—and culminating in fraudulence. As Edward describes his final infraction: " 'Writin' things down—I done something' " (*TB*, 350). For his part, George tends toward visual and aural motifs in attempting to capture the moving flux of life, stressing at every turn just where language is most likely to fall short or where it leans heavily on the realms of the senses. Most prevalent is the conceit of impression, which dominates especially in the novel's first pages ("I have got an unusual series of impressions that I want very urgently to tell," "I want to tell—*myself*, and my impressions," "Each day my accumulating impressions were added to and qualified and brought into relationship with new ones" [*TB*, 9, 12, 99, italics in the original]). As noted in chapter 1, "Voice," Wells's impressionism in *Tono-Bungay* departs from the modernist example in the extensiveness of his attempt to tether these to analysis, as in the passage about how the chaos of London is gradually brought into a theory. Still, the novel continually loops back to the field of impression, where the subjective, transient, and perceptual seem ascendant and where vantage very explicitly determines what one sees. In addition to the stress on impression, George characterizes his material by its hectic and disorganized nature, in such phrases as "agglomeration," "the notes and inconsecutive observations that make this book," "things adrift, joining on to nothing, leading nowhere" (*TB*, 11, 11, 35). Taking a familiar modernist line, in which the narrator wades into the flotsam and jetsam of language only to declare himself inadequate, George seems to be at the whim of sensory impression and the sheer superabundance of life's materials.

Then again, he is a systematizer and has at hand a decent kit of tropes to counter such overflow. Thus, for instance, as he turns to the topic of his marriage, he begins with a conceit out of accounting: "As I look back on those days in which we built up the great Tono-Bungay property out of human hope and a credit for bottles and rent and printing, I see my life as it were arranged in two parallel columns of unequal width, a wider, more diffused, eventful and various one which continually broadens out, the business side of my life, and a narrow, darker and darkling one shot ever and again with a gleam of happiness, my home life with Marion" (*TB*, 162). The metaphor does not work very well—columns don't seem likely to be diffuse nor to darken, and their mathematical shape prevents them from broadening out. But the attempt to quantify is symptomatic, with George's figures drifting toward a more solid, scientific basis than his impressionism allows. Or, to note another direction, parallel with the novel's devotion to impression is the production of a soundtrack; it is a fully aural text, with hums, whirrs, and whooshes, and of course Edward's "zzzz"ing. Tono-Bungay, a product of advertising, is also effective specifically as sound. As George first thinks, when he sees initial advertising for the product, "It was simple and yet somehow arresting. I found myself repeating the word after I had passed, it roused one's attention like the sound of distant guns. 'Tono'—what's that? and deep, rich, unhurrying;—'*Bun*-gay!'" (*TB*, 127, italics in the original). Paired with *The War in the Air*, where Wells attempts to incorporate the discordant, terrifying, often overpowering sounds of modern warfare into the text, *Tono-Bungay* gives full range to hearing, a sense often either neglected by literature or taken for granted. In all of these ways—the emphasis on impression, the evocation of sensory and cognitive overload, the countertropes, the sounds—Wells creates a textuality defined by multifariousness, overflow, circulation, and a literary infrastructure aimed to express (if not control) these properties.

It comes down, always, to change. Wellsian life, once again, is movement, ingestion (growth), and reproduction. All of these imply change, demand it; all are also haunted by the diseased versions of themselves—deterioration, cancer, sterility. The great object of *Tono-Bungay* is, in some sense, to see change as it happens, to catch it in its act, and we are back, then, to where this chapter began, the cracking of the seeds and the exuberant growth replayed on every lunar day. "The hand of change rests on it all," writes George at the outset of his story,

> unfelt, unseen; resting for a while, as it were half reluctantly, before it grips and ends the thing for ever. One frost and the whole face of things will be bare. . . . For that we have still to wait a little while. The new order may have gone far towards shaping itself, but just as in that sort of lantern show that used to be known in the village as the "Dissolving Views," the scene that is going remains upon the mind, traceable and evident, and the newer picture is yet enigmatical long after the lines that are to replace those former ones have grown bright and strong . . .
>
> (*TB*, 15–16)

Alongside Proust's colored lantern in his Combray bedroom or Eliot's magic lantern throwing "the nerves in patterns on a screen" ("Prufrock"), Wells's dissolving views join a modernist pantheon of visual signs to express a certain kind of ephemerality and pictorial unsubstantiality that leans toward but does not fully inhabit the realm of the photographic and cinematic. The ghostly picture that remains almost visible, the uncertainty of the new outline, even as it slowly emerges and deepens, is George's figure for how social orders can only just be recognized, even after the moment when the hereditary estate has been handed over to the new "tenants."

However, it also points to the novel's broader project, of attempting to portray not only what comes before or after but the process and movement and invisible realities of those exchanging temporalities. At the end of the novel, in his glide down the river, George will come back to this idea that his aim is to find the right perspective, a vantage that allows him to see totality and to see it in time as well as space:

It is curious how at times one's impressions will all fuse and run together into a sort of unity and become continuous with things that have hitherto been utterly alien and remote. That rush down the river became mysteriously connected with this book. As I passed down the Thames I seemed in a new and parallel manner to be passing all England in review.... It wasn't so much thinking at the time as a sort of photographic thought that came and grew clear.

(TB, 382)

The photographic thought, like the dissolving view or the action of time traveling or the stop-action quality of the sequence on the moon, suggests the inseparability and interpenetration of observation with its technologies. Here in *Tono-Bungay*, such insights are drawn into the novel's backward style ("all England in review") and especially into its quest for a vision of sufficient totality to compete with the entropic emphasis on decay and waste.

But of course, it does not. No matter what distance or organizing framework George is able to find, the prospect of disease continues to manifest. The same chapter that collects "all England in review" is replete with tumorous metaphors of the sort we have met before, the novel still worrying about "England as a feudal scheme overtaken by fatty degeneration and stupendous accidents of hypertrophy" (*TB*, 386). It is the reality of change, figured as decadence, that the novel cannot fully assimilate. As in so many of his works that reach for forms of totality, Wells seeks in *Tono-Bungay* to portray the whole of life, appropriating the systems that make such understanding possible—biology, chemistry, physics, evolution, economics—but something else stands out through these intersecting lines of science: the sheer fact that change cannot be halted. It is odd, in a way, that George (and Wells) comes out so virulently against the new Jewish tenants of Bladesover, given how little admiration or affection he has for the former ones. This is not a conservative longing for the old ways, for the aristocracy or the past. The early segments of the novel, with their biting satire of the Bladesover scene and spirit of admirable youthful indignation against "knowing your place," set the tone for a novel that encircles the aristocracy in no golden glow. It is, rather, the fact of supersession itself that creates the trouble. "The hand of change rests on it all," as we have already heard, "unfelt, unseen; resting for a while, as it were half reluctantly, before it grips and ends the thing for ever." What creates the charge is not "the thing," not the particular entities doing the replacing or being replaced so much as the force, "the hand of change." It is fitting for a novel about a product whose contents are irrelevant to its success that the inescapability of time itself, rather than fixed states on either side of a temporal line, should determine its tone. Yet as we have found so many times before,

Wells finds a way to dramatize as terror what he so ardently desires: change, progress, a new world that will learn from the folly of the past and then leave it all behind.

The scheme of life is a story that is always being told simultaneously from the beginning, middle, and—for Wells in *Tono-Bungay*—especially the end. Here as elsewhere in Wells's work, time passes but also loops, folds, rests. Wells never sees time in strictly directional terms. For a novel in which forward momentum has such strong purchase—since capitalism demands growth and only growth— life's many ways of resisting or checking these forces assume the form of moral fable, yet it is a moral fable without a legitimate moral authority (certainly George fails that test), and, perhaps more to the point, this is a novel half in love with the rush and whoosh of capitalism's ride. Its fetish is flight, a literal as well as figurative desire. But these gliders always sink in the end. One might fly the nets, like Stephen Dedalus, if they are nation, religion, and family, but biology admits no such escape. Wells was not the first to think of biology as destiny; he was one of the best to bore into the depths and intricacies of that truism as if, each time, it arrives as a fresh and startling discovery.

# Conclusion

---

## *The World*

How does one imagine the world? And why? Wells's answers have, I hope, emerged through these pages. Wells believed above all else that the future for humanity lay in its unification and that the imaginative work of the writer and thinker is to help generate the conditions of world harmony that will yield an indefinite future of peace and prosperity for the human species. His concept of the world partakes of all of the major strands of global thinking occupying critics today: it is, by turns, engaged with the "global" of global capitalism and its attendant inequities and imperial legacies; insistent on a planetary scope and understanding founded on astronomy, geology, history, and ecology; concerned with the age and vulnerability of the earth and its inhabitants; and fully engaged with what kinds of cultural changes and continuities will be needed to envision a unified citizenry. Wells enters our world of twenty-first-century concerns and interests on equal footing. His fifty-year career of advocating for humanity on the world scale, flawed and eccentric as it may have been, establishes him as the era's foremost literary spokesperson for the world as the final, and only, meaningful unit of cumulative effort. In concluding *Inventing Tomorrow*, we open out Wells's world orientation to consider the political forms and ethical incentives behind his humanity-scaled projects. In the end, Wells's world projects mark his most significant departure from his peers and gesture intriguingly toward us, one hundred years later.

But first, we might briefly consider the terms of global interconnectedness and imagining that best characterize Wells's thinking, and place him within the conversation animating intellectual disciplines today. Is Wells a global thinker, a planetary one, a cosmopolitan? Wells was all of these, but not exactly as we understand them, and his thinking about the regions of the globe in relation to one another, while tending to be imperial in their geographical assumptions, do not conform readily to contemporary paradigms. Critics today, in the wake of several decades of scholarship on the meanings of the global, tend to be highly nuanced and particular with these terms, such that, for instance, the notion of planetarity, currently setting the tone for literary criticism, places itself in opposition to the global. As noted in the introduction, in this conception, globalism, reflecting its emergence as master trope in the 1990s—when, with the end of the Cold War and the burgeoning of expanded markets around the world, a new era of global capitalism and its attendant cultural forms rushed into being—becomes too fully allied with the inequities of global capitalism. In a line often quoted by critics interested in the planet as a more ethically satisfactory space than the globe, Gayatri Spivak writes, "The globe is on our computers. It is the logo of the World Bank. No one lives there; and we think that we can aim to control it. The planet is in the species of alterity, belonging to another system; and we inhabit it, on loan."[1] The planet reminds us of its and our precariousness and interdependence, and critics have pointed to the release in 1968 of the famous *Earthrise* photograph (and four years later, the equally iconic *Blue Marble*) as an inauguration into this new and more ethically viable episteme, taking urgent precedence in our era of climate change. Cosmopolitanism, meanwhile, is less focused on the nature of the globe and its forms of totality than it is on the expressive terrains of those crossing linguistic and geographical borders and on an ethics derived from the sense of commonalty among the world's peoples. Most contemporary critics interested in cosmopolitanism distance themselves from Wellsian (or, as they would say, Kantian) ideals of totalizing humanism, seeing the imperialist in the universalist and a deep Western bias in the seemingly level vision of a unified world. Instead, the principle is retained with caveats, as in Rebecca Walkowitz's influential idea of "critical cosmopolitanism" or in attempts by Bruce Robbins to create a workable contemporary cosmopolitanism that can square with today's post-Enlightenment politics.[2] Overall, the basis of cosmopolitan thinking remains powerful and compelling: to recognize the equal value and demands of all, across affiliations of nation, language, and culture, and to generate from this premise essential and transformative features of our world.

These three constructs—globe, planet, cosmopole—richly counterpoised as they are in contemporary discourse, cannot be usefully disentangled when it comes to Wells, who, as we have seen in many contexts, identifies powerfully with each of them. Wells took the world's interconnectedness (technological, ecological, financial, military) as a given, in that sense engaging fully with the globalized realities of modernity. His essential cognizance of the globe as unit underlies his work across the board, from his scientific tales to his prescriptions for world governance. He was in every sense a global writer. An interest in the earth as planet, too, runs throughout Wells's work: the earth is seen from the sky, as in the opening of *The War of the Worlds*, or on Bedford's lonely return trip through space in *The First Men in the Moon*, when he "sat down to begin a vigil in that little speck of matter in infinite space that would last until [he] should strike the earth," a journey that toggles between diminishing and enlarging the individual person.[3] Throughout his work, Wells took the measure of the earth's planetary meanings, thinking about its climate, its geologic changes over the millennia, its rotations and seasons, its inhabitants (animal and otherwise), its profound vulnerabilities. Matthew Taylor rightly notes that Wells and later planetary critics "represent cataclysmic states of exception that conjure forth planetary consciousness—*and insist on planetary action*."[4]

As for cosmopolitanism, we know that Wells declared himself an unabashed adherent, distinguishing this from internationalism; as noted in the introduction, Wells claimed, "In flat contrast to [the] international school of pacifism is the cosmopolitan school . . . of which I declare myself entirely a disciple. This school thinks not in terms of states and nations but in terms of cosmopolis, the city of mankind."[5] Especially after the First World War, Wells insisted that the stakes of such cosmopolitanism were exceptionally high; to be a cosmopolitan was to leave the nation as site of loyalty and identity, turning instead to the species, joining the community of like-minded thinkers from all parts of the world in the quest to create, as he calls it, cosmopolis.

If Wells sustains global, planetary, and cosmopolitan orientations, the most encompassing and accurate descriptor for his work and aspirations nevertheless remains "world." The dream of a unified world was his ongoing project, and it was the quality of "world" itself—that sense of a human community made up of people of all races from around the seven continents, a way of thinking about humanity together in its status as species and as a potentially unified body, and the belief that the writer has a role and responsibility toward this unifying amalgam of people—that I want to stress in concluding this assessment of Wells's work and the vantage it offers on modernism and modernity.[6]

We might take, as a useful counterpoint, Jed Esty's brilliant and influential notion of England in the 1930s as a "shrinking island," an inward turning at a time of imperial retrenchment, in which England's status as object of study supersedes that of its imperial domains: "The key figures in this version of late modernism [as anthropological turn]," writes Esty, "are canonical English writers who measured the passing of British hegemony not solely in terms of a vitiated imperial humanism but also in terms of a recovered cultural particularity that is, at least potentially, the basis for both social and aesthetic renewal."[7] It is a compelling model, one that has had a shaping role in modernist studies, as critics reconsider the later modernist period and, indeed, a larger swath of the twentieth century in terms of these swings through modernist universalism, national particularism, and global power in dialectical relation with inwardness and self-scrutiny. But what if it has, in fact, explained too much—what if it has given the impression that the motivations of several modernists to renovate a certain form of culture overshadow other vital approaches to globalism and its meanings? What if the island is shrinking not because it is losing its identity as dominant world power but rather because of its speck-like quality, taken from the large scales at which one might, as a Wellsian, operate? Or, what if it is shrinking because, as one node in an interconnected world, it is not separable from the rest of the globe? Or what if it is not actually shrinking at all but rather the conception of worldwide structures of thought and identity, of notions such as global citizenship and human rights, mean that the status of being in the world is simply less tied to national origins than, say, to terrestrial or human ones? These have been the tenets of Wells's life and work, as I have been tracing them in this book. If we take Wells as one key figure to establish our models, along with Esty's trio of Woolf, Eliot, and Forster, we might see the dynamics of place, identity, and the imagination according to these much more open and outward-looking paradigms. "We do not stand alone," Wells believed, "we signify as parts of a universal and immortal development."[8] Or again, in the words of one of his many fictional alter-egos, "All history is the record of an effort in man to form communities. . . . There seems no natural and proper limit to a human community. . . . From the first dawn of the human story you see man . . . *pursuing the boundary of his possible community.*"[9] This vision of England's (or any nation's) position as one cell in an ever-enlarging body was capacious and far-reaching. At the same time, it had to engage with the actual structures of world alliances, especially the British Empire.

The signal fact of England's geopolitical orientation during Wells's life, empire has a strange and equivocal place across his writings, as we have been finding over the course of this analysis. It is there, most prominently, in the form of allegory. Given the preponderance of world systems across his thinking, it is striking how infrequently he addresses empire directly and how memorably he makes empire visible instead through allegory. Most dramatic are the allegorical dimensions of *The Island of Doctor Moreau*, where, as we saw in chapter 4, allegory was both inescapable and also beside the point, elbowed out by literalization, and the multiple allegories that sustain and deconstruct *The War of the*

*Worlds*, which establishes the analogical correlation between Martian/English as an essential technique for interpreting and assessing the story. Wells did write directly about empire at times, as in his 1914 essay "Will the Empire Live?" (Answer: only if the English engender a sense of unity among the diverse people it governs. "If it is to survive . . . everyone who wants to read science or history or philosophy, to come out of the village life into wider thoughts and broader horizons, to gain appreciation in art, must find ready to hand, easily attainable in English, all there is to know and all that has been said thereon.")[10] He also frequently castigates Kipling and his school of imperial bullying, as he saw it, along with the political classes for their obtuse conservatism; neither of these forms boded any future. These views are expressed openly in his work, but he seems to have done his real imperial thinking in his allegories, which so often defy the affordances of the form and push straight to the point, exposing the violent power politics its inequities perpetuate around the world.

In *The War of the Worlds*, as we recall, the comparisons begin with the opening lines, which set up the principle of allegorical reading, whereby the Martians are to be understood as akin to one or another group, fantastical creatures from another planet very clearly meant to tell us something about our own geopolitical dynamics. Beginning with the opening lines, in which we learn that the Martians are watching our oblivious movements across the reaches of space, ready to invade and colonize, they are overtly made analogous to human beings (such as the reader), treating their helpless subjects in the same way people typically treat theirs, notably animals, or, with even less thought, those microscopic creatures that swarm in a drop of water. The pattern continues relentlessly throughout the novel. Over and over we are told that the Martians' handling of their human victims is exactly as callous as how people behave toward wasps, ants, cattle, sheep, and so on. And Wells goes farther, explicitly likening the Martians' exterminatory approach to their human victims to the English treatment of indigenous Tasmanian people, whom the English had participated in wiping out. In being asked to see oneself in these creatures, with their gigantic heads, lumpish bodies, and giant tentacles, not to mention their blood-drinking habits and exceedingly violent tactics, we may feel shocked into action, even if, at the same time, we cannot avoid a grimace or perhaps a laugh.[11]

But the key observation for us, in considering Wells's allegorical method of approaching empire, is that in all of this rampant allegorizing, the understanding of empire remains consistent and on the surface. As the Martians are to us, so we are to X; they are us and we are they. All of this is stated in the first paragraph, and over the course of the narrative it does not change much, despite the back and forth about who is occupying which role at what point and the active misidentification readers undoubtedly feel toward the Martians. We do not, in other words, gain deeper access to the question of imperial domination than this basic exposure of imperial conquest as simple violence, self-serving and leaning toward extremity. But perhaps this is the point about empire: what we are meant to learn *is* what we already knew.

If allegories, comparisons, riffs, and analogies continually yield a familiar story, what Wells does need to explore is how this circular logic about empire and exploitation can be reconsidered in the light of his world schemes. In this sense Oswald in *Joan and Peter* is a key figure, a Wellsian double who is also an old imperialist, back from his years in Africa and seeing to the education of his wards, Joan and Peter. Oswald makes a passionate case for the world state, but he struggles to get a handle on how empire might connect with this greater world harmony, given the violence and depredation of empire as it is actually prosecuted. As a stepping stone, however, it provides the key transitional logic: "the time has come for our people now to go on from Empire and from Monroe doctrine, great as these ideas have been, to something still greater; the time has come for us to hold out our hands to every man in the world who is ready for a disciplined freedom. The German has dreamt of setting up a Caesar over the whole world. Against that we now set up a disciplined world freedom. For our- selves and all mankind . . ." (*JP*, 569, ellipsis in the original). It was, in fact, a persistent idea for Wells, that the empire might provide the grounds on which his world state would be built, only to fall away once the new structure is in place.

Or put it this way: empire functions as, in effect, *itself the allegory* for what Wells is hoping to install across the world. In Wells's view, no historical empire has ever instantiated the harmonious world state for which he advocates, but they act as iterations, false starts, mutations, perversions, not-quites. Let us recall Wells's frequent lament in *The Outline of History*: the greatest disappointments in history, without question, are leaders like Alexander and Napoleon who, in Wells's formulation, had drawn near the brink of the kind of peaceful, educated, extended human community of his aspirations yet always disastrously fell short, succumbing instead to vanity, intrigue, and violence. And the British Empire, when Wells does discuss it, tends to fall into similar patterns, with the para- mount sense being its waste and stunted imaginary. We might say, then, that the prospect of world unity under present circumstances stands, in relation to Wells's dreams, in a similar relation as the island of Dr. Moreau or the reign of the Martians stands to the British Empire. The model is one of likeness and difference, distorted mirrors, the uncanniness that is such a hallmark of Wells's science fiction. In this sense, empire is not so much missing from Wells's presentation as haunting it. And this helps contextualize, too, Wells's vitriol against the Catholic Church, which reached manic form during World War II; Catholicism, as a movement with worldwide aspirations and an imperial past, stood as a taunting double to his own secular ideal of unity.

If empire occupies a hide-and-seek place across his work, the other most potent model of world unity among Wells's cohort was socialism, and this he is quite willing to consider, argue with and against, variously claim and disown. Wells was always a socialist and identified as such by his contemporaries, even if he rarely credited socialism with the practical prospect of world unification that he sought and that, in different terms, also stood behind socialism for many of its exponents. Definitively not a Marxist, he critiqued Marx over and over in his writings, disagreeing with the central idea of class conflict, among other issues (and when he met with Stalin in 1934, lecturing him on Marx's errors, an admonition that not surprisingly fell on deaf ears). Thus the various Marxist/communist internationals had much less appeal to Wells as a platform for his own world projects than one might have expected. Wells's branch of socialism was always eclectic, and his Fabian training, despite his noisy break with the group and a great deal of critical and parodic rancor toward his former peers, nevertheless left its mark on him; he was largely a gradualist and even more importantly, as Duncan Bell has forcefully argued, a pragmatist.[12] For all of this, socialism was essential to Wells's beliefs about the future and the world because he espoused its essential principles: public control of the world's resources, equality, education, and the importance of disestablishing many existing institutions. "Socialism for me," he wrote in a typical statement, "is a common step we are all taking in the great synthesis of human purpose. It is the organisation, in regard to a great mass of common and fundamental interests, that have hitherto been dispersedly served, of a collective purpose. . . . Socialism is to me no more and no less than the awakening of a collective consciousness in humanity" (FLT, 130, 132). One can see, given the idiosyncrasy of this usage, how easily socialism can lose many of its familiar markers, to become a kind of likeness and precursor for Wells's own ideal order. The imperial is there in Wells's work at a different register, then; a possible world toward which his futures both tilt and tilt away, a kind of other and self to his dreams. Given the dialectical cast of all of Wells's thought, it is only to be expected that his world state would find its mirrors in a socialist-themed paradise and also, perhaps more tellingly, in the violent universe of empire.

But whatever the precursor, and indeed whatever the outcome, Wells's idea of a unified world was always founded on education: education would get us there, it would be a hallmark of the new phase in history, and it would signal that reaching to the heavens that closes out so many of his utopian visions, the sign that the culmination of optimism is not decadence but continued work, discovery, and change. "The main battle before it [world unity]," he wrote in 1934,

> is an educational battle, a battle to make the knowledge that already exists accessible and assimilable and effective. The world has moved from the horse-cart and the windmill to the aeroplane and dynamo but education has made no equivalent advance. The new brains that are pouring into the world are being caught by incompetent and unenlightened teachers, they are being waylaid by the marshalled misconceptions of the past, and imprisoned in rigid narrow historical and political falsifications.[13]

The way forward, for Wells, was clear. Education must become universal, in two senses: universal in that it would be common and available across the globe, and universal in stressing the unifying facts of the world. The unifying disciplines, in Wells's view, were above all science and history, specifically the shared history of mankind, as well as philosophy. Such a model of universalism flies directly in the face of today's contemporary values, where the individuality and diversity of global cultures are precisely their point of entry into any idea of global curriculum. Wells's world, by contrast, is one that moves in and toward the common, gathering in and being built out of diversity rather than celebrating it distinctively. Central to these questions was the idea of a common language, something Wells considered periodically over the course of his writings. In *A Modern Utopia*, to recall an early example, Wells is clear that "the language of Utopia will no doubt be one and indivisible. . . . I fancy it will be a coalesced language, a synthesis of many . . . a profuse vocabulary into which have been cast a dozen once separate tongues."[14] Many of Wells's writings about the future and the world state consider variations on what kind of shared language will or should be developed for his united global people. In writings after *A Modern Utopia*, this language is often speculated to be English (or perhaps Basic English), seemingly for pragmatic rather than ideological reasons, though Wells can wax suspiciously poetical about the "English-speaking world," and his world state in *The Holy Terror* explicitly begins as an Anglo-American alliance. The late-nineteenth-century movements that created universal languages, including the founding of Esperanto in 1887 by Ludwig Lazarus Zamenhof, shared with Wells the overriding goal of unifying the world in the name of peace and mutuality.

Beyond the question of language, universal education in Wells's work is not an afterthought but a site of real urgency. "Human history becomes more and more a race between education and catastrophe": we remember these words from *The Outline of History* and have heard their dialectical resonance all through this study, as these two principles, unequal and nonsimilar, jostle, draw apart, reconnect, and stand off as antagonists. Education pits itself against catastrophe insofar as it pulls people away from war and enmity; that is the key for Wells. His educational agenda, full to the brim from the end of World War I until his death, ranged across different realms but always carried that essential idea that people can and must be taught in a certain spirit, only then to be capable of joining together beyond national claims into a human community.

And they must be taught science. It may be difficult today to appreciate what a small part of the school and university curriculum science played in elite institutions in England before the Second World War. For most of Wells's writing life, to his endless frustration, training in the sciences—biology, chemistry, physics, astronomy, geology—was a specialist vocation (such as in his own case), often treated with suspicion in relation to its threat to a Christian worldview, even fifty years after Darwin, and still associated, in many quarters, with the trades. Wells's advocacy for science and science education was firm and wide ranging, and the scientific community welcomed him into its ranks. The British Academy made him president of the education wing when it was founded in 1936, and he used the occasion of his presidential address to test out his radical ideas about curriculum and the World Brain. His old friend Richard Gregory, the longtime editor of *Nature*, saw Wells as a fellow traveler, and the two collaborated on many projects, small and large, over the decades of their friendship. E. Ray Lankester, a zoologist, evolutionary biologist, and science educator, was also a longtime friend and collaborator, and one of the expert contributors to *The Outline of History*. Wells and Gregory were active in a variety of scientific and science-educative causes over the years, all the way into World War II, when they collaborated on a "Charter of Scientific Fellowship" (1941) whose core precepts articulate the universal nature of science, its critical importance, its necessary autonomy, its connection to liberty and well-being. Science, as the charter invokes it, may be used by fascists, but that borrowing is always, in some fundamental way, a perversion of its tenets ("People of all races and classes of society have contributed to the development of natural forces and resources and the understanding of the universe and mankind's relationships to it," in the charter's words).[15] Wells never strayed from the belief that science was and must be the structure of thought to take the world forward collectively.

We have seen how Wells's educational principles inflect all of his genres, some of which are explicitly educative, such as his works in the popular disciplines, others (many) of which carry educational passages or overtones, and then there were the broad cultural projects aimed at fostering new kinds of education, locally as well as globally. Locally, a primary instance is Wells's long-term involvement with Oundle School (the model for Job Huss's school in *The Undying Fire*), a progressive school run by the innovative headmaster F. W. Sanderson, to which Wells sent his sons and was devoted, conferring with Sanderson on the curriculum and other aspects of the school, providing financial support, and proselytizing for its work. For Wells, Sanderson and his school offered everything that he advocated: a sweeping away of what he felt were the tired old subjects and manners of rote learning, replaced by a vibrant curriculum centering on modern scientific subjects, history, literature, and philosophy. All were taught via collaboration (as in the school's "Scientific Conversaziones"). Most centrally, the school saw itself as a node in a larger creative synthesis, in reciprocal contact with the local community, and looking out onto the world in a spirit of connectedness. Wells was particularly moved by Sanderson's effort, aborted at his sudden death in 1922, to build a "Temple of Vision" at the school, which would provide students with a space for thought and meditation in a setting that told the story of humanity as a single, evolving unit. Sanderson and Oundle were a kind of incarnation of what Wells advocated for and about education. "I think him beyond question the greatest man I have ever known with any degree of intimacy," Wells wrote of Sanderson, high praise given the personal affinities Wells nurtured with so many exceptional people.[16]

Like his idol Huxley, the great scientific educator of the previous generation, Wells took his message about scientific and world education on the road: his educational mission was the subject of lectures, pamphlets, occasional pieces, books, radio broadcasts, even film, to the extent that films such as *Things to Come* and *The Man Who Could Work Miracles* have pedagogical aims. And then there was the World Brain, which collated his ideas about collecting and disseminating knowledge into his plan for a universal encyclopedia whose ultimate function would be to educate the world under new auspices. The encyclopedia, we recall, was to diverge in key respects from existing ones, largely in terms of its continuous updating, its benefiting from new technology, and its connection to thinkers and institutions in all parts of the world. The World Brain "would be the mental background of every intelligent man in the world. It would be alive and growing and changing continually under revision, extension and replacement from the original thinkers in the world everywhere.... It would hold the world together mentally."[17] And Wells believed, as he always did with his utopian visions, that the scheme was practicable and reasonable, thanks to the new technology of microfilm and more generally the ability to reproduce and disperse materials easily and economically. For Wells and the World Brain, the age of mechanical reproduction is a key enabling condition for human collectivity. "There is no practical obstacle whatever now to the creation of an efficient index to *all* human knowledge, ideas and achievements, to the creation, that is, of a complete planetary memory for all mankind," he argued, passionate about its potential. "The whole human memory can be, and probably in a short time will be, made accessible to every individual. . . . This is no remote dream, no fantasy. It is a plain statement of a contemporary state of affairs. It is on the level of practicable fact" (*WB*, 86, 87, italics in the original). The realist of the fantastic, always.

Of course, worlds do not have brains, and Wells's recourse to the metaphor of the collective as a singular body can be disconcerting, especially since it so closely allies with the rhetoric of fascism and other totalitarian movements of the time. His reliance on elites to bring about the revolution, too, has conservative affinities, and some of Wells's followers, unlike Wells himself, would later become infatuated by fascism. Still, metaphorizing the world as a single unit formed a critical part of Wells's thinking well before the Encyclopedia became his focus, including in the 1910s and '20s, when he tested out ideas like the "mind of the [human] race" (*Boon*, 1915) or the "common mental being of our [human] race" (*The World of William Clissold*, 1926), and in his large attempt to consider how to write human lives as part of a species. As he wrote in 1908, "It is not the individual that reproduces himself, it is the species that reproduces through the individual and often in spite of his characteristics. The race flows through us, the race is the drama and we are the incidents. . . . We are episodes in an experience greater than ourselves" (*FLT*, 102). Wells worked throughout his genres to imagine the collective as such, to harness its potential and dismantle the force of its internal parts. The educative project is thus full of paradoxes, as Wells seeks to educate individuals into thinking themselves deindividuated, or to teach that the complexities of the past can add up to a simpler future, or, ultimately, to consider how the immense diversity of the world, as revealed by science, also yields clear laws, patterns, and shared meanings.

For Wells, the ultimate lesson was a simple one, itself a corollary, in his estimation, of the way science works: the saving value of unity. He was constantly holding out for his dream space, the "World City of Mankind," which his biographers Jeanne and Norman MacKenzie see as a secularization of the New Jerusalem (*FLT*, 141). Thus, the familiar warning (in 1921):

> The urgent need for a great creative effort has become apparent in the affairs of mankind. It is manifest that unless some unity of purpose can be achieved in the world, unless the ever more violent and disastrous incidence of war can be averted, unless some common control can be imposed on the headlong waste of man's limited inheritance of coal, oil, and moral energy that is now going on,

the history of humanity must presently culminate in some sort of disaster, repeating and exaggerating the disaster of the great war, producing chaotic social conditions, and going on thereafter in a degenerative process towards extinction.[18]

And in positive terms (from a character in a 1937 novel):

I am bound to believe . . . that this world community will be growing in knowledge, power, beauty, interest, steadily and delightfully. They will be capable of knowledge I cannot even dream about; they will gain powers over space, time, existence, such as we cannot conceive . . . such a great life ahead as will make the whole course of history up to the present day seem like a crazy, incredible nightmare before the dawn.[19]

Wells's readers knew that he, if no one else, could see such "sanity," as he believed it to be, in the midst of world horrors or, rather, that he would find an imaginative bridge between destruction and utopia.

Yet I am pressed to ask, a century later, how his goal for world unification might still matter. What is the value of his view that wars and catastrophe can and must ultimately generate their very antithesis? There may be no direct line from Wells to us in this regard, but his legacy, in other ways, can be found throughout the culture, at those limit points when the temporality of war and peace seems most mutable and enriched with possibility. Throughout these chapters, we have found the idea of war's ending lodged in various spaces of the imagination—the war that *will* end war—and these help collate a range of scenarios and open horizons for thinking about peace. The bedrock view, too, that any person has the authority to intervene in the conception of the world resonates for us in the twenty-first century, with social media unleashing new forms of activism and political organization. With the World Brain, Wells comes close enough to our current models of the democratization of knowledge and information to seem uncanny, but ultimately what signifies less is his prescience than to see how ideals of peace and unification might reinfuse our own. For his contemporaries, it was this accordion-like movement close to a collective dream, and then back away from its realities or comfort level, that characterized his cultural leadership.

Certainly by the 1930s, some commentators felt that Wells's ideal of the world state and his view that war must lead to peace had grown stale and repetitive. Such a judgment derives, in part, from Wells's habitual recasting of the familiar dichotomy: either we are doomed as a species or we are saved, and if so, it will be from collectivizing the globe and taking science as our foundation. As George Orwell complained, in a 1941 essay in which he accuses Wells of losing touch with the genuine threats of the contemporary world, "Much of what Wells has imagined and worked for is physically there in Nazi Germany. The order, the planning, the State encouragement of science, the steel, the concrete, the aeroplanes, are all there, but all in the service of ideas appropriate to the Stone Age. Science is fighting on the side of superstition. But obviously it is impossible for Wells to accept this. It would contradict the world-view on which is own works are based."[20] Orwell is right about one thing in his accusations: Wells did hang on tenaciously to his idea of a planned world, and he did replay his earlier formulae at each new historical juncture. Here he is in 1940, in the preface to *The Rights of Man*, not so much using similar language from decades before as declaring exactly how and why such a return is necessary:

> Even then [in 1917–1918] there was a world-wide feeling that a great revolution in human affairs was imminent; the phrase "a war to end war" expressed that widely diffused feeling.... But that revolution did not realize itself.... Now ... we are back to something very like 1914 and the decisive question before our species is whether this time it will set its face resolutely towards that drastic remoulding of ideas and relationships, that world revolution, which it has shirked for a quarter of a century.[21]

The principle of continuity is overt; Wells still avidly believes, as he did after the First World War, that only unity will save humanity, and he still hopes to capture the emergency of mass warfare to shock people into sharing his view. At the same time, this very passage comes in the context of Wells's declaration of human rights, an undertaking that dramatically advances his earlier efforts, reminding us, contra Orwell, that Wells was consistently updating, modernizing, and rethinking the nature of globalism and the meaning of world citizenship.[22]

What that citizenship entails, here in *The Rights of Man*, is a form of universalized freedom that catapults Wells straight into the postwar world, in fact into our world. The declaration is also referred to as the Sankey Declaration, named for its official sponsor, Lord Sankey, and, as Wells stresses, it represents a collaborative project. At the same time, it bears all the hallmarks of Wells, its primary drafter and disseminator. The declaration consists of ten precepts, following a short preamble, and these are, irrespective of "race or colour," the right to food, housing, clothing, medical care; the right to education; protection of property; protection from misrepresentation and from secret government/police dossiers;

the right to work and to choice in work; the right to movement; the right to buy and sell; freedom from imprisonment without trial; freedom from violence, torture, and sterilization; and the creation of a global legal code to define and enforce these rules. Each of these is spelled out in a paragraph. Though gender is not mentioned, the use of the word "man" is explicitly noted in the paratext as gender inclusive: "using 'man' of course to cover every individual male or female, child or adult, of the species" (*RM*, 14). In the book, too, Wells includes his initial letters to the *Times* that had set in motion the revision and final publication of the declaration. These letters, as noted in chapter 2, argue that at times of great social change and confusion, the Western societies (as he calls them) have historically chosen to restate their basic tenets. Citing the Magna Carta, the American Declaration of Independence, and the French Declaration of the Rights of Man, Wells names the present as one such moment, a time for fundamental assessments and for reclaiming the moral authority of the culture.

There is much to give us pause in this short book, which brims with a sense of moral urgency and employs a rubric distinctive of World War II–era crisis. Some of his ideas, such as freedom of movement, have a familiar Wellsian ring; others sound a new and pressing note, as in the clauses protecting people from imprisonment, loss of freedom, and secret state files. In his capacity as president of PEN, Wells was also deeply involved during these totalitarian years in protecting and rescuing threatened writers. Notably, he is willing to adapt the constituents of global harmony to evolving principles and necessities and to an accounting with the world situation. If he remains stubbornly insistent in his idea that catastrophe must ultimately give us peace, the balance between collective and individual shifts in fascist-era texts like this one, to assert a new formula for individual protection and autonomy. As we have seen, the swings between individual and collective have offered an underlying structure to Wells's thought and writing, and in the opening years of World War II, Wells was ready to reassert a more person-focused model of world belonging, as the forces of history press in the direction of protecting individual rights. These were new directions and a bracing contemporary language, though the motivation and understanding of how and why such rights must be claimed echo throughout Wells's work, picking up, too, on key ethical norms running through Western thought. As Joseph Slaughter notes, "Wells was updating a classical idea that seems to be native to most (if not all) human moral and cultural traditions: war should only be prosecuted in the name of, and for the ends of, peace. For Wells," he reflects, "this is not just any peace, but a perpetual international peace characterized and guaranteed by the universal observance and enjoyment of human rights. A version of Wells' humanitarian war aims were formalized in international law with the adoption of the United Nations General Assembly in 1948."[23] In Slaughter's influential *Human Rights, Inc.: The World Novel, Narrative Form, and International Law*, moreover, he shows that the normalization of human rights has been effected in partnership with the bildungsroman, hence closely linked to literature.[24] But in 1940, the era of human rights had not yet taken hold of world organizations or of the literary imagination.[25]

What is most remarkable about *The Rights of Man*, finally, and what returns us to the overriding question of this book—how does reading Wells change our assessment of this fifty-year period in literary history?—is its unabashed claims on the moral imagination of its time. Wells, as we have seen so many times before, set literature on a path to social amelioration, seeing its *forms* as mutable and impermanent but its power and purpose as firm. This is in many ways the dominant idea that emerges from a reading of Wells's works, that writing need not be diffident, that change need not seem impossible. Over and over, Wells returned to the precept that "there is nothing absolutely unattainable in world law and world justice. More men are capable of realizing this than was ever possible at any previous time. And to be aware of a need is to be half-way toward its satisfaction. We call this stir toward a new order, this refusal to drift on in the old directions, unrest, but rather is it hope which disturbs the world" (*OH*, 2:574–75). Such transformative power may not be limited to the written word, but for Wells, it begins there; his gifts lay in writing, not in political organization. At the same time, literature will only have such broad efficacy if its own parameters are expansive. What counts as literature? Modernism pressed us to ask that question, as we know ("If a writer were a free man and not a slave . . ."), and so does Wells. Popular history? Pamphlet? Film script? Declaration of rights? Martin Puchner has named the manifesto the "poetry of the revolution," and there is no reason why Wells's declaration should not stand proudly in that company.[26] His work on behalf of human rights, following on decades of efforts to end war and bring together a world polity, persists as the last in a long series of literary innovations following and perpetuating his large plans for world peace. Wells's experimentation with form was, in that sense, pragmatic. If received convention does not offer forms to herald in the new world, then one is called to break them up, create new ones, twist and bend and remake literary forms. The point about literature was not to refine it; it was to turn it to account. As against the will to perfection in literary canons, Wells averred, "what I write *goes now*— and will presently die" (*EA*, 532, italics in original).

And what about Wells the person—do we need to extol him or believe in the direction of his work in order to be Wellsians? My answer, of course, is no. In the end, it is a way of scrutinizing, demanding, inventing, and imagining. Wells's old friend Conrad had written that he wanted, above all, to "make you see." Wells also constructs a new line of sight, but much more than this, he offers a vista *for* literature, a challenge. To take a cue from Wells is to pressure ourselves to ask what our idea of a better future might be and how, with the tools at our hands, we might seek to create it. Wells's categories and particular aspirations may not be ours, and his shortcomings are all too visible, but his work is a spur to construct one's own visions for things to come (to borrow his term) and to wonder what kind of writing might now be available to the imagination to launch such projects. It is both modest and immodest: modest because one recognizes the daunting forces that stand in the way of human happiness, peace, and harmony, Wells's goals for us, his successors, and immodest because what Wells teaches is that being one small person is, really, an illusion. It was Wells's view, as we know, that each of us is above all a member of the species, or of the human race, and that each thus contributes to its longevity and prosperity. For all of his attunement to the miniscule nature of our planet in the huge realms of space and time—not to mention the scale of any one single person—still, Wells reminds us that a tiny voice might seem less infinitesimal as it ripples and sounds through a larger space and being, the world. I do not know whether my reader will be convinced that Wells is one of the greatest and most innovative writers of the century. I hope that, in considering Wells's lifetime of writing, that reader— you—will feel motivated to ask of literature, what can and should it do for the world, for tomorrow?

# Notes

## INTRODUCTION

1. In fact, Wells's first publications came as early as 1886, but we might take 1895, the book publication date of *The Time Machine*, as the opening of his major writing career.

2. H. G. Wells, *The Outline of History: Being a Plain History of Life and Mankind*, 2 vols. (New York: Macmillan, 1920), 1:vii.

3. H. G. Wells, *Experiment in Autobiography: Discoveries and Conclusions of a Very Ordinary Brain (Since 1866)* (New York: Macmillan, 1934), 7. Cited hereafter as *EA*.

4. Virginia Woolf, *The Common Reader* (New York: Harcourt Brace Jovanovich, 1984), 150, 154. "Modern Fiction" was written in 1919, first published in 1921, and later collected in *The Common Reader* in 1925.

5. H. G. Wells, *An Englishman Looks at the World: Being a Series of Unrestrained Remarks Upon Contemporary Matters* (1914; fasc. ed., Charleston, SC: BiblioBazaar, 2016), 145–46, italics in the original. Cited hereafter as *ELW*.

6. Other primary manifestos in English literature, frequently anthologized and read today, were produced by Eliot, Forster, Lawrence, Pound, and James.

7. On manifestos and modernism, see Janet Lyon, *Manifestoes: Provocations of the Modern* (Ithaca, NY: Cornell University Press 1999); and Martin Puchner, *Poetry of the Revolution: Marx, Manifestos, and the Avant-Gardes* (Princeton, NJ: Princeton University Press, 2006).

8. That his son Frank Wells and great-grandson Simon Wells both became filmmakers is an added item of interest in the genealogy of Wells and film. By 1937, film adaptations had been made of *The Island of Doctor Moreau*, *The Invisible Man*, *The Passionate Friends*, *Kipps*, *The First Men in the Moon*, and "The Man Who Could Work Miracles"; his own major film, *Things to Come*, was released in 1936. Subsequent years have seen too many adaptations around the world to count.

9. Virginia Woolf, *Three Guineas* (San Diego: Harcourt Brace Jovanovich, 1966), 43; Woolf *The Diary of Virginia Woolf*, vol. 5, *1936–1941* (New York: Harcourt Brace Jovanovich, 1984), 53; George Orwell, *Essays* (New York: Knopf, 2002), 372.

10. Quoted in Patrick Parrinder, ed., *H. G. Wells: The Critical Heritage* (London: Routledge and Kegan Paul, 1972), 332.

11. Wells Collection, University of Illinois Rare Book and Manuscript Library, C-238. Wells and Churchill's is a complex relationship, richly exhumed by the British historian Richard Toye. See

Richard Toye, "'The Great Educator of Unlikely People': H. G. Wells and the Origins of the Welfare State," in *No Wealth but Life: Welfare Economics and the Welfare State in Britain, 1880–1945*, ed. Roger Backhouse and Tamotsu Nishizawa (Cambridge: Cambridge University Press, 2010), 161–88; Richard Toye, "H. G. Wells and Winston Churchill: A Reassessment," in *H. G. Wells: Interdisciplinary Essays*, ed. Steven McClean (Cambridge: Cambridge Scholars Publishing, 2008), 147–61; John Toye and Richard Toye, "One World, Two Cultures? Alfred Zimmern, Julian Huxley, and the Ideological Origins of UNESCO," *History* 95, no. 3 (2010); Richard Toye, "H. G. Wells and the New Liberalism," *Twentieth Century British History* 19, no. 2 (2008): 308–31. For a brief online discussion, see University of Cambridge Research, "Churchill Borrowed Some of His Biggest Ideas from H. G. Wells," November 27, 2006, http://www.cam.ac.uk /research/news/churchill-borrowed-some-of-his-biggest-ideas-from-hg-wells.

12.    Christopher Frayling, *Things to Come* (London: British Film Institute, 1995), 17.

13.    The claim for *The Outline* as one of the most widely read history books excludes textbooks. In fact, Wells envisioned *The Outline* as a kind of textbook and was disappointed that it was not taken up by schools.

14.    Quoted in Charles M. Tung, "Baddest Modernism: The Scales and Lines of Inhuman Time," *Modernism/modernity* 23, no. 3 (2016): 536.

15.    Peter Kemp, *H. G. Wells and the Culminating Ape: Biological Imperatives and Imaginative Obsessions* (1982; London: Macmillan, 1996), 4.

16.    Duncan Bell, "Pragmatic Utopianism and Race: H. G. Wells as Social Scientist," *Modern Intellectual History* (2017): 22.

17.    Thus Bernard Bergonzi, in an influential early study, writes exclusively of "the young Wells," who, he declares, "was, in essentials, a *fin de siècle* writer." See Bergonzi, *The Early H. G. Wells: A Study of the Scientific Romances* (Manchester: Manchester University Press, 1961), 3.

18.    Wells was born in 1866 and died in 1946, at the age of seventy-nine. Yeats, for comparison: 1865–1939.

19.    Qtd. in Norman MacKenzie and Jeanne MacKenzie, *The Life of H. G. Wells: The Time Traveller* (London: Hogarth, 1987), 143.

20.    Of course, I recognize that "modernism" is not a single, simple moniker or an easily reducible quantity. I hope my readers will recognize that, as a student and scholar of the period, dismissing or oversimplifying modernism is not my purpose. We all know that modernism won; at stake, in the wake of seventy years of modernist aesthetics dominating in the matter of literary value, is to make an experiment (isn't that what modernism was supposed to be about?) and to see what happens when we are willing to play with the idea of our familiar modernism as the narrower, more nationalist, more turf obsessed, perhaps even less inventive of the day's innovators.

21.    As discussed more fully hereafter, this not being a biographical study, I am less concerned to document the specific interactions of Wells with modernists, though some of these will be treated along the way, than to show how his work and modernism can be read and understood together. For discussion of these relationships, see Nicholas Delbanco, *Group Portrait: Joseph Conrad, Stephen Crane, Ford Madox Ford, Henry James, and H. G. Wells* (New York: William Morrow, 1982); J. R. Hammond, *H. G. Wells and Rebecca West* (New York: Harvester, 1991); Linda Dryden, *Joseph Conrad and H. G. Wells: The Fin-de-Siècle Literary Scene* (London: Palgrave Macmillan, 2015); and Linda R. Anderson, *Bennett, Wells, and Conrad: Narrative in Transition* (Houndmills: Macmillan, 1988).

22.    Modernists attacked him as a matter of course. In addition to Woolf, T. S. Eliot can be found sneering at Wells in his *New Criterion*. In its opening editorial, Eliot promised that these pages would not feature the likes of Wells. T. S. Eliot, "The Idea of a Quarterly Review," *New Criterion* 4, no. 1 (February 1926): 6.

23. David James and Urmila Seshagiri, "Metamodernism: Narratives of Continuity and Revolution," *PMLA* 129, no. 1 (2014): 87.

24. Frank Budgen, *James Joyce and the Making of "Ulysses"* (New York: Harrison Smith, 1934), 21.

25. At the annual Modernist Studies Association conference in 2012, I led a seminar entitled "Major Minor Modernism," the premise of which was to consider writers who had been major figures in the period but who have now slipped out of the field. The category elicited excellent papers, and the seminar participants demonstrated that this category extends very fruitfully beyond Wells.

26. *The Commonsense of World Peace* was given as a lecture in the Reichstag in Berlin earlier that year. Of *Democracy Under Revision* being published by Hogarth, Woolf writes in her diary "this is a great rise in the world for us." Virginia Woolf, *The Diary of Virginia Woolf*, vol. 3, *1925–1930* (New York: Harcourt Brace Jovanovich, 1980), 128.

27. Another tantalizing connection or near miss: according to Wells's biographer, David C. Smith, Virginia and Leonard Woolf were invited to be in the audience for Wells's initial BBC appearance, its first with a live audience. However, I have not been able to ascertain if they in fact were present and therefore assume they were not.

28. Woolf, *Diary*, 3:90, 5:53.

29. E. M. Forster, *Aspects of the Novel* (San Diego: Harcourt, 1955), 72.

30. For discussion of this relationship and its ramifications for literature, see Dryden, *Joseph Conrad and H. G. Wells*. We might note that some see the unpleasant portrait of the Eastern European sea captain in *Tono-Bungay* as a caricature of Conrad.

31. Joseph Conrad, *The Secret Agent: A Simple Tale* (1907; London: Penguin, 2007), 2.

32. Wells Collection, University of Illinois Rare Book and Manuscript Library, C400-35.

33. Quoted in Dryden, *Joseph Conrad and H. G. Wells*, 21.

34. Joseph Conrad to H. G. Wells, September 6, 1898, in H. G. Wells, *The Correspondence of H. G. Wells*, vol. 1, *1880–1903*, ed. David. C. Smith (London: Pickering and Chatto, 1998), 320–21.

35. Wellsian echoes can be found in other works by Conrad, too. We might note that though Conrad was older than Wells, Wells nevertheless acted as something of a patron early on, favorably reviewing both *Almayer's Folly* and *An Outcast of the Islands*, Conrad's first novels.

36. This relationship has received some treatment from biographers and literary critics. See Hammond, *H. G. Wells and Rebecca West*; and, for their letters, Gordon N. Ray, *H. G. Wells and Rebecca West* (New Haven, CT: Yale University Press, 1974).

37. Delbanco, *Group Portrait*, 18–19.

38. Forster, *Aspects*, 163.

39. Leon Edel and Gordon N. Ray, *Henry James and H. G. Wells: A Record of Their Friendship, Their Debate on the Art of Fiction, and Their Quarrel* (Urbana: University of Illinois Press, 1958), 104.

40. H. G. Wells, *Boon: The Mind of the Race, The Wild Asses of the Devil, and The Last Trump; Being a First Selection from the Literary Remains of George Boon, Appropriate to the Times* (1915; facsimile repr. London: Fisher Unwin, 1920), 101, ellipses in the original.

41. We cannot, by contrast, imagine Woolf advancing the proposition that her novel should sit with Lily Briscoe's painting in the attic or the servant's quarters. Notably, Wells repeated this language of himself as a journalist in one of his lunches with Woolf and her circle, as she reports in her diary in 1926.

42. The neglect of Wells today can be tabulated in various ways. The MLA bibliography lists just twenty-nine books (monographs, edited collections, or collections of his own writings) with his name in the title published in the last thirty years (compare this with 240 for Woolf over the same period), and the number of articles with Wells's name in the title ever to appear in the premier journal *Modernism/modernity* is zero. When one includes thematic books in which author names do not appear in the title but that focus on a handful of writers from the period (the majority of

academic monographs), the disparity between Wells's appearance and that of Woolf and her peers is far starker. As for the specialist journal *The Wellsian*, my own research library (Columbia University) did not subscribe to it until I requested it.

43. Even the Penguin series has cut back; both *Ann Veronica* and *The New Machiavelli* have been pulled from print, a casualty of shockingly low sales. Fortunately for readers, given their huge dissemination during his life, Wells's books are readily available and affordable for purchase online, either in out-of-print editions or in the form of reprints.

44. As an example: in later years Forster described his 1909 dystopic short story, "The Machine Stops," as a response to "one of the earlier heavens of Wells"; one wonders what he could have been reading, though, since no works written at that time match Forster's suggestion. Cited in P. N. Furbank, *E. M. Forster: A Life* (London: Cardinal, 1991), 162.

45. Even such proud Wellsians as Darko Suvin, Bernard Bergonzi, and Roger Luckhurst, who credit Wells with founding the primary literary and cognitive ideas at the basis of science fiction, are quick to distance themselves from the vast bulk of his later/other writing. Here is Bergonzi: "I am assuming as axiomatic that the bulk of Wells's published output has lost whatever *literary* interest it might have had, and is not likely to regain it in the foreseeable future, whatever value it may possess for the social historian or the historian of ideas." *The Early H. G. Wells*, 165.

46. Debra Rae Cohen, "Getting the Fame Into the Picture: Wells, West, and the Mid-War Novel," *The Space Between* 8, no. 1 (2012): 89.

47. Patrick Parrinder's work is particularly important and extensive, with key scholarly volumes such as *H. G. Wells: The Critical Heritage* (London: Routledge and Kegan Paul, 1972); and Patrick Parrinder and John S. Partington, eds., *The Reception of H. G. Wells in Europe* (London: Continuum, 2005), along with other edited collections such as Patrick Parrinder and Christopher Rolfe, eds., *H. G. Wells Under Revision* (Selinsgrove, PA: Susquehanna University Press, 1990); his own monographs, *Shadows of the Future: H. G. Wells, Science Fiction, and Prophecy* (Syracuse, NY: Syracuse University Press, 1995); and *H. G. Wells* (Edinburgh: Edinburgh University Press, 1970); important work in science-fiction studies with a strong Wellsian component such as Patrick Parrinder, ed., *Learning from Other Worlds: Estrangement, Cognition, and the Politics of Science Fiction and Utopia* (Durham, NC: Duke University Press, 2001); and his superb editing of the 2005 Penguin series. Also see John S. Partington, *Building Cosmopolis: The Political Thought of H. G. Wells* (Aldershot: Ashgate, 2003).

48. J. R. Hammond, *H. G. Wells and the Modern Novel* (Houndmills: Macmillan, 1988).

49. Simon J. James, *Maps of Utopia: H. G. Wells, Modernity, and the End of Culture* (Oxford: Oxford University Press, 2012), xi.

50. Wells himself used the terms "scientific romance" or "fantasia of possibility," "science fiction" being a later coinage.

51. Darko Suvin, introduction to *H. G. Wells and Modern Science Fiction*, ed. Darko Suvin, assoc. ed. Robert M. Philmus (Lewisburg, PA: Bucknell University Press, 1977), 28–29.

52. Roger Luckhurst, *Science Fiction* (Cambridge: Polity, 2005), 31.

53. The phrase comes in a letter: "O! Realist of the Fantastic, whether you like it or not. And if you want to know what impresses me it is to see how you contrive to give over humanity into the clutches of the Impossible and yet manage to keep it down (or up) to its humanity, to its flesh, blood, sorrow, folly. *That* is an achievement! In this little book you do it with an appalling completeness. I'll not insist upon the felicity of incident. This must be obvious even to yourself. Three of us have been reading the book . . . and we have been tracking with delight the cunning method of your logic. It is masterly—it is ironic—it is very relentless—and it is very true." Wells Collection, University of Illinois Rare Book and Manuscript Library, C 400-11.

54. H. G. Wells, preface to *The Scientific Romances of H. G. Wells* (London: Victor Gollancz, 1933), viii, italics in the original, ellipses added.

55. One might register the convergences between modernism and science fiction around the issue of estrangement. Patrick Parrinder notes that "since the formalists, estrangement has usually been interpreted as a sign of experimental and Modernist art. Picasso's painting of the head of a woman showing both eyes on the same side of the nose is an example of what would commonly be called an estrangement effect." Patrick Parrinder, "Revisiting Suvin's Poetics of Science Fiction," in *Learning from Other Worlds*, ed. Parrinder, 37.

56. See Darko Suvin, *Metamorphoses of Science Fiction: On the Poetics and History of a Literary Genre* (New Haven, CT: Yale University Press, 1979).

57. Cited in Richard Ellmann, *James Joyce* (Oxford: Oxford University Press, 1983), 414.

58. H. G. Wells, "James Joyce," *New Republic*, March 10, 1917.

59. Wells makes other appearances in *Ulysses* as well. In "Circe," during Bloom's moment of political ascendency, he orates: "I stand for the reform of municipal morals and the plain ten commandments. New worlds for old [the title of a book by H. G. Wells from 1908]. Union of all, jew, moslem and gentile. Three acres and a cow for all children of nature. Saloon motor hearses. Compulsory manual labour for all. All parks open to the public day and night. Electric dishscrubbers. Tuberculosis, lunacy, war and mendicancy must now cease. General amnesty, weekly carnival with masked license, bonuses for all, esperanto the universal language with universal brotherhood [two major Wellsian principles, as everyone knew]. No more patriotism or barspongers and dropsical impostors. Free money, free rent, free love and a free lay church in a free lay state [all Wells's causes, though not as closely identified with him]." James Joyce, *Ulysses* (1922; New York: Random House, 1986), 399.

60. H. G. Wells to James Joyce, November 23, 1928, in H. G. Wells, *The Correspondence of H. G. Wells*, vol. 3, *1919–1934*, ed. David. C. Smith (London: Pickering and Chatto, 1998), 277. We should note that Smith's volume misquotes this letter, with the penultimate paragraph ending "To me it is a dreadful end." Copies of the original letter, held at the University of Illinois Rare Book and Manuscript Library, confirm "dead" over "dreadful."

61. E. M. Forster, *Two Cheers for Democracy* (New York: Harcourt, 1951), 67.

62. Virginia Woolf, *To the Lighthouse* (1927; San Diego: Harcourt, 1981), 161.

63. Even the "world" of "world literature," to take what might seem a counterdirection, is always on guard against the prospects of imperialism, standardization, or totalization. The turn to planetary over global paradigms is thus offered in a spirit of antitotalizing principles, a shift "from *globe* as financial-technocratic system toward *planet* as world-ecology." Amy J. Elias and Christian Moraru, "Introduction: The Planetary Condition," in *The Planetary Turn: Relationality and Geoaesthetics in the Twenty-First Century* (Evanston, IL: Northwestern University Press, 2015) xiv, italics in the original.

64. Mark Wollaeger, introduction to *The Oxford Handbook of Global Modernisms*, ed. Mark Wollaeger and Matthew Eatough (New York: Oxford University Press, 2012), 12.

65. Paul K. Saint-Amour, "Weak Theory, Weak Modernism," *Modernism/modernity* 3, no. 3 (2018): 440.

66. H. G. Wells, *The Open Conspiracy: Blue Prints for a World Revolution* (London: Victor Gollancz, 1928), 33; cited hereafter as *OC*.

67. H. G. Wells, *The Common Sense of World Peace* (London: Hogarth, 1929), 18, 22, 26.

68. Today, when scholars have begun to rethink the scales and timeframes through which history and the present can be known, under the rubrics especially of the Anthropocene and the planetary, Wells's extensive writings in these modes spring back to vibrant relevance. Matthew A. Taylor writes that "like Dipesh Chakravarty, Wai Chee Dimock, Gayatri Chakravorty Spivak, and other contributors to the 'planetary turn' . . . , Wells fashions possible worlds out of the husk of an apocalyptic globalization, offering a redeemed telluric scope as a means of non-self-destructive unification. He, like them, inverts the negative image of global conflict to picture an affirmative planetarity." Matthew A. Taylor, "At Land's End: Novel Spaces and the Limits of Planetarity," *NOVEL:*

*A Forum on Fiction* 49, no. 1 (2016): 124. Similarly, Charles Tung ("Baddest Modernism") finds Wells an originator and contributor to broader modernist efforts to think in new scales about space and time, cued specifically to the planet. For a discussion of *The Time Machine* as a "romance of the anthropocene," see Aaron Rosenberg, "Romancing the Anthropocene: H. G. Wells and the Novel of the Future," *NOVEL: A Forum on Fiction* 51, no. 1 (2018): 79–100.

69.    H. G. Wells, *World Brain* (Garden City, NY: Doubleday, 1938), 40–41. Cited hereafter as *WB*.

70.    As a general rule, in Wells's works, race means the human race. There are exceptions, which I will note when referencing them. His most extensive treatment of race per se is the chapter "The Races of Mankind" in *The Outline of History.*

71.    H. G. Wells, *The World of William Clissold: A Novel at a New Angle* (London: Ernest Benn, 1926), 87–88, 89–90. Cited hereafter as *WC*.

72.    T. S. Eliot, "Tradition and the Individual Talent" (1921), in *The Sacred Wood and Major Early Essays* (Mineola, NY: Dover, 1998), 29; W. B. Yeats, "Ideas of Good and Evil" (1903), in *Essays and Introductions* (New York: Macmillan, 1961), 36.

73.    H. G. Wells, *The Time Machine* (1895; London: Penguin, 2005), 84.

74.    Wells, *The Outline of History*, 1:4, italics in the original.

75.    See Frederic Jameson, "Modernism and Imperialism," in Terry Eagleton, Frederic Jameson, and Edward Said, *Nationalism, Colonialism, and Literature* (Minneapolis: University of Minnesota Press, 1990).

76.    Modernist studies has become acutely interested in such approaches, as, for instance, in the searching analysis of Jed Esty and Colleen Lye into the question of "peripheral realisms," by which they mean an approach to totality always conscious of its limitations, played out around the world; Cóilín Parsons's account of how "planetarity . . . is an incomplete endeavor, and yet we can recognize the already existing tendrils of planetarity in modernism"; or Tung's sense that "well before the recent 'speculative turn' in philosophy . . . modernism began to inject into the moment and literary form a scaling up and a scoping out to inhuman times." See Jed Esty and Colleen Lye, "Peripheral Realisms Now," *Modern Language Quarterly* 73, no. 3 (September 2012): 269–88; Cóilín Parsons, "Planetary Parallax: *Ulysses*, the Stars, and South Africa," *Modernism/modernity* 24, no. 1 (2017): 82; and Tung, "Baddest Modernism," 519. See also the *Modernism/modernity* print plus special issue on scale and form: https://modernismmodernity.org/forums/scale-and-form.

77.    H. G. Wells, *Early Writings in Science and Science Fiction*, ed. Robert M. Philmus and David Y. Hughes (Berkeley: University of California Press, 1975), 20–21. Cited hereafter as *EWS*.

78.    See Paul K. Saint-Amour, *Tense Future: Modernism, Total War, Encyclopedic Form* (New York: Oxford University Press, 2015).

79.    Frayling, *Things to Come*, 17.

80.    Wells Collection, University of Illinois Rare Book and Manuscript Library, C-238.

81.    H. G. Wells, *The War in the Air* (1980; London: Penguin, 2005), 73. Cited hereafter as *WA*.

82.    Keith Williams, *H. G. Wells, Modernity, and the Movies* (Liverpool: Liverpool University Press, 2007), 1.

83.    For discussion of literary modernism and the modernization of the home, see Victoria Rosner, *Machines for Living* (New York: Oxford University Press, forthcoming).

84.    Le Corbusier, *The Radiant City* (New York: Orion, 1964), 181, italics in the original.

85.    For a discussion of the brief connection between Le Corbusier and *Things to Come*, see Frayling, *Things to Come.*

86.    I wish to thank Therese Cox for initially drawing my attention to the Wells–Le Corbusier connection and for pointing me to the BBC anecdote.

87.    And if we believe Paul Saint-Amour, we should add pianola to this list. See Paul K. Saint-Amour, "*Ulysses* Pianola," *PMLA* 130, no. 1 (January 2015): 15–36.

88.    On modernism and media, a large field, see, for instance, Katherine Biers, *Virtual Modernism: Writing and Technology in the Progressive Era* (Minneapolis: University of Minnesota Press, 2013); Debra Rae Cohen, Michael Coyle, and Jane Lewty, eds., *Broadcasting Modernism* (Jacksonville: University of Florida Press, 2009); Mark Goble, *Beautiful Circuits: Modernism and the Mediated Life* (New York: Columbia University Press, 2010); Andreas Huyssen, *After the Great Divide: Modernism, Mass Culture, Postmodernism* (Ann Arbor: University of Michigan Press, 1986); Julian Murphet, *Multimedia Modernism: Literature and the American Avant-Garde* (Cambridge: Cambridge University Press, 2009); Michael North, *Camera Works: Photography and the Twentieth-Century Word* (Oxford: Oxford University Press, 2005); and Mark Wollaeger, *Modernism, Media, and Propaganda: British Narrative from 1900–1945* (Princeton, NJ: Princeton University Press, 2006).

89.    In our era of fake news, cyberbullying, cyberterrorism, hacking, and the rest, one returns to Wells's essential insight about the potentially disastrous realities that follow when technology leads and thought about it lags well behind. With driverless cars and an entirely online world in sight, a Wellsian would wonder, will it ever be possible to understand first and apply later?

90.    H. G. Wells, *The King Who Was a King: The Book of a Film* (London: Ernest Benn, 1929), 17.

91.    Laura Marcus, *The Tenth Muse: Writing About Cinema in the Modernist Period* (Oxford: Oxford University Press, 2007), 47–48.

92.    For an excellent discussion of Wells and the BBC, see Todd Avery, *Radio Modernism: Literature, Ethics, and the BBC, 1922–1938* (Hampshire: Ashgate, 2006), 75–109.

93.    Hilda Mattheson to H. G. Wells, June 19, 1929, BBC Archive, http://www.bbc.co.uk/archive /hg_wells/12421.shtml.

94.    Quoted in MacKenzie and MacKenzie, *The Life of H. G. Wells*, 117.

95.    H. G. Wells, "The Novel of Ideas," in *Babes in the Darkling Wood* (New York: Alliance Book Company, 1940), xii–xiii.

96.    On the robust topic of self-help in the United States, see Alfred H. Katz, *Self-Help in America: A Social Movement Perspective* (New York: Twayne, 1993); Micki McGee, *Self-Help, Inc.: Makeover Culture in America* (Oxford: Oxford University Press, 2005); and Sandra K. Dolby, *Self-Help Books: Why Americans Keep Reading Them* (Urbana: University of Illinois Press, 2005).

97.    MacKenzie and MacKenzie, *The Life of H. G. Wells*, 41.

98.    See Peter J. Bowler, *Science for All: The Popularization of Science in Early-Twentieth-Century Britain* (Chicago: University of Chicago Press, 2009).

99.    To name one reader of *The Science of Life*: Virginia Woolf, whom Hermione Lee describes on several occasions as reading Wells as part of her self-education in the sciences. Woolf critics have tended to seize on her reading of other scientists, such as James Jeans, in considering works like *The Waves*, seeing Wells only as an antagonist, rarely as an influence or stimulator of her thought.

100.    The most scholarly biographies are David C. Smith, *H. G. Wells: Desperately Mortal, a Biography* (New Haven, CT: Yale University Press, 1986); MacKenzie and MacKenzie, *The Life of H. G. Wells*; and Michael Sherborne, *H. G. Wells: Another Kind of Life* (London: Peter Owen, 2010). Others include Lovat Dickson, *H. G. Wells: His Turbulent Life and Times* (New York: Atheneum, 1969); Michael Draper, *H. G. Wells* (Houndmills: Macmillan 1987); Anthony West, *H. G. Wells: Aspects of a Life* (London: Hutchinson, 1984); Geoffrey West, *H. G. Wells: A Sketch for a Portrait* (London: Gerald Howe, 1930), Wells's authorized biography; and W. Warren Wagar, *H. G. Wells: Traversing Time* (Middletown, CT: Wesleyan University Press, 2004).

101.    H. G. Wells, *Anticipations of the Reaction of Mechanical and Scientific Progress Upon Human Life and Thought* (London: Harper and Brothers, 1902), 324.

102.    Rupert Hart Davis, *Hugh Walpole: A Biography* (London: Macmillan, 1952), 68, qtd. in Dryden, *Joseph Conrad and H. G. Wells*, 110.

## 1. VOICE

1.  Jonathan Rose, *The Intellectual Life of the British Working Classes* (New Haven, CT: Yale University Press, 2001), 139.

2.  For Wells's influence on the English political scene, see several works by Richard Toye: "'The Great Educator of Unlikely People': H. G. Wells and the Origins of the Welfare State," in *No Wealth but Life: Welfare Economics and the Welfare State in Britain, 1880–1945*, ed. Roger E. Backhouse and Tamotsu Nishizawa (Cambridge: Cambridge University Press, 2012), 161–88; "H. G. Wells and the New Liberalism," *Twentieth Century British History* 19, no. 2 (2008): 156–85; "H. G. Wells and Winston Churchill: A Reassessment," in *H. G. Wells: Interdisciplinary Essays*, ed. Steven McClean (Newcastle: Cambridge Scholars Publishing, 2008), 147–61. David Smith's biography also details Wells's relationships with the political elite: David Smith, *H. G. Wells: Desperately Mortal* (New Haven, CT: Yale University Press, 1986).

3.  This number of two million is given by several of Wells's biographers: Michael Draper, *H. G. Wells* (New York: St. Martin's, 1988); and Norman MacKenzie and Jeanne MacKenzie, *The Life of H. G. Wells: The Time Traveller* (London: Hogarth, 1987), 324.

4.  See Patrick Parrinder and John S. Partington, eds., *The Reception of H. G. Wells in Europe* (London: Continuum, 2005).

5.  "A world figure with a world audience," in Lovat Dickson's phrase. Lovat Dickson, *H. G. Wells: His Turbulent Life and Times* (New York: Atheneum, 1969), 282.

6.  See Rebecca Walkowitz, *Born Translated: The Contemporary Novel in an Age of World Literature* (New York: Columbia University Press, 2015).

7.  George Orwell, *Essays* (New York: Knopf, 2002), 372.

8.  In attempting to uncover key aspects of this voice, I will be focusing on his texts themselves, rather than extending an empirical analysis of his readers or their reactions to his works (an audience study of the sort Rose so admirably practices). Such a sociology of reading, in the context of an analysis of the publishing market in the period, would contribute to a broader picture of Wells as a writer who spoke to diverse readers and evaded the more familiar configurations of high-, middle-, and lowbrow.

9.  H. G. Wells, *The Time Machine* (New York: Penguin, 2005), 39–40. Cited hereafter as *TM*.

10. Of his biographers, Jeanne and Norman MacKenzie go furthest in tracing his thought and writing almost entirely to his personal history and, even more specifically, to his young childhood.

11. Maud Ellmann, *The Poetics of Impersonality: T. S. Eliot and Ezra Pound* (Brighton: Harvester, 1987).

12. As an example of extreme self-misrecognition, we might note that Wells typically flew off the handle at the suggestion of autobiographical content in his works.

13. For discussion of the roman à clef in modernism, with a nod toward Wells in its introduction, see Seth Latham, *The Art of Scandal: Modernism, Libel Law, and the Roman à Clef* (New York: Oxford University Press, 2009).

14. His sexual autobiography is published as *H. G. Wells in Love: Postscript to an Experiment in Autobiography*, ed. G. P. Wells (London: Faber, 1984).

15. H. G. Wells, *Love and Mr. Lewisham: The Story of a Very Young Couple* (London: Weidenfield & Nicols, 2010), 2. Cited hereafter as *LL*.

16. H. G. Wells, *The History of Mr. Polly* (New York: Penguin, 2005), 76, 186. Cited hereafter as *MP*.

17. The inn is based in part on one of the few places Wells as a child had experienced physical beauty and a bit of easy, natural pleasure, Surly Hall, his uncle Tom's inn.

18. Richard Higgins, "Feeling Like a Clerk in H. G. Wells," *Victorian Studies* 50, no. 3 (2008): 457–75.

19. Robert Caserio, "Abstraction, Impersonality, Dissolution," in *The Cambridge Companion to Modernist Autobiography*, ed. Maria DiBattista and Emily O. Wittman (Cambridge: Cambridge University Press, 214), 197–214.

20. Michel de Montaigne, *Essays*, trans. J. M. Cohen (London: Penguin, 1993), 23.

21. H. G. Wells, *The First Men in the Moon* (London: Penguin, 2005), 129, ellipses in the original, quotes marking internal dialogue.

22. Qtd. in Patrick Parrinder, ed., *H. G. Wells: The Critical Heritage* (London: Routledge and Kegan Paul, 1972), 246.

23. Harvey N. Quamen, "Unnatural Interbreeding: H. G. Wells's *A Modern Utopia* as Species and Genre," *Victorian Literature and Culture* 33 (2005): 67.

24. H. G. Wells, *A Modern Utopia* (New York: Penguin, 2005), 246–247, italics in the original, to signal the Owner's voice. Cited hereafter as *MU*.

25. Wells came back to *The Republic* repeatedly in his writings (an example: he has the protagonist of *The Research Magnificent* give a copy to his future wife, and her reaction to it helps confirm his choice).

26. One could name many such examples: in *The World of William Clissold*, Clissold remarks derisively that his cousin "Wells" had made a hash of the idea of God in one of his recent books (*WC*, 92–93); Oswald in *Joan and Peter* dismisses various contemporary thinkers, including Wells, whom he waves away as a "counter-jumper." H. G. Wells, *Joan and Peter: The Story of an Education* (New York: Macmillan, 1922), 273, cited hereafter as *JP*.

27. H. G. Wells, *The Island of Doctor Moreau* (London: Penguin, 2005), 131. Cited hereafter as *IDM*.

28. H. G. Wells, *Tono-Bungay* (London: Penguin, 2005), 9, 12, 11, 11. Cited hereafter as *TB*.

29. It was C. F. G. Masterman who coined that term, having just read *Tono-Bungay* and with it in mind.

30. Waste is a central metaphor in the novel, named as such by George, and it is an important theme throughout Wells's corpus. I will discuss the topic of waste in chapter 4.

31. H. G. Wells, *Mr. Britling Sees It Through* (New York: Macmillan, 1917), 428–29, all italics and ellipses in the original. Cited hereafter as *MB*.

32. It is possible that they are meant to read as "And make an End to them." I thank the anonymous reader at Columbia University Press for this suggestion.

33. Branka Arsić, *Bird Relics: Grief and Vitalism in Thoreau* (Cambridge, MA: Harvard University Press, 2016), 12–13.

34. H. G. Wells, *An Englishman Looks at the World, Being a Series of Unrestrained Remarks Upon Contemporary Matters* (Charleston, SC: Bibliobazaar, 2016), 145, 146.

35. Robert Caserio, "The Novel as a Novel Experiment in Statement: The Anticanonical Example of H. G. Wells," in *Decolonizing Tradition: New Views of Twentieth-Century "British" Literary Canons*, ed. Karen R. Lawrence (Urbana: University of Illinois Press, 1992), 91.

36. H. G. Wells, *The Undying Fire: A Contemporary Novel* (New York: Macmillan, 1919), 60. Cited hereafter as *UF*.

37. Advertising is a big theme in Wells's works; *Tono-Bungay*, *The World of William Clissold*, and *The Sleeper Awakes* offer especially lavish and exceptionally prescient visions of the future of/as advertisement. For the most influential work on advertising and modernism, see Jennifer Wicke, *Advertising Fictions: Literature, Advertisement, and Social Reading* (New York: Columbia University Press, 1988).

38. A similar configuration organizes *Things to Come*, in the person of Theotocopulos the artist/philosopher who leads the opposition against the benevolent world state that Wells, again, would seem wholeheartedly to endorse—except that he gives Theotocopulos such wonderful language and charisma, and a following too.

39. A similar point can be made about Wells's main themes, especially in the scientific romances: they typically come to revolve around a central contradiction or self-division. Much of the best criticism of his works focuses on these divisions. Even John Cary, who initially attacks Wells vigorously, adds a second Wells chapter in which he changes the tune, regarding him ultimately as self-divided on his approach to mass culture.

40. H. G. Wells, *The Outline of History*, 2 vols. (New York: Macmillan, 1920), 2:594. Cited hereafter as *OH*.

41. As an aside to Wells's treatment of the submarine as the epitome of human ingenuity turning to sadistic cruelty: his choice of the submarine might recall readers (today and when the novel was published) of the person to whom Wells was most often compared in his first years of writing, Jules Verne. At the center of *Twenty-Thousand Leagues Under the Sea* (and later *The Mysterious Island*) is a real wonder of man's making, the *Nautilus*, a submarine that showcases the most admirable feats of engineering, culture, art, and the scientific imagination. Verne may not have been on Wells's mind, of course—there were plenty of real submarines to inspire him—but there is a sense, I think, of Wells refuting the easy optimism of his forebear in favor of the more haunted and complex pessimism/optimism of his own work.

42. Susan Sontag borrowed the phrase for an early essay on science fiction. Susan Sontag, "The Imagination of Disaster," *Commentary*, October 1965, 42–48.

43. H. G. Wells, *The World Set Free* (New York: E. P. Dutton, 1914), 139. Cited hereafter as *WSF*.

44. H. G. Wells, *The War of the Worlds* (New York: Penguin, 2005), 7. Cited hereafter as *WW*.

45. Jed Esty, "Modernist Worlds at War: Wells, Welles, Spielberg, and Anglo-American Paranoia," unpublished paper, Rutgers University, New Brunswick, NJ, October 2013.

46. As a later example, Mina Loy uses the word "infusoria" in "Lunar Baedeker."

47. T. S. Eliot, *The Waste Land* (New York: Norton, 2001), 5.

48. T. S. Eliot, *Selected Prose of T. S. Eliot* (San Diego: Harcourt, 1975), 65, italics in the original.

49. These scenes are suggestive of the film *The Wizard of Oz* (1939), when Dorothy watches the tornado from her window as on a screen. L. Frank Baum's book from 1896 does not mention Dorothy looking out from the flying house, this being one of many instances of filmic self-consciousness characterizing Fleming's movie.

50. Keith Williams, *H. G. Wells, Modernity, and the Movies* (Liverpool: Liverpool University Press, 2007), 1, 2.

51. Laura Marcus, *The Tenth Muse: Writing About Cinema in the Modernist Period* (Oxford: Oxford University Press, 2007), 45, 44.

52. H. G. Wells, *The Complete Short Stories of H. G. Wells* (London: Ernest Benn, 1970), 283, 282. Cited hereafter as *Stories*.

53. It seems the model, in all of these ways, for Forster's "The Other Side of the Hedge" (1911).

54. H. G. Wells, *The Invisible Man* (New York: Dover, 1992), 91. See Deaglán Ó Donghaile, *Blasted Literature: Victorian Political Fiction and the Shock of Modernism* (Edinburgh: Edinburgh University Press, 2011). For discussion of political violence in the context of dynamite, anarchism, and terrorism, see also my *At the Violet Hour: Modernism and Violence in England and Ireland* (New York: Oxford University Press, 2012), 83–129.

55. Maren Tova Linett, *Bodies of Modernism: Physical Disability in Transatlantic Modernist Literature* (Ann Arbor: University of Michigan Press, 2016), 63.

56. Wells felt rage and contempt for Kipling's imperial tales, which he believed did appreciable harm. Wells took Kipling's model of English superiority and what he viewed as Kipling's espousal of bullying and violence against Britain's colonial subjects as a primary foil to his own ideal of world unity.

57. The story's ending is ambiguous; in the original version, an injured and weak Nunez climbs out of the valley, watching the glory of the setting sun from a cliff above the village, opting for death and sight rather than an operation to have his eyes removed; in a later revision, Wells has the valley destroyed by landslide while Nunez and Medina-saroté escape.

58. H. G. Wells, *The Country of the Blind, Typescript of Film Scenario*, 2nd rev., p. 10, New York Public Library, Berg Collection

59. To clarify, this passage does not describe the Bladesover estate, the one in whose aura George grows up. Bladesover is modeled on Up Park, where Wells's mother worked as a ladies' maid and his father as a gardener.

## 2. CIVILIAN

1. H. G. Wells, *The War in the Air* (1908; New York: Penguin, 2005), 126. Cited hereafter as *WA*.

2. I am using the term "civilian" in this sense of noncombatant (*OED*: "a non-military man or official"), a usage first reported in 1766. Following the root word "civil" takes us first to the community of citizens (civil society/life), to civilization, and to civility. The attributes that cluster in these separate terms are all embedded in the sense of urgency, crisis, and conviction in the civilian story I am telling in this chapter.

3. Mary Favret, *War at a Distance: Romanticism and the Making of Modern Wartime* (Princeton, NJ: Princeton University Press, 2009).

4. In today's wars, civilians represent an astonishing 75 percent or more of total deaths, a percentage that has been steadily rising since World War I (WWI: 20%; WWII: 50%). All numbers provided in Daniel Rothbert, Karina V. Korostelina, and Mohammed D. Cherkaoui, eds., *Civilians and Modern War: Armed Conflict and the Ideology of Violence* (London: Routledge, 2012), 3. The editors stress that civilian deaths are not always answerable to "the brute force of bullets or bombs, but the deprivation of essential needs caused by the condition of war—[including] disease and the effects of famine" (3–4).

5. H. G. Wells, *First and Last Things: A Confession of Faith and Rule of Life* (New York: G. P. Putnam's Sons, 1908), 102.

6. H. G. Wells, *Washington and the Hope of Peace* (London: W. Collins, 1922), 154. Cited hereafter as *WHP*.

7. See my *At the Violet Hour: Modernism and Violence in England and Ireland* (New York: Oxford University Press, 2012).

8. See, for instance, I. F. Clarke, *Voices Prophesying War, 1763–1984* (New York: Oxford University Press, 1966); I. F. Clarke, *The Pattern of Expectation, 1644–2001* (London: Cape, 1979); I. F. Clarke, ed., *The Tale of the Next Great War, 1871–1914: Fictions of Future Warfare and of Battles Still to Come* (Syracuse, NY: Syracuse University Press, 1995); and I. F. Clarke, ed., *The Great War with Germany, 1890–1914: Fictions and Fantasies of the War-to-Come* (Liverpool: Liverpool University Press, 1997).

9. It may be hard for us to remember today, but in the interwar period, Wells was viewed as one of England's most important and influential pacifists. For modernist scholars, part of our amnesia is again traceable to Woolf, who portrays Wells in *Three Guineas* as a sexist, rather than as a pacifist. One of my goals, as I hope is clear, is to see these two great advocates for peace and world harmony as allies, rather than opponents.

10. Trutz von Trotha, " 'The Fellows Can Just Starve': On Wars of 'Pacification' in the African Colonies of Imperial Germany and the Concept of 'Total War,' " in *Anticipating Total War: The German and American Experiences, 1871–1914*, ed. Manfred F. Boemeke, Roger Chickering, and Stig Förster (Cambridge: Cambridge University Press, 1999), 417, 418–19.

11. H. G. Wells, *Anticipations of the Reaction of Mechanical and Scientific Progress Upon Human Life and Thought* (New York: Harper, 1902), 200, 201, 203. Cited hereafter as *Ant*.

12. Ian F. W. Beckett, "Total War," in *War, Peace, and Social Change in Twentieth-Century Europe*, ed. Clive Emsley, Arthur Warwick, and Wendy Simpson (Milton Keynes: Open University Press, 1989), 32.

13. Roger Chickering, "Total War: The Use and Abuse of a Concept," in *Anticipating Total War*, 15.

14. See Favret, *War at a Distance*; and Paul K. Saint-Amour, *Tense Future: Modernism, Total War, Encyclopedic Form* (Oxford: Oxford University Press, 2017).

15. For discussion of the Washington conference in several historical contexts, see Andrew Webster, "From Versailles to Geneva: The Many Forms of Interwar Disarmament," *Journal of Strategic Studies* 29, no. 2 (2006): 225–46; Erik Goldstein and John Maurer, eds., *The Washington*

*Conference, 1921–22: Naval Rivalry, East Asian Stability, and the Road to Pearl Harbor* (London: Frank Cass, 1994); and Robert Gordon Kaufman, *Arms Control During the Pre-Nuclear Era: The United States and Naval Limitation Between the Two World Wars* (New York: Columbia University Press, 1990).

16. For discussion of "the bombsite" as a location of exceptional meaning both in the lead-up to war and in its aftermath, with a reading of 1930s and '40s British literature in and around its contours, see Leo Mellor, *Reading the Ruins: Modernism, Bombsites, and British Culture* (Cambridge: Cambridge University Press, 2011).

17. For discussion of the Rising in *Ulysses*, see Enda Duffy, *The Subaltern Ulysses* (Minneapolis: University of Minnesota Press, 1994); and Saint-Amour, *Tense Future*.

18. Jan Mieszkowski, *Watching War* (Stanford, CA: Stanford University Press, 2012).

19. Jeffrey Richards, "*Things to Come* and Science Fiction in the 1930s," in *British Science Fiction Cinema*, ed. Ian Hunter (London: Routledge, 1999), 19.

20. See Richards, "*Things to Come* and Science Fiction in the 1930s," for this view.

21. On *Metropolis*, Wells had much to say. In a review of the film in the *New York Times* in 1927, upon its English-language release, Wells pointed out how Fritz Lang had borrowed heavily from him; he mentions *The Sleeper Awakes*, the clearest case, and we can also add *The Time Machine*. For all such alleged borrowing, Wells had great contempt for the histrionic and conservative (and we might also assume, religious) nature of the film. In the preface to his published screenplay of *Things to Come*, he makes a point of denigrating the designs of *Metropolis* and promising that his film will be something of an anti-*Metropolis*. See H. G. Wells, *Things to Come: A Film by H. G. Wells* (New York: Macmillan, 1935). Cited hereafter as *TTC*.

22. The film was cut substantially from its original version. The lines just quoted are taken from the published screenplay; they are not included in the final film version.

23. Richard Rhodes, *The Making of the Atomic Bomb* (New York: Simon and Schuster, 2012), 13.

24. Mark Morrison, too, in his study of alchemy's strange place in economic and scientific thinking in the modernist era, sees *The World Set Free* at the center of the storm, noting Wells's generative place in the imaginative activity of the early nuclear scientists. See Mark S. Morrison, *Modern Alchemy: Occultism and the Emergence of Atomic Theory* (Oxford: Oxford University Press, 2007), 152–55.

25. H. G. Wells, *The World Set Free: A Story of Mankind* (New York: E. P. Dutton, 1914), 138–39, all but final ellipses in the original, passage in dialogue. Cited hereafter as *WSF*.

26. Tim O'Brien, *The Things They Carried* (New York: Broadway Books, 1990), 87.

27. In prescient fashion, Wells saw the bombs as creating long-lasting pollution of the cities where they fall, such that they are, ultimately, abandoned, and new cities built further from the smoldering remains.

28. In the contemporary era, such speculative works with a future-historical perspective are common, especially within the canon of eco-apocalypse writings.

29. Jesse Matz, *Literary Impressionism and Modernist Aesthetics* (Cambridge: Cambridge University Press, 2001), 8–9.

30. Mieszkowski, *Watching War*, 69.

31. Bert certainly channels Wells in some ways (they share a name and a birthplace), yet Wells also layers several alter egos into the text, including Lieutenant Kurt, the likeable Anglicized German whose year of biological education in London serves as a tip-off for his author's affinity and similarity.

32. Here we might note how this novel presages later war films, such as *Saving Private Ryan* (Steven Spielberg, 1998), which work to convey the vast noise of war, something soldiers of the First World War regularly reported. It is not always successful, perhaps, to notate these sounds, but Wells does attempt to stretch his medium to accommodate sound as one of the critical perceptual features of

the new warfare. Within modernism, sound studies is a growing area; see, for instance, Sam Halliday, *Sonic Modernity: Representing Sound in Literature, Culture, and the Arts* (Edinburgh: Edinburgh University Press, 2013); Ann Thompson, *The Soundscape of Modernity: Architectural Acoustics and the Culture of Listening in America, 1900–1933* (Cambridge, MA: MIT Press, 2002); Daniel Morat, ed., *Sounds of Modern European History: Auditory Cultures in Nineteenth- and Twentieth-Century Europe* (New York: Berghahn Books, 2014); and Patricia Pye, *Sound and Modernity in the Literature of London, 1880–1918* (London: Palgrave Macmillan, 2017).

33. Favret, *War at a Distance*, 15; Mary L. Dudziak, *War Time: An Idea, Its History, Its Consequences* (New York: Oxford University Press, 2014), 13.

34. Sympathy is a major topic in Victorian studies. For a superb account that updates the classic trope, see Rae Greiner, *Sympathetic Realism in Nineteenth-Century British Fiction* (Baltimore, MD: Johns Hopkins University Press, 2012).

35. *Crome Yellow* is known today mostly for furnishing Eliot's *The Waste Land* with the progenitor of Madame Sosostris, one "Sesostris," a fake fortune teller at the county fair, impersonated by the same Scogan who speaks here.

36. Aldous Huxley, *Crome Yellow* (New York: Barnes and Noble, 2004), 91.

37. Robert Crossley, "Wells's Common Readers," in *Critical Essays on H. G. Wells*, ed. John Huntington (Boston: G. K. Hall, 1991), 178, 174.

38. On Woolf as a civilian writing about war, see David Bradshaw, "Woolf's London, London's Woolf," in *Virginia Woolf in Context*, ed. Bryony Randall and Jane Goldman (Cambridge: Cambridge University Press, 2012); Marina MacKay, *Modernism and World War II* (Cambridge: Cambridge University Press, 2007); Marina MacKay, "The Lunacy of Men, the Idiocy of Women: Woolf, West, and War," *NWSA Journal* 15, no. 3 (2003): 124–44; Gill Plain, *Women's Fiction of the Second World War: Gender, Power, and Resistance* (New York: St. Martin's, 1996); J. Ashley Foster, "Subverting Genres and Virginia Woolf's Political Activism: *Three Guineas* as Peace Testimony," *Virginia Woolf Miscellany* 83 (2013): 20–23; Christine Froula, *Virginia Woolf and the Bloomsbury Avant-Garde: War, Civilization, Modernity* (New York: Columbia University Press, 2005); Jessica Berman, *Modernist Commitments: Ethics, Politics, and Transnational Modernism* (New York: Columbia University Press, 2011); Jessica Berman, "*Three Guineas* and the Politics of Interruption," in *A Companion to Virginia Woolf*, ed. Jessica Berman (Hoboken, NJ: John Wiley & Sons, 2016); Bette London, "Posthumous Was a Woman: World War I Memorials and Woolf's Dead Poet's Society," *Woolf Studies Annual* 16 (2010): 45–70; and John Whittier-Ferguson, "Repetition, Remembering, Repetition: Virginia Woolf's Late Fiction and the Return of War," *Modern Fiction Studies* 57, no. 2 (Summer 2011): 230–53.

39. For discussion of these two works together, see Debra Rae Cohen, "Getting the Fame Into the Picture: Wells, West, and the Mid-War Novel," *The Space Between* 8, no. 1 (2012): 85–107.

40. Matching's Easy is modeled on the town of Easton Glebe, where Wells was then living, which became something of a tourist attraction in the years of the novel's success.

41. Wells also gives a curiously Orientalist guise to the scene of the archduke's assassination. "It occurred at an open space by a river that ran through a cramped Oriental city, a city spiked with white minarets and girt about by bare hills under a blazing afternoon sky" (*MB*, 79).

42. We should perhaps clarify here some convergences and differences between Wells's approach to the Belgian civilian trauma and the more familiar propaganda usages of these "atrocities." Both dwell on gruesome violence against civilians. Wells's style is of course literary (the focus on a bone in the street, say, rather than the famous image of the soldiers bayoneting children), and the incorporation of the slowly arriving, shocking, and confusing news from Belgium into his story of the English village is part of its overall developmental structure and of its deepening and humanizing relation to the war.

43. See Judith Butler, *Precarious Life: The Powers of Mourning and Violence* (London: Verso, 2004).

44.  Marianne Hirsch, "Presidential Address 2014—Connective Histories and Vulnerable Times," *PMLA* 129, no. 3 (2014): 337.

45.  Anna Lowenhaupt Tsing, *The Mushroom at the End of the World: On the Possibility of Life in Capitalist Ruins* (Princeton, NJ: Princeton University Press, 2015), 29.

46.  One thinks, too, of Elaine Scarry's idea that the injured bodies in war play a crucial role in affixing meanings and ensuring outcomes; in the midst of a war, there is a period when the meanings that will accrue to those bodies remain unfixed. Wells is not waiting for someone else to determine that substance.

47.  Paul Fussell cites Hugh's killing in terms of the British tradition of uniformity and its ironic effects; he is killed through a loophole in the sandbag, easily visible to the Germans. Paul Fussell, *The Great War and Modern Memory* (London: Oxford University Press, 1975), 79.

48.  *All Quiet on the Western Front*, with its exemplary sequences when Paul Baümer identifies with the French soldier he has killed, and later with the starving Russian prisoners he guards, was only published in 1929 (in English that same year), and the vast majority of the war literature that has defined the genre similarly emerged well after 1918.

49.  Fussell, *The Great War and Modern Memory*, 164.

50.  For riveting discussion of hands and war, see Santanu Das, *Touch and Intimacy in First World War Literature* (Cambridge: Cambridge University Press, 2006).

51.  Wilfred Owen, "The Poet in Pain," in *The Poems of Wilfred Owen*, ed. Jon Stallworthy (London: Chatto, 1990), 88.

52.  H. G. Wells, *The War That Will End War* (New York: Duffield, 1914), 14, 58–59. Cited hereafter as *WEW*.

53.  It is an interesting fact, given this construction of civilians taking the reins from politicians, that Wells may have been spurred to write "The War That Will End War" by a meeting he had with Lloyd George in the first days of August, when, as Gary Massinger puts it in a study of propaganda and the First World War, "Lloyd George urged Wells to write something that would move Americans to give greater support to the British cause." Gary Massinger, *British Propaganda and the State in the First World War* (Manchester: Manchester University Press, 1992), 189.

54.  Mark Wollaeger, *Modernism, Media, and Propaganda: British Narrative from 1900 to 1945* (Princeton, NJ: Princeton University Press), 14–15.

55.  Lovat Dickson, *H. G. Wells: His Turbulent Life and Times* (New York: Atheneum, 1969), 232.

56.  Norman MacKenzie and Jeanne MacKenzie, *The Life of H. G. Wells: The Time Traveller* (London: Hogarth, 1987), 198.

57.  Favret, *War at a Distance*, 30, 31.

58.  Moreover, Wells regularly predicted during the war years that if the peace was botched, another war would indeed soon follow. Like so many others, Wells found an essential genius and bedrock truth in John Maynard Keynes's *The Economic Consequences of the Peace* (1919).

59.  It should also be said, somewhat paradoxically, that Wells shared the national self-deception that it would be short.

60.  H. G. Wells, *The Peace of the World* (London: Daily Chronicle, 1915), 30. Cited hereafter as *PW*.

61.  H. G. Wells, *In the Fourth Year: Anticipations of a World Peace* (New York: Macmillan, 1918), 1. Cited hereafter as *IFY*.

62.  Of interest to our ongoing analysis of Wells and modernism, we note here that his work on behalf of the League brought him into touch with Leonard Woolf, with whom he collaborated again in the 1930s in their shared antifascist activism, though they also had their spats.

63.  H. G. Wells et al., "The Idea of a League of Nations," *Atlantic*, January 1919, 14 (pg. in online reprint).

64.  In the Washington essays, again these are called "teachers and writers . . . parents and talkers and all who instruct and make and change opinion" (*WHP*, 154).

65.  H. G. Wells, *The Open Conspiracy: Blue Prints for a World Revolution* (London: Victor Gollancz, 1928), 31; H. G. Wells, *The Outline of History: Being a Plain History of Life and Mankind* (New York: Macmillan, 1920), 2:572.

66.  Tsing, *The Mushroom at the End of the World*, 29; Butler, *Precarious Life*, xii.

67.  H. G. Wells, *The Rights of Man; or, What Are We Fighting For?* (repr., London: Penguin, 1940), 7.

## 3. TIME

1.  I am less concerned in this chapter to explore in detail the sources for Wells's many ideas about time than to reveal and develop those ideas. One figure who should be named up front, however, is J. W. Dunne, whose *An Experiment with Time* (1927) was one of Wells's key texts, in his later works, as he thought about temporal play and movement. For discussion of the long-lasting dialogue between Wells and Dunne and of Dunne's influence more broadly, see Darryl Jones, "J. W. Dunne: The Time Traveller," in *Literature and Modern Time: Technological Modernity, Glimpses of Eternity, Experiments with Time*, ed. Trish Ferguson (London: Palgrave Macmillan, 2019).

2.  "A Vision of the Past" can be found in H. G. Wells, *H. G. Wells: Early Writings in Science and Science Fiction*, ed. Robert M. Philmus and David Y. Hughes (Berkeley: University of California Press, 1975), 153–57. Cited hereafter as *EWS*.

3.  Stephen Kern, *The Culture of Time and Space, 1880–1914* (Cambridge, MA: Harvard University Press, 1983), 29.

4.  To name just three exquisite arguments: Frank Kermode posits modernism's sense of endings as its distinguishing feature; Jed Esty sees late modernism struggling "to give narrative form, aesthetic meaning, or spiritual value to time"; and Paul Saint-Amour has argued that a distinctive "tense future," or attitude of foreboding anticipation of destruction, is one of modernism's primary developments. Frank Kermode, *The Sense of an Ending: Studies in the Theory of Fiction* (Oxford: Oxford University Press, 1967); Jed Esty, *A Shrinking Island: Modernism and National Culture in England* (Princeton, NJ: Princeton University Press, 2003), 116; Paul Saint-Amour, *Tense Future: Modernism, Total War, Encyclopedic Form* (New York: Oxford University Press, 2015).

5.  Wyndham Lewis, *Time and Western Man* (Boston: Beacon, 1957), 15.

6.  Thomas Mann, *The Magic Mountain*, trans. John E. Woods (New York: Random House, 1995), 102.

7.  Kern, *The Culture of Time and Space*, 16. Of this necessary synchronicity, Georg Simmel wrote in his classic essay "The Metropolis and Mental Life": "the technique of [modern] metropolitan life is unimaginable without the most punctual integration of all activities and mutual relations into a stable and impersonal time schedule." Georg Simmel, *The Sociology of Georg Simmel*, trans. and ed. Kurt H. Wolff (Glencoe, IL: Free Press, 1950), 413.

8.  Adam Barrows, *The Cosmic Time of Empire: Modern Britain and World Literature* (Berkeley: University of California Press, 2010), 2.

9.  Mark R. Hillegas, *The Future as Nightmare: H. G. Wells and the Anti-utopians* (New York: Oxford University Press, 1967), 4.

10.  The full quote: "From Leibniz's discovery of the subconscious via the Romantic psychology of night and primeval past to the psychoanalysis of Freud, essentially only 'backward dawning' has previously been described and investigated. People thought they had discovered that everything present is loaded with memory, with past in the cellar of the No-Longer-Conscious. What they had not discovered was that there is in present material, indeed in what is remembered itself, an impetus and a sense of being broken off, a brooding quality and an anticipation of

Not-Yet-Become; and this broken-off and broached material does not take place in the cellar of consciousness, but on its Front." Ernst Bloch, *The Principle of Hope*, trans. Neville Plaice, Stephen Plaice, and Paul Knight (Cambridge MA: MIT Press, 1986), 11.

11.  Reinhart Koselleck, in considering early modernity, sees the cutting off of prophecy as a sign of its historical temporality, noting, for instance, that "the genesis of the absolutist state [in the sixteenth century] is accompanied by a sporadic struggle against all manner of religious and political predictions . . . a rigorous politics had succeeded in gradually eliminating from the domain of political consideration and decision making the robust religious expectations of the future that had flourished after the decline of the Church." Reinhart Koselleck, *Futures Past: On the Semantics of Historical Time*, trans. Keith Tribe (New York: Columbia University Press, 2004), 16.

12.  Heather Love, *Feeling Backward: Loss and the Politics of Queer History* (Cambridge, MA: Harvard University Press, 2007), 8.

13.  Nor would the restless soul of "Sailing to Byzantium," for all the poem's ending with "to come," ever escape the life cycle of "whatever is begotten, born, and dies."

14.  Sarah Cole, *At the Violet Hour: Modernism and Violence in England and Ireland* (New York: Oxford University Press, 2012).

15.  Cole, *At the Violet Hour*; Saint-Amour, *Tense Future*.

16.  H. G. Wells, *The Time Machine* (London: Penguin, 2005), 91. Cited hereafter as *TM*.

17.  Vincent Sherry, *Modernism and the Reinvention of Decadence* (Cambridge: Cambridge University Press, 2015), 103. For more on decadence and *The Time Machine*, see Theresa Jamieson, "Working for the Empire: Professions of Masculinity in H. G. Wells's *The Time Machine* and R. L. Stevenson's *Dr. Jekyll and Mr. Hyde*," *Victorian Network* 1, no. 1 (Summer 2009): 72–90.

18.  Aaron Rosenberg, "Romancing the Anthropocene: H. G. Wells and the Genre of the Future," *NOVEL: A Forum on Fiction* 51 (2018): 81.

19.  H. G. Wells, *Journalism and Prophecy, 1893–1946*, ed. W. Warren Wagar (Boston: Houghton Mifflin, 1964), 8. Cited hereafter as *JP*.

20.  In fact, Wells mentions his Pall Mall article in *The War of the Worlds*, a classic case of his self-referential intertextuality. H. G. Wells, *The War of the Worlds* (London: Penguin, 2005), 127.

21.  In the 1880s and '90s, Wells followed the scientific consensus in predicting the eventual freezing over of the earth, a stance that he would later mildly regret, as the discovery of radiation eventually countermanded the necessity for the sun's warmth to be dissipating. Interestingly, in *The Undying Fire* (1919), though, Wells has Job Huss return to the vision of a freezing earth, considering evolution's endpoint in a scene reminiscent of the late sequences in *The Time Machine*: "Always the day drags longer and longer and always the sun radiates its energy away. A time will come when the sun will glow dull red in the heavens, shorn of all its beams, and neither rising nor setting. A day will come when the earth will be as dead and frozen as the moon." H. G. Wells, *The Undying Fire: A Contemporary Novel* (New York: Macmillan, 1919), 107–8.

22.  Earlier in the nineteenth century, estimates of the earth's age (and hence of its longevity) were much more varied, with some scientists predicting demise within only thousands of years. But such a short duration had been firmly superseded in scientific thought by the time Wells was studying science in the 1880s. On the subject of Malthus, it should be added that Wells was deeply affected by Malthusian forecasts, and this took him in both progressive and conservative directions.

23.  For discussion of the world-as-book conceit, see Rosenberg, "Romancing"; and Simon J. James, *Maps of Utopia: H. G. Wells, Modernity and the End of Culture* (Oxford: Oxford University Press, 2012), 38–76.

24.  H. G. Wells, *Certain Personal Matters* (London: Lawrence and Bullen, 1898), 178. Cited hereafter as *CPM*.

25. H. G. Wells, Julian S. Huxley, and G. P. Wells, *The Science of Life*, 2 vols. (New York: Doubleday, 1931), 1:596. Cited hereafter as *SL*.

26. Virginia Woolf, *Moments of Being* (San Diego: Harcourt, 1985), 72; T. S. Eliot, *Four Quartets* (San Diego: Harcourt, 1971), 58.

27. The speech was also published as an essay in *Nature* and in the *Smithsonian Institution Record*.

28. H. G. Wells, *Social Anticipations* (New York: Vanguard, 1927), 61–62. Cited hereafter as *DF*.

29. At a lecture in London at the Lyceum Club in 1911, Marinetti was introduced by Wells, though by then their different views of Mussolini and fascism created some tension.

30. F. T. Marinetti, *Marinetti: Selected Writings*, ed. R. W. Flint, trans. R. W. Flint and Arthur A. Coppotelli (New York: Farrar, Straus and Giroux, 1972), 82, 55, 56.

31. "It is one thing to write in a style which is already popular, and another to hope that one's writing may eventually become popular." T. S. Eliot, *The Use of Poetry and the Use of Criticism* (Cambridge, MA: Harvard University Press, 1994), 22.

32. See T. H. Huxley, *Science and Culture and Other Essays* (New York: D. Appleton, 1882), 135–55.

33. Saint-Amour, *Tense Future*, 236–37.

34. E. M. Forster, *Aspects of the Novel* (San Diego: Harvest, 1955), 125.

35. Herodotus, *The Histories*, trans. Aubrey de Sélincourt (London: Penguin, 2003), 261–62.

36. H. G. Wells, *Anticipations of the Reaction of Mechanical and Scientific Progress Upon Human Life and Thought* (New York: Harper, 1902), 3–4. Cited hereafter as *A*.

37. E. M. Forster, *The Eternal Moment and Other Stories* (San Diego: Harcourt, 1956), 3.

38. Branka Arsić, *Bird Relics: Grief and Vitalism in Thoreau* (Cambridge, MA: Harvard University Press, 2016), 36.

39. H. G. Wells, *What Is Coming: A Forecast of Things After the War* (New York: Macmillan, 1916), 1 (pg. not identified). Cited hereafter as *WIC*.

40. H. G. Wells, *The Food of the Gods* (London: Hesperus, 2013), 253–54. Cited hereafter as *FG*.

41. H. G. Wells, *First and Last Things: A Confession of Faith and a Rule of Life* (New York: Putnam, 1908), 37.

42. Darko Suvin, introduction to *H. G. Wells and Modern Science Fiction*, ed. Darko Suvin, assoc. ed. Robert M. Philmus (Lewisburg, PA: Bucknell University Press, 1977), 27.

43. H. G. Wells, *Men Like Gods* (New York: Macmillan, 1923), 169.

44. H. G. Wells, *The Complete Short Stories of H. G. Wells* (London: Ernest Benn, 1970), 936. Cited hereafter as *CSS*.

45. Louise Hornby, *Still Modernism: Photography, Literature, Film* (New York: Oxford University Press, 2017), 112. It should be said that Hornby does not credit Wells with such insights. She cites "The New Accelerator" in her introduction as an example of modernist veneration of speed (against which her concept of stillness is posed), a strange reading of a story that, in many ways, embodies the principles she is exploring in her book.

46. Garrett Stewart, *Between Film and Screen: Modernism's Photo Synthesis* (Chicago: University of Chicago Press, 1999).

47. I am assuming familiarity with the period trope of degeneration, since criticism on the subject, with Max Nordau's *Degeneration* (1894) as touchstone, has been a staple since the 1980s. See, for instance, Stephen Arata, *Fictions of Loss in the Victorian Fin de Siècle* (New York: Cambridge University Press, 1996); J. Edward Chamberlin and Sander L. Gilman, *Degeneration: The Dark Side of Progress* (New York: Columbia University Press, 1985); Susan J. Navarette, *The Shape of Fear: Horror and the Fin de Siècle Culture of Decadence* (Lexington: University Press of Kentucky, 1998); Marja Härmänmaa and Christopher Nissen, eds., *Decadence, Degeneration, and the End: Studies in the European Fin de Siècle* (New York: Palgrave Macmillan, 2014); Piers J. Hale, *Political Descent: Malthus, Mutualism, and the Politics of Evolution in Victorian England* (Chicago:

University of Chicago Press, 2014); and Stephan Karschay, *Degeneration, Normativity, and the Gothic at the Fin de Siècle* (New York: Palgrave Macmillan, 2015).

48.　For discussion of the Victorian museum, see Annie E. Coombes, *Reinventing Africa: Museums, Material Culture, and Popular Imagination in Late Victorian and Edwardian England* (New Haven, CT: Yale University Press, 1994); Barbara J. Black, *On Exhibit: Victorians and Their Museums* (Charlottesville: University Press of Virginia, 2000); Carla Yanni, *Nature's Museums: Victorian Science and the Architecture of Display* (Princeton, NJ: Princeton Architectural Press, 2005); Lara Kriegel, *Grand Designs: Labor, Empire, and the Museum in Victorian Culture* (Durham, NC: Duke University Press, 2007); and David N. Livingstone and Charles W. J. Withers, *Geographies of Nineteenth-Century Science* (Chicago: University of Chicago Press, 2011).

49.　The dinosaur bones are placed right at the entryway, as they were in the Natural History Museum in London, which contained skeletons throughout its huge halls, and like the American Museum of Natural History in New York, where the signature skeleton still towers proudly at the main entrance on Central Park West, in the Theodore Roosevelt Hall.

50.　H. G. Wells, *The Croquet Player* (New York: Viking, 1937), 64. Cited hereafter at *CP*.

51.　H. G. Wells, *Ann Veronica* (London: Penguin, 2005), 185–86. Cited hereafter as *AV*.

52.　H. G. Wells, *The World of William Clissold: A Novel at a New Angle* (London: Ernest Benn, 1926), 106–7. Cited hereafter as *WWC*.

53.　For discussion of these issues, see Christine Froula, *Virginia Woolf and the Bloomsbury Avant-Garde: War, Civilization, Modernity* (New York: Columbia University Press, 2005); and my *At the Violet Hour*, 197–286.

54.　For primitivism and modernism, see Marianna Torgovnick, *Gone Primitive: Savage Intellects, Modern Lives* (Chicago: University of Chicago Press, 1990); Elazar Barkan and Ronald Bush, ed., *Prehistories of the Future: The Primitivist Project and the Culture of Modernism* (Stanford, CA: Stanford University Press, 1995); Carole Sweeney, *From Fetish to Subject: Race, Modernism, and Primitivism, 1919–1935* (Westport, CT: Praeger, 2004); Elizabeth Hutchinson, *The Indian Craze: Primitivism, Modernism, and Transculturation in American Art, 1890–1915* (Durham, NC: Duke University Press, 2009); Jack Flam and Miriam Deutch, ed., *Primitivism and Twentieth-Century Art: A Documentary History* (Berkeley: University of California Press, 2003). Individual modernist authors, too, have been well discussed in the context of primitivism. See Marc Manganaro, "Dissociation in 'Dead Land': The Primitive Mind in the Early Poetry of T. S. Eliot," *Journal of Modern Literature* 13, no. 1 (March 1986): 97–110; Louis A. Sass, " 'The Catastrophes of Heaven': Modernism, Primitivism, and the Madness of Antonin Artaud," *Modernism/modernity* 3, no. 2 (April 1996): 73–91; and Robin Hackett, *Sapphic Primitivism: Productions of Race, Class, and Sexuality in Key Works of Modern Fiction* (New Brunswick, NJ: Rutgers University Press, 2004).

55.　D. H. Lawrence, *The Rainbow* (New York: Penguin, 1983), 193.

56.　Virginia Woolf, *The Waves* (San Diego: Harcourt, 1959), 289.

57.　James Joyce, *Ulysses* (New York: Random House, 1986), 34, 42.

58.　T. S. Eliot, *Four Quartets* (San Diego: Harcourt, 1971), 23.

59.　See Gillian Beer, *Open Fields: Science in Cultural Encounter* (Oxford: Clarendon, 1996), esp. "Forging the Missing Link," 115–45.

60.　T. S. Eliot, *Selected Prose of T. S. Eliot* (San Diego: Harcourt, 1975), 64.

61.　Joseph Conrad, *Heart of Darkness* (London: Penguin, 2007), 105, 108.

62.　Thomas Hardy, *Tess of the D'Urbervilles* (London: Penguin, 2003), 395.

63.　Eliot, *Selected Prose*, 39.

64.　The term was first used by Yi-Fu Tuan in 1974. See Yi-Fu Tuan, *Topophilia: A Study in Environmental Perceptions, Attitudes, and Values* (New York: Columbia University Press, 1990), 23.

65. Kitty Hauser, *Shadow Sites: Photography, Archaeology, and the British Landscape, 1927–1951* (New York: Oxford University Press, 2007), 1, 2, italics in the original.

66. Karin Sanders, *Bodies in the Bog and the Archaeological Imagination* (Chicago: University of Chicago Press, 2009), 15, italics in the original.

67. D. H. Lawrence, *Phoenix II: Uncollected, Unpublished, and Other Prose Works* (Harmondsworth: Penguin, 1978), 434.

68. Another contender would be: "Across this wilderness, which is now the great plain of Europe, wandered a various fauna. At first there were hippopotami, rhinoceroses, mammoths, and elephants. The sabre-toothed tiger was diminishing toward extinction. Then, as the air chilled, the hippopotamus, and then other warmth-loving creatures, ceased to come so far north, and the saber-toothed tiger disappeared altogether. The wooly mammoth, the wooly rhinoceros, the musk ox, the bison, the aurochs, and the reindeer became prevalent, and the temperate vegetation gave place to plants of a more arctic type. The glaciers spread southward to the maximum of the Fourth Glacial Age (about 50,000 years ago) and then receded again. In the earlier phase, the Third Interglacial period, a certain number of small family groups of men (Homo Neanderthalensis) and probably of sub-men (Eoanthropus) wandered over the land, leaving nothing but their flint implements to witness to their presence. . . . As the weather hardened to its maximum of severity, the Neanderthal men, already it would seem acquainted with the use of fire, began to seek shelter under rock ledges and in caves—and so leave remains behind them. Hitherto they had been accustomed to squat in the open about the fire, and near their water supply. But they were sufficiently intelligent to adapt themselves to the new and harder conditions. (As for the sub-men, they seem to have succumbed to the stresses of this Fourth Glacial Age altogether. At any rate, the rudest type of Palaeolithic implements presently disappears)." *OH*, 1:76.

69. Woolf was also reading *The Science of Life* in the mid-1930s, and though she may not have read all 1,500 pages, the sections on the evolution of man also bring to mind the mood and metaphors of *Between the Acts*.

70. Of interest to those tracking *Between the Acts* is also this comment in "The Grisly Folk": "With the spring grass and foliage came great herds of reindeer, wild horses, mammoth, elephant, and rhinoceros, drifting northward from the slopes of the great warm valley that is now filled up with water—the Mediterranean Sea. It was in those days before the ocean waters broke into the Mediterranean that the swallows and a multitude of other birds acquired the habit of coming north, a habit that nowadays impels them to brave the passage of the perilous seas that flow over and hide the lost secrets of the ancient Mediterranean valleys." *CSS*, 610.

71. At the same time, Wells was one of the very few to remain suspicious of the Piltdown hoax and so comes out well in that instance. The Piltdown remains were first discovered in 1912, generating great archeological interest and debate. Though there were always skeptics, it was not until 1953 that scientists concluded definitively that the artifacts had been planted and the find was a hoax. Most archeologists had bought it.

72. Carl L. Becker, *Everyman His Own Historian: Essays on History and Politics* (New York: F. S. Crofts, 1935), 178. The essay was first published in the *American Historical Review* in July 1921.

73. E. M. Forster, review in *Athenaeum*, July 1920, quoted in *H. G. Wells: The Critical Heritage*, ed. Patrick Parrinder (London: Routledge, 1972), 253. Cited hereafter as Parrinder, *Critical Heritage*.

74. H. G. Wells, *Tono-Bungay* (London: Penguin, 2005), 99–100.

75. William T. Ross, *H. G. Wells's World Reborn: The Outline of History and Its Companions* (Selinsgrove, PA: Susquehanna University Press, 2002). Ross, along with Cary, makes a case for Wells's racism, seeing in Wells all the worst aspects of his culture's attitude to race and empire.

76. For a view of *The Outline* as expressing "a thoroughgoing technological determinism," see Aaron Worth, "Imperial Transmissions: H. G. Wells, 1897–1901," *Victorian Studies* 53, no. 1 (2010): 66.

77. In *Aspects of the Novel*, which has Wells much in view, Forster borrows these bards from *The Outline* as his paradigmatic cavemen. See E. M. Forster, *Aspects of the Novel* (San Diego: Harcourt, 1955), 26.

78. It is a subject of regular critique. Here is Carl Becker: "It comes to this, that Mr. Wells is too much aware of being himself part of the cosmic process, is too intent upon shaping and improving that process, is too much in the game, to be willing to stand, aloofly wrapped in the blanket of intellectual curiosity, on the side lines." Becker, *Everyman His Own Historian*, 185. Or Forster: "The religious experiences of Wells, like those of Mr. Britling, have been little more than a visit to a looking-glass in whose area he has seen an image of himself which imitates his gestures and endorses his deficiencies." Parrinder, *Critical Heritage*, 253–54.

79. Virginia Woolf, *Jacob's Room* (London: Penguin, 1992), 31.

80. Parrinder, *Critical Heritage*, 252.

81. Virginia Woolf, *The Common Reader* (San Diego: Harcourt, 1984), 147.

82. Parrinder, *Critical Heritage*, 250–51.

83. Belloc published a rejoinder to Wells in 1926 entitled "A Companion to Mr. Wells's 'Outline of History,'" which Wells answered in the form of his own small book, "Mr. Belloc Objects," followed by more from Belloc, "Mr. Belloc Still Objects." It was to these publications that Eliot was responding in his commentary in *The Criterion* in 1927.

84. See A. B. McKillop, *The Spinster and the Prophet: H. G. Wells, Florence Deeks, and the Case of the Plagiarized Text* (New York: Four Walls Eight Windows, 2000).

85. Peter Novick, *That Noble Dream: The "Objectivity Question" and the American Historical Profession* (Cambridge: Cambridge University Press, 1988), 1.

86. *Symposium of Opinions Upon* The Outline of History, *by H. G. Wells: Views of Historians* (New York: National Civic Federation, 1922).

87. The 1911 *Britannica* was a famous and contentious work of its own. Saint-Amour in *Tense Future* argues that it contributed to the phenomenon of modernist encyclopedic fiction, so another interesting cross-hatching of Wells and modernism, especially in terms of his advocating for the World Brain in the 1930s.

88. Cliona Murphy, "H. G. Wells: His History, the People and the Historians," *The Wellsian* (1996): 43.

89. Lisa Fluet, "Modernism and Disciplinary History: On H. G. Wells and T. S. Eliot," *Twentieth-Century Literature* 50, no. 3 (Fall 2004): 286, 253.

90. T. S. Eliot, "Recent Books," *The New Criterion: A Quarterly Review* 5 (1927): 253.

91. Becker, *Everyman His Own Historian*, 186.

92. Becker, *Everyman His Own Historian*, 190, italics in the original.

93. We have noted, from the first page of this study, a pervasive energy in the attacks on Wells, stemming typically from the needs felt by other writers to clear space for themselves and their movements. *The Outline* engendered its own subset of such rejoinders. I would note, in this respect, the strikingly inaccurate reflections of A. J. P. Taylor on Wells's career, in which his multiform misreading of *The Outline* provides the context. Bizarrely, for instance, he states that "Wells wrote [*The Outline*] to demonstrate that knowledge was superior to art and literature," that Wells "like[s] to think that the Better Side wins," that Wells thought "The Romans were . . . more civilized or more enlightened than the Greeks," and, strangest of all, that Wells thought men could be biologically changed, that is by evolution, in the short run. It is hard to understand. A. J. P. Taylor, "The Man Who Tried to Work Miracles," in *Critical Essays on H. G. Wells*, ed. John Huntington (Boston: G. K. Hall, 1991), 133, 129. Originally published in *Listener*, July 21, 1966.

94. David C. Smith, *H. G. Wells: Desperately Mortal, a Biography* (New Haven, CT: Yale University Press, 1986), 260. Smith's account of responses to *The Outline* is excellent.

95. Fernand Braudel, *The Mediterranean and the Mediterranean World in the Age of Philip II*, trans. Siân Reynolds (New York: Harper and Row, 1995), 1:18.

96.    Fred Spier, *Big History and the Future of Humanity* (Malden: Wiley-Blackwell, 2010), ix, 2.

97.    David Christian and William H. McNeil, *Maps of Time: An Introduction to Big History* (Berkeley: University of California Press, 2004), 3.

98.    Wai Chee Dimock, *Through Other Continents: American Literature Across Deep Time* (Princeton, NJ: Princeton University Press, 2008), 3–4.

99.    T. S. Eliot, *Selected Prose of T. S. Eliot* (San Diego: Harcourt, 1975), 177.

100.   H. G. Wells, *The Open Conspiracy: Blue Prints for a World Revolution* (London: Victor Gollancz, 1928), 104–5.

101.   Wells worked toward educational reform and expansion in many different forums. This will be discussed in the conclusion.

102.   George Orwell, *Essays* (New York: Knopf, 2002), 370.

103.   Another such lapse is his essentially ethnographic (as distinct from historical or ethical) regrets about the wiping out of native South American populations by the conquering Spaniards.

## 4. BIOLOGY

1.    H. G. Wells, *The First Men in the Moon* (London: Penguin, 2005), 51. Cited hereafter as *FMM*.

2.    H. G. Wells, *The Outline of History*, 2 vols. (New York: Macmillan, 1920), 2:594. Cited hereafter as *OH*.

3.    Michael R. Page, *The Literary Imagination from Erasmus Darwin to H. G. Wells: Science, Evolution, Ecology* (Burlington, VT: Ashgate, 2012), 150.

4.    For a discussion of scientists in Wells's work, see Patrick Parrinder, "Men Who Could Work Miracles: The Tragicomedy of Wellsian Science Fiction," *Foundation* 46, no. 127 (2017): 33–42; and Anne Stiles, "Literature in *Mind*: H. G. Wells and the Evolution of the Mad Scientist," *Journal of the History of Ideas* 70, no. 2 (April 2009): 317–39.

5.    H. G. Wells, *The Food of the Gods* (London: Hesperus, 2013), 11–12. Cited hereafter as *FG*.

6.    H. G. Wells, *The Science of Life* (New York: Doubleday, 1931), 2:967. Cited hereafter as *SL*.

7.    See Anna Lowenhaupt Tsing, *The Mushroom at the End of the World: On the Possibility of Life in the Capitalist Ruins* (Princeton, NJ: Princeton University Press, 2015).

8.    H. G. Wells, *The Conquest of Time* (1942; Amherst, NY: Prometheus, 1995), 53. Cited hereafter as *CT*.

9.    H. G. Wells, *A Modern Utopia* (London: Penguin, 2005), 64. Cited hereafter as *MU*.

10.   There is a long bibliography on modernism's attraction and repulsion to unruly desire, materialist excess, the full dilemma of what separates and attaches ripeness from/to rottenness (within, moreover, a much longer Western tradition). A small selection includes Laura Frost, *The Problem with Pleasure: Modernism and Its Discontents* (New York: Columbia University Press, 2015); Maurizia Boscagli, *Stuff Theory: Everyday Objects, Radical Materialism* (New York: Bloomsbury, 2014); Christopher Schmidt, *The Poetics of Waste: Queer Excess in Stein, Ashbery, Schuyler, and Goldsmith* (New York: Palgrave Macmillan, 2014); Colleen Lamos, *Deviant Modernism: Sexual and Textual Errancy in T. S. Eliot, James Joyce, and Marcel Proust* (Cambridge: Cambridge University Press, 1998); and on *The Waste Land* in particular, Harriet Davidson, "Improper Desire: Reading *The Waste Land*," in *The Cambridge Companion to T. S. Eliot*, ed. David Moody (Cambridge: Cambridge University Press, 1994), 121–31.

11.   Schmidt, *The Poetics of Waste*, 1.

12.   Or here is *The Outline of History*'s version:

> Now here it will be well to put plainly certain general facts about this new thing, *life*, that was creeping in the shallow waters and intertidal muds of the early Palaeozoic period, and which is perhaps confined to our planet alone in all the immensity of space.
>
> Life differs from all things whatever that are without life in certain general aspects. There are the most wonderful differences among living things to-day, but all living things

past and present agree in possessing a *certain power of growth*, all living things *take nour-ishment*, all living things *move about* as they feed and grow, though the movement may be no more than the spread of roots through the soil, or of branches in the air. Moreover, living things reproduce; they give rise to other living things, either by growing and then dividing or by means of seeds or spores or eggs or other ways of producing young. *Repro-duction* is a characteristic of life.

(*OH*, 1:16, italics in the original)

13.  H. G. Wells, *A Text-Book of Biology* (London: W. B. Clive, 1893), vii.

14.  H. G. Wells, *Ann Veronica* (London: Penguin, 2005), 5. Cited hereafter as *AV*.

15.  Leon Edel and Gordon N. Ray, eds., *Henry James and H. G. Wells: A Record of their Friendship, Their Debate on the Art of Fiction, and Their Quarrel* (Urbana: University of Illinois Press, 1958), 266–67, italics in the original.

16.  H. G. Wells, *The Future in America: A Search After Realities* (New York: Harper, 1906), 4, 3. Cited hereafter as *FA*.

17.  Virginia Woolf, *The Common Reader* (New York: Harcourt, 1984), 152; Edel and Ray, *Henry James and H. G. Wells*, 267.

18.  H. G. Wells, *The Island of Doctor Moreau* (London: Penguin, 2005), 94. Cited hereafter as *IDM*.

19.  Jeanne and Norman MacKenzie note that the closest Wells came to a personal interaction with Huxley at the Normal School was to hold a door open for him. Meanwhile, however, the paternal and professional relationship Wells later developed with Julian Huxley might make for a juicy addition to the psychological story of these men.

20.  But the point about Wells's attachment to evolution can easily be misconstrued. To take a partic-ularly extreme case, the famous historian A. J. P. Taylor wrote in a 1966 commentary on Wells's career that Wells failed to understand the basics of evolution, asserting that Wells believed man could evolve within a few hundred years to suit Wells's own plans for the future. It is a spectacu-larly wrongheaded discussion. A. J. P. Taylor, "The Man Who Tried to Work Miracles," in *Critical Essays on H. G. Wells*, ed. John Huntington (Boston: G. K. Hall, 1991), 127–35.

21.  Roslynn D. Haynes, *H. G. Wells: Discoverer of the Future: The Influence of Science on His Thought* (New York: NYU Press, 1980), 16.

22.  Michael R. Page, *The Literary Imagination from Erasmus Darwin to H. G. Wells: Science, Evolu-tion, Ecology* (Farnham: Ashgate, 2012), 151.

23.  Leon Stover, "Applied Natural History: Wells v. Huxley," in *H. G. Wells Under Revision*, ed. Pat-rick Parrinder and Christopher Rolfe (Selinsgrove, PA: Susquehanna University Press, 1990), 125.

24.  Huxley and Darwin represent the most prominent, though far from the only, scientific influences on Wells's thought. For a discussion of Wells and a variety of scientific debates of the 1890s, see John McNabb, "The Beast Within: H. G. Wells, *The Island of Doctor Moreau*, and Human Evolu-tion in the mid-1890s," *Geological Journal* 50 (2015): 383–97.

25.  H. G. Wells, *Early Writings in Science and Science Fiction*, ed. Robert M. Philmus and David Y. Hughes (Berkeley: University of California Press, 1975), 211. Cited hereafter as *EWS*.

26.  H. G. Wells, *The Undying Fire* (New York: Macmillan, 1919), 140, 157, italics in the original. Cited hereafter as *UF*.

27.  Here Wells shows his debt, in particular, to Ray Lankester, the evolutionary biologist whose book *Degeneration: A Chapter in Darwinism* (1880) is particularly germane. For a discussion of Wells and Lankester, see Richard Barnett, "Education or Degeneration: E. Ray Lankester, H. G. Wells, and *The Outline of History*," *Studies in History and Philosophy of Science Part C: Studies in History and Philosophy of Biological and Biomedical Sciences* 37, no. 2 (June 2006): 203–29.

28.  On Victorian character building, see, for instance, John Chandos, *Boys Together: English Public Schools, 1800–1864* (New Haven, CT: Yale University Press, 1984); David Newsome, *Godliness*

and *Good Learning: Four Studies on a Victorian Ideal* (London: Murray, 1961); J. A. Mangan, *The Games Ethic and Imperialism: Aspects of the Diffusion of an Ideal* (New York: Viking, 1985); and Michael Rosenberg, *The Character Factory: Baden-Powell and the Origins of the Boy Scout Movement* (New York: Pantheon, 1986).

29. In the conclusion, I will turn to some of Wells's iterations of a world community. These differ across the works, and the question of what role the British Empire might be playing in establishing the new order is never entirely stable over his texts. Here, the New Republic is imagined more or less as encompassing the Empire and the United States, the English-speaking world.

30. H. G. Wells, *Mankind in the Making* (New York: Scribner, 1918), 19. Cited hereafter as *MM*. Italics in the original.

31. Martin Danahay, "Wells, Galton, and Biopower: Breeding Human Animals," *Journal of Victorian Culture* 17, no. 4 (December 2012): 478.

32. John Carey, *The Intellectuals and the Masses: Pride and Prejudice Among the Literary Intelligentsia, 1880–1939* (London: Faber and Faber, 1992), 119, 134.

33. We might note, once again, the cross-pollination of technology with literary method, with this portion of text envisioned as pure radio transmission.

34. All quoted in Patrick Parrinder, ed., *H. G. Wells: The Critical Heritage* (London: Routledge, 1972), 51, 50, 43–44.

35. Peter Kemp, *H. G. Wells and the Culminating Ape: Biological Imperatives and Imaginative Obsessions* (London: Macmillan, 1996).

36. H. G. Wells, "Preface," in *The Works of H. G. Wells* (New York: Scribner, 1927), 2:ix.

37. Parrinder, *Critical Heritage*, 331.

38. Paul A. Cantor and Peter Hufnagel, "The Empire of the Future: Imperialism and Modernism in H. G. Wells," *Studies in the Novel* 38, no. 1 (Spring 2006): 52. See also Jennifer DeVere Brody, *Impossible Purities: Blackness, Femininity, and Victorian Culture* (Durham, NC: Duke University Press, 1998); Timothy Christensen, "The Bestial Mark of Race in *The Island of Dr. Moreau*," *Criticism* 46, no. 4 (Fall 2004): 575–95; John Rieder, *Colonialism and the Emergence of Science Fiction* (Middletown, CT: Wesleyan University Press, 2012); Payal Taneja, "The Tropical Empire: Exotic Animals and Beastly Men in *The Island of Dr. Moreau*," *English Studies in Canada* 39, no. 2/3 (June–September 2013): 139–59.

39. Margaret Atwood's excellent introduction to Penguin *The Island of Doctor Moreau* includes a discussion of the import of some of these literary forebears and adds others, such as "Goblin Market." Margaret Atwood, introduction to H. G. Wells, *The Island of Doctor Moreau* (London: Penguin, 2005), xiii–xxvi.

40. For a brilliant discussion of the freak in American culture, see Rachel Adams, *Sideshow USA: Freaks and the American Cultural Imagination* (Chicago: University of Chicago Press, 2001).

41. H. G. Wells, "The Limits of Individual Plasticity," *Saturday Evening Review*, January 19, 1895; reprinted in *EWS*, 39.

42. Kimberly W. Benston, "Sacrifice, Anthropomorphism, and the Aims of (Critical) Animal Studies," *PMLA* 124, no. 2 (2009): 551.

43. Thomas Mann, *The Magic Mountain*, trans. John E. Woods (New York: Random House, 1996), 215. Interestingly, Hans's reaction to the hand echoes the reaction of Anna-Bertha Röntgen, whose husband Wilhelm had discovered the X-ray, on first seeing the results: "I have seen my own death." Quoted in Lauren Redniss, *Radioactive: Marie and Pierre Curie, A Tale of Love and Fallout* (New York: Harper Collins, 2011), 42.

44. H. G. Wells, *The War of the Worlds* (London: Penguin, 2005), 168.

45. Holly Henry, *Virginia Woolf and the Discourse of Science: The Aesthetics of Astronomy* (Cambridge: Cambridge University Press, 2003), 7.

46. Cóilín Parsons, "Planetary Parallax: *Ulysses*, the Stars, and South Africa," *Modernism/modernity* 24, no. 1 (2017): 76.

47. H. G. Wells, *First and Last Things: A Confession of Faith and a Rule of Life* (New York: Putnam, 1908), 40, italics in the original. Cited hereafter as *FLT*.

48. Enda Duffy, "Rush: Biomodernism, Stress, and the Sensation of Time," unpublished manuscript, delivered in Leuven, Belgium, 2015.

49. Enda Duffy, "High Energy Modernism," in *Moving Modernisms: Motion, Technology, and Modernity*, ed. David Bradshaw, Laura Marcus, and Rebecca Roach (Oxford: Oxford University Press, 2016), 87.

50. H. G. Wells, *The World Set Free: A Story of Mankind* (New York: Dutton, 1914), 15, 34–37.

51. As Michael Whitworth notes, the accumulating work that opened radioactivity up to the general understanding, with its core precept of the insubstantiality of matter, could not be attributed singly and sensationally to an individual intellect, the way relativity typically was (and is) to Einstein, nor does its meaning have quite the immediacy in shattering earlier, common-sense scientific principles as relativity held. Michael H. Whitworth, *Einstein's Wake: Relativity, Metaphor, and Modernist Literature* (Oxford: Oxford University Press, 2001). For a survey of the history of radiation and its literary manifestations, see chapter 5, "Invisible Men and Fractured Atoms," 146–69.

52. H. G. Wells, "The Endowment of Motherhood," *An Englishman Looks at the World* (Charleston, SC: BiblioBazaar, 2016), 196–200.

53. Wells Collection, University of Illinois, Rare Book and Manuscript Library, WF 1. An alternative explanation for his being pushed out of the Fabian Society is that he made it a habit to have sexual affairs with the daughters of some of its most prominent members, such as Amber Reeve and Rosamond Bland. Yet a third possibility is that Wells had to leave the Fabian Society because he wanted to take it over, in a battle of wills with its more established members, such as George Bernard Shaw, a friend as well as nemesis, and especially Beatrice and Sydney Webb, the group's leaders.

54. All quoted in Parrinder, *The Critical Heritage*, 169–70, 158, 161.

55. D. H. Lawrence, *The Letters of D. H. Lawrence* (Cambridge: Cambridge University Press, 1979), 1:339. Italics in the original.

56. It is thus particularly welcome that Broadview has recently published a teaching edition of *Ann Veronica* (2015), edited by Carey Snyder.

57. Parrinder, *Critical Heritage*, 158.

58. Victoria Rosner, *Modernism and the Architecture of Private Life* (New York: Columbia University Press, 2012).

59. Cited in Allison Pease, *Modernism, Feminism, and the Culture of Boredom* (Cambridge: Cambridge University Press, 2102), 52.

60. On the biographical front, Wells is, as usual, strongly present. Capes is clearly Wells, though loosely. Wells also taught in the university and met his second wife, Amy Catherine Robbins (Jane), when she was his student and he too was married at the time.

61. James Joyce, *Ulysses* (New York: Random House, 1986), 89.

62. H. G. Wells, *Tono-Bungay* (London: Penguin, 2005), 381. Cited hereafter as *TB*.

63. H. G. Wells, *Mr. Britling Sees It Through* (New York: Macmillan, 1916), 121, ellipses in the original. Cited hereafter as *MB*.

64. Wilfred Owen, "Futility," in *The Poems of Wilfred Owen*, ed. Jon Stallworthy (London: Chatto, 1990), 135.

65. H. G. Wells, *The Salvaging of Civilization: The Probable Future of Mankind* (New York: Macmillan, 1921), 13.

66. H. G. Wells, *Things to Come: A Film by H. G. Wells* (New York: Macmillan, 1935), 155.

67. H. G. Wells, *World Brain* (New York: Doubleday, 1938), 35.

68.  Angelique Richardson, *Love and Eugenics in the Late Nineteenth Century: Rational Reproduction and the New Woman* (Oxford: Oxford University Press, 2003).

69.  Maurizia Boscagli, *Stuff Theory: Everyday Objects, Radical Materialism* (New York: Bloomsbury, 2014), 233.

70.  For a discussion of Wells and Galton that stresses these divergences, see Martin Dahanay, "Wells, Galton, and Biopower: Breeding Human Animals," *Journal of Victorian Culture* 17, no. 4 (December 2012): 468–79.

71.  H. G. Wells, "Discussion," *Journal of American Sociology* 10, no. 1 (July 1904): 10–11.

72.  This literary-critical term was coined in Charles Masterman's book *The Condition of England* (1909). Wells's friend Masterman read his works as they came out, and the just-published *Tono-Bungay* was on his mind when he completed his diagnosis of the English social cosmos.

73.  These sequences would film very naturally—one imagines a quick-cut montage of factories growing, areas of operation expanding, crates being packed according George's patented new method, typewriter girls tapping away, Edward and Susan moving from their small flat into the first and second of their ever-larger abodes, and always the imperial comparison, with its maps and war metaphors, providing an ongoing allegory.

74.  Edward Mendelson, introduction to H. G. Wells, *Tono-Bungay* (London: Penguin, 2005), xxiii.

75.  William Kupinse, "Wasted Value: The Serial Logic of H. G. Wells's *Tono-Bungay*," *NOVEL: A Forum on Fiction* 33, no. 1 (Fall 1999): 64.

76.  Kupinse, "Wasted Value," 66.

77.  James Longenbach, *Modernist Poetics of History: Pound, Eliot, and the Sense of the Past* (Princeton, NJ: Princeton University Press, 1987), 11.

## CONCLUSION: THE WORLD

1.  Gayatri Spivak, *Death of a Discipline* (New York: Columbia University Press, 2003), 51.

2.  As Bruce Robbins puts it, "Like nations, cosmopolitanisms are now plural and particular. Like nations, they are both European and non-European, and they are weak and underdeveloped as well as strong and privileged. And again like the nation, cosmopolitanism is *there*—not merely an abstract ideal, like loving one's neighbor as oneself, but habits of thought and feeling that have already shaped and been shaped by particular collectivities, that are socially and geographically situated, hence both limited and empowered" (italics in the original). Bruce Robbins, "Introduction Part I: Actually Existing Cosmopolitanism," in *Cosmopolitics: Thinking and Feeling Beyond the Nation*, ed. Pheng Cheah and Bruce Robbins (Minneapolis: University of Minnesota Press, 1998), 2. See also Rebecca Walkowitz, *Cosmopolitan Style: Modernism Beyond the Nation* (New York: Columbia University Press, 2007).

3.  H. G. Wells, *The First Men in the Moon* (London: Penguin, 2005), 145.

4.  Matthew A. Taylor, "At Land's End: Novel Spaces and the Limit of Planetarity," *NOVEL: A Forum on Fiction* 49, no. 1 (2016): 126, italics in the original.

5.  H. G. Wells, *The Common Sense of World Peace* (London: Hogarth, 1929), 26.

6.  Here I am less interested in plugging Wells into contemporary debates about world literature than in denoting his own significant engagement with the world as such. Readers with investments in the current world literature conversation might note, however, some points of interest, involving his world readership and his placement at the center of a publishing network headquartered in London and New York.

7.  Jed Esty, *A Shrinking Island: Modernism and National Culture in England* (Princeton, NJ: Princeton University Press, 2004), 3.

8. H. G. Wells, *First and Last Things: A Confession of Faith and Rule of Life* (New York: G. P. Putnam's Sons, 1908), 103. Cited hereafter as *FLT*.

9. H. G. Wells, *Joan and Peter: The Story of an Education* (New York: Macmillan, 1922), 563–64, italics in the original, ellipses added. Cited hereafter as *JP*.

10. H. G. Wells, *An Englishman Looks at the World*, facsimile ed. (Charleston, SC: BiblioBazaar, 2016), 40–41. Here we might pause to note both the overlap and departure of Wells's ideal with the larger nineteenth- and twentieth-century principles of westernizing colonial subjects through education, under the aegis of "civilization," a project that has been thoroughly critiqued by postcolonial scholars such as Gauri Viswanathan, *Masks of Conquest: Literary Study and British Rule in India* (New York: Columbia University Press, 1989); and Priya Joshi, *In Another Country: Colonialism, Culture, and the English Novel in India* (New York: Columbia University Press, 2002). Imperial policy no doubt paved the way for Wells to develop and spread such ideas, but it should also be stated that Wells's goal was not domination, the creation of a subject race, or the extension of England over the globe. His humanism no doubt today raises the specter of bad faith, but its effort was, I believe, not reducible to a version of imperial control or false humanistic consciousness.

11. Here they (we) are: "They were . . . the most unearthly creatures it is possible to conceive. They were huge round bodies— or rather, heads—about four feet in diameter, each body having in front of it a face. This face had no nostrils—indeed, the Martians do not seem to have had any sense of smell—but it had a pair of very large, dark-coloured eyes, and just beneath this a kind of fleshy beak. In the back of this head or body—I scarcely know how to speak of it—was the single tight tympanic surface, since known to be anatomically an ear, though it must have been almost useless in our denser air. In a group round the mouth were sixteen slender, almost whip-like tentacles, arranged in two bunches of eight each." H. G. Wells, *The War of the Worlds* (London: Penguin, 2005), 124–25. Cited hereafter as *WW*.

12. Duncan Bell, "Pragmatism and Prophecy: H. G. Wells and the Metaphysics of Socialism," *American Political Science Review*, published online, December 20, 2017, 1–14.

13. H. G. Wells, *Experiment in Autobiography: Discoveries and Conclusions of a Very Ordinary Brain (Since 1866)* (New York: Macmillan, 1934), 670. Cited hereafter as *EA*.

14. H. G. Wells, *A Modern Utopia* (London: Penguin, 2005), 21–22.

15. Quoted in D. L. Smith, *H. G. Wells: Desperately Mortal* (New Haven, CT: Yale University Press, 1986), 489.

16. H. G. Wells, *The Story of a Great Schoolmaster* (London: Chatto and Windus, 1924), 1.

17. H. G. Wells, *World Brain* (New York: Doubleday, 1938), 20–21.

18. H. G. Wells, *The Salvaging of Civilization: The Probable Future of Mankind* (New York: Macmillan, 1921), 13.

19. H. G. Wells, *Star Begotten: A Biological Fantasia* (New York: Viking, 1937), 199.

20. George Orwell, *Essays* (New York: Knopf, 2002), 371.

21. H. G. Wells, *The Rights of Man; or, What Are We Fighting For?* (London: Penguin, 2015), 2–3.

22. Orwell, in the same essay, seems to dismiss the declaration, decrying "the usual rigmarole about the World State, plus the Sankey Declaration, which is an attempted definition of fundamental human rights, of anti-totalitarian tendency. Except that he is now especially concerned with federal world control of air power, it is the same gospel as he has been preaching almost without interruption for the past forty years, always with an air of angry surprise at the human beings who can fail to grasp anything so obvious." Orwell, *Essays*, 368–69.

23. Joseph Slaughter, "Humanitarian Reading," in *Humanitarianism and Suffering: The Mobilization of Empathy*, ed. Richard Ashby Wilson and Richard D. Brown (Cambridge: Cambridge University Press, 2009), 88–89.

24. See Joseph Slaughter, *Human Rights, Inc.: The World Novel, Narrative Form, and International Law* (New York: Fordham University Press, 2007).

25. When the United Nations was debating its Universal Declaration, it noted on the floor Wells's *Rights of Man* as one of two "private" precursors.

26. Martin Puchner, *Poetry of the Revolution: Marx, Manifestos, and the Avant-Gardes* (Princeton, NJ: Princeton University Press, 2006).

# Bibliography

Adams, Rachel. *Sideshow USA: Freaks and the American Cultural Imagination.* Chicago: University of Chicago Press, 2001.

Anderson, Linda R. *Bennett, Wells, and Conrad: Narrative in Transition.* Houndmills: Macmillan, 1988.

Arata, Stephen. *Fictions of Loss in the Victorian Fin de Siècle.* New York: Cambridge University Press, 1996.

Arsić, Branka. *Bird Relics: Grief and Vitalism in Thoreau.* Cambridge, MA: Harvard University Press, 2016.

Atwood, Margaret. Introduction to H. G. Wells, *The Island of Doctor Moreau* (London: Penguin, 2005), xiii–xxvi.

Avery, Todd. *Radio Modernism: Literature, Ethics, and the BBC, 1922–1938.* Hampshire: Ashgate, 2006.

Barkan, Elazar, and Ronald Bush, ed. *Prehistories of the Future: The Primitivist Project and the Culture of Modernism.* Stanford, CA: Stanford University Press, 1995.

Barnett, Richard. "Education or Degeneration: E. Ray Lankester, H. G. Wells, and *The Outline of History.*" *Studies in History and Philosophy of Science Part C: Studies in History and Philosophy of Biological and Biomedical Sciences* 37, no. 2 (June 2006): 203–29.

Barrows, Adam. *The Cosmic Time of Empire: Modern Britain and World Literature.* Berkeley: University of California Press, 2010.

Becker, Carl L. *Everyman His Own Historian: Essays on History and Politics.* New York: F. S. Crofts, 1935.

Beckett, Ian F. W. "Total War." In *War, Peace, and Social Change in Twentieth-Century Europe,* edited by Clive Emsley, Arthur Warwick, and Wendy Simpson. Milton Keynes: Open University Press, 1989.

Beer, Gillian. *Open Fields: Science in Cultural Encounter.* Oxford: Clarendon, 1996.

Bell, Duncan. "Pragmatic Utopianism and Race: H. G. Wells as Social Scientist." *Modern Intellectual History* (2017): 1–33.

——. "Pragmatism and Prophecy: H. G. Wells and the Metaphysics of Socialism." *American Political Science Review* 112, no. 2 (2017): 409–22.

Benston, Kimberly W. "Experimenting at the Threshold: Sacrifice, Anthropomorphism, and the Aims of (Critical) Animal Studies." *PMLA* 124, no. 2 (2009): 548–55.

Bergonzi, Bernard. *The Early H. G. Wells: A Study of the Scientific Romances.* Manchester: Manchester University Press, 1961.

Berman, Jessica. *Modernist Commitments: Ethics, Politics, and Transnational Modernism.* New York: Columbia University Press, 2011.

——. "*Three Guineas* and the Politics of Interruption." In *A Companion to Virginia Woolf*, ed. Jessica Berman. Hoboken, NJ: John Wiley & Sons, 2016.

Biers, Katherine. *Virtual Modernism: Writing and Technology in the Progressive Era*. Minneapolis: University of Minnesota Press, 2013.

Black, Barbara J. *On Exhibit: Victorians and Their Museums*. Charlottesville: University Press of Virginia, 2000.

Bloch, Ernst. *The Principle of Hope*. Translated by Neville Plaice, Stephen Plaice, and Paul Knight. Cambridge, MA: MIT Press, 1986.

Boscagli, Maurizia. *Stuff Theory: Everyday Objects, Radical Materialism*. New York: Bloomsbury, 2014.

Bowler, Peter J. *Science for All: The Popularization of Science in Early-Twentieth-Century Britain*. Chicago: University of Chicago Press, 2009.

Bradshaw, David. "Woolf's London, London's Woolf." In *Virginia Woolf in Context*, edited by Bryony Randall and Jane Goldman, 229–42. Cambridge: Cambridge University Press, 2012.

Braudel, Fernand. *The Mediterranean and the Mediterranean World in the Age of Philip II*. 2 vols. Translated by Siân Reynolds. New York: Harper and Row, 1995.

Brody, Jennifer DeVere. *Impossible Purities: Blackness, Femininity, and Victorian Culture*. Durham, NC: Duke University Press, 1998.

Budgen, Frank. *James Joyce and the Making of "Ulysses."* New York: Harrison Smith, 1934.

Butler, Judith. *Precarious Life: The Powers of Mourning and Violence*. London: Verso, 2004.

Cantor, Paul A., and Peter Hufnagel. "The Empire of the Future: Imperialism and Modernism in H. G. Wells." *Studies in the Novel* 38, no. 1 (Spring 2006).

Carey, John. *The Intellectuals and the Masses: Pride and Prejudice Among the Literary Intelligentsia, 1880–1939*. London: Faber and Faber, 1992.

Caserio, Robert. "Abstraction, Impersonality, Dissolution." In *The Cambridge Companion to Modernist Autobiography*, edited by Maria DiBattista and Emily O. Wittman, 197–214. Cambridge: Cambridge University Press.

——. "The Novel as a Novel Experiment in Statement: The Anticanonical Example of H. G. Wells." In *Decolonizing Tradition: New Views of Twentieth-Century "British" Literary Canons*, edited by Karen R. Lawrence, 88–109. Urbana: University of Illinois Press, 1992.

Chamberlin, J. Edward, and Sander L. Gilman. *Degeneration: The Dark Side of Progress*. New York: Columbia University Press, 1985.

Chandos, John. *Boys Together: English Public Schools, 1800–1864*. New Haven, CT: Yale University Press, 1984.

Chickering, Roger. "Total War: The Use and Abuse of a Concept." In *Anticipating Total War: The German and American Experiences, 1871–1914*, edited by Manfred F. Boemeke, Roger Chickering, and Stig Förster, 13–28. Cambridge: Cambridge University Press, 1999.

Chinitz, David. *T. S. Eliot and the Cultural Divide*. Chicago: University of Chicago Press, 2003.

Christensen, Timothy. "The Bestial Mark of Race in *The Island of Dr. Moreau*." *Criticism* 46, no. 4 (Fall 2004): 575–95.

Christian, David, and William H. McNeil. *Maps of Time: An Introduction to Big History*. Berkeley: University of California Press, 2004.

Clarke, I. F., ed. *The Great War with Germany, 1890–1914: Fictions and Fantasies of the War-to-Come*. Liverpool: Liverpool University Press, 1997.

——. *The Pattern of Expectation, 1644–2001*. London: Cape, 1979.

——. *The Tale of the Next Great War, 1871–1914: Fictions of Future Warfare and of Battles Still to Come*. Syracuse, NY: Syracuse University Press, 1995.

——. *Voices Prophesying War, 1763–1984*. New York: Oxford University Press, 1966.

Cohen, Debra Rae. "Getting the Fame Into the Picture: Wells, West, and the Mid-War Novel." *The Space Between* 8, no. 1 (2012): 85–107.

Cohen, Debra Rae, Michael Coyle, and Jane Lewty, eds. *Broadcasting Modernism*. Jacksonville: University of Florida Press, 2009.

Cole, Sarah. *At the Violet Hour: Modernism and Violence in England and Ireland*. New York: Oxford University Press, 2012.

Conrad, Joseph. *Heart of Darkness*. London: Penguin, 2007.

——. *The Secret Agent: A Simple Tale*. London: Penguin, 2007.

Coombes, Annie E. *Reinventing Africa: Museums, Material Culture, and Popular Imagination in Late Victorian and Edwardian England*. New Haven, CT: Yale University Press, 1994.

Crossley, Robert. "Wells's Common Readers." In *Critical Essays on H. G. Wells*, edited by John Huntington, 170–79. Boston: G. K. Hall, 1991.

Daly, Nicholas. *Modernism, Romance, and the Fin de Siècle: Popular Fiction and British Culture*. Cambridge: Cambridge University Press, 2000.

Danahay, Martin. "Wells, Galton, and Biopower: Breeding Human Animals." *Journal of Victorian Culture* 17, no. 4 (December 2012): 468–79.

Das, Santanu. *Touch and Intimacy in First World War Literature*. Cambridge: Cambridge University Press, 2006.

Davidson, Harriet. "Improper Desire: Reading *The Waste Land*." In *The Cambridge Companion to T. S. Eliot*, ed. David Moody, 121–31. Cambridge: Cambridge University Press, 1994.

Davis, Rupert Hart. *Hugh Walpole: A Biography*. London: Macmillan, 1952.

Delbanco, Nicholas. *Group Portrait: Joseph Conrad, Stephen Crane, Ford Madox Ford, Henry James, and H. G. Wells*. New York: William Morrow, 1982.

Dickson, Lovat. *H. G. Wells: His Turbulent Life and Times*. New York: Atheneum, 1969.

Dimock, Wai Chee. *Through Other Continents: American Literature Across Deep Time*. Princeton, NJ: Princeton University Press, 2008.

Dolby, Sandra K. *Self-Help Books: Why Americans Keep Reading Them*. Urbana: University of Illinois Press, 2005.

Draper, Michael. *H. G. Wells*. Houndmills: Macmillan, 1987.

Dryden, Linda. *Joseph Conrad and H. G. Wells: The Fin-de-Siècle Literary Scene*. London: Palgrave Macmillan, 2015.

Dudziak, Mary L. *War Time: An Idea, Its History, Its Consequences*. New York: Oxford University Press, 2014.

Duffy, Enda. "High Energy Modernism." In *Moving Modernisms: Motion, Technology, and Modernity*, edited by David Bradshaw, Laura Marcus, and Rebecca Roach, 83–97. Oxford: Oxford University Press, 2016.

——. "Rush: Biomodernism, Stress, and the Sensation of Time." Unpublished manuscript, delivered in Leuven, Belgium, 2015.

——. *The Subaltern "Ulysses."* Minneapolis: University of Minnesota Press, 1994.

Edel, Leon, and Gordon N. Ray. *Henry James and H. G. Wells: A Record of Their Friendship, Their Debate on the Art of Fiction, and Their Quarrel*. Urbana: University of Illinois Press, 1958.

Elias, Amy J., and Christian Moraru. "Introduction: The Planetary Condition." In *The Planetary Turn: Relationality and Geoaesthetics in the Twenty-First Century*, edited by Amy J. Elias and Christian Moraru, xi–l. Evanston, IL: Northwestern University Press, 2015.

Eliot, T. S. *Four Quartets*. San Diego: Harcourt, 1971.

——. "The Idea of a Quarterly Review." *New Criterion* 4, no. 1 (February 1926).

——. "Recent Books." *The New Criterion: A Quarterly Review* 5 (1927): 253–59.

——. *The Sacred Wood and Major Early Essays*. Mineola, NY: Dover, 1998.

——. *Selected Prose of T. S. Eliot*. San Diego: Harcourt, 1975.

——. *The Use of Poetry and the Use of Criticism*. Cambridge, MA: Harvard University Press, 1994.

——. *The Waste Land*. New York: Norton, 2001.

Ellmann, Maud. *The Poetics of Impersonality: T. S. Eliot and Ezra Pound*. Brighton: Harvester, 1987.

Ellmann, Richard. *James Joyce*. Oxford: Oxford University Press, 1983.

Esty, Jed. "Modernist Worlds at War: Wells, Welles, Spielberg, and Anglo-American Paranoia." Unpublished paper, delivered at Rutgers University, New Brunswick, NJ, October 2013.

——. *A Shrinking Island: Modernism and National Culture in England.* Princeton, NJ: Princeton University Press, 2004.

Esty, Jed, and Colleen Lye. "Peripheral Realisms Now." *Modern Language Quarterly* 73, no. 3 (September 2012): 269–88.

Favret, Mary. *War at a Distance: Romanticism and the Making of Modern Wartime.* Princeton, NJ: Princeton University Press, 2009.

Flam, Jack, and Miriam Deutch, ed. *Primitivism and Twentieth-Century Art: A Documentary History.* Berkeley: University of California Press, 2003.

Fluet, Lisa. "Modernism and Disciplinary History: On H. G. Wells and T. S. Eliot." *Twentieth-Century Literature* 50, no. 3 (Fall 2004): 283–316.

Forster, E. M. *Aspects of the Novel.* San Diego: Harcourt, 1955.

——. *The Eternal Moment and Other Stories.* San Diego: Harcourt, 1956.

——. *Two Cheers for Democracy.* New York: Harcourt, 1951.

Foster, J. Ashley. "Subverting Genres and Virginia Woolf's Political Activism: *Three Guineas* as Peace Testimony." *Virginia Woolf Miscellany* 83 (2013): 20–23.

Frayling, Christopher. *Things to Come.* London: British Film Institute, 1995.

Frost, Laura. *The Problem with Pleasure: Modernism and Its Discontents.* New York: Columbia University Press, 2015.

Froula, Christine. *Virginia Woolf and the Bloomsbury Avant-Garde: War, Civilization, Modernity.* New York: Columbia University Press, 2005.

Furbank, P. N. *E. M. Forster: A Life.* London: Cardinal, 1991.

Fussell, Paul. *The Great War and Modern Memory.* London: Oxford University Press, 1975.

Goble, Mark. *Beautiful Circuits: Modernism and the Mediated Life.* New York: Columbia University Press, 2010.

Goldstein, Erik, and John Maurer. *The Washington Conference, 1921–22: Naval Rivalry, East Asian Stability, and the Road to Pearl Harbor.* London: Frank Cass, 1994.

Greiner, Rae. *Sympathetic Realism in Nineteenth-Century British Fiction.* Baltimore, MD: Johns Hopkins University Press, 2012.

Hackett, Robin. *Sapphic Primitivism: Productions of Race, Class, and Sexuality in Key Works of Modern Fiction.* New Brunswick, NJ: Rutgers University Press, 2004.

Hale, Piers J. *Political Descent: Malthus, Mutualism, and the Politics of Evolution in Victorian England.* Chicago: University of Chicago Press, 2014.

Halliday, Sam. *Sonic Modernity: Representing Sound in Literature, Culture, and the Arts.* Edinburgh: Edinburgh University Press, 2013.

Hammond, J. R. *H. G. Wells and Rebecca West.* New York: Harvester, 1991.

——. *H. G. Wells and the Modern Novel.* Houndmills: Macmillan, 1988.

Hardy, Thomas. *Tess of the D'Urbervilles.* London: Penguin, 2003.

Härmänmaa, Marja, and Christopher Nissen, eds. *Decadence, Degeneration, and the End: Studies in the European Fin de Siècle.* New York: Palgrave Macmillan, 2014.

Hauser, Kitty. *Shadow Sites: Photography, Archaeology, and the British Landscape, 1927–1951.* New York: Oxford University Press, 2007.

Haynes, Roslynn D. *H. G. Wells: Discoverer of the Future: The Influence of Science on His Thought.* New York: NYU Press, 1980.

Henry, Holly. *Virginia Woolf and the Discourse of Science: The Aesthetics of Astronomy.* Cambridge: Cambridge University Press, 2003.

Herodotus. *The Histories.* Trans. Aubrey de Sélincourt. London: Penguin, 2003.

Higgins, Richard. "Feeling Like a Clerk in H. G. Wells." *Victorian Studies* 50, no. 3 (2008): 457–75.

Hillegas, Mark R. *The Future as Nightmare: H. G. Wells and the Anti-Utopians*. New York: Oxford University Press, 1967.

Hirsch, Marianne. "Presidential Address 2014—Connective Histories and Vulnerable Times." *PMLA* 129, no. 3 (2014): 330–38.

Hornby, Louise. *Still Modernism: Photography, Literature, Film*. New York: Oxford University Press, 2017.

Huntington, John. *Critical Essays on H. G. Wells*. Boston: G. K. Hall, 1991.

Hutchinson, Elizabeth. *The Indian Craze: Primitivism, Modernism, and Transculturation in American Art, 1890–1915*. Durham, NC: Duke University Press, 2009.

Huxley, Aldous. *Crome Yellow*. New York: Barnes and Noble, 2004.

Huxley, T. H. *Science and Culture and Other Essays*. New York: D. Appleton, 1882.

Huyssen, Andreas. *After the Great Divide: Modernism, Mass Culture, Postmodernism*. Ann Arbor: University of Michigan Press, 1986.

James, David, and Urmila Seshagiri. "Metamodernism: Narratives of Continuity and Revolution." *PMLA* 129, no. 1 (2014): 87–100.

James, Simon J. *Maps of Utopia: H. G. Wells, Modernity, and the End of Culture*. Oxford: Oxford University Press, 2012.

Jameson, Frederic. "Modernism and Imperialism." In *Nationalism, Colonialism, and Literature*, by Terry Eagleton, Frederic Jameson, and Edward Said. Minneapolis: University of Minnesota Press, 1990.

Jamieson, Theresa. "Working for the Empire: Professions of Masculinity in H. G. Wells's *The Time Machine* and R. L. Stevenson's *Dr. Jekyll and Mr. Hyde*." *Victorian Network* 1 (2009): 72–90.

Jones, Darryl. "J. W. Dunne: The Time Traveller." In *Literature and Modern Time: Technological Modernity, Glimpses of Eternity, Experiments with Time*, edited by Trish Ferguson. London: Palgrave Macmillan, 2019.

Joshi, Priya. *In Another Country: Colonialism, Culture, and the English Novel in India*. New York: Columbia University Press, 2002.

Joyce, James. *Ulysses*. 1922. New York: Random House, 1986.

Karschay, Stephan. *Degeneration, Normativity, and the Gothic at the Fin de Siècle*. New York: Palgrave Macmillan, 2015.

Katz, Alfred H. *Self-Help in America: A Social Movement Perspective*. New York: Twayne, 1993.

Kaufman, Robert Gordon. *Arms Control During the Pre-Nuclear Era: The United States and Naval Limitation Between the Two World Wars*. New York: Columbia University Press, 1990.

Kemp, Peter. *H. G. Wells and the Culminating Ape: Biological Imperatives and Imaginative Obsessions*. 1982. London: Macmillan, 1996.

Kermode, Frank. *The Sense of an Ending: Studies in the Theory of Fiction*. Oxford: Oxford University Press, 1967.

Kern, Stephen. *The Culture of Time and Space, 1880–1914*. Cambridge, MA: Harvard University Press, 1983.

Koselleck, Reinhart. *Futures Past: On the Semantics of Historical Time*. Translated by Keith Tribe. New York: Columbia University Press, 2004.

Kriegel, Lara. *Grand Designs: Labor, Empire, and the Museum in Victorian Culture*. Durham, NC: Duke University Press, 2007.

Kupinse, William. "Wasted Value: The Serial Logic of H. G. Wells's *Tono-Bungay*." *NOVEL: A Forum on Fiction* 33, no. 1 (Fall 1999): 51–72.

Lamos, Colleen. *Deviant Modernism: Sexual and Textual Errancy in T. S. Eliot, James Joyce, and Marcel Proust*. Cambridge: Cambridge University Press, 1998.

Latham, Seth. *The Art of Scandal: Modernism, Libel Law, and the Roman à Clef*. New York: Oxford University Press, 2009.

Lawrence, D. H. *The Letters of D. H. Lawrence*. Cambridge: Cambridge University Press, 1979.

——. *Phoenix II: Uncollected, Unpublished, and Other Prose Works*. Harmondsworth: Penguin, 1978.

——. *The Rainbow*. New York: Penguin, 1983.

Le Corbusier. *The Radiant City*. New York: Orion, 1964.

Lewis, Wyndham. *Time and Western Man*. Boston: Beacon, 1957.

Linett, Maren Tova. *Bodies of Modernism: Physical Disability in Transatlantic Modernist Literature*. Ann Arbor: University of Michigan Press, 2016.

Livingstone, David N., and Charles W. J. Withers. *Geographies of Nineteenth-Century Science*. Chicago: University of Chicago Press, 2011.

London, Bette. "Posthumous Was a Woman: World War I Memorials and Woolf's Dead Poet's Society." *Woolf Studies Annual* 16 (2010): 45–70.

Longenbach, James. *Modernist Poetics of History: Pound, Eliot, and the Sense of the Past*. Princeton, NJ: Princeton University Press, 1987.

Love, Heather. *Feeling Backward: Loss and the Politics of Queer History*. Cambridge MA: Harvard University Press, 2007.

Luckhurst, Roger. *Science Fiction*. Cambridge: Polity, 2005.

Lyon, Janet. *Manifestoes: Provocations of the Modern*. Ithaca, NY: Cornell University Press, 1999.

MacKay, Marina. "The Lunacy of Men, the Idiocy of Women: Woolf, West, and War." *NWSA Journal* 15, no. 3 (2003): 124–44.

——. *Modernism and World War II*. Cambridge: Cambridge University Press, 2007.

MacKenzie, Norman, and Jeanne MacKenzie. *The Life of H. G. Wells: The Time Traveller*. London: Hogarth, 1987.

Mangan, J. A. *The Games Ethic and Imperialism: Aspects of the Diffusion of an Ideal*. New York: Viking, 1985.

Manganaro, Marc. "Dissociation in 'Dead Land': The Primitive Mind in the Early Poetry of T. S. Eliot." *Journal of Modern Literature* 13, no. 1 (March 1986): 97–110.

Mann, Thomas. *The Magic Mountain*. Translated by John E. Woods. New York: Random House, 1995.

Marcus, Laura. *The Tenth Muse: Writing About Cinema in the Modernist Period*. Oxford: Oxford University Press, 2007.

Marinetti, F. T. *Marinetti: Selected Writings*. Edited by R. W. Flint. Translated by R. W. Flint and Arthur A. Coppotelli. New York: Farrar, Straus and Giroux, 1972.

Massinger, Gary. *British Propaganda and the State in the First World War*. Manchester: Manchester University Press, 1992.

Matz, Jesse. *Literary Impressionism and Modernist Aesthetics*. Cambridge: Cambridge University Press, 2001.

McClean, Steven. *H. G. Wells: Interdisciplinary Essays*. Newcastle: Cambridge Scholars, 2008.

McGee, Micki. *Self-Help, Inc.: Makeover Culture in America*. Oxford: Oxford University Press, 2005.

McKillop, A. B. *The Spinster and the Prophet: H. G. Wells, Florence Deeks, and the Case of the Plagiarized Text*. New York: Four Walls Eight Windows, 2000.

McNabb, John. "The Beast Within: H. G. Wells, *The Island of Doctor Moreau*, and Human Evolution in the Mid-1890s." *Geological Journal* 50 (2015): 383–97.

Mellor, Leo. *Reading the Ruins: Modernism, Bombsites, and British Culture*. Cambridge: Cambridge University Press, 2011.

Mieszkowski, Jan. *Watching War*. Palo Alto, CA: Stanford University Press, 2012.

Montaigne, Michel de. *Essays*. Trans. J. M. Cohen. London: Penguin, 1993.

Morat, Daniel, ed. *Sounds of Modern European History: Auditory Cultures in Nineteenth- and Twentieth-Century Europe*. New York: Berghahn Books, 2014.

Morrison, Mark S. *Modern Alchemy: Occultism and the Emergence of Atomic Theory*. Oxford: Oxford University Press, 2007.

Murphet, Julian. *Multimedia Modernism: Literature and the American Avant-Garde*. Cambridge: Cambridge University Press, 2009.

Murphy, Cliona. "H. G. Wells: His History, the People, and the Historians." *The Wellsian* 19 (1996): 36–47.

Navarette, Susan J. *The Shape of Fear: Horror and the Fin de Siècle Culture of Decadence.* Lexington: University Press of Kentucky, 1998.

Newsome, David. *Godliness and Good Learning: Four Studies on a Victorian Ideal.* London: Murray, 1961.

North, Michael. *Camera Works: Photography and the Twentieth-Century Word.* Oxford: Oxford University Press, 2005.

Novick, Peter. *That Noble Dream: The "Objectivity Question" and the American Historical Profession.* Cambridge: Cambridge University Press, 1988.

O'Brien, Tim. *The Things They Carried.* New York: Broadway Books, 1990.

Ó Donghaile, Deaglán. *Blasted Literature: Victorian Political Fiction and the Shock of Modernism.* Edinburgh: Edinburgh University Press, 2011.

Orwell, George. *Essays.* New York: Knopf, 2002.

Owen, Wilfred. *The Poems of Wilfred Owen.* Edited by Jon Stallworthy. London: Chatto, 1990.

Page, Michael R. *The Literary Imagination from Erasmus Darwin to H. G. Wells: Science, Evolution, Ecology.* Burlington, VT: Ashgate, 2012.

Parrinder, Patrick. *H. G. Wells.* Edinburgh: Edinburgh University Press, 1970.

——, ed. *H. G. Wells: The Critical Heritage.* London: Routledge and Kegan Paul, 1972.

——, ed. *Learning from Other Worlds: Estrangement, Cognition, and the Politics of Science Fiction and Utopia.* Durham, NC: Duke University Press, 2001.

——. "Men Who Could Work Miracles: The Tragicomedy of Wellsian Science Fiction." *Foundation* 46 (2017): 33–42.

——. "Revisiting Suvin's Poetics of Science Fiction." In *Learning from Other Worlds: Estrangement, Cognition, and the Politics of Science Fiction and Utopia*, edited by Patrick Parrinder, 36–50. Durham, NC: Duke University Press, 2001.

——. *Shadows of the Future: H. G. Wells, Science Fiction, and Prophecy.* Syracuse, NY: Syracuse University Press, 1995.

Parrinder, Patrick, and John S. Partington, eds. *The Reception of H. G. Wells in Europe.* London: Continuum, 2005.

Parrinder, Patrick, and Christopher Rolfe, eds. *H. G. Wells Under Revision.* Selinsgrove, PA: Susquehanna University Press, 1990.

Parsons, Cóilín. "Planetary Parallax: *Ulysses*, the Stars, and South Africa." *Modernism/modernity* 24, no. 1 (2017): 67–85.

Partington, John S. *Building Cosmopolis: The Political Thought of H. G. Wells.* Aldershot: Ashgate, 2003.

Pease, Allison. *Modernism, Feminism, and the Culture of Boredom.* Cambridge: Cambridge University Press, 2012.

Plain, Gill. *Women's Fiction of the Second World War: Gender, Power, and Resistance.* New York: St. Martin's, 1996.

Puchner, Martin. *Poetry of the Revolution: Marx, Manifestos, and the Avant-Gardes.* Princeton, NJ: Princeton University Press, 2006.

Pye, Patricia. *Sound and Modernity in the Literature of London, 1880–1918.* London: Palgrave Macmillan, 2017.

Quamen, Harvey N. "Unnatural Interbreeding: H. G. Wells's *A Modern Utopia* as Species and Genre." *Victorian Literature and Culture* 33 (2005): 67.

Rainey, Lawrence. *Institutions of Modernism: Literary Elites and Public Culture.* New Haven, CT: Yale University Press, 1998.

Ray, Gordon N. *H. G. Wells and Rebecca West.* New Haven, CT: Yale University Press, 1974.

Redniss, Lauren. *Radioactive: Marie and Pierre Curie, A Tale of Love and Fallout.* New York: Harper Collins, 2011.

Rhodes, Richard. *The Making of the Atomic Bomb.* New York: Simon and Schuster, 2012.

Richards, Jeffrey. "*Things to Come* and Science Fiction in the 1930s." In *British Science Fiction Cinema*, edited by Ian Hunter, 28–44. London: Routledge, 1999.

Richardson, Angelique. *Love and Eugenics in the Late Nineteenth Century: Rational Reproduction and the New Woman*. Oxford: Oxford University Press, 2003.

Rieder, John. *Colonialism and the Emergence of Science Fiction*. Middletown, CT: Wesleyan University Press, 2012.

Robbins, Bruce. "Introduction Part I: Actually Existing Cosmopolitanism." In *Cosmopolitics: Thinking and Feeling Beyond the Nation*, edited by Pheng Cheah and Bruce Robbins, 1–19. Minneapolis: University of Minnesota Press, 1998.

Rose, Jonathan. *The Intellectual Life of the British Working Classes*. New Haven, CT: Yale University Press, 2001.

Rosenberg, Aaron. "Romancing the Anthropocene: H. G. Wells and the Genre of the Future." *NOVEL: A Forum on Fiction* 51, no. 1 (2018): 79–100.

Rosenberg, Michael. *The Character Factory: Baden-Powell and the Origins of the Boy Scout Movement*. New York: Pantheon, 1986.

Rosner, Victoria. *Machines for Living*. New York: Oxford University Press, forthcoming.

——. *Modernism and the Architecture of Private Life*. New York: Columbia University Press, 2005.

Ross, William T. *H. G. Wells's World Reborn: The Outline of History and Its Companions*. Selinsgrove, PA: Susquehanna University Press, 2002.

Rothbert, Daniel, Karina V. Korostelina, and Mohammed D. Cherkaoui. *Civilians and Modern War: Armed Conflict and the Ideology of Violence*. London: Routledge, 2012.

Saint-Amour, Paul K. *Tense Future: Modernism, Total War, Encyclopedic Form*. New York: Oxford University Press, 2017.

——. "*Ulysses* Pianola." *PMLA* 130, no. 1 (2015): 15–36.

——. "Weak Theory, Weak Modernism." *Modernism/modernity* 3, no. 3 (2018): 437–59.

Sanders, Karin. *Bodies in the Bog and the Archaeological Imagination*. Chicago: University of Chicago Press, 2009.

Sass, Louis A. "'The Catastrophes of Heaven': Modernism, Primitivism, and the Madness of Antonin Artaud." *Modernism/modernity* 3, no. 2 (April 1996): 73–91.

Schmidt, Christopher. *The Poetics of Waste: Queer Excess in Stein, Ashbery, Schuyler, and Goldsmith*. New York: Palgrave Macmillan, 2014.

Sherborne, Michael. *H. G. Wells: Another Kind of Life*. London: Peter Owen, 2010.

Sherry, Vincent. *Modernism and the Reinvention of Decadence*. Cambridge: Cambridge University Press, 2015.

Simmel, Georg. *The Sociology of Georg Simmel*. Edited by Kurt H. Wolff. Glencoe, IL: Free Press, 1950.

Slaughter, Joseph. *Human Rights, Inc.: The World Novel, Narrative Form, and International Law*. New York: Fordham University Press, 2007.

——. "Humanitarian Reading." In *Humanitarianism and Suffering: The Mobilization of Empathy*, edited by Richard Ashby Wilson and Richard D. Brown, 88–89. Cambridge: Cambridge University Press, 2009.

Smith, David C. *H. G. Wells: Desperately Mortal, a Biography*. New Haven, CT: Yale University Press, 1986.

Sontag, Susan. "The Imagination of Disaster." *Commentary*, October 1965, 42–48.

Spier, Fred. *Big History and the Future of Humanity*. Malden, MA: Wiley-Blackwell, 2010.

Spivak, Gayatri. *Death of a Discipline*. New York: Columbia University Press, 2003.

Stewart, Garrett. *Between Film and Screen: Modernism's Photo Synthesis*. Chicago: University of Chicago Press, 1999.

Stiles, Anne. "Literature in *Mind*: H. G. Wells and the Evolution of the Mad Scientist." *Journal of the History of Ideas* 70, no. 2 (April 2009): 317–39.

Stover, Leon. "Applied Natural History: Wells v. Huxley." In *H. G. Wells Under Revision*, ed. Patrick Parrinder and Christopher Rolfe. Selinsgrove, PA: Susquehanna University Press, 1990.

Suvin, Darko, ed. *H. G. Wells and Modern Science Fiction*, assoc. ed. Robert M. Philmus. Lewisburg, PA: Bucknell University Press, 1977.

——. *Metamorphoses of Science Fiction: On the Poetics and History of a Literary Genre*. New Haven, CT: Yale University Press, 1979.

Sweeney, Carole. *From Fetish to Subject: Race, Modernism, and Primitivism, 1919–1935*. Westport, CT: Praeger, 2004.

*Symposium of Opinions Upon* The Outline of History, *by H. G. Wells: Views of Historians*. New York: National Civic Federation, 1922.

Taneja, Payal. "The Tropical Empire: Exotic Animals and Beastly Men in *The Island of Dr. Moreau*." *English Studies in Canada* 39, no. 2/3 (June–September 2013): 139–59.

Taylor, A. J. P. "The Man Who Tried to Work Miracles." In *Critical Essays on H. G. Wells*, edited by John Huntington, 127–35. Boston: G. K. Hall, 1991.

Taylor, Matthew A. "At Land's End: Novel Spaces and the Limit of Planetarity." *NOVEL: A Forum on Fiction* 49, no. 1 (2016): 115–38.

Thompson, Ann. *The Soundscape of Modernity: Architectural Acoustics and the Culture of Listening in America, 1900–1933*. Cambridge, MA: MIT Press, 2002.

Torgovnick, Marianna. *Gone Primitive: Savage Intellects, Modern Lives*. Chicago: University of Chicago Press, 1990.

Toye, John, and Richard Toye. "One World, Two Cultures? Alfred Zimmern, Julian Huxley, and the Ideological Origins of UNESCO." *History* 95, no. 3 (2010): 308–31.

Toye, Richard. " 'The Great Educator of Unlikely People': H. G. Wells and the Origins of the Welfare State." In *No Wealth but Life: Welfare Economics and the Welfare State in Britain, 1880–1945*, edited by Roger Backhouse and Tamotsu Nishizawa, 161–88. Cambridge: Cambridge University Press, 2010.

——. "H. G. Wells and the New Liberalism." *Twentieth Century British History* 19, no. 2 (2008): 156–85.

——. "H. G. Wells and Winston Churchill: A Reassessment." In *H. G. Wells: Interdisciplinary Essays*, edited by Steven McClean, 147–61. Cambridge: Cambridge Scholars, 2008.

Tratner, Michael. *Modernism and Mass Politics: Joyce, Woolf, Eliot, Yeats*. Stanford, CA: Stanford University Press, 1995.

Tsing, Anna Lowenhaupt. *The Mushroom at the End of the World: On the Possibility of Life in Capitalist Ruins*. Princeton, NJ: Princeton University Press, 2015.

Tuan, Yi-Fu. *Topophilia: A Study in Environmental Perceptions, Attitudes, and Values*. New York: Columbia University Press, 1990.

Tung, Charles M. "Baddest Modernism: The Scales and Lines of Inhuman Time." *Modernism/modernity* 23, no. 3 (2016): 515–38.

Viswanathan, Gauri. *Masks of Conquest: Literary Study and British Rule in India*. New York: Columbia University Press, 1989.

Wagar, W. Warren. *H. G. Wells: Traversing Time*. Middletown, CT: Wesleyan University Press, 2004.

Walkowitz, Rebecca. *Born Translated: The Contemporary Novel in an Age of World Literature*. New York: Columbia University Press, 2015.

——. *Cosmopolitan Style: Modernism Beyond the Nation*. New York: Columbia University Press, 2007.

Webster, Andrew. "From Versailles to Geneva: The Many Forms of Interwar Disarmament." *Journal of Strategic Studies* 29, no. 2 (2006): 225–46.

Wells Collection, University of Illinois Rare Book and Manuscript Library.

Wells, H. G. *Ann Veronica*. London: Penguin, 2005.

——. *Anticipations of the Reaction of Mechanical and Scientific Progress Upon Human Life and Thought*. New York: Harper, 1902.

——. *Boon, the Mind of the Race, the Wild Asses of the Devil, and the Last Trump; Being a First Selection from the Literary Remains of George Boon, Appropriate to the Times*. 1915. London: Fisher Unwin, 1920. Facsimile.

——. *Certain Personal Matters*. London: Lawrence and Bullen, 1898.

——. *The Common Sense of World Peace.* London: Hogarth, 1929.

——. *The Complete Short Stories of H. G. Wells.* London: Ernest Benn, 1970.

——. *The Conquest of Time.* Amherst NY: Prometheus, 1995.

——. *The Correspondence of H. G. Wells.* Edited by David C. Smith. 4 vols. London: Pickering and Chatto, 1998.

——. *The Country of the Blind, Typescript of Film Scenario [Second Revision].* New York Public Library, Berg Collection.

——. *The Croquet Player.* New York: Viking, 1937.

——. "Discussion." *Journal of American Sociology* 10, no. 1 (1904): 10–11.

——. *Early Writings in Science and Science Fiction.* Edited by Robert M. Philmus and David Y. Hughes. Berkeley: University of California Press, 1975.

——. *An Englishman Looks at the World, Being a Series of Unrestrained Remarks Upon Contemporary Matters.* Charleston, SC: BiblioBazaar, 2016. [London: Cassell, 1914.]

——. *Experiment in Autobiography: Discoveries and Conclusions of a Very Ordinary Brain (Since 1866).* New York: Macmillan, 1934.

——. *First and Last Things: A Confession of Faith and Rule of Life.* New York: G. P. Putnam's Sons, 1908.

——. *The First Men in the Moon.* London: Penguin, 2005.

——. *The Food of the Gods.* London: Hesperus, 2013.

——. *The Future in America: A Search After Realities.* New York: Harper, 1906.

——. *H. G. Wells in Love: Postscript to an Experiment in Autobiography.* Edited by G. P. Wells. London: Faber, 1984.

——. *The History of Mr. Polly.* New York: Penguin, 2005.

——. *In the Fourth Year: Anticipations of a World Peace.* New York: Macmillan, 1918.

——. *The Invisible Man.* New York: Dover, 1992.

——. *The Island of Doctor Moreau.* London: Penguin 2005.

——. "James Joyce." *New Republic,* March 10, 1917.

——. *Joan and Peter: The Story of an Education.* New York: Macmillan, 1922.

——. *Journalism and Prophecy, 1893–1946.* Edited by W. Warren Wagar. Boston: Houghton Mifflin, 1964.

——. *The King Who Was a King: The Book of a Film.* London: Ernest Benn, 1929.

——. *Love and Mr. Lewisham: The Story of a Very Young Couple.* London: Weidenfield & Nicols, 2010.

——. *Mankind in the Making.* New York: Scribner, 1918.

——. *Men Like Gods.* New York: Macmillan, 1923.

——. *A Modern Utopia.* London: Penguin, 2005.

——. *Mr. Britling Sees It Through.* New York: Macmillan, 1916.

——. "The Novel of Ideas." In *Babes in the Darkling Wood.* New York: Alliance Book Company, 1940.

——. *The Open Conspiracy: Blue Prints for a World Revolution.* London: Victor Gollancz, 1928.

——. *The Outline of History.* 2 vols. New York: Macmillan, 1920.

——. *The Peace of the World.* London: The Daily Chronicle, 1915.

——. Preface to *The Scientific Romances of H. G. Wells.* London: Victor Gollancz, 1933.

——. Preface to *The Works of H. G. Wells.* New York: Scribner, 1927.

——. *The Rights of Man; or, What Are We Fighting For?* London: Penguin, 1940.

——. *The Salvaging of Civilization: The Probable Future of Mankind.* New York: Macmillan, 1921.

——. *The Science of Life.* New York: Doubleday, 1931.

——. *Social Anticipations.* New York: Vanguard, 1927.

——. *Star Begotten: A Biological Fantasia.* New York: Viking, 1937.

——. *The Story of a Great Schoolmaster.* London: Chatto & Windus, 1924.

——. *A Text-Book of Biology.* London: W. B. Clive, 1893.

——. *Things to Come: A Film by H. G. Wells.* New York: Macmillan, 1935.

——. *The Time Machine.* London: Penguin, 2005.

——. *The Time Machine*. New York: Penguin, 2005.

——. *Tono-Bungay*. London: Penguin, 2005.

——. *The Undying Fire: A Contemporary Novel*. New York: Macmillan, 1919.

——. *The War in the Air*. 1908. London: Penguin, 2005.

——. *The War of the Worlds*. London: Penguin, 2005.

——. *The War That Will End War*. New York: Duffield, 1914.

——. *The World Set Free: A Story of Mankind*. New York: E. P. Dutton, 1914.

——. *The World of William Clissold: A Novel at a New Angle*. London: Ernest Benn, 1926.

——. "A Vision of the Past." In *H. G. Wells: Early Writings in Science and Science Fiction*, edited by Robert M. Philmus and David Y. Hughes, 153–57. Berkeley: University of California Press, 1975.

——. *Washington and the Hope of Peace*. London: W. Collins, 1922.

——. *What Is Coming: A Forecast of Things After the War*. New York: Macmillan, 1916.

——. *World Brain*. New York: Doubleday, 1938.

Wells, H. G., et al. "The Idea of a League of Nations." *The Atlantic*, January 1919, 14.

Wells, H. G., Julian S. Huxley, and G. P. Wells. *The Science of Life*. 2 vols. New York: Doubleday, 1931.

West, Anthony. *H. G. Wells: Aspects of a Life*. London: Hutchinson, 1984.

West, Geoffrey. *H. G. Wells: A Sketch for a Portrait*. London: Gerald Howe, 1930.

Whittier-Ferguson, John. "Repetition, Remembering, Repetition: Virginia Woolf's Late Fiction and the Return of War." *Modern Fiction Studies* 57, no. 2 (Summer 2011): 230–53.

Whitworth, Michael H. *Einstein's Wake: Relativity, Metaphor, and Modernist Literature*. Oxford: Oxford University Press, 2001.

Wicke, Jennifer. *Advertising Fictions: Literature, Advertisement, and Social Reading*. New York: Columbia University Press, 1988.

Williams, Keith. *H. G. Wells, Modernity, and the Movies*. Liverpool: Liverpool University Press, 2007.

Wollaeger, Mark. Introduction to *The Oxford Handbook of Global Modernisms*, edited by Mark Wollaeger and Matthew Eatough, 3–24. New York: Oxford University Press, 2012.

——. *Modernism, Media, and Propaganda: British Narrative from 1900 to 1945*. Princeton, NJ: Princeton University Press.

Woolf, Virginia. *The Common Reader*. New York: Harcourt Brace Jovanovich, 1984.

——. *The Diary of Virginia Woolf*, vol. 3, *1925–1930*, vol. 5, *1936–1941*. New York: Harcourt Brace Jovanovich, 1980.

——. *Jacob's Room*. London: Penguin, 1992.

——. "Mr Bennett and Mrs Brown." In *Selected Essays*. New York: Oxford University Press, 2008.

——. *Moments of Being*. San Diego: Harcourt Brace Jovanovich, 1985.

——. *To the Lighthouse*. San Diego: Harcourt Brace Jovanovich, 1981.

——. *Three Guineas*. San Diego: Harcourt Brace Jovanovich, 1966.

——. *The Waves*. San Diego: Harcourt Brace Jovanovich, 1959.

Worth, Aaron. "Imperial Transmissions: H. G. Wells, 1897–1901." *Victorian Studies* 53, no. 1 (2010): 65–89.

von Trotha, Trutz. *Anticipating Total War: The German and American Experiences, 1871–1914*. Edited by Manfred F. Boemeke, Roger Chickering, and Stig Förster. Cambridge: Cambridge University Press, 1999.

Yanni, Carla. *Nature's Museums: Victorian Science and the Architecture of Display*. Princeton, NJ: Princeton Architectural Press, 2005.

# Index